D0875791

Exporting Capitalism

EXPORTING CAPITALISM

Private Enterprise and US Foreign Policy

ETHAN B. KAPSTEIN

HARVARD UNIVERSITY PRESS
Cambridge, Massachusetts
London, England
2022

For Anne, Laura, Nina, and Felicity

Copyright © 2022 by the President and Fellows of Harvard College
All rights reserved
Printed in the United States of America

First printing

Library of Congress Cataloging-in-Publication Data
Names: Kapstein, Ethan B., author.
Title: Exporting capitalism : Private enterprise and US foreign policy /
Ethan B. Kapstein.
Description: Cambridge, Massachusetts : Harvard University Press, 2022. |
Includes bibliographical references and index.
Identifiers: LCCN 2021039638 | ISBN 9780674251632 (cloth)
Subjects: LCSH: Investments, American—Developing countries—History—
20th century. | Investments, American—Developing countries—History—
21st century. | Capitalism—Developing countries—History—20th century. |
Capitalism—Developing countries—History—21st century. | United States—
Foreign economic relations—Developing countries—History—20th century. |
United States—Foreign economic relations—Developing countries—
History—21st century.
Classification: LCC HF1456.5.D44 K37 2022 | DDC 337.730172 / 4—dc23
LC record available at https://lccn.loc.gov/2021039638

Contents

Preface   *vii*

Introduction: Exporting Capitalism   1

1 Private Enterprise, International Development, and the
  Cold War   17

2 Private Sector Development in the Shadow of War: Taiwan
  and Korea   39

3 Capitalism, Colonialism, or Communism? Private Enterprise
  in Latin America, 1950–1965   67

4 "Storm over the Multinationals": Foreign Investment from
  Nixon to Reagan   93

5 Capitalism Triumphant: Private Enterprise and the
  New World Order   117

6 Exporting Capitalism to Fragile States   154

7 Dueling Capitalisms? Private Enterprise and the
  China Challenge   186

8 The Future of Private Sector Development   205

Notes   227
Index   273

Preface

The way of economic life which goes by the name of private
enterprise is the sound and true gospel.

—US AMBASSADOR MERWIN BOHAN, 1954

The United States has long believed that private enterprise is crucial for
economic growth. So deep is this belief that the United States has sought
to spread it around the world, including to developing countries. Yet in
many settings the private sector has failed to flourish. Why is that the
case, and what can the United States and the international community
do to help it take root? These are among the questions I address in this
book.

For me, that topic goes beyond academic or theoretical interest. Prior to
the COVID-19 pandemic, I spent much of my time visiting projects backed
by multinational corporations and foreign aid agencies that had as their
objective private sector development; and by the time this book is published,
I hope to be back in the field! A seemingly new objective of donors and
investors, "private sector development," is meant to supplement or even
supplant foreign aid as a driver of economic growth and poverty reduction. Some of the relevant projects that have I studied over the years include
SABMiller's brewing of a novel type of beer in Uganda (Eagle Lager) that
made intensive use of local cassava and thus local farmers, instead of imported hops; Newmont Mining's encouragement of local entrepreneurs surrounding its Ahafo iron ore mine in Ghana; and Coca-Cola's long-standing
efforts in many countries to create "inclusive" domestic value chains running
from agriculture to final distribution.[1] I have also worked in the former Soviet
Union on the conversion of defense plants to commercial activity and in

conflict-affected countries including Afghanistan, where US policy makers hoped that spurring private enterprise would lead to economic growth and job creation, contributing to peace. Prior to becoming an academic, I worked as an international banker, supporting private sector development directly in such countries as Brazil.

As I examined the economics of these and many other programs, I realized that some were more successful than others in catalyzing the private sector; similar interventions in two different places generated two very different results. Why was that the case? To what extent did the economic structure of a country shape the attitudes of its elites toward private investment? And that led to an even larger, "so what" question: under what conditions did private enterprise programs *within* a country lead to systemic or political-economic transformation *of* the country? What is the relationship between micro, firm-level interventions and macro political-economic change?

In contemplating these issues, I also discovered that private sector development wasn't such a new policy objective after all. In fact, it's probably fair to say that no line of effort in US foreign aid policy is of longer-standing than private enterprise promotion. US government efforts to address private sector development went back at least to the postwar Marshall Plan, while the multilateral International Finance Corporation (IFC) was founded in 1956 with that very purpose. Now that the international community was rediscovering private enterprise as a key component of development policy, I wondered what previous experiences might teach us, in the hope of making contemporary policies and programs most effective. That motivation was given further impetus by the creation in 2018 of the new US International Development Finance Corporation (DFC), whose objective is to support private sector–led investment in developing countries, in contrast to China's state-led model of economic growth.

This book tells the story of Washington's persistent efforts to encourage private enterprise in the developing world and so-called transition economies of Central and Eastern Europe (note that I do *not* emphasize short-term capital flows via portfolio investments or bank loans in this study). It has done so both by motivating foreign direct investment (FDI) and the creation of local firms, and more generally by encouraging the creation of an amenable "investment climate." The US government, of course, has also sought to export capitalism through a variety of other policies, including international trade agreements and foreign aid programs aimed at building institutions like judiciaries and enforceable property rights (and many scholars would argue that the United States has used its military power and intelligence services for this purpose as well). Not surprisingly, the outcomes of these efforts have varied across time and space; after all, the beliefs and aspirations of policy makers may not necessarily map neatly onto the reality they confront in a given place.

For one thing, leaders in the developing world have not always shared Washington's enthusiasm regarding private enterprise; alternative economic ideologies, often coupled with political efforts to concentrate industrial power in the hands of government officials and state-owned enterprises, meant that fostering private sector growth has not always and everywhere been a policy priority. For another, American business leaders have often proved unwilling to follow Washington's lead when it came to investing in the developing world. Instead, these executives worked to further their own interests and corporate strategies, which usually emphasized the wealthier industrial world, or a handful of the larger developing economies or those with specific resources like petroleum. As a consequence, the US government's ability to export capitalism through private enterprise has been repeatedly constrained by the preferences of leaders in the developing world on one hand and those of executives of US multinational corporations on the other.

The structural conditions found in developing countries also play a major role in shaping the environment for private enterprise. Private sector development, for example, has proved much more difficult in countries that rely heavily on natural resources and that are mired in violent conflict. Conversely, in countries where the local elites are invested in a wide range of economic activities—and where at least some are committed to long-term investment schemes as opposed to short-term rent-seeking—the chances of promoting private sector–led growth are much greater. Indeed, the economic structure of these elites will play a decisive role in determining the success of private enterprise. Donor nations that seek to promote private enterprise would do well to consider these structural and related political economy issues as they devise their policies and programs. To put this starkly, if the preferences of local elites are not closely aligned with those of foreign donors, the chances of programmatic success are severely limited.

This book is broken into nine chapters, each of which is meant to elicit key "lessons" for contemporary policy makers. In the Introduction, I discuss the concept of private sector development and why it has held such a persistent attraction for American officials. Chapter 1 focuses on the ideas that shaped US foreign economic policy toward private enterprise during the Cold War, reminding us that many of the policies that are today touted as "new" have a long lineage. Chapter 2 examines private investment in the context of the "developmental" or "*dirigiste*" states of Taiwan and South Korea, where central governments sought to maintain a heavy hand on their economies as they dealt with both internal and external threats. Chapter 3 examines the long-standing Latin American ambivalence toward foreign direct investment (at least in some sectors) while Chapter 4 focuses on how Presidents Nixon, Carter, and Reagan dealt with the problem of "economic nationalism" and the related threats of expropriation of American property. In Chapter 5, I analyze the post-communist transition, when capitalism finally seemed to triumph—and with it, democracy, highlighting the American belief in the linkage between the two. Chapter 6 picks up the thread of this story in conflict-affected states like Afghanistan and Iraq, where American officials hoped that private enterprise would similarly act as a force for peace and the creation and maintenance of democratic institutions. Chapter 7 examines private sector development with a focus on the DFC and the China challenge. The final chapter provides conclusions and policy recommendations.

As this summary hopefully makes clear, my purpose here is not to write a history of the multinational corporation or of government efforts to regulate that form of business organization. I also give relatively short shrift to "corporate social responsibility" and the role of firms in providing support for community needs. Instead, I focus squarely on the problem of how US officials sought to motivate the spread of private enterprise in a number of different settings, and how effective these policies have been.

I decided to write this book following a brief stint with the US government. Prior to entering government, I was engaged in a project with several collaborators on private enterprise in Afghanistan, and as a follow-up I codirected a project for the United Kingdom's Department for International Development on private sector development in Afghanistan, Iraq, and Pakistan. Once I arrived in Washington, I became aware of discussions (although I took no part in them) regarding the new International Development Finance Corporation, which replaced the Overseas Private Investment Corporation founded under President Nixon. Upon returning to academic life in late 2018, I felt compelled to write up a proposal to the Smith Richardson Foundation to help fund the work of researching and writing this book, and I am once again grateful to Marin Strmecki and his colleagues for their support. Further support has been provided by Princeton University, including funding from the Princeton Institute for International and Regional Studies for work on fragile states and the Undergraduate Dean's Office at the Princeton School of Public and International Affairs and the Department of Politics for research assistance. My research in Afghanistan has been supported by the World Bank and by the Department of Defense through its Minerva Research Initiative.

Many people have provided crucial assistance along this road, including my fellow directors of the Empirical Studies of Conflict program: Jacob Shapiro, Eli Berman, and Col. (Ret.) Joseph Felter, and my Princeton colleagues

David Baldwin, Miguel Centeno, Amaney Jamal, Steve Kotkin, and Cecilia Rouse. Baldwin's intellectual imprint, in particular, is all over this book, and I am grateful for the time we've shared together over the years discussing economic statecraft (and working on a new edition of his classic work). He also provided a detailed reading of an earlier draft of the manuscript, which led to numerous corrections and improvements. Similarly, historian David Painter of Georgetown University, a great student of the issues raised in this book, provided penetrating comments on an earlier draft of the manuscript. At Arizona State, I wish to thank President Michael Crow, along with Ann Florini, Mark Green, Sanjiv Khagram, Jonathan Koppell, and Don Siegel, who are all sources of inspiration and support; I am proud to be associated with an institution that combines the excitement of a Silicon Valley start-up with the foundational principles of academic excellence and student inclusivity. I am also grateful to the many librarians and archivists who so quickly responded to my information requests, especially during the COVID-19 pandemic!

Outside the academy, Neil Gregory of the IFC and Beata Javorcik of the European Bank for Research and Development (on leave from Oxford) have been extremely helpful to me, not just to this project but over many years. I have learned volumes about private sector development through my collaboration with Rene Kim and his colleagues at the firm of Steward Redqueen, and I am grateful to the many firms and development agencies that have sought our assistance.

Research support for this project has been ably provided by Princeton doctoral student Zenobia Chan, MPA student Michelle Nedashkovskaya, research assistant Adityamohan Tantravahi, and undergraduates Judy Koo and Cai Markham. My daughter Nina Kapstein did great work in helping compile sources for the endnotes. In Jess McCann I found a terrific editor who helped structure and improve the text. Ian Malcolm of Harvard University Press was an early advocate of this project, and I am grateful to him for all his support; it's great to be back with the Press after a long absence! Thanks are also due to Olivia Woods at the Press for all her help in moving the book toward production. A special shout-out is due to the anonymous reviewers of the manuscript, who went way beyond any reasonable call of duty in providing incredibly detailed, insightful, and truly helpful critiques of earlier drafts; the Syndics of Harvard University Press added many productive comments as well. Portions of Chapter 1 were first published as "Private Enterprise, International Development, and the Cold War," *Journal of Cold War Studies,* Volume 22, Number 4, Fall 2020, pp. 113–145. I thank the anonymous reviewers who provided many useful comments on that text and the MIT Press for publishing the article.

One of the most joyful aspects of writing this book was that it led me to reread much of the work of my great mentor Raymond Vernon and recall our many conversations on related topics. I am forever blessed by the memories of the relationship I forged with him over our years working together on Harvard's Economics and National Security Program. I also recall with gratitude my opportunity to study with Alfred Chandler, whose brilliance was only matched by his kindness. Samuel Huntington, who served as the director of Harvard's Olin Institute and recruited me when he learned of my interest in bringing together research in economics and national security, has also written powerfully on many of the issues addressed here. I still miss my regular discussions with Sam; working with him was one of the greatest honors and opportunities of my life.

Deep thanks are due to Benedicte Callan, who has suffered through too many discussions on topics related to this book. But I dedicate this book to my four daughters—Anne, Laura, Nina, and Felicity—as partial thanks for all the cherished moments we've shared and for being so forgiving of their dad when he was at work. I know they will bring as much happiness to their loved ones as they have to me.

Introduction

Exporting Capitalism

The whole free world needs capital; America is its largest source.
—Dwight D. Eisenhower, Special Message to Congress,
6 January 1955[1]

In october 2018, the US Congress passed the BUILD Act,[2] establishing the new International Development Finance Corporation (DFC). Capitalized at some $60 billion, the DFC's stated economic purpose is to promote "development by supporting foreign direct investment [FDI] in underserved types of projects, regions, and countries."[3] Its larger geopolitical purpose, however, is to challenge China's Belt and Road Initiative (BRI), which is a $1 trillion global infrastructure program. As then –Vice President Mike Pence said of DFC, "we'll be giving foreign nations a just and transparent alternative to China's debt-trap diplomacy."[4]

Washington insiders in both government and business have characterized DFC as a sea change in American foreign assistance policy. Ray Washburne, former head of the Overseas Private Investment Corporation (OPIC, which DFC replaces), said that its creation "launches a new era in development finance,"[5] while USAID administrator Mark Green held out its promise to "catalyze market-based, private-sector development, spur economic growth in less-developed countries, and advance the foreign-policy interests of the United States."[6] Senator Bob Corker (R-Tenn.), who cosponsored the bipartisan BUILD Act, claimed that the founding of DFC heralds the end of traditional, government-to-government foreign aid programs. These programs, he proclaimed, could now "set the goal of putting themselves out of business."[7] For its part, the US Chamber of Commerce, representing the views of its corporate members, wrote in support of the BUILD Act that it "would leverage the U.S. private sector's expertise and investment capital to generate economic growth in the developing world and provide tangible benefits for American companies selling their goods and services there." In so doing, it would "advance U.S. national security and economic interests."[8]

The purpose of this book is to examine these claims about the promise of private enterprise as an instrument for international development. The ideas animating the DFC are hardly revolutionary, but instead represent the continuation of a persistent effort to catalyze private sector development on behalf of Washington's geopolitical and geoeconomic objectives—an effort that was at the focal point of foreign assistance policy during the early years of the Cold War and that, with some ebbs and flows, has remained a policy objective ever since. For at least a decade beginning in the late 1940s, the US government believed that foreign investment could fuel economic growth in the developing world, and in so doing counter the existential threat posed by international communism.[9] As President Dwight D. Eisenhower said in a 1955 address to Congress, "An increased flow of United States private investment funds abroad . . . would do much to offset the false but alluring promises of the Communists."[10]

In promoting FDI, Washington's "theory of change" was that American firms would catalyze economic growth through FDI, in turn motivating local entrepreneurs to invest in the supply chains and support functions that these corporations required. Jobs, incomes, exports, and tax revenues would be generated as a result. Economists would later refer to this process as one of creating "linkages" between foreign and domestic firms. By promoting linkages, countries would enjoy faster rates of development.[11] More recently, the United States has sought to grow private firms organically, without depending so much on the catalyzing power of multinational firms.

Generating growth in the developing world through private enterprise was not solely of material or economic interest to Washington; it did not arise solely out of a desire for the developing world's commodities or market potential. Equally if not more important, it promised a number of political and national security spin-offs, including a pro-American foreign policy orientation, and perhaps eventually democracy (and, more recently, policy makers have held out its potential for promoting peace and more gender equality in such countries as Afghanistan). This causal chain reflected key tenets of modernization theory, one of whose advocates, W. W. Rostow of the Massachusetts Institute of Technology, was an influential academic who would help shape US foreign aid policy before going on to become a national security adviser to Presidents Kennedy and Johnson.[12] As Richard N. Cooper has written of American statecraft in the early Cold War, "the principal instruments for preventing the spread of Communism by nonmilitary means involved building an international economic system conducive to economic prosperity," which required the spread of trade and private enterprise.[13]

This quest for private sector development was, of course, securely nested within American ideology as well—by a persistent belief in the superiority of political-economic systems based on liberal, democratic-capitalist institutions. In fact, one of the most striking things about US development policy is its continually expressed belief in private sector–led growth. What David Baldwin wrote in 1966 remains equally relevant today: "To representatives of the less developed nations it must seem that the United States never tires of citing the advantages—real and imagined—of an economic system based on private enterprise."[14]

This market-oriented ideology did not just help shape foreign economic policy during the Cold War, when the United States allegedly faced an existential threat from "international communism," but it has also remained prominent during the subsequent eras of globalization and neoliberalism, and today is a key instrument in challenging China's "Belt and Road" model of economic development. Indeed, while American officials were not usually blinded by economic ideology—at the end of the day, they generally recognized the art of the possible in a given setting—in some cases the ideologues among them had the scope to advance policies that made little sense given the facts on the ground. In Iraq, for example, US officials believed that they could replicate the "shock therapy" models imported from post–Cold War Eastern Europe in the hope of creating a private sector–led market economy.

What lessons can foreign policy officials today, including those running the DFC, draw from this history, in particular as they seek to confront China in the developing world? What core interests and ideas motivated Washington's underlying philosophy of international development? And what does this history tell us about the relationship between the American government, the developing world, and US-based multinational corporations, which has been a contentious topic among scholars over many decades?[15] These are among the questions this book will address.

To preview the general argument, Washington's long-standing private enterprise project has had only mixed success, providing today's international development community (which encompasses bilateral and multilateral development agencies along with foreign aid implementers and private foundations) many lessons regarding effective vs. ineffective policy interventions. That track record reflects in part the clash between the policy preferences of the Executive Branch on the one hand and the interests of private sector firms and of many local elites in developing countries on the other, not to overlook the foreign economic policy preferences of the US Congress as well, which I will show sometimes conflicted with those of the President. Whereas the US government believed that foreign investment could drive the economic growth of developing countries, multinational firms have generally been interested in only a handful of those countries as investment destinations.[16] Investing in developing economies has simply not been a priority for most of them, no matter a particular country's geostrategic importance to the White House and Foggy Bottom. As a result, FDI flows have often lagged behind the amounts that Washington had hoped for, with major consequences for the government's philosophy of foreign assistance.

Further, structural conditions within recipient nations have often shaped the opportunities for private enterprise. Countries that rely heavily on natural resources, and those in the midst of violent conflict, for example, have proved to be particularly challenging settings for growing the private sector. No less problematic, the kleptocratic rulers of all-too-many countries have exploited national economies as a source of private gains rather than as a seedbed for inclusive growth, dampening the prospects for entrepreneurship. Conversely, in countries in which the elites have a diverse set of economic interests, and where incentives exist to pursue long-term investment schemes rather than engage in short-term rent-seeking, the promise of private sector development is much greater. In sum, certain places have proved more hostile, and some more welcoming, to private sector development than others, largely reflecting underlying structural conditions and the related political economy of elite interests.

At the same time, we will also see that Washington has sometimes exaggerated a recipient government's hostility to private enterprise. A policy of blocking foreign investment in some "strategic" sectors like petroleum, for example, did not necessarily mean that multinational corporations and local firms weren't welcome by host governments in others. In that context, it should be recalled that the US government also actively screens, and sometimes prevents, foreign investment, especially when it "threatens" national security.

The story presented here demonstrates, contrary to Robert Gilpin's famous assertion, that American firms have *not* served as reliable "instruments of American global hegemony."[17] In fact, the evidence presented in this book casts doubt upon the ability of the United States to impose its policies, even on supposedly "weak" states (or even those that it has occupied militarily), when preferences and priorities differ. And for their part, developing countries have varied enormously over time and space in their demand for private capital and ability to attract it. In several cases, notably among countries within the former Soviet orbit in Central and Eastern Europe, former hostility toward the private sector turned into a more welcoming embrace as the political economy of their regimes changed.

Despite the crucial differences in the economic policies and trajectories of the world's developing regions (and even within Latin America, East

Asia, and Sub-Saharan Africa, there has been of course great diversity in both policies and outcomes), it is also important to be cognizant of the commonalities among the world's poorest countries that played a major role in shaping the contours of US policy.[18] In fact, some generalizations about the postwar developing world, no matter the region, are fairly robust, such as the need of the poorest countries to import foreign capital in some form (i.e., either as grants, loans, or investments) given the "gap" between domestic savings and investment requirements. After all, by definition, developing countries lacked savings, and thus savings had to be mobilized through some combination of domestic and international effort.

American policy makers also discovered that developing country leaders, as a general rule, did not believe that FDI was a substitute for government-to-government assistance; instead, different sources of capital were needed for the production of public vs. private goods. These leaders urged Washington to accept the proposition that foreign aid and private enterprise were complementary rather than competitive; aid-funded infrastructure, for example, would attract more investment. At the United Nations, where developing world leaders often expressed similar views on foreign assistance, they called for "external grant aid to finance 'low-yielding . . . social and economic overhead projects' basic to economic development."[19] It would take many years for American policy makers to accept that official aid represented something beyond a failure of recipient nations to harness private capital. As President Eisenhower liked to say, foreign assistance was the equivalent of putting money in a "tin cup."[20]

The purpose of this Introduction is to lay the groundwork for the case study chapters that follow, which analyze private sector development across a wide range of settings in the hope of generating some overarching findings. In so doing, I define key terms, and present some of the arguments that have been made over the years by scholars on behalf of a growth model based on private enterprise. I then lay out the fundamental principles and ideas that have guided American policy makers in their approach to international economic development.

What Is Private Sector Development?

Private sector development has become a big business in its own right. According to Daniel Runde and Aaron Milner at the Center for Strategic and International Studies, the development finance institutions (DFIs), which include such organizations as the International Finance Corporation, the European Bank for Reconstruction and Development, the Asian

Development Bank, and the Inter-American Development Bank, now commit something close to $90 billion per annum on private sector projects, including equity investments, loans, and guarantees. Much of this funding flows to local banks, which in turn are expected to lend to local private sector firms, including small and medium-sized enterprises (SMEs).[21]

But what is meant by the "private sector" and "private sector development"? Even if precise definitions remain elusive, we must begin by providing some parameters around these and other key terms which will be used throughout the book. For as we will see in a moment, terms like these, which seem relatively straightforward to define, are perhaps less clear than imagined. USAID, for example, provides the following definition of "private sector":

- For profit, commercial entities and their affiliated foundations;
- Financial institutions, investors and intermediaries;
- Business associations and cooperatives;
- Micro, small, medium, and large enterprises that operate in the formal and informal sectors;
- American, local, regional, and multinational businesses; and
- For profit approaches that generate sustainable income.

According to this definition, a state-owned enterprise (SOE) that operates at a profit could be construed as operating in the private sector. That, in turn, has implications for both policy and data collection. American policy makers, for example, have generally been uncomfortable providing financial support to SOEs (e.g., through Export-Import Bank financing of their imports); but as we will see, they have nonetheless swallowed their reservations and done so at various times when it was politically expedient. From a data-gathering perspective, a commonly used proxy measure for private sector activity among researchers is "credit to the private sector," or loans provided by banks to local firms. But the World Bank warns that "for some countries, these claims include credit to public enterprises."[22] While I generally define the private sector and private enterprise as firms that are owned by private actors rather than by the government (and to further confuse things, it must be admitted that private *ownership* does not necessarily equate to private *control*), I want to be upfront about some of these definitional complexities (also note that I focus on firms that produce or serve consumers as opposed to governments; thus, I do not discuss US defense industries in this book, although they have certainly played a role in industrialization through co-production and technology transfer arrangements, particularly among military allies).[23]

Private sector development (PSD), in turn, is "defined" in that wonderfully bureaucratic fashion as "a discipline and area of programmatic work focused on strengthening the business-enabling environment for the private sector to drive inclusive economic growth . . . PSD often focuses on supporting regulatory reforms that improve business and investment climates, providing public goods that help strengthen the broader private sector, and/or facilitating investment from companies."[24]

In fact, in the foreign assistance community, private sector development has taken on a multitude of meanings, many of which—it should be emphasized—ironically imply an active role for the state. It should also be recalled that the "foreign assistance community" goes well beyond official bilateral donors and multilateral development finance institutions to include foundations (e.g., the Gates Foundation, which holds approximately $37 billion in assets); foreign aid "implementers," or those responsible for executing agency programs in the field, some of which, like Mercy Corps, now have venture capital arms that invest directly in developing countries; multinational corporations and banks that promote local industry and develop supply chains through their activities; and an array of social entrepreneurs who are engaged in "impact investing." Taken together, a short list of what constitutes PSD in the contemporary world would include the following items:

- Improving the investment climate
- Direct financing by development agencies to local companies, especially SMEs
- Providing indirect financing to companies by capitalizing local banks
- Development-related activities by multinational enterprises (sometimes called "inclusive," "bottom-of-the-pyramid," or "value chain" strategies)
- Building financial and equity markets
- Promoting development finance for infrastructure, especially through public-private partnerships (PPPs)
- Blended finance (i.e., finance that combines public and private funds)
- Social entrepreneurship and impact investment
- Some activities of export-import banks (e.g., lending to local enterprises in the developing world)
- Microfinance

As this list suggests, it is important to be clear regarding what we mean by PSD in our discussion, as all of the above activities have fallen under that umbrella term at one time or another. We will also see how the concept of PSD has expanded over time. During the early Cold War years, for example, US policy makers focused their attention on the role of FDI in international development, for reasons I describe in the following section and country case studies. More recently, the development community has placed greater emphasis on organically promoting private enterprise, perhaps in recognition of the limits of FDI flows to the world's poorest and most fragile countries. Still, even in places like Afghanistan and Iraq, US officials have expressed great hopes for the role that foreign investors can play in local economies. More recently, President Joe Biden has urged American-based multinationals like Microsoft to invest in Central America in the hope of promoting economic activity there, in turn reducing the northward flood of immigrants.[25]

As an additional note, I should flag for readers that I do not emphasize the role of microfinance in this book, despite its prominence as a vehicle for PSD in such countries as Iraq. This is because I consider microfinance to be primarily focused on poverty reduction rather than growing private enterprise. Alex Counts of the Grameen Foundation has written, "The most straightforward measure of microfinance's social impact is clients' economic status," as opposed, say, to the number of firms created.[26] Few microfinanced businesses ever evolve into formal companies. Several studies have even concluded that it does little to lift people out of poverty, as the funds are primarily used for immediate consumption needs rather than productive investment.[27] Again, my emphasis is on growing private enterprise rather than on social policies, though of course development officials have hoped and believed that private sector development would lead to poverty reduction via job creation and economic growth.

Whereas traditionally the international community relied heavily on FDI to promote development (the fourth point on the preceding list), and while multinational firms continue to provide important developmental "services" through their "linkages" to local economies—as described in more detail below—the development finance institutions (DFIs) and bilateral aid agencies have really emphasized the first three items. First, improving the investment climate, which, as we will see, has been a prominent concept throughout the period studied here; second, directly providing capital injections to local firms, particularly SMEs; and third, injecting funds into local banks or investment companies (which also implies that the government has put into place the kinds of regulations required to supervise such institutions). These three activities are interrelated, and there is an underlying logic to them. After all, if the investment climate is hostile to private enterprise, then providing credit is a futile exercise. Nonetheless, an important point that I will make throughout the book is that interventions of this type are based on some heroic assumptions about the role of local governments in promoting entrepreneurship and private enterprise; one of our main tasks is gaining a better understanding of the political-economic conditions that favor private sector development.

Why Private Sector Development?

One question that might be reasonably asked is, why has Washington been so insistent about promoting private enterprise in the first place?[28] Why did American officials have any preferences at all over a foreign government's domestic economic policies, so long as those countries maintained a pro-US foreign policy orientation and had sufficient growth to quell domestic instability? As President Eisenhower himself said, the United States "did not need to fear a socialized state as something inimical to us in itself."[29] What did it matter if countries emphasized SOEs over the private sector, or the building up of social infrastructure (e.g., education, health care, housing, public utilities and transportation) over FDI? Why were Americans so convinced of the benefits of their private sector prescription?

A number of answers present themselves, both pragmatic and ideological in nature. From a practical standpoint, American officials did, and the DFC suggests that they still do, possess what students of international development would now call a "theory of change" when it comes to encouraging private enterprise in general and FDI in particular. It's a theory that has proved remarkably resilient since its elaboration during the early Cold War era, carrying over from one administration to the next.[30] And unlike some theories dreamed up in Washington, this one also generated a distinguished academic pedigree to back it up—launching a research program on the role of FDI in spurring economic growth that continues to the present day.[31]

In brief, this theory posits that FDI by multinational firms provides the catalyst for local private enterprise in recipient nations, creating a substantial multiplier effect in terms of employment, incomes, productivity gains, tax revenues, and, in many cases, export earnings. In creating these benefits, foreign investors brought with them technology and organizational skills that were otherwise difficult for developing countries to obtain. Already in the "Grey Report" of 1950 on US foreign economic policy, these were highlighted among other arguments on behalf of foreign investment.[32]

Why did officials believe that private investment would catalyze growth in host markets, particularly when coupled with foreign trade—and promotion of international trade was, of course, the other crucial pillar of US foreign economic policy? Underlying this belief in the power of FDI was the theory of "linkages," meaning that this type of investment created "backward linkages" or induced demand for "inputs" (e.g., agricultural commodities) while also creating "forward linkages" or "outputs" (e.g., the creation of distribution networks). As one of the great proponents of linkage theory, Albert Hirschman, wrote in 1958, "Development policy must attempt to enlist these well-known backward and forward effects."[33] The promotion of FDI as the key element in US development assistance seemed to fit that bill for several reasons.

First, foreign capital was deemed essential to development because, by definition, the world's poorest countries lacked adequate savings to fuel their investment needs. Recall the Keynesian identity that savings = investment. If a country had little by way of savings (since in poor countries people use their small incomes to meet immediate consumption needs, with little left over for savings), it would have hardly any investment. This meant that developing countries had to find ways to "import" foreign savings—in the form of foreign aid, bank loans, private investment, or some combination thereof. With the US government insistent on limiting foreign aid allocations for both budgetary and ideological reasons, countries had little choice but to rely on private sources of funding—a seeming fact of life that many developing world leaders resented and would fight against.

Second, beyond its role in augmenting domestic savings, foreign investors could bring a number of additional benefits to developing countries—including cutting-edge technology and new modes of economic organization. They often paid higher salaries than local firms, and they also paid taxes, though of course they might use "transfer pricing" techniques to limit their overall tax burden. To the extent that these firms engaged in exports, they helped generate foreign exchange as well. Some of these firms, particularly in Latin America, would also engage in "import-substituting industrialization" (ISI), whereby they manufactured products locally for domestic consumption—reducing imports and the demand for foreign exchange—which was often in short supply.

Third, Hirschman also pointed to certain political economy benefits of foreign investment. Public investment, he noted, was inevitably subject to "pork barrel" distribution, as it was used to generate political benefits for local politicians and elites rather than to serve broader economic objectives. It gave elites prestigious jobs with access to resources that were all too often used for personal enrichment rather than corporate profitability. In turn, these elites would reward the politicians who helped them gain their positions, creating a cycle that was virtuous for themselves but vicious for development. At times donors have sought to break these cycles, while at others they have thrown up their hands in despair.

Foreign investors, in contrast, had to choose projects that would be profitable, and in so doing they invested in sectors and regions that promised to maximize earnings. As these firms expanded, they in turn uplifted their local suppliers of goods and services. In that way, FDI served the cause of economic development—as if by an "invisible hand," the selfish interests of foreign investors created widespread social benefits! Note that Hirschman believed that foreign investors were most useful in the early stages of development; he feared that over time, monopolistic foreign investment could actually place a chokehold on local firms, preventing them from upgrading to higher value-added activities. FDI thus had, in his view, an expiration date, and he even proposed an organization that would be responsible for the orderly transfer of multinational assets to local entrepreneurs.[34]

The emphasis of private enterprise, then, responded to many of Washington's most pressing concerns regarding how best to promote economic progress in the developing world, which was of strategic concern to the extent that anti-American forces could take advantage of poverty and unrest in these countries. It required only limited taxpayer funds (in the form of various subsidies to encourage such investment), and it was expected to promote local entrepreneurship and, in turn, economic growth, which was viewed by officials as an important contributor to political stability and a long-run driver of democratization. However, the United States would discover that all these attractions would not necessarily convince developing world leaders to prioritize it over official, government-to-government economic assistance.

The US insistence on the importance of private enterprise arose within a broader ideational and ideological context that shaped, and continues to shape, American foreign assistance policy. In fact, one of the most remarkable observations about these developmental ideas, as first identified by David Baldwin in 1966, is how resilient they have proved to be: we will see similar themes repeated over and over by policy makers from the late 1940s to the present day.[35] In particular, Baldwin emphasized three interrelated ideas that American have consistently advocated: first, that developing countries "themselves are primarily responsible for their own economic development," or the principle of "self-help" (or what USAID now calls "self-reliance");[36] second, that growth depends on private rather than state capital; and third, that the "main obstacle retarding the flow of private capital . . . was the absence of a 'favorable climate of investment.'"[37]

The American ideology that I focus on in this book concerns the superiority of the private enterprise system over all contenders. Legal scholar Scott Bowman writes of the United States: "Throughout the history of the republic, the corporation has served as the primary agent for economic development and expansion, at home and abroad."[38] Historian Lawrence Glickman calls free enterprise "an essential American ideal."[39] In his memoirs, Dwight Eisenhower wrote that his philosophy on how to promote economic growth was powerfully shaped by the American experience, as if this could be readily transferred abroad: "Our economic strength had developed," he wrote, "historically, freely and without artificial and arbitrary government controls."[40] As a USAID policy document put it, "a private enterprise economy is . . . the most efficient means of achieving broad-based economic development."[41]

In Louis Hartz's view, Washington's insistence on exporting free enterprise reflected its "totalitarian" mind-set, its righteousness about possessing the one and only model of political economy. This set of "Lockean" beliefs had been deeply rooted since the country's founding, but they were undoubtedly amplified and strengthened during the Cold War, when the American system confronted an alternative global ideological challenge in the form of communism. Even worse, communism was seemingly attractive to many developing nations—especially given the apparent success of the Soviet Union and then Mao's China in rapidly industrializing their economies and dragging them out of poverty. The United States had no choice but to export capitalism, lest the world fall prey to this contending worldview.

As Hartz stressed, free enterprise (or what he also called "Algerism," after the nineteenth-century writer Horatio Alger, who mythologized the American bootstrap economy) was not just another way of organizing production: It was, for Americans, the *only* way. And that stance was not based on its material fruits alone, as bountiful as these were, but rather because it was the only form of economic organization that simultaneously motivated and safeguarded individual liberty.[42] Americans had no doubt about the singular greatness of their political economy.

But a Hartz powerfully put it, "The question is not whether our history has given us something to 'export,' but whether it has given us the right thing. And this question has to be answered in the negative."[43] For Hartz, the paradox—or even tragedy—of the American creed of democratic capitalism was that it extolled the unique circumstances under which it had emerged while also being convinced of its universal applicability. The novelist Robert Stone (perhaps cribbing from Hartz?) put it this way: "I think what's best about my country is not exportable."[44] Focusing more narrowly on democracy promotion, Nancy Bermeo has concluded that "democracy is not exportable," adding to doubts about the ability of the United States—despite all its military and economic power—to translate these resources into preferred foreign policy outcomes.[45]

This book urges us to reconsider such sweeping conclusions by analyzing the conditions under which efforts to export capitalist institutions succeeded and when they failed. In particular, we will examine the underlying economic conditions, including commodity dependence (the infamous "natural resources curse"), violent conflict, and the economic structure of local elites, that seem to shape the environment for private enterprise. Investors who put capital at risk must have some confidence that their property rights will be respected, but sadly that is not the case everywhere. Along these lines, a recent econometric study of political risk insurance unsurprisingly shows that firms are more likely to file claims for losses in countries which suffer violent conflict or depend heavily on resource rents.[46] These are the places where companies most often lose their assets either through destruction or expropriation. The analysis presented here supports these hypotheses, while going further to argue that in such places private sector development is less likely to take root in the first place.

While American officials usually recognized the challenges associated with encouraging investment in certain political-economic environments, their faith in the gospel of free enterprise would often overcome any such reservations. For alongside its contributions to material well-being, Americans have often expressed the belief that the free-market economy, with its ability to deliver sustainable growth, was a system capable of overcoming political divisions within societies and bringing harmony to them by creating an ever-expanding pie. To American officials, most social grievances were ultimately rooted in unresolved economic problems. As Franklin Roosevelt said in a January 1941 address to Congress, "economic problems . . . are the root cause of the social revolution which is today a supreme factor in the world."[47] Solving those economic problems through growth-generating policies became a core mission of post–World War II US foreign policy. Charles Maier has written in his brilliant essay, "The Politics of Productivity," that the stress on "economic growth arose out of the very terms in which Americans resolved their own organization of economic power . . . agreement on production and efficiency had helped bridge deep divisions at home."[48]

More generally, Americans have linked together economic and political freedom. Milton Friedman wrote in a famous 1961 essay "that economic arrangements play a dual role in the promotion of a free society. On the one hand, 'freedom' in economic arrangements is itself a component of freedom broadly understood, so 'economic freedom' is an end in itself to a believer in freedom. In the second place, economic freedom is also an indispensable means toward the achievement of political freedom."[49] A generation later, USAID echoed Friedman by stating: "A society in which individuals have freedom of economic choice, freedom to own the means of production, freedom to compete in the market place, freedom to take economic risk for profit and freedom to receive and retain the rewards of economic decisions is a fundamental objective of the AID, program in less developed countries." Moreover, USAID stressed the political implications of this policy: "A society in which economic power is widely dispersed is more likely to be one in which transfer of political power by election is permitted than in a society where exclusion from political power carries with it exclusion from economic power."[50] We will see that this view of the interlinkage between economic and political freedom reappears time and again throughout the history recounted here. That view has been severely challenged with the rise of China, whose economic liberalization has, at least for now, failed to generate the political freedom that was once widely expected by policy makers and pundits.

The ideology of private and free enterprise has thus provided a roadmap for American policy makers, setting the feasible routes that they can take to promote international development and growth. And while American officials were not, for the most part, ideologues, we will discover some notable exceptions to that rule, cases where economic ideology blinded officials to the facts on the ground. This seems to have occurred, for example, in Iraq, where dismantling SOEs (in part by refusing to finance them) was high on the American policy agenda, despite the fact that these firms were important sources of local employment. One of the tensions explored throughout this study is that between pragmatic policy making and America's political-economic ideology.

How successful has private sector development been around the world? Figure I.1 provides some tantalizing evidence to consider. Using "credit to the private sector" as a proxy measure for private sector activity, we can see that East Asia and the Pacific is by far the most dynamic of the world's regions in this respect (and obviously this vast region, like the others listed here, is made up of a great diversity of countries, so any sweeping generalizations must keep that in mind). Further analysis also suggests that East Asia is the region in which FDI has had the strongest association with the rise in credit, suggesting that this may be where linkages were the strongest; and note that in the conclusion we will revisit the structural conditions which seem to influence the prospects for private sector development.[51] Is it a coincidence that this area has also become the epicenter of global economic growth? If so, why did it ultimately provide a hospitable environment for

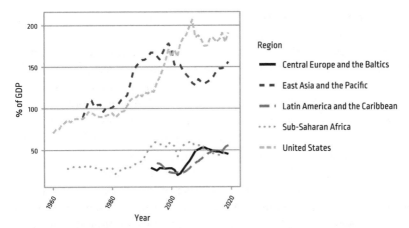

Data source: World Bank, "World Development Indicators," https://datacatalog.worldbank.org/dataset/world
-development-indicators.

FIGURE I.I   Credit to the Private Sector since 1960, Selected Regions

private enterprise, after a period of initial hostility as described in Chapter 2? What underlying conditions distinguish it from other regions? These are among the questions we will address in this book.

Conclusions

The purpose of this chapter has been to provide an intellectual roadmap for the book. It provides a rationale for why "history matters" (or should matter) to contemporary policy makers, and suggests some of the transcendent ideas that have guided (and continue to guide) American approaches to economic development, including self-help, private sector–led growth, and creation of a favorable investment climate. For much of the history that we will explore, Washington further believed that multinational corporations would fuel development through their linkages with local firms, and its assistance policies aimed to encourage such FDI.

At the same time, I have highlighted some of the constraints on Washington in promoting private sector development. For one thing, some developing countries had different priorities for their economic policy, and different ideologies about how growth could most effectively be achieved. For another, American executives of multinational firms have largely eschewed the developing world—outside a handful of countries—given investment opportunities elsewhere. These constraints, when interacting with such underlying structural conditions as dependence on natural resources or protracted violent conflict, limited the effectiveness of US policies aimed at private sector development.

Some other constraints, of course, were self-inflicted by Washington itself. Protectionism of key sectors of the American economy, for example, limited multinational interest in investing in export-oriented industries abroad so long as the US market was closed. Aid and trade policies were often incoherent, a situation that has hardly been remedied.

In Chapter 1 I provide some background history that will inform the country case studies that follow. In particular, I examine private sector development during the Truman and Eisenhower administrations, a period that saw the United States introduce a number of incentives to multinational firms to invest in the developing world. This period also saw the birth of the International Finance Corporation, a new institution (founded in 1956) whose sole focus would be on growing private enterprise. Despite these efforts, these administrations would confront the constraints previously described, leading them to recognize that private sector development had to be supplemented by foreign aid.

1

Private Enterprise, International Development, and the Cold War

An increased flow of United States private investment funds abroad . . . would do much to offset the false but alluring promises of the Communists.

—President Dwight D. Eisenhower, Message to Congress, 1955

Fresh off his stunning upset over Thomas Dewey in the election of 1948, President Harry S. Truman was searching for a big idea to animate his inaugural address. That idea eventually emerged from a relatively lowly State Department official named Benjamin Hardy, who had to circumvent several layers of bureaucracy to get his contribution up to the White House. Hardy thought that Truman should emphasize a positive program that would harness the energies of American corporations and charitable organizations on behalf of the world's developing nations, building on some modest efforts along these lines that the United States was funding in Latin America. This appealed to a president who sought to cast his own vision on the international system, allowing him to step out from the shadow of his predecessor, Franklin D. Roosevelt.[1]

Truman recognized that the US government had economic, moral, and geopolitical interests in promoting the growth of the world's developing nations, including those grappling with postcolonial independence, and the famous "Point Four" of his 1949 inaugural address pledged American assistance to this great task. In particular, Truman thought that the United States should mobilize the nation's science, technology, and capital in an effort to transform developing world economies. In Truman's words, "I believe that we should make available to peace-loving peoples the benefits of our store of technical knowledge in order to help them realize their aspirations for a better life. And, in cooperation with other nations, we should foster capital investment in areas needing development."

At the same time, Truman wanted to reassure the developing world about his intentions: "The old imperialism—exploitation for foreign profit—has no place in our plans. What we envisage is a program of development based on the concepts of democratic fair-dealing."[2] The United States had no intention of replacing the European powers as these countries began the often arduous process of decolonization, but instead would act to support their growth.

The Point Four announcement caught some members of Truman's administration off guard. They did not anticipate that the President would seek to take on new international initiatives, particularly in regions that seemed distant to many Americans. But beyond American participation in European reconstruction through the Marshall Plan (and note that some developing nations, including Taiwan, received Marshall Plan aid), Truman was aware of the potential strategic challenges posed by a growing number of newly independent nations. In 1945, the United Nations had 51 members; that number increased to 76 by 1955, and by 1961 it would grow to 104. These new states would certainly become targets for communist influence.

Driving US policy toward the developing world was postwar decolonization—which, in fact, had been one of Roosevelt's wartime objectives—alongside the emerging Cold War with the Soviet Union and the threat posed by communist China following Mao Tse-tung's victorious peasant revolution in 1949.[3] The advent of the Korean War in 1950, in which Beijing of course actively participated by sending troops, would further stimulate US concerns with the stability and security of developing countries, particularly those in East Asia and other suppliers of "critical" raw materials to the American economy and its defense industries. A "Soviet economic offensive" in the developing world, beginning in the mid-1950s, would add more fuel to American efforts to promote international economic growth.[4]

The Cold War also brought into sharp relief the ideological frames that shaped US development policy, which revolved around the fundamental concepts of "self-help" and private enterprise.[5] After all, the conflict with communism was also a war of ideas, as emphasized in one of the founding documents of the period, National Security Council report 68 (NSC-68).[6] The Cold War provided Washington with an opportunity to extol the many virtues of its free-market approach to economic organization, contrasting it with the communist world's "command and control" model. To once again cite David Baldwin, the United States never tired "of citing the advantages—real and imagined—of an economic system based on private enterprise."[7]

Yet US policy was also powerfully shaped and constrained by postwar fiscal concerns, which placed added pressure on officials to emphasize private enterprise and foreign direct investment (FDI) as drivers of development. With Congress unwilling to fund a massive foreign aid program beyond the Marshall Plan, the Truman administration had no choice but to encourage American investors to go overseas, and it elaborated a number of policies and subsidies designed to motivate them to do so. Still, the failure of American business to respond to these incentives at the levels necessary to meet developing world investment needs would lead Washington to reconsider its reluctance to providing foreign aid, and eventually to the creation of a "permanent" foreign assistance bureaucracy, the United States Agency for International Development (USAID), in 1961.

This chapter describes and analyzes the broad contours of US development policy during the first two decades of the Cold War, emphasizing why the center of that effort shifted from private enterprise toward government-to-government official development assistance (ODA) as the decade rolled on. In sketching this history, we will see the limits placed on the American state's policies by both business leaders and developing world governments. That is one theme that re-emerges time and again throughout this book.

The first section of the chapter examines the instruments that Washington devised in order to propel overseas investment. In the second, I turn to the Eisenhower administration's tortured path toward founding the International Finance Corporation (IFC) in 1956. While the idea of launching an IFC had been around since the Truman presidency, it had languished in Washington for lack of support. I explore how and why attitudes toward the IFC changed during the 1950s.

The chapter thus provides both the historical background for the country case chapters that follow, along with an outline of some of the enduring issues that US policy makers have faced. One of the main lessons of this history is straightforward: US policies to promote private enterprise around the world, as with the new Development Finance Corporation (DFC), have deep roots, going back at least to the earliest days of the Cold War. Studying that history could prove useful to all those charged with advancing American interests in the global economy, and help them to recognize that many of the issues being debated today are hardly novel.

Catalyzing Private Investment

At the end of World War II, the world economy lay in ruins. Much of Western Europe and East Asia had been shattered by the fighting, and Washington's initial belief in a quick recovery was soon shaken.[8] The hopes pinned on the United Nations to serve as the cornerstone of a new era of global peace and prosperity were also quickly squashed by the emerging Cold War with the Soviet Union. While these troubles would eventually lead to the June 1947 announcement of the Marshall Plan for European recovery, Washington had no intention of doing anything on a comparable scale for developing countries. The Marshall Plan bestowed limited funding to select Asian economies, including China and South Korea; officials seemed to believe that the rest of the developing world, which continued to include many colonies, would indirectly benefit from assistance to the European metropole.[9]

This is not to say that the United States was indifferent to their plight. Washington sought to promote international development for a host of humanitarian, economic, and security reasons; in fact, these were inextricably linked for American officials, given a deeply rooted belief that economic grievances were the primary reason for political instability. As President Truman put it in 1950, "poverty, misery and insecurity are the conditions on which communism thrives."[10]

Planning for the postwar economy had begun during the war itself, and the fruits of these efforts were made manifest at the Bretton Woods negotiations of 1944. There, the international community agreed to create an International Monetary Fund (IMF) in the interest of ensuring financial stability, and an International Bank for Reconstruction and Development (IBRD, or World Bank) to provide loans for recovery. For our purposes, it is critical to point out that one objective of the World Bank, as set forth in its articles of agreement, was to "promote foreign direct investment." Specifically, it was expected to carry out that task "by means of guarantees or participations in loans and other instruments made by private investors."[11] The reasons for the inclusion of this article were straightforward: developing countries had to mobilize foreign savings in order to meet their investment needs, and if official development assistance was not forthcoming or sufficient, then governments had little choice but to attract private funds from abroad.[12]

Fortunately, over the course of the war, a "surplus" pool of capital in the United States had emerged and was waiting to be deployed overseas. As a 1945 report by a US House special committee put it, "After the war, extensive foreign investments by the United States will have important benefits . . . to the rest of the world. The scarcity of capital in underdeveloped countries . . . will provide a large opportunity for American investments."[13] Assistant Secretary of State William Clayton made a similar point in a 1946 speech, saying that "It is essential that American capital . . . make a major contribution over a long time to the increase of production and wealth in many countries. . . . We cannot long continue to enjoy great wealth and prosperity, with most of the world lying prostrate from the war."[14]

Yet there were many impediments to moving American capital overseas, especially to the world's poorest nations. First, drawing on the British colonial experience, the State Department was concerned American investors might "exploit" developing nations, causing political problems between Washington and host governments and creating an opening for communist penetration. In order to create a buffer between the US government and foreign investors, the State Department began to give serious thought to calling for the creation of a United Nations Investment Board that would serve as a mediator between investors and host governments, ensuring that foreign investments were being made "for desirable purposes."[15]

Second, and perhaps more intractable, were the host of risks associated with FDI, including the lack of convertible currencies and exchange controls; the fear of expropriation without adequate compensation; double taxation; and the presence of high tariffs in industrial countries that discouraged developing world exports. Even during the 1944 Bretton Woods talks, the US Treasury advisor Harry Dexter White warned that private investors "had suffered too many losses" in the developing world in the past to justify any hope that large sums could again be mobilized.[16]

In order to address these problems, in 1945 the US government created an interagency Foreign Investment Policy Committee with the express purpose of elaborating a set of proposals that would assuage the investment community on the one hand and potential developing world recipients on the other. Working in consultation with the American business community, these proposals would soon come to reflect the concerns of investors more than those of recipient nations. Thus, references to "desirable investments" would soon become increasingly muted in official policy discourse.

Fundamentally, American firms wanted the following from developing nations before investments could proceed: market access, national treatment, quick and fair compensation in the event of nationalization or expropriation, avoidance of double taxation, and the ability to repatriate profits in dollars. Given the war's dislocation and their own economic policies, very few countries were willing or able to promise that they could meet these demands. This helps to explain why many developing world governments were dubious about relying on private investment and instead insisted on receiving official foreign aid as their first priority.

Still, the Foreign Investment Policy Committee continued to seek ways to remove the blockages to direct investment, and during the late 1940s it turned to an old tool for assistance: the Treaty of Friendship, Commerce, and Navigation (FCN). The Committee had come to the view that foreign investment should serve several purposes beyond simply making profits for multinational firms, including the promotion of "good international relations" and the upgrading of "skills and technology" in recipient nations. The best way to foster these various objectives while ensuring that developing world governments met their commitments to investors would be through treaty arrangements. In the words of Kenneth Vandevelde, who has carried out the most comprehensive study of the FCN in US foreign policy, "by 1948, the State Department knew that it wanted to obtain increased treaty protection for foreign investment . . . foreign investment policy called for national treatment; . . . prompt, adequate and effective compensation for expropriated property; and a prohibition on exchange controls."[17] President Truman's 1949 announcement of the new Point Four program for encouraging developing world economic growth further catalyzed these treaty efforts.

According to Truman, his "bold new program" would make "the benefits of our scientific advances and industrial progress available for the improvement and growth of underdeveloped areas. . . . Our aim should be to help the free peoples of the world, through their own efforts, to produce more food, more clothing, more materials for housing, and more mechanical power to lighten their burdens." However, Point Four would not be driven by government alone: "With the cooperation of business, private capital, agriculture, and labor in this country, this program can greatly increase the industrial activity in other nations and can raise substantially their standards of living."[18]

Following the announcement of Point Four, leading policy makers in the Truman Administration scurried to clarify what the United States had promised and the role that various parties were expected to play in the program's execution. In a memo to the President, Secretary of State Dean Acheson emphasized his understanding "that neither technical cooperation activities nor measures to foster capital investment be allowed to give an impression that the United States Government thereby becomes obligated to supply the funds needed to finance economic development. The US cannot accept the ultimate responsibility for seeing that economic development really takes place. This responsibility must . . . rest unmistakably on the nations desiring development."[19] As Acheson sought to emphasize, the overarching principle of self-help would not be forgotten!

Self-help, in turn, meant mobilizing private enterprise—both local and foreign—to provide the capital, technology, and ideas needed for development. As Acheson said in a 1949 speech, "This country has been built by private initiative, and it remains a land of private initiative. The preponderance of our economic strength depends . . . upon the abilities and morale of private citizens." Acheson believed that all nations could draw appropriate lessons from this experience.[20]

Sadly, Acheson admitted in a press briefing that "many places" had demonstrated a "failure" to create the conditions that would invite private investment in the first place. He warned those governments that closed their doors to foreign investors: "It is no solution to say, 'Well, the private sector won't do it, therefore the government must.'"[21] In Acheson's view, the problem wasn't a shortage of capital; it was the failure of developing countries to create a business environment that invited the economic participation of private investment. This meant that developing countries needed to prioritize improving their "investment climate."[22] Thus, alongside the Point Four program, the US government emphasized the importance of self-help, private enterprise, and creating an attractive "investment climate." We will see these themes re-emerge in American policy discourse time and again.

Hearings in Congress also sought to clarify the role of government vs. business in Point Four programming. While hardly a monolithic entity, American business had strong views when it came to foreign assistance, if witness testimony at congressional hearings provides any evidence (and, of course, witnesses are selected by congressional committees to elicit particular perspectives). According to a study by McLellan and Woodhouse, these witnesses "were agreed that 'technical cooperation programs should be authorized only with foreign countries which have indicated their firm intention to cooperate in fostering private enterprise.'" That view was bolstered by Representative (and later Secretary of State) Christian Herter (R-MA), who stated: "I think it is of the utmost importance to let foreign nations know that . . . there is a limit to which this country will go in supplying government funds, unless those nations are willing to be reasonable from the point of view of possible private investments."[23]

Nowhere in these statements can a recognition be found that the international system might also play a decisive role in shaping the economic trajectory of the world's poorest nations, and with it the willingness of multinational executives to invest there. Certainly, the United States had taken the lead after World War II in creating a new international trade regime, which was supposed to serve as the main engine for lifting countries out of poverty and generating global economic growth.[24] But for developing countries, the promise of that regime was limited by protectionism within the leading economic powers themselves. Protectionism in the industrial nations discouraged foreign investors who sought export-oriented platforms in the developing world; to put this somewhat differently, US protectionism was at odds with Washington's objective of promoting FDI.

In particular, protectionism limited the ability of these nations to exercise their comparative advantage to export commodity foodstuffs and labor-intensive goods like textiles; further, the provision of "food aid" by the United States and Western European nations beginning in the 1950s— generally surpluses that their farmers wanted to remove from inventories— often hurt developing world producers by undercutting them.[25] Even worse, "tariff escalation" in the industrial world discouraged investment in value-added production. Tariffs on chocolate, for example, were higher than they were on cocoa beans. This meant that there was little incentive to build, for example, food processing plants in developing countries.[26] As historian Robert Pollard has stated, "by retaining substantial trade barriers" against developing countries and refusing to support the creation of a new International Trade Organization to regulate world trade, "Congress undermined the Truman Administration's . . . development program for the Third World."[27] And while developing countries may have been important sources of "strategic raw materials," American officials were sensitive to the fact that the production and export of these commodities might have a smaller development impact than would manufactures.

A related barrier to growth was created by the economic structure of many developing countries, with their heavy reliance on commodity production and export. In the late 1940s, two economists in the United Nations system— Raul Prebisch in Santiago and Hans Singer in New York—independently elaborated what has since become known as the Prebisch-Singer hypothesis with respect to international trade, a theory that has been contested by economists ever since its publication. Prebisch and Singer posited that developing countries inevitably confronted declining terms of trade, and thus they were forced to export more and more natural resources in order to import fewer and fewer manufactured goods.[28] The answer was obvious: import-substituting industrialization (ISI), in which firms, operating behind high tariff barriers, would displace imported manufactures and stimulate economic diversification.

The call for ISI was also amplified by the so-called dollar shortage that gripped many nations after World War II. Given the widespread economic devastation that the war had produced, the United States became the global supplier for many goods and services. These products, however, had to be paid for in dollars, and few countries had the economic capacity to generate the cash needed to pay for imports invoiced in the American currency. Indeed, the dollar shortage was a major factor behind the elaboration of the Marshall Plan, among other emergency foreign assistance programs.[29]

There was thus a contradiction at the heart of American development policy. On the one hand, the United States assumed that nations could grow through self-help, and that trade provided the vehicle for that uplifting process—but on the other, it had erected significant protectionist barriers that impeded international commerce. Given Congress's protectionism, this contradiction could not be easily resolved. As it became more apparent that private sector–led trade and investment could not be an equal substitute for aid as the driver of economic growth, American officials would slowly come to recognize the need for a formalized program of government-to-government foreign assistance extending beyond an "emergency" period of recovery.[30]

But that lesson was still to come. During the Truman and (first) Eisenhower administrations, policy makers believed that private capital would flow in sufficient amounts to meet the investment needs of the developing world.[31] These needs were great. According to a group of experts brought together by the United Nations in 1951, the developing world would require about $19 billion of investment per annum to achieve annual growth rates of just 2 percent (an amount less than population growth in some countries). Given developing world savings rates, only $5 billion of this could be expected to come from domestic sources (recall once again the Keynesian identity that savings is equal to investment). International agencies and investors would therefore have to contribute $14 billion annually to meet that target. This difference between domestic savings and overall investment needs became widely known in the development community as the "investment gap." This was an influential concept in development circles, shaping the first generation of postwar foreign assistance programming aimed at catalyzing economic growth. In retrospect, some economists like William Easterly have argued it was ultimately counterproductive, encouraging many inefficient "white elephant" projects, whereas a better emphasis might have been on productivity instead.[32]

In an attempt to stimulate more FDI to meet these needs, the Truman administration initially devised three incentive schemes, drawing on input from the business community as to which policy innovations would be most effective in leading them overseas. These three schemes consisted of tax breaks, investment guarantees, and investment treaties.[33] Among the policies that might "catalyze private investment" most effectively, American business in the late 1940s and early 1950s concentrated their lobbying efforts on tax breaks, specifically tax reductions when it came to earnings from developing world subsidiaries and branches. According to Marina von Neumann Whitman, "A number of powerful business organizations and government advisory groups . . . argued that such favorable tax legislation would be the most effective way to increase foreign investment quickly and substantially. Such a tax reduction or elimination . . . would not only have a tremendous psychological incentive effect, but would also permit returns to increase to a point where they would outweigh the extra risks of foreign investment."[34] In fact, this proposal simply extended to other developing nations the reductions that were already in place for earnings in Latin America and pre-Maoist China and a deferral of tax payments until profits were remitted to the parent company.

As Whitman points out, these policy proposals were quickly attacked by some Republicans in Congress, among other critics, as corporate subsidies that were also patently unfair because they privileged investments in poor regions over rich ones. But these targeted subsidies spoke directly to the foreign policy objectives of the tax program. Again, in a political and ideological environment where neither President Truman nor his successor, Dwight Eisenhower, could muster much support for official foreign aid to the developing world (though this is less true of Eisenhower's second administration, during which business leaders began to voice their support for a more ambitious aid program),[35] it would need to rely on the private sector to cover the investment gap these countries faced. If lower tax rates were needed to stimulate more foreign investment, then the administration had no choice but to support that incentive.

The second policy innovation was investment guarantees. In fact, guarantee schemes had existed for many decades before World War II, but these generally protected bondholders against default risk and were usually provided by private insurers. During the 1920s and 1930s, Western governments had devised many new schemes to encourage exports, which mainly covered nonpayment risks; the US Export-Import (EXIM) Bank, for example, was founded in 1934 with this as one of its mandates.

The real innovation of the late 1940s and early 1950s was to provide government insurance against political risk, including wars, expropriations, and currency inconvertibility. Specifically, the government would provide firms with dollars in the event of local currency losses. Since many local currencies at this time were effectively inconvertible, the government hoped that this form of insurance would motivate firms to invest in places where they might not otherwise invest. Further, as Whitman emphasizes, an additional purpose of having the US government provide the insurance was to reduce the risk, rather than simply to price it. It was hoped that foreign governments would be less likely to nationalize, expropriate, or attack American firms if they knew that Washington was acting as their guarantor.[36]

Business criticism, however, mounted around these guarantee schemes as they began to take shape. First, many businesses were reluctant to share the information required in the insurance application with the US government. Second, some executives were concerned that "delicate political problems may result if the Government refuses guaranties on investment projects in one country while approving some in another." Third, there were debates over which agency should administer a program of this type; while the EXIM Bank was authorized by Congress to provide this function during the 1950s, it would pass to USAID a decade later and eventually to the Overseas Private Investment Corporation (OPIC) following its establishment in 1971.[37]

In any case, the guarantee scheme was little used during its first years of operation.[38] According to Raymond Mikesell, between 1948 and 1956 total insurance contracts amounted to just $124 million, "and less than 10 percent of these covered investments in the less developed countries. Thus far the results of the program have been disappointing."[39]

The final innovation was the investment treaty, which, as previously mentioned, had an earlier incarnation in the many treaties of "friendship, commerce, and navigation" that the United States had signed over the years, including with developing countries. But the protection afforded industry in these earlier documents, which focused mainly on trade, was often ill defined, and the changing international situation made it increasingly unlikely that the United States would willingly use military force or "gunboat diplomacy" to protect American investors as it had done in the past (although it would make use of the CIA partly for that purpose in several places, including Iran, Guatemala, and Chile).[40] Accordingly, a new emphasis was placed on drawing up investment treaties that specified the obligations of investors and recipient governments, including provisions for mediation in the event that the two parties could not reach agreement over how to settle differences. Truman's State Department stated that the United States would "expect any countries receiving [insurance] guaranties to enter into such treaties with us."[41]

However, as Foggy Bottom discovered upon starting to negotiate these investment treaties as early as 1949, there was "considerable reluctance on the part of governments to enter into . . . commitments for giving assurance to private investment."[42] These governments did not necessarily share Washington's preference for private enterprise, and the apparent economic success of the Soviet Union offered a very different economic model that some developing world leaders found intriguing. This effect was magnified as Moscow began to increase its foreign aid and trade promotion activities—the so-called Soviet economic offensive of the mid-1950s.[43] As a result, historian Pollard concludes, the FCNs "were a resounding flop: only eight countries—Ethiopia, Greece, Iran, Israel, Korea, Muscat and Oman, Nicaragua, and Panama—had ratified the treaties by 1963."[44]

In light of the lack of interest among a number of developing countries with respect to attracting foreign investment, in 1951 Congress urged that "the removal of restrictions and obstacles to foreign private investment be made a condition for receiving United States aid."[45] The Truman administration took up these concerns at the United Nations, but there "the representatives of most of the underdeveloped nations made it clear . . . that in their view large-scale public aid was necessary before conditions attractive to foreign investment could be created . . . in any case they much preferred capital assistance from public rather than private sources."[46] American officials were again taken aback by the doubts many developing world representatives expressed with respect to private enterprise and the priority they gave to official grants and long-term loans.

By the closing years of the Truman administration, the promise of private capital fueling international development had not materialized. As Figure 1.1 shows, total FDI by American firms never reached even $1 billion in any year between 1946 and 1952. Further, over half the amount invested flowed to Canada; the largest developing region, Latin America, received only 25 percent of overall funding. This was far below the amounts

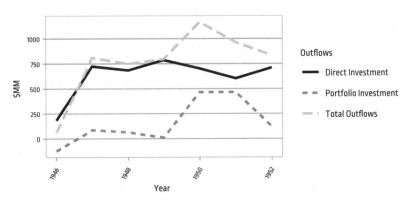

Data sources: Department of Commerce, *Balance of Payments of the United States 1949–1951* (Washington, DC: Department of Commerce, 1952), 91–100, 156; Department of Commerce, *Survey of Current Business* (Washington, DC: Department of Commerce, March 1953), 8–9, drawn from Gardiner Patterson and John Gunn, *Survey of U.S. International Finance, 1952* (Princeton, NJ: Princeton University Press, 1953), 124.

FIGURE 1.1   US Capital Outflows, 1946–1952, in Millions of Dollars ($MM)

needed to close the investment gap. The reluctance of American business to invest overseas at a time when many profitable opportunities still existed at home, coupled with foreign resistance to the private sector and a "dollar shortage" that made it difficult to import capital inputs to foreign subsidiaries, served to undermine the US government's preferred approach to international development. Protectionism within the United States also made export-oriented investments unattractive for many commodities and finished goods. Accordingly, the incoming Eisenhower administration would have to seek out new ideas.

The Eisenhower Administration and Private Investment

While President Truman had signaled that international development was one of his administration's priorities, in fact the resources allocated to that policy were paltry. The administration's total request to Congress for the FY1952 Point Four program was only $79 million, and of the appropriated amount, only about half would actually be expended in the field. The Korean War and the need for rearmament took precedence in Washington over the expansion of foreign aid programs. But developing countries "expressed dissatisfaction" with the American effort and called for "large amounts of capital assistance."[47]

Under the new Eisenhower administration, these pleas did not fall upon deaf ears. According to historian Burton Kaufman, "the United States became more attentive to the problems of Third World Countries and assumed greater responsibilities for meeting their economic needs . . . the economic development of the Third World became one of the administration's highest priorities."[48] This conviction was largely the product of Eisenhower's evolving views regarding the communist threat to the developing world and how that might impact American security, especially at a time when the American military was relying more heavily upon the raw materials these countries provided.[49]

Further, as W. W. Rostow has written, following the death of Stalin in 1953, the Soviet economic offensive was rapidly expanding to a number of developing countries and regions where the United States had vital strategic interests, such as Iran, India, and even Latin America.[50] Initially, however, a president who had sworn his devotion to balanced budgets could hardly lend his support to major increases in bilateral foreign aid, and these programs went against his market-oriented priors in any case.

Instead, Eisenhower believed that a combination of increased trade and FDI would "assure economic growth and prosperity."[51]

Eisenhower had already signaled his approach to international development in his 1953 inaugural address. He'd stated that the United States "shall strive to foster everywhere, and to practice ourselves, policies that encourage productivity and profitable trade. For the impoverishment of any single people in the world means danger to the well-being of all other peoples."[52]

His emphasis on free trade, however, was not an easy sell domestically. Any expansion of world trade would require reductions in US tariffs; this was strongly opposed by many Republicans in Congress, who were led by Senate majority leader Robert Taft (R-OH), a staunch isolationist and protectionist. As a consequence, the administration deferred any major action on trade policy in 1953, accepting a one-year extension of the President's trade negotiating authority, and instead appointed a commission (named the Randall Commission, after its chairman, Clarence Randall, CEO of Inland Steel Company) charged with conducting an overall review of foreign economic policy.[53]

Remarkably, the Randall Commission recommended that "economic aid on a grant basis should be terminated as soon as possible."[54] Most economic aid at that time flowed to a recovering Western Europe, and the sums allocated to the developing world were insignificant by comparison. Further, within the developing world, the plurality of funds went to Asian countries; funding for Sub-Saharan Africa, in contrast, was negligible, as Washington relied upon the European countries to provide funding (see Figure 1.2). The implication of Randall's recommendation was, naturally, that trade and investment must play a larger role in US foreign economic policy.

With respect to trade, however, the Randall Commission recognized the political climate of the times was not ripe for major changes in US policy. As they put it, "We are fully aware of the arguments for free trade. It is sufficient to say that, in our opinion, free trade is not possible under the conditions facing the United States today."[55] Instead, the commission emphasized granting the President greater authority to negotiate multilateral trade agreements.

Given the limitations the commission placed on aid and trade as vehicles for economic development, it only followed that "the United States Government should make clear that primary reliance must be placed on private investment to undertake the job of assisting in economic development abroad."[56] Accordingly, the commission suggested that the United States should use the diplomatic corps as, in effect, representatives of the private sector, who would school local governments on the conditions which would

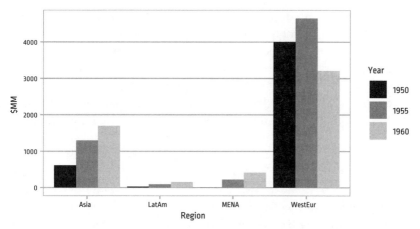

Data source: USAID, Foreign Assistance "Green Book," https://pdf.usaid.gov/pdf_docs/PBAAJ833.pdf.

FIGURE 1.2   US Foreign Aid by Region (Military Excluded), 1950–1960, in Millions of Dollars ($MM)

make their countries most conducive to such investment. It further argued that the United States should relax any antitrust laws that constrained firms from creating joint ventures overseas.

On March 30, 1954, President Eisenhower took a slightly refined version of the Randall Commission's recommendations and delivered them to Congress as an address dedicated to US foreign economic policy.[57] On trade, the President called for "the gradual and selective revision of our tariffs" through multilateral negotiations. But it was "investment abroad" that would achieve multiple US objectives, including trade expansion, the maintenance of American employment, the securing of mineral resources, and the strengthening of "the economies of foreign countries."

Given "the great importance of private investment to our foreign economic policy," Eisenhower called for further changes in taxation that would make such investment even more appealing. In line with the Randall Commission, he also said that private investors would have "full diplomatic support," including through the negotiation of investment treaties. As for grant aid, Eisenhower echoed the recommendation for eliminating it, insisting that "dollar grants are no solution" to development problems.[58]

The private investment theme was taken up in April in an article for *Foreign Affairs* written by Harold Stassen, director of the newly established Foreign Operations Administration, which succeeded the short-lived Mutual Security Agency. He reiterated that "an important objective of our foreign economic policy in the years ahead must be to stimulate the flow of

private investment into those areas of the world where the need is greatest."
Stassen noted that during the postwar era, the vast majority of US FDI in
the developing world had been aimed at exploiting natural resources, particularly as the price of these commodities skyrocketed during the Korean
War. He expressed hope that FDI would diversify into manufacturing and
into countries that did not rely primarily on commodity exports. In addition
to the US actions already outlined by President Eisenhower for encouraging
investment, he also insisted upon the necessity of having local governments
adopt investor-friendly policies, lecturing that "we hope it will be realized
that private investment is the best, indeed the only, means of supplying adequate funds to do the job for which the underdeveloped countries are clam-
oring."[59] Public assistance, it seemed, would not be forthcoming.

Overall, as Rostow has written, "1954 was a . . . somewhat regressive
year in foreign aid."[60] Despite the Eisenhower administration's belief in the
strategic importance of development in light of the communist threat, it
continued to rely on private investment as the elixir for growth. And while
the amount of capital flowing to the developing world was on the rise, increasing from $6.1 billion in 1950 to $7.3 billion in 1953, it still lagged
far below the amounts required to fill the $19 billion investment gap.[61]

Nonetheless, confronted by a new "Soviet economic offensive" and developing world demands for more assistance, by the fall of 1954 an Eisenhower economic adviser asked Randall, who was now also acting as coun-
selor to the President, whether he would be open "to new thinking in the
[development] field. Mr. Randall replied affirmatively."[62] One aspect of that
"new thinking" would be US support for an International Finance Corporation (IFC), to be housed within the World Bank. But to get approval for
the IFC, the administration would first have to overcome opposition both
at home and abroad.

Origins of the International Finance Corporation

In fact, the IFC had been initially proposed in 1951—probably by the World
Bank, which recognized its own shortcomings with respect to private sector
development.[63] Even though the World Bank's Articles of Agreement called
upon it to "promote foreign investment," its capacity to do so was limited
by constraints within its charter, especially in terms of its inability to take
equity stakes in private companies and projects. An IFC would expand
upon the World Bank's limited ability to catalyze the private sector in developing countries. It also had the added benefit of being a multilateral
organization, which could assuage the fears of those foreign leaders who

viewed American efforts to promote direct investment as a Trojan horse for more sinister or imperialist attempts to control and manipulate local politics and economics.[64]

Still, the Truman administration had "strongly opposed the IFC concept" when an advisory board on international development chaired by Nelson Rockefeller sought US government support for the idea.[65] First, the United States did not want to be the sole funder of such an initiative, which was certain to be the case during these early postwar years. Second, business leaders feared that the IFC would "encroach upon a field that should be reserved for private enterprise." Third, business executives, along with many public officials (including those at the Treasury and Federal Reserve Board), were uncomfortable with the melding of public and private dollars in foreign investments.[66] This melding would blur the difference between the public and private sectors and muddle the American idea that these were, and should remain, separate spheres of activity.

Likewise, developing countries themselves were not pushing for the creation of the IFC; instead, they sought higher levels of public funding via foreign aid transfers.[67] They lobbied the United Nations for the creation of a "special fund for grants in aid and for low-interest, long-term loans." However, the United States was firmly against this proposal, with the State Department taking the position that "circumstances do not permit the establishment of an international grant fund at this time."[68]

Now it was the Eisenhower administration's turn to review the case for an IFC. It initially decided to punt on the issue, with the State Department instructing its UN representatives in June 1953 to "frankly admit that the United States government has not yet formulated its position on the IFC proposal."[69] As with the Truman administration, the IFC's opponents both within and outside of government continued to argue that it was not the public sector's role to make direct investments in private enterprise for the sake of economic development. The National Foreign Trade Council, a business organization, "maintained that the Unites States government 'must make it clear, by word and action,' that American public funds would not be used for development and investment projects which . . . could be financed by private capital.'"[70] A year later, the debate within the administration continued, and in July 1954 the National Advisory Council (NAC, an interagency body responsible for international economic policy established after World War II) determined that the United States should report to the UN that it was "unconvinced that the establishment at this time of an International Finance Corporation is either . . . necessary or desirable."[71]

However, the world had not stopped for Washington and its new president. At the UN, developing countries were moving ahead with their call for a "Special UN Fund for Economic Development" (SUNFED), which the United States continued to resist. The US representative to the UN's Economic and Social Council (EcoSoc) had already reported in the summer of 1953 that as a result of Washington's failure to be take a more positive stance toward international development, the United States was becoming "the focus of resentment by the underdeveloped countries."[72] In October 1954, the US representative was urging Washington "that U.S. position [regarding the IFC] be changed."[73]

By November, the NAC had indeed changed its position; it now recommended "United States participation in an International Finance Corporation." The NAC noted that its reconsideration was due to the urging of Washington's ambassador to the UN (former Senator Henry Cabot Lodge, R-MA), while the State Department added that it "was willing to support the . . . proposal, largely because of the importance to the United States of avoiding a perpetual negative position" with respect to development initiatives. For his part, Federal Reserve Board chairman William McChesney Martin continued to express skepticism about the IFC, stating that he "remained unconvinced that the IFC . . . had economic merit"—but he added that he would support it if the NAC "felt it necessary to approve the proposal on political grounds."[74] Once some important changes were made to its lending principles to curb its ability to make loans to state-owned enterprises, a number of leading American bankers and business leaders came around to accepting the new organization.[75]

The United States announced its official support of the IFC at a meeting of Latin American finance ministers in late November 1954. There, Secretary of Treasury George Humphrey recognized that the proposal for an IFC had been "under study for several years." After all this deliberation, the Eisenhower administration was now prepared to "ask the Congress to support United States participation in such a corporation. We have in mind an institution organized as an affiliate of the International Bank, with an authorized capital of $100 million to be contributed by those members of the International Bank who wish to subscribe."[76] President Eisenhower himself discussed the importance of the IFC proposal in a January 1955 congressional address on foreign economic policy.[77] The following year, the new institution would be established as part of the World Bank.

With the United States now committed to the IFC's creation, the Eisenhower administration once again indicated to the international community that it "intended to rely on the private sector to promote economic development abroad."[78] Eisenhower also hoped that the developing world's demand to establish a SUNFED for grants and soft (low-interest) loans would diminish. However, that proved not to be the case. Many developing coun-

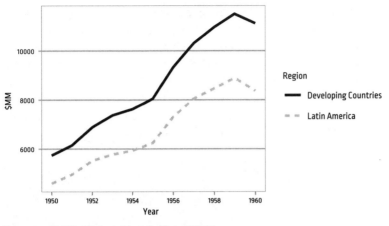

Data sources: Statistical Abstract of the United States; BEA data.

FIGURE 1.3   US FDI in Developing Countries and Latin America, 1950–1960, in Millions of Dollars ($MM)

tries continued to express skepticism about the role that the private sector should, and could, play in driving economic growth, meaning that their appetite for public funds had not changed.[79] Would the Eisenhower administration need to reconsider its position, or would it ultimately be proven right about the role of foreign investment as a driving force for capital mobilization?

To some extent, this latter question can be answered in the affirmative. During the administration's years in office, the stock of US FDI in the developing world increased from $7.3 billion in 1953 to $11.1 billion in 1960, with the vast majority directed to Latin America (see Figure 1.3).[80] Still, the total amount of FDI flowing to developing countries remained far below the $19 billion that the UN had estimated necessary to meet investment and growth targets, and the bulk of it went to a handful of countries.

For its part, the IFC would make only a small contribution to closing the investment gap. In fiscal year 1960–1961 it made $6.2 million in new investments, bringing the total since its founding to $44.4 million. Indeed, the IFC devoted its annual report that year to "some problems of industrial operations in developing countries," citing the small size of many local markets, the financial problems these countries faced, and in some cases the conflicts that arose between domestic and foreign firms.[81] Despite Washington's best efforts, foreign investment would not flow in sufficient amounts to meet developing world needs.

One issue that the IFC did *not* highlight was the lack of interest in foreign investment on the part of several developing world governments. This lack of interest was of central concern to US policy makers, who grew frustrated with their inability to change the situation. As a member of the US delegation to the UN wrote in late 1954, "There is no seeming disposition on the part of any of the underdeveloped countries to rely on private capital . . . while giving lip service to its flow most of them in practice do little to attract it. Many . . . underdeveloped countries consider foreign private capital as a form of colonialism."[82]

Turning to Foreign Aid

Taking this delegate's sweeping generalization with a grain of salt, there were economic and political reasons beyond fears of colonialism for developing world skepticism regarding reliance on foreign investment. One that was widely prevalent during the postwar years was "export pessimism," or the view that the inevitable decline in the terms of trade for commodity exporters meant that they had no choice but to build up domestic markets for locally produced manufactures through their own protectionist policies, or "import-substituting industrialization (ISI)."[83] But ISI should not be equated with protection against FDI; indeed, some governments (e.g., that of Brazil) welcomed foreign investors into their ISI schemes (usually in sectors other than natural resources, with a particular encouragement of investment in manufacturing), and the firms could earn large profits in these captive markets.[84] At the same time, to the extent that multinational enterprises sought to establish export platforms in the developing world, export pessimism necessarily discouraged these types of investment.[85]

How should the United States respond when FDI was either insufficient or deemed by local rulers to be undesirable, especially in those cases where the country in question was of strategic interest to Washington? By the end of Eisenhower's first term, Cold War competition in the developing world was growing ever more intense. The Suez debacle of November 1956—in which France and Great Britain joined Israel in attacking Egypt and seizing the Canal Zone in response to President Gamal Nasser's nationalization of that waterway—demonstrated that Europe's colonial impulse had not died. Eisenhower was slowly coming around to the realization that the United States would have to offer more than the promise of private investment if it was to keep developing countries out of the communist orbit; it would have to provide direct foreign aid in the form of soft loans as well. This was becoming all the more necessary as demands for a SUNFED continued to rise in the United Nations.[86]

Accordingly, Eisenhower submitted a Fiscal Year 1958 proposal for foreign assistance to Congress that included $500 million for what became the Development Loan Fund (DLF), which provided funding for industrial projects, and an additional $300 million for a "special assistance" fund for "economic and military emergencies."[87] As its name suggests, the DLF provided loans, not grants, for projects that were expected to have broad, developmental effects (e.g., electrification). It was hoped that US multinationals would become actively engaged in these projects, but in a retrospective analysis of the DLF upon its termination in 1961, USAID reported that "DLF's effort to encourage activity by US private enterprise in less developed countries was its least successful endeavor."[88] That being said, we will see examples in the following chapters of how DLF loans were put to use in the service of local industrialization.

In the event, these requests were not greeted warmly by the Congress. There, Eisenhower's requests were slashed, with only $300 million approved for the DLF. As Republican Senator H. Alexander Smith of New Jersey put it, "This is a devastating defeat . . . for the president."[89] Yet even an underfunded DLF represented a sea change in American foreign assistance policy. The long-standing belief that private sector funds would suffice to meet developing world demands was evaporating. Under Secretary of State Herter expressed this new perspective when he said in 1957 that "it would be unrealistic to plan on a complete substitution of private investment for economic assistance programs."[90]

Conclusions

During the early years of the Cold War, the United States government pinned most of its hopes for economic development on the private sector. US-based foreign investors, Washington believed, would be eager to enter developing countries and displace the capital-starved European companies that had once controlled local and regional supply chains. Undoubtedly they needed some incentives, including tax breaks and investment guarantees, but these policies and programs would be sufficient to open the floodgates of America's financial resources. In so doing, American capitalism would counter the communist economic challenge.

That vision reflected a development policy that revolved around self-help, private enterprise, and improvement of the investment climate as its core principles. But this ideological underpinning was ill suited to the postwar economic environment in several important respects. First, the international economy was in a shambles at the war's end, and the task of global market reconstruction was far greater than the postwar planners in Washington had anticipated. Second, and related, the world suffered a "dollar shortage" that made foreign investments uninviting, as multinational firms were hesitant to operate in countries with inconvertible currencies. Third, investment opportunities in the United States were ample and profitable; there was no capitalist "necessity" to invest overseas. Fourth, the Soviet Union and communist China offered developing world leaders an alternative vision of economic growth and management—one that Moscow in particular would promote through its foreign assistance and trade policies during the 1950s. Finally, the newly independent countries of the developing world were seeking to free themselves of their colonial shackles, and a number of them were skeptical of Western policies that emphasized foreign investment and private enterprise, which they saw as instruments of colonial policy. All these factors led to skepticism regarding the efficacy and/or desirability of the private investment prescription Washington was trying to write.

On some levels, developing country doubts about the promise of private investment proved correct. As we have seen, the amount of FDI flowing to the developing world during the 1950s was far below the levels required to overcome the investment gap, even if it steadily increased during that decade. The paucity of international funds, coupled with enduring protectionism in the United States and Western Europe, led developing countries to believe that they indeed had to rely on "self-help" in order to generate sustained growth, but with the state rather than private enterprise at the core of economic policy and activity. This, in turn, provided intellectual support (and in some cases the underlying rationale) for policies of economic nationalism, including import-substituting industrialization and the establishment of state-owned enterprises.

Yet it is dangerous to paint the developing world's economic experience with a broad brush. Latin America and East Asia, for example, followed very different development models, and even within these regions there was great political and economic diversity. Similarly, the African continent witnessed myriad experiments with economic policy. Still, nearly all developing countries shared a determination to industrialize and shrink their agricultural sectors using the levers of public policy to the extent possible.[91] We will now turn to our country case studies in order to probe more deeply the question of where the American call for private sector development was welcomed and where it was eschewed.

2

Private Sector Development in the Shadow of War

Taiwan and Korea

What has happened on Taiwan is what we want to see happen throughout Africa and Asia and Latin America.

—USAID ADMINISTRATOR DAVID BELL, 1965[1]

DURING THE LATE 1940s and early 1950s, some countries that had previously been considered marginal to the containment of communism by US public officials, including South Korea and Taiwan, became indispensable American allies. Given the security environment in East Asia, Washington was compelled to concoct a development formula that would enable Seoul and Taipei to defend themselves without placing an undue strain on their—or the American—economies. What President Eisenhower said of South Korea in 1953 also reflected his views of Taiwan: "I am convinced that the security interests of the United States clearly indicate the need to act promptly not only to meet immediate relief needs but also to begin the long-range work of restoring the . . . economy to health and strength."[2]

How could the United States support economic recovery and growth in East Asia without placing unreasonable burdens on American taxpayers? The only answer was greater foreign direct investment (FDI) and private sector development. In a 1952 meeting with President Chiang Kai-shek, for example, a State Department official said that Washington was "encouraging American private investment on Taiwan." He further noted that "continuing economic aid from the United States . . . would be dependent upon their carrying out sound economic policies,"[3] which naturally included "more private investment."[4]

But the *dirigiste* regimes in Taiwan and South Korea were not necessarily amenable to the concept of private sector development that the United States was promoting. Governments in postwar East Asia tended to place less emphasis on private enterprise, and more on state-led development, than Washington did. Growing a free market, with independent, private firms at its core, simply wasn't a priority for governments seeking to gain control over their polities.[5] Neither Chiang nor Korean leader Syngman Rhee placed the growth of private enterprise at the center of their economic concerns or objectives.

Instead, what both Chiang and Rhee wanted was to exercise firm control over their respective economies. This was partly for reasons of national security—they believed that the state had to direct scarce capital to the sectors most crucial for military power—but politics loomed large as well. Both men believed that economic power was a necessary component of political power; or to put this somewhat differently, their political power would be compromised in an environment that gave free reign to entrepreneurship and private investment. As Park has written, "the dirigiste state did not wish to yield control of the economy."[6]

In retrospect, given their security environment and their antimarket economic policies, it seems incredible that Taiwan and South Korea were among the group of countries that created an "East Asian miracle" of growth with equity. Searching for the sources of that miracle, scholars have cited any number of policies and background conditions, including, inter alia, land reform; literacy campaigns and investment in human capital; the legacy of "good" colonial institutions bequeathed by Japan, like enforceable property rights; entrepreneurial "cultures"; foreign assistance and technology transfer; the communist threat and American security umbrella; technocratic, growth-oriented governments that created "developmental states"; the export-orientation of industry; the role of new economic ideas; and postwar population growth.[7]

Yet what role did Washington's encouragement of private enterprise play in this rapid economic expansion? How did the United States use its foreign aid as a lever to push for more private sector development in countries that were recalcitrant about promoting it? These are the questions we examine in this chapter.[8]

As I will show, growing the private sector was an important objective of the United States, which was basically the sole provider of economic assistance to Taiwan and Korea during the early Cold War era. But the United States could not unilaterally impose its preferences, despite its seeming leverage in these cases; thus, negotiations between the United States and local governments led to assistance packages that sequenced a reform process, with private sector development often targeted for the later stages, once other policies and programs had been put into place. Still, the United States had no compunction when it came to encouraging these governments to promote private enterprise as soon as possible, and it provided high-powered incentives for them and local entrepreneurs to do so. As a US Senate report noted, "The very giving and receiving of aid are major infringements on sovereignty,"[9] and Washington felt obliged for ideological and fiscal reasons to advance its private enterprise formula for development.

US aid to Taiwan and South Korea shored up both economies at a critical juncture. According to one scholar, "There is little doubt that, without massive U.S. support . . . neither South Korea nor Taiwan could have survived as nation-states."[10] For his part, Tsai states that "the top priority of the Kuomingtang (KMT) regime during the early 1950s was simply 'security' and 'survival.'" He argues that Chiang harbored few grand economic ambitions at this time beyond keeping his people fed; thus the early focus on land reform, and the use of aid to pay for food imports, as discussed in more detail below.[11] Even if these viewpoints appear too extreme, they do point to the crucial role that aid played a time when these economies had to finance massive defense expenditures while trying to meet the minimal needs of their civilian populations.

Nonetheless, even in a situation where the United States had as much leverage with foreign governments as it could ever hope to muster, Washington's ability to shape their economic policies faced severe limits. The leaders of South Korea and Taiwan had their own ideas about how to organize an economy, and these ideas were inextricably intertwined with their pressing political, economic, and military concerns. Taiwan and Korea would emphasize state-directed economic programs that also served their enormous defense requirements, and to the extent private enterprise was allowed to develop, it would be under government tutelage.[12] As Kim reminds us, "aid transfers are not a unilateral transfusion by aid givers, but are a mutual bargain between donors and recipients."[13]

The history presented in this chapter also provides rich insights into the conflicts that emerged between the broad policy lines being advanced by distant officials in Washington and the situation that American diplomats and experts confronted on the ground in their assigned countries. Washington painted its policies in ideologically tinted brush strokes, yet these often provided only the haziest of sketches for the detailed canvas being prepared by the country teams in real time. These teams had to work on a daily basis under the constraints imposed by the domestic political economy, and their ability to align a given policy with Washington's preferences was limited. In that sense, the analysis here is in partial contrast to Bruce Cumings's important argument regarding Taiwan and Korea, "Often it was difficult to know if natives or Americans were writing the plans and policies." The evidence presented here suggests that the "natives" had far more ability to shape policy than implied in that quote, a crucial point that Americans would relearn in every country they have sought to influence.[14]

That being said, American policymakers did exercise some influence over local officials, probably accelerating their acceptance of more private enterprise than they would have otherwise preferred. They did so in part through the astute use of its aid funding, as we will see in the following sections. The United States also rolled out Point Four programs, such as technical-assistance training, which brought hundreds of Taiwanese citizens (including, it must be said, many who were born on the mainland, as they were favored by the KMT) to America, while supporting the development of advanced research institutes in Korea; these programs expanded the available pool of human capital, which was in terribly short supply during the early Cold War in both countries.[15] In what follows we first consider Taiwan, then South Korea, before offering some lessons from this history for contemporary policy makers.

US Foreign Aid and Private Enterprise in Taiwan

Taiwan was colonized by Japan in the late nineteenth century and remained under Tokyo's tutelage until 1945. The impact of this colonial legacy on postwar economic growth remains contested among scholars, but some good institutions were undoubtedly bequeathed to the island, including a fairly strong property rights regime (the island had good cadastral surveys, which greatly facilitated the land reform process undertaken with American encouragement during the early 1950s) and an educational system that reached deeper into the lower classes than in many Asian countries. In 1950, for example, Taiwan's literacy rate of 50 percent was far above that found in India. The country's 1953 GDP per capita of some $220, however, was, by some estimates, below the levels found at that time in such countries as Kenya and Ghana.[16] Only in the early 1960s did Taiwan regain its pre–World War II living standards.[17]

With the end of World War II and the defeat of Imperial Japan, Taiwan reverted to becoming a province of China. But a split between the KMT party and communist forces on the mainland led to civil war, and some of the Nationalist forces began to flee to the island. Their relations with the established Taiwanese were hardly cordial, and in March 1947 a revolt broke out that took thousands of lives.[18] By the time KMT leader Chiang Kai-shek fled to Taiwan in 1949, these local tensions had eased somewhat; still, the KMT was loathe to cede too much economic power to the established Taiwanese, and that political objective would play a major role in subsequent economic policies.[19]

But Chiang's immediate worry was a Maoist invasion from the mainland—one that he would likely have to face without any outside intervention and perhaps in the presence of internal party dissension. For throughout 1949 and 1950, Chiang faced two crises: an internal crisis of KMT leadership and the external threat from Beijing. Even worse for the KMT, the United States did not greatly involve itself in Taiwan's problems until the outbreak of the Korean War in June 1950. The Joint Chiefs of Staff did not believe that Taiwan was of sufficient strategic importance to defend from attack, leaving Secretary of State Dean Acheson to half-heartedly float the idea that it become a UN trusteeship (as the United States had also proposed for Korea). Taiwan, the State Department believed, would ultimately fall to the communists, owing to KMT corruption, military incompetence, and alienation of the local Taiwanese—so America's refusal to fight on behalf of its freedom seemed only sensible.[20] On 17 May 1950, the US Consul General in Taipei, Robert Strong, sent a telegram to Secretary of State Dean Acheson, saying, "In opinion of attachés and myself fate of Taiwan sealed," as an invasion was believed to be imminent.[21]

Once the Korean peninsula became embroiled in war, the threat from international communism seemed much graver than previously believed, and Washington's strategic calculus changed. As President Truman stated on 27 June, "communism has passed beyond the use of subversion to conquer independent nations and will now use armed invasion and war."[22] Suddenly, it was in the national interest to provide Taiwan with a security umbrella and to support its economic development as well; as Wu asserts, "it is no exaggeration to say that the Korean War . . . saved Taiwan."[23] The US Senate would also put the issue of economic assistance to Taiwan in defense terms: "Regardless of the labels pasted on . . . aid, the whole of it adds up to an operation in support of our military."[24] Henceforth, Taiwan would become a linchpin of Washington's anti-Maoist strategy in East Asia.

The KMT's early economic policies reflected a combination of Sun Yat-sen's philosophy and the realities confronting the government on the ground. Sun had adopted a socialist orientation toward economic development back in the nineteenth century, and he had decreed that China's modernization must rest upon the pillars of land reform, industrialization, and state intervention.[25] These were the very pillars that the KMT adopted in Taiwan, motivated in large part by the government's desperate need for streams of revenue. Accordingly, the large Japanese firms on the island were nationalized at the war's end and brought under state control. The space for private enterprise was limited by several factors, including tensions between mainlanders and native Taiwanese (who constituted a large share of the business owners), a lack of credit, and uncertainty about the island's future.[26]

As a result, during the early postwar years, "Taiwan had one of the largest public sectors outside the Communist Bloc. Throughout the 1950s, state corporations accounted for 50 percent or more of industrial production. The average share of the public sector in gross fixed capital formation from 1951 to 1980 was 30.9 percent . . . only India had a higher percentage."[27] Beyond the companies nationalized following Japan's defeat, new state-owned enterprises (SOEs) were created to build infrastructure and provide public services, as well as to engage in banking and finance.

The immediate task facing Taiwan after the war was the restoration of agricultural and industrial production. The economy had been "seriously damaged" by allied bombing, curbing output of desperately needed commodities. Given the shortage of goods and services, rampant inflation took hold, while foreign exchange and gold reserves were quickly being depleted to pay for imports. On top of all these issues, the economy had to put itself on a war footing and support large outlays for troops and defense expenditures.[28]

American economic assistance to Taiwan (then commonly referred to as Formosa) after 1949 was initially carried out by the Economic Cooperation Administration (ECA), the organization created to administer Marshall Plan aid to Western Europe. This gave it some independence from the State Department; of course, Congress had created it for that very purpose, as many in that body doubted the ability of those at State to run efficient economic programs. The ECA was led by a businessman, Paul Hoffman, formerly of Studebaker, and he recruited many business executives to work under him. In fact, ECA had sought to continue operating in China following the communist revolution there, viewing economic assistance as a "last bridge" between Washington and Beijing.[29] That hope, of course, was shattered, and the ECA would ultimately move all its operations to Taiwan.

Taiwan's immediate need was to import critical commodities, chiefly food and medicine. Between 1949 and 1951, the ECA provided $75 million to finance these imports; technical assistance was also focused on restoring agricultural production in an effort to conserve foreign exchange. It was Taiwan's good fortune that the head of the ECA mission, and US representative on the Joint Commission on Rural Reconstruction (JCCR), which had been established under the China Aid Act of 1948 to promote rural development, was the distinguished agricultural specialist and old China hand Dr. Raymond Moyer. He would play a key role in Taiwan's famed land reform program, something he had already urged Chiang to undertake on the mainland.

Indeed, a notable aspect of the US aid program was that it enjoyed remarkable continuity in leadership. Officials stayed on Taiwan for several years, getting to know the country, its people, and its elite. At the same time, many of Taiwan's technocrats had been educated in the United States; the first head of the JCCR, Dr. Chiang Monlin, for example, had received his doctorate at Columbia University (where one of his professors was John Dewey), and many JCCR members had old-school ties through their agricultural studies at Cornell.[30]

During this early recovery stage, Taiwan looked largely inward for its economic development, only turning to export-led growth in the 1960s and 1970s. Taiwan's earliest industrial policies focused on import substitution, again driven by the island's disastrous foreign exchange position.[31] According to a United Nations report, "In 1950 government revenue was sufficient to cover only about three-fifths of government expenditure, leaving a deficit amounting to about 15 per cent of the national income."[32] Given these exigencies, as Cullather argues, "In Taiwan, U.S. officials were forced to jettison free-market nostrums from the start and collaborate with Chinese officials" in creating a unique, state-directed political economy that was designed to meet the government's fiscal needs while minimizing the burden on American taxpayers. While I will show that the United States pursued private sector development despite KMT intransigence, his crucial point that the United States had to adapt to local conditions and preferences is one that I also emphasize here and in subsequent country case studies.[33]

In an important sense, the postwar crisis atmosphere in Taiwan played into the KMT's political and bureaucratic interests. It allowed the state to develop a strong, independent bureaucracy, limited only by the lack of qualified personnel and sufficient finance. It should be noted that these strengths and weaknesses also played into US hands once Washington took an interest in Taiwan's recovery and growth. It meant that Washington could work with a relatively autonomous state, insert its own experts into the decision-making process, and use its economic aid as a lever for winning desired reforms. As a US Senate report stated, the "implementation of these decisions is facilitated by Government ownership or control of almost every significant economic activity."[34] There were few pesky interest groups outside of government to contend with, and any opposition groups led by members of the established Taiwanese population had already been brutally suppressed before Chiang arrived from the mainland.

But what ideas animated American economic assistance in Taiwan? While ideological preferences certainly played some role in shaping US policy there, the island's security requirements certainly came first, along with the lessons that American and Taiwanese officials had drawn from the China debacle. In particular, the United States believed that Chiang's inability to put a meaningful land reform program in place was at least partly responsible for the KMT's defeat on the mainland, along with the party's overall ineptitude and corruption. These fundamental failings had to be addressed if the KMT was to avoid a repeat performance. As it turned out, the KMT would go on to assign very competent officials to leading economic positions, which indicated to Washington that Chiang had at least learned something of value from his defeat.[35]

Of all the reforms that postwar Taiwan undertook at Washington's behest, perhaps none is so celebrated as land reform. As previously noted, the United States had already urged the KMT to pursue agricultural reforms on the mainland, considering rural unrest to be the fuel feeding the Maoist revolution.[36] So important was the land issue that the United States had established China's JCCR in 1948 to deal with it; this organization would go on to play a significant role in shaping the postwar Taiwanese economy once it moved its operations to the island in December 1949.

With Chiang's relocation to Taipei, land reform became both economically urgent and politically feasible, as the KMT was less beholden to the landlords who had played such a big political role on the mainland. Conveniently, Taiwanese landlords were already viewed as Japanese lackeys, and in any event were not a power resource for the party; restive peasants, stuck paying heavy rents, were no longer willing to serve in thrall to them. The population spurt that occurred as mainlanders flooded the island placed increased pressure on agriculture to deliver foodstuffs, while Taiwan's precarious foreign exchange position made it impossible to depend heavily on additional imports. As previously noted, US aid would cover much of Taiwan's essential import needs during the early 1950s.

Land reform proceeded in three stages between 1949 and 1953. First, farm rents were reduced; second, public lands were sold; finally, a "Land to the Tiller" program was initiated to limit the amount of land that could be held by landlords, resulting in a widespread transfer of land to tenant farmers.[37] This entire effort was supported by the JCCR, which also advocated for the creation of farmers' associations that would be controlled by the new smallholders.

Land reform was a critical element in Taiwan's shift toward an industrial economy. For their part—and key to future private sector development—landlords were paid in industrial bonds, forcing a shift in their allocation of capital. Some specific success stories are mentioned in what follows. As

Ho put it, "land reform . . . helped Taiwan to move capital resources from agriculture to the rest of the economy—a transfer that is central to the development process."[38] This possibility of diversifying elite assets was a key element in Taiwan's success and in Washington's ability to find allies in its quest for private sector development. By the time the land reform had been completed, less than 10 percent of landlord income came from the land, while the number of tenant farmers fell from 41 to 16 percent.[39] The United States further induced these landlords to invest in industry by providing foreign aid in support of capital investment; in fact, US foreign aid totaled over one-third of all gross capital investment in Taiwan during the 1950s. From a sectoral perspective, aid "accounted . . . for 68% of total investment in public utilities, 28% in transportation and communication, and 24% in manufacturing."[40]

Gray agrees that land reform in Taiwan "played a key role in . . . subsequent industrialization."[41] With rising agricultural productivity, farmers again began to export commodities like sugar, generating foreign exchange that could be used to import industrial and agricultural inputs. Incidentally, the land reform among other policy efforts also contributed to the creation of a relatively egalitarian society from an income standpoint, curbing if not eliminating the appeal of any radical movements that sought to exploit economic grievances.[42]

This shift from agriculture to industry was given further impetus by US trade policy, which gave Taiwan improved access to the US market through the multilateral tariff reductions negotiated in the General Agreement on Tariffs and Trade (GATT).[43] As Baldwin and Nelson put it, "As far as trade policy is concerned, Taiwan did not receive any special treatment in the early postwar years. However, since part of the U.S. strategy of strengthening non-communist countries was to engage in trade-liberalizing negotiations through the GATT process, and since developing countries were not required to make reciprocal cuts in their own duties, Taiwan and other developing countries enjoyed improved access to U.S. markets without having to open up their own markets."[44] The growth of Taiwan's exports to the United States during the late 1950s is astounding, rising from a mere $7.2 million in 1953 to $51.5 million in 1961. Entrepreneurs were given added incentives to engage in exports when a major shift in the foreign exchange regime was introduced in the late 1950s, which abandoned the overvalued currency (which of course was attractive for an import-dependent country) in favor of competitive exchange rates.[45]

At the same time, US advisors encouraged Taipei to accept more FDI on the island, which would provide local elites with further opportunities to profit from industrial expansion. Starting from a very low base, the amount of FDI flowing into Taiwan tripled during the 1950s, and by the 1960s it constituted over 17 percent of all manufacturing. The largest providers of FDI were Japan and the United States; major companies like Singer Sewing Machine came to Taiwan at this time, bolstering confidence among potential investors in the island's political and economic stability. Over time, these foreign investors would establish linkages with local entrepreneurs, as discussed in more detail below.[46]

The role of the United States in Taiwan's economic miracle has, of course, been touched upon and debated for many years,[47] but few scholars have focused on its promotion of private sector development, though in his oft-cited work Neil Jacoby certainly emphasizes its importance to American aid officials.[48] But before continuing with the specifics of private sector development, one further point is worth noting, namely, the strategic interaction between Washington and Taipei. On the one hand, the United States had a "dominant strategy" for supporting Taiwan (at least after the Korean War), giving Taipei leverage in its dealings with Washington that wouldn't have existed had the country not held such geopolitical importance. At the same time, Washington was ambivalent toward the KMT regime. There was always the possibility that an American administration would eventually reach out to the mainland and offer diplomatic recognition in an effort to isolate the Soviet Union; indeed, American officials continuously debated the conditions under which they might recognize Beijing throughout the 1950s. This gave the KMT additional incentives to take American policy recommendations seriously. In sum, Taiwan provided a seemingly favorable environment for advancing American influence.

On the other, the KMT remained stubborn in adopting and carrying out the policies that were in *its* interest, even if those policies were at odds with American preferences—or, at the limit, even seemed irrational to US officials. What Nancy Tucker has written about US military advice to Chiang during World War II—when military leaders advocated the creation of a modern army that could go on the offensive against Japan—could equally apply to economic policy: "Chiang did not want a modern army with effective officers who owed their loyalty to the institution and the country rather than to him personally."[49] Tucker's insight brings us to the heart of the political economy of foreign assistance: that the recipient, given its own objective function, may simply not be interested in adopting the ideas that accompany the principal's cash. This remains a crucial lesson for US policy makers to contemplate.

So what were those ideas in the Taiwanese case? Jacoby, an early student of US aid policy in Taiwan, asserts that "the two major thrusts of AID influence were to elevate development as a Chinese national goal and to foster private enterprise."[50] The two, of course, were interrelated, and they get at the heart of the nexus between foreign assistance and economic development. After all, to adopt a development perspective means to think beyond the immediate future—to invest in policies, programs, and institutions that may only bear fruit in some distant future. Indeed, one might say that the key to development is to shift society (or at least the political and economic elite) from a philosophy of short-term "predation" or rent-seeking to one of long-term investment.

This was particularly challenging in the Taiwanese case because, in Tucker's words, Chiang "preferred to view economic policies in Taiwan as temporary measures designed to create a reliable base for efforts to return to the mainland . . . it appeared a waste to devote time, attention, and resources to island-specific plans." Tucker goes on to quote a refugee who made this point in evocative terms in 1953: "You think about it (returning to the mainland) every time you start to do anything, even such a simple thing as putting in a vegetable garden. . . . Am I not surrendering to despair if I put in trees—am I not admitting to myself that I may be here forever?"[51]

Similar to gardeners deciding whether to plant trees, entrepreneurs must decide whether to make "lumpy" capital investments that often take years to pay off. Private enterprise is often absent in the developing world, or is only found only in a very few sectors, because governments have not made—or lack the credibility of making—the sorts of long-run investments (e.g., in infrastructure and property rights protections) that support a healthy investment climate. As a consequence, businesses will instead operate to make a "fast buck"; they must extract rather than invest. Further, the KMT had a reputation of being corrupt and inept; who would invest in the long term while the island was governed by such a gang and faced such a powerful enemy in Mao's China?

According to Jacoby, "AID . . . played a vital role in the adoption of policies" by Taipei "under which the private sector burgeoned in both industry and agriculture." As previously noted, however, this private enterprise "thrust" did not represent the KMT's policy preferences, and certainly not in their early years on the island. Jacoby asserts that, recognizing both the immediate economic and security problems facing Taipei and KMT intransigence, the US "emphasis on private enterprise came during the latter part of the aid period, after the environment and Chinese attitudes were favorable."[52] Thus, he argues that private sector development followed on the heels of other priorities, including land reform, macroeconomic stabilization, the building of infrastructure, and investment in such public goods as education. The evidence, however, does not quite support that claim; indeed, as previously noted, privatization of at least some Taiwanese industry was an essential part of the land reform program.

As previously noted, at the war's end the Chinese government national-ized four Japanese-owned industries: Taiwan Pulp and Paper Corporation, Taiwan Cement Corporation, Taiwan Agricultural and Forestry Develop-ment Corporation, and Taiwan Industrial and Mining Corporation. With the introduction of the Land-to-the-Tiller program, the government pro-mulgated a "Statute for Transforming SOEs into Privately Owned Enter-prise," which served as the basis for all future privatization efforts. Under this program, landlords received shares in these corporations as part of their compensation package. According to the Mutual Security Mission to China (MSM/C), this transfer "to private hands involved the government divesting itself of approximately $40 million worth of shares."[53] More to the point, MSM/C emphasized that this action promoted the "trends toward private enterprise." Given that these investments could take years to become profitable, it forced the recipients to adopt a long-run per-spective, especially in light of Taiwan's underdeveloped capital markets at this time.

For his part, Cullather deems the privatization program undertaken alongside land reform a failure. He argues that "the state compelled land-lords to surrender their property in return for overvalued shares in four public enterprises. Most shares immediately lost half their value. Share-holders enjoyed no proprietary privileges, and the firms continued under the same management." Still, he recognizes that the state did begin to launch a number of new ventures that were turned over to private hands in the ensuing years.[54]

In fact, some of these newly privatized companies proved quite profit-able, forming the basis for future Taiwanese fortunes. In particular, Taiwan Cement Corporation, which was a recipient of a $3 million loan from the Development Loan Fund (DLF),[55] more than doubled its production in the ten years following its privatization, and shareholders saw the values of their stock double over that time period. The landholding Gu family were major investors in Taiwan Cement, who "used that company . . . as a foun-dation for creating a business empire."[56] During this period, Taiwan actu-ally became one of the world's largest producers of cement and a net ex-porter of this commodity.

Even more important, the transformation of these companies set Taiwan on a path toward embracing private enterprise. By 1964, of Taiwan's 12,000 industrial plants, more than 80 percent were in private hands, up from less than 30 percent in 1949.[57] Overall, Hamilton and Kao state that "most of these industries had their origins in the period of land reform."[58]

Taiwan's industrial development started from a very low base. The economy had long been dominated by agricultural production, and as late as 1957, industrial products constituted only 7 percent of total exports. According to the US aid mission in Taiwan, industrial development "from 1950 onward can be divided roughly into three phases: the rehabilitation, or postwar reconstruction period, from 1949–1952; the basic facilities build-up or foundation-strengthening stage, beginning in 1951 and not yet concluded; and third, the comprehensive industrial expansion effort that begin in 1953."[59]

During the years 1953–1956, the US government provided US$162 million and NT$2,062 billion in direct project aid to the industrial development effort, as well as an additional $62 million in nonproject aid. This constituted about 45 percent of total capital investment in industry for that period, a remarkable sum. Local entrepreneurs contributed about 17 percent of all capital, with the remaining amount coming from the government. About 40 percent of these US grants were used for power generation, with fertilizer production receiving another 15 percent; transportation projects received 7 percent of the funding. MSM/C estimated that 16 percent of local currency funds were devoted to increasing production in the commodity and manufacturing industries.[60] The major targets for private investment were textiles, chemicals, cement, paper and board, glass, and electrical appliances—the latter being a precursor to what would become one of Taiwan's great export success stories. Of the fourteen DLF loans made to Taiwan between 1957 and 1961, five went to private enterprise (including the Taiwan Cement Corporation, as previously noted). Among these, one was a shipbuilding joint venture with the US firm Ingalls.

In addition to major grants for large capital-intensive projects, the US mission also launched a "Small Industry Loan Program" that made highly subsidized loans to local companies. Between 1954 and 1958, 643 private firms received a total of US$6.3 million and NT$111 million for project finance, crucial at a time when credit was largely controlled by the government.[61] To my knowledge, this program has not been noted by previous scholars, yet it provides further evidence of US efforts to pursue its private enterprise agenda.

Private enterprise continued to expand, at least in terms of numbers of firms being created, during the 1950s despite the government's lukewarm or even hostile attitude toward it. But that did not imply any rollback of the state. In fact, the relative role of state-owned enterprises was rising, from 29 percent of gross capital formation in 1951 to nearly 33 percent ten years later.[62] Still, according to the local aid mission, "Of the twenty thousand or more factories in operation at the end of 1957, approximately one-third came into being after 1952, the great majority of them privately financed."[63] State-owned enterprise, in contrast, tended to focus on the provision of public goods like power generation and transportation. Indeed, powering this industrial drive was a trebling of electricity production.

The United States provided not just direct financial assistance to Taiwanese firms and entrepreneurs, but technical assistance as well. A host of industrial advisers were brought to the island under contract with the J.G. White Engineering Corporation, including experts in a variety of technical fields like pulp and paper milling, iron and steel production, telecommunications, and shipbuilding. Some 2,700 managers were sent from Taiwan for training to the United States, which in retrospect Taipei considered to be one of the most effective contributions to the nation's growth.[64] Related, the United States established a China Productivity Center (CPC), which provided consultation services in the interest of increasing firm output; many of its specialists were among those who traveled to the United States to visit American firms, learning about their operations and managerial techniques. The CPC also provided guidance on export markets for Taiwanese products.[65] Studies of technical assistance programs in other settings have highlighted their contribution to industrial productivity.[66]

What is perhaps most impressive when one reviews the evidence on US support for Taiwan is how comprehensive it was. It covered both agriculture and industry, and within industry it promoted myriad sectors. It financed public goods, including power production and transportation, public health programs, education, and of course defense. It provided technical advice on both macroeconomic and microeconomic policies, using experts who were widely respected by their Taiwanese counterparts.

Of all the industries supported by US assistance, the local aid mission deemed the growth of cotton textiles "most striking."[67] Aid was given to buy new equipment and to import raw cotton under a preferential exchange rate regime (Taiwan had multiple exchange rates at this time). While industrial output climbed dramatically for many industries during the mid-1950s, cotton yarn production was the clear winner, doubling between 1952 and 1957.

Haggard emphasizes the coherence of US policies, stating that textile policies incorporated "technical assistance from American engineering firms, imported power looms . . . and US aid in the form of raw cotton." The United States, as previously noted, also made loans to firms for plant expansion. The KMT stepped in to ensure that cotton was allocated to the different companies through a quota system, reflecting its fear that a "free market" in cotton could be "taken advantage of by speculators and profiteers."[68] This point about policy coherence is also an essential lesson for today's development officials.

Bureaucratically, US assistance was so important that the leading economic body in Taiwan for many years was the Council for United States Aid (CUSA), a body that had left the mainland with the KMT. Running parallel to the JCCR, CUSA "functioned outside the regular ministries, selecting and overseeing the implementation of aid-funded projects and coordinating aid imports with project needs."[69] It was highly autonomous and technocratic. However, this does not mean that internal conflicts over policy directions and priorities were absent, or that decisions were taken free of political considerations.

As previously noted, one of the cleavages within Taiwan's government and between the KMT and the United States concerned the role of private enterprise. These differences in opinion were both economic and political in nature. From an economic standpoint, some government officials doubted local entrepreneurs' ability to grow industrial companies. They cynically went so far as to support the transfer of state-owned enterprises to landlords because they were convinced that these firms would fail, demonstrating that the government had to run industry after all. Politically, Haggard emphasizes concerns within the KMT that private sector growth "would inevitably strengthen the native Taiwanese, who then might use their economic power for political ends. The United States, on the other hand, saw the strengthening of the private sector as contributing to long-run political stability by co-opting the Taiwanese into the system."[70]

What emerged from this pulling and hauling—both within the KMT itself and between the KMT and the US government—was a mixed economy with the state controlling overall investment policy and retaining a monopoly in certain sectors. Specifically, "the government monopolies included electric power, sugar [traditionally the country's major export], petroleum, tobacco and alcoholic beverages. Principal industrial products [run by the private sector] included processed foods, textiles, plywood, chemicals, plastics, cement, fertilizer, iron and steel."[71] Even in the private sector, however, the government ruled with a heavy hand by controlling imports and, in some cases, the allocation of final products, especially those that served as intermediate goods for other industries.

Yet another aspect of US policy was to encourage FDI; as we have seen throughout this book, FDI was, in fact, a major pillar of US economic development strategy. Again, one might be skeptical about the KMT's interest in attracting foreign investment given its desire to control the economy, and Cullather quotes a 1960 congressional delegation that complained about the government's "extreme interference in the conduct of business."[72] However, he also notes the significant growth in US FDI from $2 million in

1959 to $50 million in 1965. By 1969, foreign investment in Taiwan had climbed to $505 million, again mainly coming from the United States and Japan.[73] Still, FDI constituted a relatively small share of the economy.

During the postwar period Taiwan passed three laws to incentivize FDI, in 1954, 1959, and 1960. These laws, inter alia, exempted FDI from income tax for five years, limited the corporate tax rate, excluded a significant share of investments from taxable income and allowed for accelerated depreciation, provided for free capital repatriation after two years, and provided guarantees against expropriation. As another inducement, the US Agency for International Development (USAID) had created an investment guarantee program to motivate FDI. Further, an export processing zone (EPZ) was opened in 1966 after many years of internal wrangling. Opponents of the EPZ argued that it would create an unlevel playing field between foreign and local firms, exploit "cheap" Taiwanese labor, and erode sovereignty given the "extraterritorial" nature of the EPZ. With the termination of US foreign aid in 1964, and the emergence of EPZs in such places as Hong Kong, these objections were ultimately overcome.[74]

Why did Taiwan become more open to FDI during the 1960s? The role of the United States in this process cannot be understated. As Yu argues, by the mid-1950s the Taiwanese economy was "experiencing a number of difficulties" including sluggish growth and investment. He notes that Washington "was concerned by these developments, as well as the ongoing aid burden. It was clear that the United States could not continue to subsidize the economy," thus it "had a direct interest in promoting both exports and investment that would substitute for the . . . winding down of foreign aid."[75] Haggard and Zheng date the origins of the US focus on FDI to the late 1950s, following the Second Straits Crisis over Quemoy and Matsu (August 1958–January 1959), after which "aid officials began to outline a package of reforms that would ultimately allow Taiwan to graduate from foreign aid." They state that the "crucial statute" that came out of these reforms was the Statute for Encouragement of Investment of 1960, which created a set of subsidies and incentives, mainly tax incentives, for domestic and foreign investors.[76]

Reviewing the environment on Taiwan for FDI in 1970, Schreiber concluded that "Taiwan currently presents a situation to American businessmen of profitable opportunity and minimal risk." This is a remarkable statement when one contemplates the country's postwar history of fragile geopolitics and intrusive economics. He further noted a "confluence of interest of both the US and Chinese governments vis-à-vis American private capital," which contributed to giving comfort to potential investors, including those from Japan, which was the source of much of Taiwan's FDI.[77]

But to what extent were American officials correct to emphasize FDI as a key element in Taiwanese growth? To what extent did FDI create linkages with the local economy, especially given its "enclave" position—at least initially—in an EPZ? If so, what form did these linkages take? Did FDI promote new capital investment, improve productivity via the transfer of technology and know-how, or some combination of the two?

While the existing studies generally support the existence of linkages, which in turn contributed to Taiwanese growth, they differ somewhat on the importance of the various channels. Thus, in what remains the most comprehensive study of FDI linkages in Taiwan, Schive finds that FDI contributed through both technology transfer and local content purchases, though he emphasizes the former. Focusing on the case of consumer electronics, Lowe and Kenney similarly find these dual effects, noting that both US and Japanese companies actively transferred technology to local suppliers while also supporting the training of their managers and technicians (they contrast the Taiwanese experience with that of Mexico, which they argue experienced fewer spillover effects from FDI owing to the lack of indigenous firms with which FDI could partner). In the most sophisticated econometric analysis of FDI linkages, Chan finds that technology transfer was a more significant contributor to economic growth than the local content sourcing that drove new capital formation. Overall, Schive concludes that FDI "has played an important role in Taiwan's modern economic development."[78]

The case of Taiwan, then, provides a pointed case study for policy makers today who are seeking to promote private sector development. It suggests that even when foreign officials hold tremendous leverage over local leaders, they are nonetheless in a bargaining situation whose outcome is not preordained by the apparent imbalance in power. Differing policy preferences and ideologies will shape what domestic rulers are willing to accept in exchange for foreign aid, and rulers who are relatively insulated from societal pressures will have even greater ability to craft outcomes in their favor.

Still, even in these conditions, donors may find the "moving parts" within an economy who may be incentive-compatible with their interests. In Taiwan, landlords could be moved off the land and incentivized to invest in local industry. Officials could be made to recognize that aid was temporary and that Taiwan would suffer an enormous economic hit when it ended. Managers and engineers could be trained in best practices, returning to their ministries and firms with productivity-enhancing ideas, some of which were most effectively practiced in private enterprise or in partnership with foreign investors. All this, however, required a fair degree of policy coherence on the part of the United States.

It also required time. Yet another important lesson that emerges from the Taiwan case is that building influence and trust requires intimate knowledge of the local society and, in particular, its elites. Accordingly, many American officials spent years in Taiwan developing the sorts of relationships that ultimately enabled them to craft and execute incentive-compatible policies. Today, when many American officials do exceedingly short tours in a given place, that lesson is well worth remembering.

War and Recovery in Korea

While sharing certain similarities—including a history of Japanese colonization, a precarious postwar security environment, and massive amounts of US economic and military assistance—Taiwan and South Korea took different paths on their respective roads to economic recovery and sustainable growth. Per a hasty US-Soviet agreement, Korea had emerged from World War II as a divided land, soon thereafter pitting North against South in a bitter war that failed to settle the ongoing issue of peninsular reunification; that war and its aftermath would also have far-reaching economic ramifications. The 1953 armistice that followed created an extremely uneasy peace, one that both North and South Koreans exploited for their own political purposes. American officials had an even more conflictual relationship with Korean leader Syngman Rhee than they did with Taiwan's Chiang Kai-shek, further muddying the policy waters. Still, while Chiang created a long period of political and economic stability, albeit under martial law, this was something that eluded Korea's rulers until the late 1980s and the achievement of a durable democratic system.[79]

The American Military Government (AMG) that arrived in Korea in September 1945 had scant knowledge of the country or how to prepare for postwar occupation.[80] The military commander, General John K. Hodge, was an Illinois farm boy who had served in the Far East during World War II; his political advisor, Merrell Benninghoff, was a specialist on Japan.[81] During the war, Roosevelt had pursued the idea of an "international trusteeship" for Korea, which was his general approach to the problem of dealing with former European and Japanese colonies. He had not anticipated its permanent division into North and South.[82]

However, the fractious nature of Korean politics had already been apparent during the war, and this would be a source of continuing instability for more than a decade after the war's end. The Korean Provincial Government was established in exile in China but it was not viewed by American policy makers as widely representative. In the period between Japan's surrender and the establishment of the military government, a People's Republic of Korea (PRK), with a differing set of leading personalities, sprung up on the peninsula. This party also sought recognition from Washington, again without success.[83]

The international situation compounded the domestic impediments to reaching a Korean settlement. For reasons of military expedience during the last stages of the Pacific War, the United States and the Soviet Union had agreed to accept their respective Instruments of Surrender from Japanese forces along a line defined by the 38th parallel; the Soviets would take over control from the Japanese to the North, and the Americans to the South.[84] The United States had hoped to avoid a German-type "zonalization" of Korea, but negotiations with the Soviets over Korea's final status did not achieve a shared view; some historians have seen this failure as an early warning sign of the ensuing Cold War.[85] In addition, Americans were sharply divided on the strategic value of Korea. Observing the political chaos on the peninsula in 1947, for example, George Kennan recommended that "we cut our losses and get out."[86]

The division of Korea into North and South posed fundamental problems for economic recovery. The industrial heartland of the peninsula was in the North, which was also the center of electricity production. The loss of access to the North's industry and electricity, coupled with the South's own collapse of industrial output owing to the lack of capital and needed inputs, left the South bereft of consumer goods, causing hyperinflation. As Haggard summarizes the situation facing postwar South Korea, the number of manufacturing establishments had fallen by 44 percent, manufacturing employment had dropped by 60 percent, and industrial output overall was just 20 percent of 1940 levels.[87]

US assistance thus focused on getting food and fuel to Korea in order to contain the immediate economic crisis and the political instability it was fueling; American officials were particularly concerned that the economic disruption in the South was feeding communist agitation there. Suk Tai Suh asserts that "foreign economic aid played a vitally important role in alleviating poverty, disease, and social unrest" at this time.[88] But in terms of longer-run economic planning, the possibility of reunification between North and South meant that both the United States and the government of Syngman Rhee were initially reluctant to invest resources into capital-intensive industries that might prove redundant.

Instead, the United States turned its attention to land reform. Korea had been colonized by Japan since 1910, and during the ensuing decades the Japanese amassed agricultural land in the country, controlling 1.4 million farms and an estimated 15 percent of all farmland by 1945.[89] According to historian Ronald Spector, "Under Japanese rule, Korea's rice production, collection and pricing were controlled by the colonial government. At least 80 percent of all Korean farmers rented all or part of the land."[90] With its occupation the United States would promote a "land to the tiller" program as it had done in Taiwan (and Japan); this program, while more modest than those in other East Asian economies, nonetheless provided a fragile financial basis for a new industrialization drive.

At the war's end, "Korean agriculture was a mess. . . . About 3 percent of the population owned two-thirds of the arable land. Farms were small, and farming methods were primitive. More than half of all farmers were tenants who worked their rented land under conditions that made sharecroppers in the American South appear almost affluent."[91] The PRK government sought to dispossess the landlords and give local tenants "land at no cost."[92] According to US advisor Benninghoff, the common denominator in Korean politics at this time was the idea of "seizing Japanese property, ejecting the Japanese from Korea and achieving immediate independence."[93]

Recognizing the potency of agricultural discontent, a "major agrarian rebellion" had erupted in 1946, which involved over 2 million people spread across the country. The North Koreans had already launched a major program of land redistribution under Soviet tutelage, and the AMG quickly responded to demands for reform in the South.[94] Guided in part by what historian David Ekbladh calls "New Deal principles of social justice,"[95] the AMG restricted rent payments to no more than one-third of the crop, down from the 50–60 percent that landlords had demanded. AMG then consolidated all Japanese-held farmland and, along with Japanese-owned mines and industrial concerns, created the New Korea Company. In 1948, Japanese lands were transferred to a newly established National Land Administration, which began to sell the land to the peasants. By September of that year, over 505,000 households owned land in South Korea, representing a small but growing share of the country's estimated 11 million tenant farmers.[96]

However, the initial Korean land reform had created very small plots, which made it difficult for many new owner-farmers to make a living off the land. A crucial point for our purposes is that many of these farmers would ultimately provide labor for the industries that rapidly developed on the heels of the Korean War.[97] That also served the political purposes of Korean leaders who wished to provide big business with a "cheap" factor input.

From a political perspective, the organization of rural life differed significantly from that which followed the land reforms in Taiwan and Japan.

The agricultural associations that had been created in these countries along-side land reform were central to the empowerment of farmers, as they performed crucial functions managing the use of inputs like water and out-puts like the marketing of crops. In Korea, in contrast, these associations were largely directed by political appointees, and so they played a much different role. As an official at Korea's Ministry of Agriculture and Forestry put it, the main goal of land reform "was nation-state building," or strength-ening the state.[98]

Korean strongman Syngman Rhee was also adept at putting political pressure on farmers by leveraging food imports from the United States, which constituted a substantial share of the economic assistance program in some years. As Bo has written, introducing agricultural surpluses from the United States reduced food prices, a move that put farmers at a disad-vantage but was applauded by urban elites and workers, and that helped feed the industrialization drive.[99] Further, lacking the rural industries that dotted Japan, for example, Korean landlords and those tenants who did not participate in the land reform process began to leave the land altogether and move to the industrial cities.[100] Like the nineteenth-century British corn laws, this was, in fact, a central objective of the 1950 Land Reform Act.

As Shin writes, "The Land Reform Act originally intended to help land-lords to transform themselves into industrial capitalists or entrepreneurs. When a landlord wanted to use his Land-value Bills as industrial capital or he applied for a loan from public financial institutions, the Minister of Fi-nance had [an] obligation to guarantee a low-interest loan. And, when a landlord wanted to buy government facilities at disposal such as factories, mines, ships, fishing grounds, breweries . . . etc., the Government had the obligation to give preference to the Land-value Bill holders."[101] Still, only 18 percent of Korean workers were in industrial employment as late as 1970, while 50 percent continued to work the land. For their part, land-lords were hesitant to invest in industry until the end of the Korean War; unfortunately, in the meantime inflation ate away at the value of their bonds.[102]

Much like Taiwan, US foreign aid was crucial to keeping Korea's economy afloat. According to Steinberg, "In various years during this period [the 1950s], the United States provided a third of the total budget for the Gov-ernment (58.4 percent in 1956) and up to 85 percent of all imports and 75 percent of total fixed capital formation. During 1952–1958, foreign aid and relief assistance provided 75 percent of Korea's imports and 8 percent of GNP."[103] As Haggard summarizes, "The significance of U.S. support . . . can hardly be overstated."[104]

But bilateral relations with Korea were far less harmonious than in Taiwan in terms of economic policy. As a US official put it, "Despite the massive U.S. assistance, there was little agreement between the governments on anything beyond the survival of the Korean state. Thus, arguments about the level and role of foreign assistance were endemic, with the Koreans attempting to expand Government activity without indigenous resource mobilization, while the United States was trying to limit both its and the Korean Governments' expenditures."[105]

The United States had not expected to be a long-term donor to Korea. The aid program established under the Economic Cooperation Administration in fiscal year 1950 (which was also responsible for executing the Marshall Plan) had called for assistance that would end in 1952–1953, after which time the country was expected to augment domestic savings through FDI and World Bank loans. Congress then reduced even the paltry funding that had been requested, stating that "further help for Korea would be useless." It just seemed that Seoul lacked the will to tackle its fundamental economic problems, including shortages and, related, inflation. Harvard economist Edward Mason has suggested that this action signaled Washington's lack of support for South Korea to Pyongyang, providing an impetus for invasion.[106]

The Korean War shattered an already struggling economy, destroying massive amounts of human and physical capital. In addition to the millions of casualties that South Korea had suffered (the precise number remains contested) and the dislocation of up to one-quarter of the population, the destruction of assets was also devastating. According to Koh, "over 17,000 industrial plants and business facilities, 4,000 schools, and 600,000 homes were destroyed; agricultural production declined by 27 percent between 1949 and 1952; and Gross National Product (GNP) declined by 14 percent during the same period. The total value of property damage was estimated at $2 billion, which was equal to South Korea's GNP in 1949."[107]

Following the 1953 armistice agreement to halt fighting on the Korean peninsula, Washington and Seoul faced the enormous task of economic recovery in the South. Charged by President Eisenhower with developing a plan for American participation in the reconstruction effort, the State Department's Henry Tasca sought to place this technical issue in a broader strategic context. Despite testy relations between Eisenhower and the mercurial Korean leader Syngman Rhee, Tasca argued that the United States had no choice but to provide generous foreign assistance for the war-torn nation; if it did not, the consequences would reverberate far beyond the Korean peninsula. As Tasca stated, "If the people of the free world, particularly of the Far East, were led to believe that comparable resistance to aggression might mean only . . . future hardships . . . the present defense of the U.S. could be gravely affected in other parts of the world by a deterioration of the will to resist and the desire to remain free."[108] In Tasca's view, American abdication would only leave a huge vacuum for the communists to fill.

Given the ever-present communist threat to the South, the United States was unwilling to abandon the country despite the ever-present tensions with its leader, Rhee; instead, it launched a massive economic assistance program. According to Mason, "foreign assistance played a major role in the Korean economy. It financed nearly 70 percent of total imports from 1953 through 1962. It was equal to nearly 80 percent of total fixed capital formation and to 8 percent of GNP."[109]

The US assistance program approved by President Eisenhower followed the recommendations of the Tasca mission. Tasca's report began as follows: "The security interests of the United States require the strengthening of the economy of the Republic of Korea." While the United States sought to reduce the fiscal burdens associated with its large military presence on the peninsula, Washington's underlying concern was that the country's poverty and instability made it a tempting target for communist infiltration.[110] These security interests dictated the general shape of the assistance program, but they also left Rhee with enough room to maneuver so as to use American funds to further his political aims.

A good example is provided by Rhee's industrial policy. In line with American ideology, Tasca recommended the speedy sale of state-owned enterprises to private investors and, more generally, the "encouragement of private enterprise." According to Lim, the "Rhee government set the conditions for the sale of these properties so as to preclude competitive bidding and to favor the interim plant managers as well as the politically well-connected. The Rhee government typically set the assessed value of the vested industrial properties at 25–30 percent of the market value."[111]

In turn, those who obtained these assets were expected to give generously to Rhee's political party, creating a feedback loop between political and economic favors. Later in the 1950s, when commercial banks were privatized, these same industrialists snapped them up, creating the conglomerates known as *chaebol*. As Lim concludes, "In the end, what passed for an economic system in Korea in the 1950s was primarily shaped by Rhee's use of policy instruments to secure and sustain his power base. The sale of vested properties resulted in windfall gains for favored businessmen and undue concentration of economic power."[112] These investments were further supported by Korea's policy of import substitution, or giving rents to domestic companies that might other face competing goods from overseas.

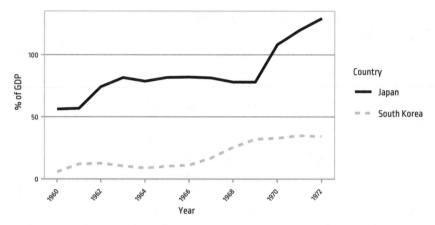

Data source: World Bank, "World Development Indicators," https://datacatalog.worldbank.org/dataset/world
-development-indicators.

FIGURE 2.1   Japan vs. South Korea: Domestic Credit to Private Sector as Percent
of GDP, 1960–1972

American support was, according to Haggard, "key" to the development
of these policies.[113] Even in these cases, however, the United States provided
Korean managers with the opportunity to travel to America to observe new
production and managerial techniques, much as it had done in Taiwan,
giving them the tools they needed to increase their firms' productivity.

But overall, Korea's industrial development followed a very different path
from that of Taiwan. Whereas Taiwan, despite heavy state direction over
the economy, eventually became home to a multitude of small-and-medium-
sized enterprises, Korea would eventually see the birth of large, family-owned
conglomerates that would control much of the country's industrial activity.
The *chaebol* were closely connected to the government and profited from
crony capitalism in the form of contracts and loans (including loans to small
and medium-sized enterprises (SMEs) made to the subsidiaries of these enterprises). As Figure 2.1 reveals, credit to the private sector in Korea remained
far below the levels found in Japan, suggesting the absence of access to finance for would-be entrepreneurs. In recent years, however, Korea has closed
the gap, with private credit increasing dramatically from these low levels. By
2000 it stood at more than 140 percent of GDP, even higher than Taiwan's
135 percent, but still lower than the 180 percent for Japan.[114]

Further, in Korea, FDI remained limited into the 1980s despite the eclipse
of US aid. According to Steinberg, "Investment has been small relative to
the size and potential of the economy because of the fear of conflict on the
peninsula, the uncertainty about the future political leadership and the po-

litical process, and past tight Government controls on investment."[115] For its part, the United States didn't really push the Koreans toward greater openness as it had done with Taipei. It was preoccupied with other pressing issues, including the ever-present threat of renewed conflict on the penin-sula; the costs of maintaining large military forces, which weighed on both the United States and the Republic of Korea; ongoing disputes between Korea and Japan (Rhee, who had led the Korean government in exile during the war, hated Japan perhaps as much as he did communist China and the Soviet Union, making talk of reconciliation nearly impossible); and the se-vere and immediate economic problems that, to Americans, signaled the threat of continued political instability.

Still, in the face of limited domestic resources for meeting investment needs and concerns that the United States might reduce its foreign assis-tance (concerns that would prove real in the early 1960s), Korea turned to the US Development Loan Fund (DLF) for loans to finance its investment programs.[116] Of the eight DLF loans made between 1957 and 1961, five went to private sector firms, including those in cement, chemicals, and tex-tiles. And as in Taiwan, some of these companies went on to become leading firms in the country. Oriental Chemical Industry (now known as OCI), for example, evolved into a major multinational firm in its own right, with for-eign subsidiaries in the United States, China, Japan, and Vietnam.[117] Yet according to Haggard and Cheng, Rhee's "Liberal party was said to have substantial interests in at least 50 percent of all private projects receiving US aid, which was later to inspire charges of illicit accumulation of wealth."[118] Kim states that "ironically, US AID loans, originally intended for devel-oping small and medium-size firms, had been crafted instead to assist large, well- established firms, some capable of obtaining other financing."[119]

The specter of an end to American aid brought many changes to Korean economic organization. New ministries were created, and an emphasis was placed on import-substituting industrialization. The Koreans used some of its foreign aid funds to launch the so-called white industries in sugar, milling, and cotton textiles. Again, rather than encourage SMEs in these sectors, the government developed monopolistic structures.[120]

Similar to Taiwan as well, Seoul began inviting FDI to the peninsula as it recognized that American aid would eventually wind down and new sources of finance were needed. Accordingly, the 1960s saw the passage of a series of laws with American encouragement (e.g., changes to the foreign exchange regime) making the Republic of Korea more inviting as a host des-tination, along with the creation of export-processing zones.[121] But as previ-ously noted, FDI remained minimal until the 1980s, as the country slowly transformed itself from an economic policy based on import substitution to one based on export orientation.[122] Yet, even at its high-water mark in 1999, FDI inflows only represented slightly more than 2 percent of GDP, suggesting that the shift to an export-oriented economy was largely driven by domestic rather than foreign firms.[123] Perhaps not surprisingly given these low levels, Kim and Hwang find little evidence that FDI has made much of a contribution to Korean economic growth, although they make note of some anecdotal evidence of technology and skill transfer from foreign to local firms that may have enhanced productivity.[124]

As this case shows, the American ability to export its style of capitalism, even at the height of its power on the peninsula, proved limited. In a June 1961 meeting with Japan's prime minister, an exasperated President Kennedy admitted "that the United States has spent a considerable amount of money in Korea with little to show for it."[125] An American assistance official concluded of the Rhee period that "the major lesson . . . about what is now called 'policy dialogue' is that there was relatively little successful policy intervention by the donor, despite the magnitude of the support."[126] Similarly, Haggard wrote: "Despite his high dependence on US aid, Rhee stubbornly resisted American advice."[127]

Thus, to use Haggard's redolent phrase, Korea traced its own "pathway from the periphery"—one that made intensive use of American foreign aid but that was only weakly shaped by donor preferences in terms of private sector development.[128] Given the immediate pressures in Korea's security environment, and finding it even more difficult than in Taiwan to identify the "moving parts" that might align Seoul's policies with those of Washington, the United States ultimately bowed to the government's priorities. Private enterprise would emerge in Korea, but it would take a distinctive form that revolved around large conglomerates.

Conclusions

During the late 1940s, few countries seemed less poised for an economic miracle than either Taiwan or Korea. For its part, the island was not only riven by internal conflicts; it was also threatened by invasion. Further, it was led by a man whose conduct on the mainland had hardly inspired confidence in his American backers, and his KMT party was widely vilified for its corruption and ineptitude. These are not the background conditions normally associated with sustained growth.

And yet Taiwan emerged from these unpromising circumstances as one of the East Asian tigers, enjoying not only rapid growth but widespread equity as well. How it did so remains a subject of debate among scholars, but clearly the combination of extensive US aid, good economic policy, and ultimately supportive international conditions all contributed to its success.

Similarly, background conditions in Korea were hardly promising in the late 1940s, and they became far worse following the outbreak of an extremely destructive war. The Korean problem was compounded by a mercurial leader who was distrusted by American officials. The friction between Washington and Seoul was so great that had the security situation not been of such overwhelming concern, it's difficult to imagine the United States offering that country any foreign aid at all.

But what role did private enterprise play in Taiwan and Korea? Much of the scholarship to date downplays it, focusing instead on the "state" and its heavy hand in directing the economy. Little credit is given to the entrepreneurs who also built these countries. In that context, a 2008 report on entrepreneurship in Taiwan provides a refreshing contrast, stating: "The entrepreneurial streak in Taiwan dates back to as early as the 1940s, when many of the Chinese businessmen and refugees fleeing the communists on the China mainland opened shops on the island, as there was no major industrial base to provide jobs."[129] That statement, of course, overlooks the critical role that local Taiwanese entrepreneurs played in building the economy as well!

Nor is FDI given much pride of place in these arguments, despite the fact that an early generation of researchers "found that FDI played an important role in Taiwan's early economic development and thus confirmed that FDI is an efficient channel of technology transfer from overseas to Taiwan."[130] Indeed, Taiwan would succeed in moving up the value chain from commodity exports to more sophisticated technologies, becoming a hub for many businesses associated with the laptop computer revolution, among other high-tech industries that took off beginning in the 1980s. Korea would similarly open itself to FDI, largely due to a desire to capture foreign technology, although economists have found less evidence of linkages in this case.

More to the point, private enterprise and FDI grew over time in importance to the Taiwanese and, to a lesser extent, Korean economies, despite political preferences in both countries to control economic activity. Concerned about letting go of the economy for both fiscal and political reasons, the KMT and its leaders in Taipei had little interest in promoting activities that they could not easily direct. Similarly, Rhee was intent on using private enterprise for his political ends.

The story of Taiwan and Korea thus illustrates both the strengths and weaknesses of America's effort to export capitalism during the Cold War. On the one hand, the United States had relatively little leverage over countries whose survival it was determined to ensure. On the other, in those cases where its economic assistance provided crucial resources to the regime, local leaders recognized the need to accommodate American interests in order to keep the money flowing. Further, in both countries the economic interests of the elites were sufficiently diversified as to make it possible for US policy makers to find points of leverage in each polity that were amenable to the private enterprise message. Related, there was a coherence to US policy that helped its effectiveness. American officials, for example, recognized that land reform would help bolster industrialization, while an open American market would make export-oriented industries attractive. The importance of policy coherence in making private sector development effective is a theme we will return to throughout this book.

Overall, it was out of these delicate trade-offs between American and local interests that public policies around private enterprise and foreign investment emerged. While neither country placed a welcome mat at the door for many years, both Taiwan and Korea ultimately come to recognize their need for foreign capital (though in Korea this would take mainly the form of bank loans to fuel domestic industries rather than FDI), especially after US aid dried up. In fact, one important lesson for USAID concerns the idea of "graduation" and the importance of this tool in getting countries to construct "self-help" strategies. As a result, private enterprise contributed to the development of each economy in its own distinctive way—perhaps to a greater extent than either Chiang or Rhee would have imagined.

3

Capitalism, Colonialism, or Communism?

Private Enterprise in Latin America, 1950–1965

The President [Eisenhower] commented that . . . the use of the term "capitalism," which means one thing to us, clearly meant to much of the rest of the world something synonymous with imperialism. We should try to coin a new phrase to represent our own modern brand of capitalism.

—NATIONAL SECURITY COUNCIL MEMORANDUM, 1958[1]

The United States was not merely "doing business" in Latin America, but was fighting a war there against Communism.

—PRESIDENT DWIGHT D. EISENHOWER, 1954[2]

ON THE NIGHT OF 24 AUGUST 1954, following a meeting with his cabinet, the embattled Brazilian president Getulio Vargas put a gun to his head and committed suicide. The note he left behind emphasized the battles he had waged on behalf of the nation's poor, which included establishing such state-owned firms as the oil monopoly Petrobras, despite international pressure to open up even the most strategic sectors of the economy to foreign investment: "After decades of being ruled and exploited by the International Economic and Financial Groups," he wrote, "I turned myself leader of a revolution and I won."[3]

Vargas's worries about foreign investment as an instrument of penetration and political influence were not without foundation. As an Assistant Secretary of State back in the Taft administration (1909–1913) said of US foreign investment, it strengthened "American influence in spheres where it ought to predominate over any other foreign influence . . . such a sphere is Latin America."[4] A generation of dependency theorists has since made sophisticated arguments about the political-economic channels through which the US metropole exercised its power over the region.[5]

In the previous chapter we examined the economic trajectories of Taiwan and Korea with specific reference to how the United States tried to use foreign aid as a tool for promoting private sector development and foreign direct investment (FDI). We saw that the United States had only mixed success in these efforts, as it engaged in policy negotiations with leaders who were bent on shoring up their regimes and saw control over the economy as a crucial tool in that endeavor. As a consequence, foreign investment in particular was discouraged in both Taiwan and Korea (more in the latter than the former) until local, import-substituting industries—many of which were state-owned enterprise—could be built up. These industries would be funded in part by US foreign aid dollars.[6]

Latin America, of course, differed from East Asia in important respects as a test bed for development. For one thing, FDI had a long history in Latin America, and it played a significant role in several countries' economies. In his pathbreaking book *Dependent Development,* Peter Evans famously argued, using Brazil as his case study, that Latin America had witnessed the formation of a "triple alliance" between multinational firms, local capital, and the state that played a determinative role in shaping the economic structure of industry.[7] Second, and related, Latin America did not receive anything like the amount of foreign aid that East Asia enjoyed after World War II, as Washington believed that private capital flows would be adequate to meet development needs. It would only recognize the need for a large aid package in the late 1950s, and, as we will see in this chapter, the relationship between US foreign aid and private investment was less coherent in the Latin American case than it was in East Asia. Third, having been liberated from Japan's colonial structure after World War II, East Asia only re-entered the global economy in a significant way in the 1970s following a major industrialization drive, initially focusing its exports on value-added, light-manufacturing sectors, which contributed to bolstering national productivity and incomes (one can imagine a counterfactual postwar world in which Taiwan, say, was forced by the United States to remain an exporter of sugar). Latin America, in contrast, was stubbornly tied to its comparative advantage in commodities, a fate that the economic structuralists deemed would be immiserating if governments did not subsidize import-substituting industrialization.[8]

In what follows I will show that these factors led to constant tensions between the United States and Latin America during the early postwar era.

As a general rule (and of course the Latin American nations differed significantly in their politics and economics), Latin leaders sought more foreign
aid for social infrastructure, which they believed would not be provided
by foreign investors. Further, they sought to protect certain "strategic" sectors from foreign investment, even as the United States said they needed
foreign capital and technology to make those sectors competitive. Finally,
many Latin leaders shared the export pessimism of the structuralist school
of international economics, leading them to adopt import-substituting industrialization (ISI) policies, which conveniently also served the rent-
seeking interests of local business elites.[9]

All told, while most Latin countries were hardly hostile to FDI and local
business enterprise, their political leaders naturally wanted to exercise
some control over the process of economic development. Whether the
policies they chose were optimal from the perspective of building linkages with that FDI are still being debated, although economists tend to
argue that in many Latin countries the failure to open economies earlier
to competition, and to invest more heavily in human capital formation,
undermined the prospects for economic diversification and sustainable growth.
In short, the political economy of many Latin American countries was not
conducive to the generation of public goods that built a sturdy foundation
for long-run development.[10]

This chapter explores American efforts to promote foreign investment
and private sector development in Latin America during the Cold War. It
highlights the role of Latin American governments in their negotiations with
Washington over development policy, and their ultimately successful efforts
in winning more foreign aid from a recalcitrant Washington. I will also
show that, despite the oft-expressed fears of American policy makers that
rising economic nationalism in the region, capped by the Cuban Revolution of 1959, would spook foreign investors, capital continued to flow south
during the Cold War years.[11] The amounts, however, were less than those
Latin America had hoped to receive to fuel its economic growth, further
solidifying the case for more foreign aid.[12]

Accordingly, President Eisenhower would ultimately accede to Latin
American demands for a regional development bank, creating the Inter-
American Development Bank (IADB), and would leave office having overseen
a dramatic increase in foreign assistance programs for the region as well.
In turn, the new Kennedy administration would repackage and bolster these
programs though an "Alliance for Progress," with the earlier emphasis on
private sector development taking a backseat to other regional policy priorities, including land reform and improvements in social policy, particularly
in the areas of education and health care.[13] This shift would, ironically, lead
the executives of American multinationals with interests in the region to

attack the Kennedy administration for its failure to do more to promote their investments.

The Latin American Economy in Depression and War

Latin America has traditionally been the largest developing world destination for US FDI, and by the 1920s, American firms had displaced their European rivals to become the region's biggest investors. A significant change by the 1920s was that Americans were now investing in ongoing operations in Latin America directly, as opposed to passively, via portfolio (or bond) investors. This was due partly to opportunities opened up by World War I as European exports to the United States were reduced and investors began to liquidate their foreign holdings, and partly to the historical legacy of an earlier period of shady Wall Street dealings that left US investors with little appetite for Latin American securities.[14]

That earlier experience, of course, had not been a happy one for those on either side of the financial transactions. Latin Americans had assumed debts they could not repay, while unsuspecting Americans had invested in worthless paper. Still, in protecting the financial interests of Wall Street (while preventing interference in Latin America on the part of European governments, whose investors were also at risk), the administration of Theodore Roosevelt intervened in several countries, taking over customs houses to ensure that debts were repaid. Later, during the Taft administration, the United States engaged in "dollar diplomacy," in which the interests of Washington and Wall Street could hardly be distinguished. While Franklin D. Roosevelt tried to change the American image through his Good Neighbor Policy, which denounced intervention, a great deal of damage to hemispheric relations had already been done, and the effects of this would frequently spill over to direct investors. As Robert Swansbrough notes, "The highly visible presence of American firms provided an immediate target for the frustration and bitterness of Latin American nationalists."[15]

Swansbrough's comment, however, reminds us of the importance of looking beyond polemics to the actual data. In fact, by 1930, US-based multinationals had invested even more in Latin America than in Western Europe—about $5.3 billion in the former versus $4.9 billion in the latter. Among the countries in that region, Cuba was the leading recipient, with $1 billion of investment; this eclipsed the traditional leader, Mexico, where the Mexican Revolution had had a chilling effect on American investors with respect to their prospects in that country. This shift in recipients was also due to the effects of World War I, which "curtailed the production of beet sugar in Europe and gave a stimulus to the Cuban cane-sugar industry. This resulted in a heavy flow of American capital into the island."[16]

The Great Depression disrupted Latin America's international economic relations and, in particular, its exports and inflows of foreign capital. Accordingly, the region turned increasingly inward, emphasizing ISI and intraregional trade as substitutes for global commerce. As a result of these measures, most countries in the region continued to enjoy economic growth throughout the 1930s, unlike the industrial powers.[17] Shut out of European markets, the United States also began to recognize the importance of Latin America to its economic well-being and national security, with President Franklin D. Roosevelt initiating his Good Neighbor Policy in 1933 and Secretary of State Cordell Hull following up with Reciprocal Trade Agreements with several countries in subsequent years.[18]

As the war in Western Europe gathered steam in the early 1940s, the United States became even more committed to Latin development. A large Export-Import (EXIM) Bank loan was approved in 1941 for the Brazilian steel mill at Volta Redonda, a government-owned enterprise that exemplified the role of the state in the nation's development. It was designed in close cooperation with American engineers, and an official American delegation would be present for its opening in 1946. Brazilians drew from Volta Redonda's success the developmental lesson that state-run firms could operate successfully in other economic sectors as well.[19]

The war years continued to stimulate Latin American economic growth. According to Rosemary Thorp, real incomes rose by 5 percent between 1940 and 1945, while the share of industry in GDP increased to nearly 17 percent.[20] Demand for commodities and raw materials was high in the United States, while limits on American exports continued to spur the continent's ISI strategies. Regional trade continued to grow, and its strong net export position meant that it accumulated significant reserves during the conflict. When these reserves were coupled with the lack of imports, the result was too much money chasing too few goods, or inflation. High levels of inflation, of course, would continue to bedevil many Latin American economies for decades to come.

Given the region's economic prospects, American investors took renewed interest in the continent during the late 1940s. As a result, direct investment grew between 1940 and 1950 from $2.7 billion to $4.7 billion.[21] The exit of German firms in sectors like pharmaceuticals provided new openings for American companies, while the postwar thirst for oil and minerals pushed firms to seek resources across the region.[22] Between 1950 and 1953, the single largest recipient of US FDI was oil-rich Venezuela, followed by growing industrial powerhouse Brazil, and then Cuba with its sugarcane and tourism infrastructure. Most other countries, however, received only paltry inflows from the United States.[23] This point about the very unequal flows of FDI is important to remember, not just for Latin America but for the developing world overall.

The war's end also signaled a sea change in US policy toward the region. During the 1930s and the war years, the United States had worked to strengthen its diplomatic, military, and economic relationships in Central and South America; it even grudgingly accepted Mexico's 1938 expropria-tion of US oil properties, in part because of concerns over that country's diplomatic relations with Nazi Germany, which remained active until the spring of 1942. Yet as the war drew toward its conclusion and it became increasingly apparent that the United States would stand alone as a global power, Washington's interest in regionalism faded (only later re-emerging as it promoted regionalism among the Western European allies). Instead, it began to emphasize a more internationalist approach to world affairs, as exemplified by the United Nations. Even though regional groupings were permitted by the UN Charter—largely at the instigation of Latin American delegates—Washington had turned its focus toward the Security Council and such economic institutions as the International Monetary Fund and World Bank as the organizations that would now organize and shape an increasingly global political economy.

Further, as Europe's postwar economic problems emerged in sharp relief—economic problems that could cause political instability as well—Washington focused its exceptional assistance efforts there, culminating in the 1948 congressional approval of the Marshall Plan. Latin America, like the United States, had emerged relatively unscathed by World War II in terms of asset destruction, and American officials deemed it unnecessary to target any aid programs toward the region. That position rankled Latin Americans, who believed that their support of the allied war effort should be repaid with another Marshall Plan directed to the continent and tailored to its specific needs.[24] In that context, recall that Taiwan, for example, was a recipient of Marshall Plan funds through the Economic Cooperation Administration.

President Truman, however, was unwilling to accept that line of argu-ment. As he told the delegates to the Inter-American Defense Conference of 1947 (the "Rio Conference"), the problems of Latin America were com-pletely different from those facing the devastated European continent. "Here," he said, "the need is for long-term economic collaboration. This is a type of collaboration in which a much greater role falls to private citizens and groups than is the case in a program designed to aid European countries to recover from the destruction of war." According to a State Department cable, the president "promised that increasing attention would be given to the economic problems of the Americas," but that these could be resolved "by private capital." These comments were not met with applause; the US embassy in Bogota reported that the official and media responses in Colombia "have been sour."[25]

Considering that this book emphasizes the agency of developing world governments in their negotiations with the United States, it is intriguing to consider Soviet views of Washington's interactions with its Latin American neighbors during the Rio Conference. According to an article published in the Soviet navy newspaper *Red Fleet* by a leading Russian student of US foreign policy, the discussion of "economic problems" at the meeting reflected "U.S. domination and military penetration and colonial policy toward Latin America. Extremely favorable moment has arrived for US economic expansion . . . under pretext of defense, Latin American states now openly at service of U.S. capital."[26] If that interpretation were true, one might have expected a bit more economic policy activism by the US delegation; after all, American private enterprise wanted the Latin nations to at least create an environment hospitable to their investments. But perhaps the Russian analyst believed that Latin America was so prostrate that it would welcome FDI on any terms that were offered, even if that meant further subservience to Washington and Wall Street.

In this context, it is also interesting to note Washington's unwillingness to take on the leading role in fighting communism in its own backyard. During a 1947 meeting with Secretary of State George Marshall, for example, the Argentine foreign minister tried to make a persuasive case for the threat that the region now faced: "he expressed the opinion that, as things now stand . . . communism will win out." This meant that Washington needed to adopt a comprehensive program to fight the communists, who "had the advantage" against Western states.

But Marshall calmly replied, "our thought was that measures against communism could best be left to the individual countries; that Communist activities varied from one country to another and each country had its own problems." Further needling the minister, he said that the attack on communism had to focus on where it was most threatening: "to stamp out the fire at its source, to remedy the economic chaos in Western Europe."[27] This perspective would be adopted in the first National Security Council document devoted to Latin America, NSC 16 of June 1948, which stated that "communism in the Americas is a potential danger, but . . . it is not seriously dangerous at the present time."[28]

The Bogota Conference, held in the spring of 1948, framed the Charter of the Organization of American States. The Latin American delegates hoped that this new institution would, according to historian Roger Trask, "provide a framework for the economic development of the American republics." Indeed, some within the State Department called for a major financial commitment to the region, including the US ambassador to Brazil, who argued that a $2 billion program be launched.

But Secretary Marshall reiterated his earlier theme. It was, he said, "beyond the capacity of the United States Government itself to finance more than a small portion of the vast development needed. The capital required through the years must come from private sources. . . . As the experience of the United States has shown, progress can be achieved best through individual effort and the use of private resources."[29] Again, we see the themes of self-help and private enterprise being repeated. This magic of the American experience was one that US officials gladly and often shared with others. It reflected the underlying optimism concerning private enterprise expressed in 1939 by a public relations executive, who claimed that "because of free enterprise, America has advanced more in the last 150 years than Europe has advanced in the last 1,000 years."[30]

Thus, during the Truman administration, the economic problems of Latin America never received the kind of attention devoted to Western Europe or East Asia. Little by way of Point Four assistance flowed to the region—between 1945 and 1952, "the twenty Latin American nations together received less economic aid . . . than did Belgium"[31]—much less loans in the anticipated amounts from the EXIM Bank.[32] Nor would Latin America be the recipient of anything like the economic largesse showered upon such East Asian countries as Taiwan and South Korea.

Rather than provide official development assistance, American officials insisted that Latin America could acquire the foreign capital it needed by creating "a suitable investment climate."[33] As historian Trask concludes of this period, "An important step that the United States might have taken during these years to encourage closer hemispheric collaboration . . . was cooperation in the establishment of a program of economic development . . . the Latin American governments considered this their greatest need and foremost objective. Had the United States cooperated, relationships within the hemisphere would have been happier."[34] But Latin America no longer had the strategic prominence it had had during World War II, and the Cold War had yet to heat up sufficiently in the region to draw Washington's attention. That situation would slowly change during the course of the two

Eisenhower administrations, ultimately leading the president to take Latin American demands for exceptional economic assistance more seriously.

Private Sector Development in Latin America

Like its predecessor, the Eisenhower administration in its early years did not hesitate to promote "the potential of the free-market system to meet U.S. [economic] objectives" for Latin America.[35] Not only did the president have an ideological commitment to the power of free enterprise, but Secretary of State John Foster Dulles had previously represented US multinational firms that operated in Latin America, like United Fruit Company, and so knew firsthand about investing in the region.[36]

Furthermore, Eisenhower's policy could ride on the back of increasing FDI, which rose from $4.7 to $6 billion from 1950 to 1953, confirming his administration's belief that private capital could play the leading role in stimulating economic growth; still, it should be noted that in 1953, Venezuela and Brazil held one-third of this stock of direct investment, with most other Latin nations receiving little FDI. Thus, in the administration's first major review of Latin American policy in 1953, the National Security Council recommended that it encourage "Latin American governments to recognize that the bulk of the capital required for their economic development can best be supplied by private enterprise and that their own self-interest requires the creation of a climate which will attract private investment."[37] Self-help, private enterprise, and a good investment climate were the keys to sustainable growth.

Yet subsequent meetings of the NSC would signal the difficulties of putting these ideas into action. Brazil, for example, had gone so far as to state in the legislation creating its national champion Petrobras that foreign firms were unwelcome in petroleum development. Bolivia had nationalized its tin mines, while Chile was embroiled in a dispute with the multinational copper producers operating in that country. A "progress report" on NSC policy in July 1953 concluded that "little further progress has been made in improving the climate for investment in the Latin American countries."[38] There was a fundamental gap between the American view that if its neighbors to the south were more welcoming of foreign capital, their development needs would be met, and the views of many Latin leaders that development required not an invisible hand but state-led investment, particularly in natural resources.

In the eyes of the Eisenhower administration, however, these differing beliefs constituted only a small roadblock that could easily be overcome.

In a 1954 "update" to its Latin policy statement, the NSC again underscored the role of private enterprise, while recognizing a modest role for foreign aid, using identical language to its earlier document:

The United States should seek to assist in the economic development of Latin America by:

a. Encouraging Latin American governments to recognize that the bulk of the capital required for their economic development can best be supplied by private enterprise and that their own self-interest requires the creation of a climate which will attract private investment.
b. Continuing the present level of International Bank loans and Export–Import Bank loans and, where appropriate, accelerating and increasing them, as a necessary supplement to foreign private investment.
c. Continuing a limited economic grant program in Latin America, including such projects as the Inter-American Highway.[39]

But despite the flows of FDI, which the Eisenhower administration viewed as being ample for development purposes, diplomatic historian Bevan Sewell notes that "tensions were beginning to emerge" between the new administration and its Latin American neighbors when it came to economic policy. According to calculations performed by the Economic Commission for Latin America (ECLA) in 1954, Latin America required $1 billion of investment capital per annum from foreign sources over the next ten years to achieve economic growth rates of 2 percent per annum; its growth in the 1950s thus far had been just half that level. ECLA hoped that international lending institutions, including the World Bank and the EXIM Bank would provide $700 million of this amount, with the rest coming from some combination of FDI and, should it be created, a new regional development bank.[40] This $1 billion figure—and the approximately $300 million per annum reserved for private capital (and note that average flows of new foreign investment to Latin America had been half that amount between 1950 and 1954)—became a focal point of discussions between Washington and Latin America when it came to target levels of investment.[41]

These discussions proved difficult. Rather than prioritizing foreign investment, Latin American leaders had formulated three economic policy goals that were at odds with those being pursued by Washington. According to administration official Marion Hardesty, these were: first, "development financing that is equal to that given to other areas of the world; second, the formation of a Pan American Bank; and third, a floor under prices paid for their commodities."[42] This is not to say that Latin governments minimized the need for private capital and investment; again, as suggested by the ECLA estimates, they simply did not believe that private capital was sufficient to meet their myriad development challenges.[43] Because of this view, Latin America in general looked to the government to play a more active role in economic development, and the region expected Washington to be supportive of those needs that FDI could not meet.

Growing US concern with the spread of "international communism" in Latin America caused the Eisenhower administration to launch an internal debate over the direction of its foreign economic policy in 1954[44] As President Eisenhower told the National Security Council in a November meeting, "You must think of our policy in Latin America as chiefly designed to play a part in the cold war against our enemies."[45] Already, beginning in 1953, the United States had started to plot the overthrow of the alleged communist President Jacobo Arbenz in Guatemala, in part due to his threat of redistributing a portion of the lands owned by United Fruit Company; he would be deposed in 1954 after considerable efforts by the CIA to prod Guatemala's military into action.[46] This case, of course, is often used as a prime example of the American state working hand in hand with multinational corporations to advance jointly held policy preferences.[47]

The immediate cause of US internal reflection on its foreign economic policy toward the region, however, was the upcoming Rio Conference—to be held for two weeks beginning in late November 1954—that would focus on the continent's economic problems and the US response to them. These discussions over US policy caused the inevitable bureaucratic battles as key officials adopted different positions, with each simultaneously seeking to emerge as the "honest broker" whose ideas would be taken to the president for his ultimate decision.

For its part, the Foreign Operations Administration (FOA), headed by former Minnesota Governor Harold Stassen, called for "dramatic new lines of action" when it came to economic policy. Some of these lines were actually standard fare, such as the FOA's emphasis that "private investment" should be the "main source of development capital . . . and that Latin America take appropriate measures to encourage this investment." But others were relatively novel (and are still relevant today), like urging "Latin American governments to seek a more equitable distribution of income." The FOA also gave its support to the long-standing Latin American demand for the establishment of a regional development bank and for higher levels of EXIM Bank lending, along with encouragement of a regional trade grouping. Overall, however, FOA "adopted the position that the economic development of Latin American countries will be best served by adherence to the principles of the private enterprise system."[48]

In preparing for Rio, Stassen began to think more deeply about the relationship between public and private capital. In particular, he asked his staff to prepare a report "to see if there is any indication whether governmental credit for developmental facilities expanded or contracted private investment." While I do not know whether such a report was ever produced—I have been unable to locate it—it does point to a question that we will see repeated again and again in Washington and that still resonates in the development community: Does official assistance "crowd in" or "crowd out" private investment? Of course, in the Latin American case, many officials doubted the need for much foreign assistance at all.[49] As Assistant Secretary of State for Latin America Henry Holland—formerly a lawyer representing US companies doing business in the region—said, "We feel that . . . programs of aid would demoralize our private . . . businesses."[50]

But other agencies—notably Treasury—thought these proposals were too bold, and ultimately, it was Treasury Secretary Humphrey—a noted fiscal conservative—who would lead the US delegation to Rio, giving him perhaps more authority over US policy in this area than he might normally have commanded as compared, say, to the Secretary of State (note that in Dulles, Eisenhower had found a secretary who "gave relatively little attention to economic relations with Latin America or other areas of the world").[51] Notably, Treasury rejected the idea of an inter-American bank. The Treasury—joined by some but not all officials at State—also rejected US participation in commodity price stabilization schemes, a position that would eventually change, with the United States becoming a member of a new International Coffee Agreement in 1963 (President Donald Trump would withdraw from the ICA in 2018). In general, Treasury also expressed reservations about "trade-diverting" regional economic integration schemes; that is, schemes that would shift the region away from trade with the United States.[52]

Unlike the FOA or the Treasury, however, the State Department highlighted the role that trade must play in Latin American development, and it emphasized that the United States must pursue a "gradual, selective reduction of trade barriers" at home. While President Eisenhower shared this objective, naturally any tariff reductions would ultimately depend on congressional approval. Finally, all agencies recommended increasing EXIM Bank lending to the region, although Assistant Secretary Holland reminded colleagues that "we have had recurring struggles in order to use the Bank as an instrument of foreign policy . . . because there is no . . . Congressional sanction for these purposes."[53]

As one might expect from such a bureaucratic tussle, the only "significant initiative" that the United States brought to the Rio Conference centered around the promise of expanded lending by the EXIM Bank. Nevertheless, as Stephen Rabe points out, the conference proceeded without acrimony—in part because the United States had already briefed Latin American heads of state on what to expect, and in part because Washington was reciting the same recipe for economic development that the region had heard for nearly a decade.

Not every official was happy with the nonoutcome. State's Richard Rubottom, who would be promoted to Assistant Secretary for Latin America in 1957, called Rio "one of the worst failures of any conference that we've ever had."[54] These officials felt that trouble was brewing on the continent, largely due to growing but unmet social aspirations. This vacuum left an opening for anti-American forces, whether nationalists or communists.

Still, most foreign policy officials felt they could look with satisfaction on the state of relations with the region. Both trade and FDI were rising, and the military regimes that were increasingly running Latin American countries were pro-American in orientation. Interestingly, these trends sparked debate within the Eisenhower administration as to whether it should put more emphasis on democracy promotion, an idea that the President supported over the "long-run," while Treasury Secretary Humphrey thought that dictatorial regimes were better for US interests;[55] for his part, Dulles was wary of meddling in the domestic politics of other countries so long as they posed no communist threat. With the US-instigated overthrow of Arbenz in Guatemala, the National Security Council could report that "Communists have no present prospect of gaining control of any Latin American state."[56]

That being said, the Soviet Union was seemingly posing a growing threat in the region. In January 1956, Moscow launched an "economic offensive" in Latin America to promote trade relations, and the propaganda value of this initiative seemed well poised to exploit the poverty and discontent found in countries across the continent. As an Eisenhower administration official put it, "There are continuing sources of irritation within the hemisphere which are exploitable for Communist propaganda purposes . . . it is important to take early action to eliminate or reduce these causes of friction."[57] A new objective for US policy was now set: to "reduce and eventually eliminate Soviet bloc and communist influence in the area."[58] In practical terms, this meant a renewed emphasis on hemispheric trade.

Yet the specter of communist revolution was not the sole driver of US policy at this time. Even before Premier Nikita Khrushchev launched his Soviet economic offensive across the developing world, a 1954 National Security Council report warned: "Recent changes in the private investment climate appear to be generally unfavorable. An intense spirit of economic nationalism continues to operate against the desire and the need for development."[59] We have already heard Vargas's last words on this topic, but earlier wake-up calls had come from the Bolivian Revolution of 1952 and subsequent nationalization of the nation's tin mines.

That event had led Secretary of State Dean Acheson to worry about "the unsettling effect . . . any confiscatory action would have on private invest-ment in Latin American, including U.S.-owned copper companies in Chile and petroleum interests in Venezuela." The United States worked hard to ensure that American investors were duly compensated for their stakes in the mines, but the collapse of tin prices in 1953 caused Bolivia's "govern-ment to panic," and it went on a public relations offensive, accusing the new Eisenhower administration of "economic imperialism" in its alleged attempt to destabilize the country. Recognizing that it needed to remedy the situa-tion, the administration worked closely with the Bolivian government to ensure a reasonable settlement that satisfied both the mining companies and the regime.[60]

Thus, it wasn't just communism that challenged the US vision of a free-enterprise Latin America; it was also the interaction of regional ideas about development with the nationalist and populist political orientations and as-pirations springing up across the region. Resentment was building across Latin America over FDI, at least in sectors that host countries considered to be strategic. There was also—or so it seemed to many of the region's leaders and economists—sound intellectual support for a more national-istic approach to economic policy. After all, by this time the great economic historian Alexander Gerschenkron had taught that "late industrializers" needed the state to mobilize capital, a lesson taken up by the UN's Eco-nomic Commission for Latin America.[61]

For their part, the Latin American countries were generally disappointed in the state of US economic policy for their region and expressed that view to Washington at every opportunity. As we have already seen, they had sought a Marshall Plan after the war and been rebuffed at every turn. Their calls for a regional development bank had likewise fallen on deaf ears, as Eisenhower administration officials felt that existing institutions, including the World Bank and the EXIM Bank, were sufficient to finance official Latin American needs. Nonetheless, throughout the 1950s the leaders of the main Latin American governments persisted in calling for the establishment of a regional or Inter-American Development Bank (IADB) to spur investment.

By early 1958, the United States was once again prepared to re-examine its economic policy toward Latin America. According to the Historian's Of-fice at the US Department of State, Dulles was "concerned by declining Latin American exports to the United States, falling prices of some impor-tant commodities produced in Latin America, and efforts by the Soviet Union to expand its trade and influence in the area." Dulles told his under secretary, Christian Herter (who would soon succeed him when Dulles lost his battle against cancer), "I doubt that we are in a good position to withstand in that part of the world a Soviet economic offensive at a time when the demand for raw materials is down and prices are very low."[62]

At Dulles's request, a State Department committee examined the scope for possible changes in US foreign economic policy to address these concerns. It did not come up with any concrete recommendations, other than to back "U.S. participation in a multilateral study" of a possible IADB. A subsequent trip to Latin America by Dulles deepened his conviction that an IADB was politically necessary, along with deeper regional economic integration—but he still faced opposition to these ideas from more fiscally conservative members of the cabinet, who feared that the United States would have to bankroll these various schemes.

The administration's attitude toward the IADB began to shift, however, following Vice President Richard Nixon's calamitous trip to South American in 1958.[63] There he and Mrs. Nixon were met with hostile crowds; in Venezuela, their car was attacked and its windows smashed, eventually forcing them to hole up inside the US embassy until the mob dispersed.

The vice president must have felt that his lack of enthusiasm for taking that trip in the first place was fully vindicated. But one lesson that Nixon drew from this experience was that many in Latin America were hostile to American-style "capitalism." As he reported to the National Security Council, "In talking to the heads of the governments in Latin America, he [Nixon] had noted that, with the exception of Stroessner in Paraguay, all of them would say, in effect, we would like to adopt policies which would invite into our country private capital from abroad and which would support the private enterprise system. Nevertheless, [newly elected Argentine president] Frondizi and the others had added that they simply could not get the support of their public for such policies. Moreover, our own Ambassadors generally agreed with this point of view."[64]

In the aftermath of the embarrassing Nixon trip, Brazilian president Kubitschek saw an opening to launch an "Operation Pan America," which resembled a Marshall Plan for the region. Kubitschek called on the United States to dedicate $40 billion to Latin America over the next twenty years; while Eisenhower was unwilling to sign on to such a program, he did send senior officials to Brazil for meetings. These officials, joined by others in the State Department (along with the president's influential brother Milton, whom he frequently employed as a personal emissary to the region), told the president that private enterprise alone could not solve the region's social problems, and that investors would not enter countries with widespread poverty and poor infrastructure.[65]

With the Nixon fiasco and the Kubitschek proposal, President Eisenhower and Secretary Dulles came around to accepting the political need to support a dedicated Inter-American Development Bank (IADB). As UN economist Sidney Dell put it, "Given the prevailing Latin American mood, thrown into relief by the reception given to the Vice-President, it must have appeared [to US officials] that the establishment of a regional development bank would constitute one rather effective method of channeling the forces of continental nationalism into productive channels."[66] While the administration still doubted the need for the IADB from an economic standpoint, it had now become a vital gesture of goodwill toward a region that had historically received little official foreign assistance.

In 1959, President Eisenhower sent a message to Congress calling for its support of the IADB. Knowing the views of many in Congress when it came to foreign aid, he made clear that "Throughout the [IADB] Agreement emphasis is given to the promotion of private investment in Latin America . . . only through the increased flow of private investment can the desired rate of progress be attained." Recall that the administration had earlier given its support to the creation of the new International Finance Corporation (IFC), whose specific mandate was private enterprise development. Indeed, it appears that the Eisenhower administration had reached the conclusion that indirect appeals to private sector development, made through multilateral or regional organizations, were more effective in convincing recalcitrant governments to improve their investment climate than a frontal assault coming out of Washington. In any event, FDI to Latin America did climb during the Eisenhower administration, even if the growth was less dramatic and less widespread across sectors and countries than had been hoped for.

As of 1959, US firms had invested over $8 billion in Latin America, as can be seen in Figure 3.1—an amount that was nearly double the $4.4 billion of investments in 1950 (or about 60% more when accounting for inflation). While much of this investment was in petroleum (mainly in Venezuela, as investments in the petroleum sector were not permitted in Brazil), minerals (especially iron ore), and manufacturing, by far the single largest sector remained public utilities, although this would change as an increasing number of governments frowned upon foreign intrusion in this sector.[67] The postwar era would in fact see a number of expropriations targeted at the public utility sector. These did not, however, seem to have any major impact on foreign investment overall.

In fact, it would be hard to understate the importance of FDI to the industrialization of some Latin American countries. In Brazil, for example, multinational firms would come to dominate such sectors as automobile production, chemicals, pharmaceuticals and electronics; by the mid-1950s,

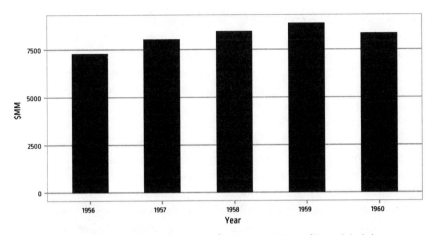

Data source: Selected Data on US Direct Investment Abroad (Washington, DC: Bureau of Economic Analysis, Department of Commerce, 1982).

FIGURE 3.1   US FDI in Latin America, 1956–1960, in Millions of Dollars ($MM)

nearly 20 percent of local sales were generated by US-based companies. While Brazilian policies could be unstable—in the early 1960s, for example, limitations were placed on divided repayments that had a chilling effect on FDI[68]—overall, the country provided a welcoming environment for these firms, which mainly operated to serve the domestic market rather than as an export hub. Indeed, despite these investments, Brazil has relied heavily on commodity exports to the present day.

Did the growth in FDI help local economies? Unsurprisingly, there is variance across and within countries with respect to the multiplier effect of these linkages, since the power of linkages depends on such factors as access to human capital and finance by local firms. A recently published study of Brazilian firms, for example, finds that only local companies with "high absorptive capacity" (meaning human capital and technological capability) have benefited the most from FDI in manufacturing. As a consequence, the state of São Paulo, for example, saw much higher average incomes than the rest of Brazil, in part because of this manufacturing boom. Overall, however, the effects of FDI at the national (or continental) level were muted by the absence of supporting institutions.[69]

But the Eisenhower administration believed that if only the country would open itself to FDI in *all* sectors, especially petroleum, it could put behind it many of the economic problems caused by its historic dependence on coffee and the volatile export earnings that coffee generated (and Washington didn't particularly care if that investment came from American firms;

perhaps it would be even better if Brazil opened itself up to European oil companies at first, to avoid charges of Yankee imperialism).[70] A sound economic policy based on foreign investment would alleviate the country's greatest challenges and bottlenecks. But successive Brazilian administrations balked, saying that opening the petroleum sector would leave them too vulnerable to leftist criticism.

The biggest shock to the Eisenhower administration's foreign economic policy was delivered in 1959 by the Cuban Revolution. Not only did it lead to the expropriation of American properties on the island, but it signaled the specter of communist revolution and growing Soviet influence elsewhere. The United States reacted by both seeking to overturn that revolution directly (an effort that dramatically failed at the Bay of Pigs in April 1961, which caused embarrassment to the new Kennedy administration) and increasing foreign aid to countries that were threatened by communist infiltration. Following meetings with sympathetic Latin American leaders, Eisenhower announced a new Social Progress Trust Fund in 1960, a $500 million program to be administered through the IADB that turned out to be a forerunner of President Kennedy's Alliance for Progress (discussed in the following section).[71] While Eisenhower continued to believe that foreign investment was critical to Latin American economic development, by the time he left office he recognized that more had to be done to quell a possible continent-wide communist revolution.

The Alliance for Progress

For the Kennedy administration, the Cuban Revolution meant that Latin America had become the epicenter of the global Cold War. Kennedy now saw Cuba as "a base for military and intelligence activities against the United States" and for "opportunistic conquests in Latin America."[72] No less important, the administration believed that Castro's declaration of independence from American domination might easily resonate with peasants, workers, and disaffected urban elites alike throughout the South, spreading political turmoil.[73]

Early in his presidency, Kennedy had thus come to believe that Latin America was "the most dangerous area in the world."[74] Under the shadow of this growing communist menace, and only weeks before launching his failed attempt to reverse the Cuban Revolution at the Bay of Pigs, Kennedy announced in March 1961 his signature foreign aid program, the Alliance for Progress. In his kickoff address, Kennedy said that the purpose of the Alliance would be "to satisfy the basic needs of the Latin American people for homes, work, land, health, and schools." He went on to say that Latin America could only "complete its revolution" if it engaged in "necessary social reforms, including land and tax reform . . . unless we broaden the opportunity of all of our people, unless the great mass of Americans share in increasing prosperity."[75] For his part, the CIA's Douglas Blaufarb called the Alliance nothing less than a "broad counterinsurgency program" for the continent.[76]

The Alliance for Progress was nested within the broader Kennedy administration effort to recast foreign aid. Even before assuming office, he created a Task Force on Foreign Economic Policy that highlighted the need for a consolidated assistance program. Foreign direct investment, which had been the focus of prior administrations when it came to international development could not be relied upon since it failed "to recognize the strength of nationalism in the underdeveloped areas."[77]

The extent of nationalist fervor, however, was perhaps exaggerated. A 1962 poll in Brazil, for example, did not find overwhelming public support for expropriations and a plurality argued on behalf of "full-worth" compensation in such cases. This survey certainly did not indicate a country full of left-wing hotheads.[78] As I will show later, the data also suggest that foreign investment continued to flow southward despite the supposed nationalist fervor that had taken hold.

Shortly after establishing himself in the Oval Office, Kennedy put a team of officials to work on recasting foreign aid, including Deputy National Security Advisor W. W. Rostow, who had gained renown during the 1950s as an intellectual architect of US foreign assistance programs while teaching at the Massachusetts Institute of Technology. A proponent of "modernization" theory, Rostow believed that the developing world's masses were demanding a better life, one that would harness the capabilities of advanced technology in order to improve productivity and living standards. As the author of *The Stages of Economic Growth* he argued that a growing number of countries around the world were achieving the conditions needed for "takeoff," and that foreign aid could provide them with the extra thrust needed.[79]

In a February memo to Kennedy, Rostow outlined the monumental problems in foreign aid that the new administration faced. The assistance program it inherited was like "the New Haven Railway, pouring out large sums to keep afloat, but with neither a defined forward objective nor the fresh capital to move toward it. We begin with a program that is almost wholly defensive in character and one which commands neither the resources, the administration, nor the criteria designed to move the underdeveloped countries toward sustained economic growth."[80]

In keeping with the Kennedy mantra, he proposed a "new look" for foreign aid. This included a commitment to multilateralism (the Kennedy administration thought it was high time for Europe to contribute more to international development, and indeed in 1961 Kennedy would launch a
"Decade of Development" at the United Nations, calling upon the industrial nations to target a certain percentage of their GNP for foreign aid)
and urging a shift in the developing world to longer-run thinking and
planning:

> The goal is to help other countries learn how to grow. Aid ends when self-
> sustained growth is achieved and borrowing can proceed in normal commer-
> cial ways; e.g., Mexico. This notion can be made an effective basis for a new
> non-colonial approach of the Atlantic Community to the southern half of the
> world; and even relatively poor countries, who have passed the take-off, can
> contribute—in technical assistance if not in long-term capital; e.g., Mexico,
> Israel, Philippines, as well as Japan. . . . The crucial element here is the new
> criteria we wish applied in granting aid. Aid shall go to those who have devel-
> oped at home the capacity to absorb capital productively.[81]

Besides the condescending professorial tone that Rostow adopts here, the
memo is also notable by his failure to mention any explicit role for FDI.

On 22 March 1961, President Kennedy gave a special address to Congress on foreign aid. There he called for a new, unified aid organization,
higher levels of spending, and national development planning: "The instrument of primary emphasis—the single most important tool" for carrying
out aid objectives, he said, will be "long-term development loans at low or
no interest," made available by a recapitalized Development Loan Fund.
Again, foreign investment was never mentioned explicitly by the president,
other than in the context of a brief mention of maintaining existing insurance programs.

While the Alliance for Progress has been widely viewed by scholars (and
probably pundits as well) as a Washington-inspired program, more recent
historiography has emphasized its Latin American roots.[82] In fact, ever since
the launching of the Marshall Plan in 1948, Latin leaders (like Brazilian
president Kubitschek) and economists (including Raul Prebisch) had lobbied for something similar on the continent. According to Griffith-Jones,
this group "called on the U.S. to cooperate with those Latin American countries willing to make structural social and economic changes (with particular emphasis on land tenure, education and tax reform); to capture the
support of the masses, by convincing them 'with clear and palpable evidence that the program is not motivated by a desire to create lucrative fields
of investment for foreign private capital', and to launch an external pro-

gram of long-term supplementary capital assistance and commodity price stabilization."[83]

In fact, the role of important foreign direct investors in Latin America, like the Rockefellers, in shaping the Alliance has been contested. As Griffith-Jones has put it, "'Liberal' historians stress the . . . absence of corporate influence in the Alliance for Progress program. They correctly point out that the program, drafted by international bureaucrats, academic specialists and politicians, had hardly any reference to US private investment. This attitude was not an oversight, but a response from the Kennedy administration to the warning given by Latin American economists not to appear as furthering investments of US foreign investors through the Alliance."[84] For his part, Darnton writes, "By the time Kennedy was elected and US leaders decided that the threats posed by the Cuban revolution demanded a major response, the deck of options was stacked in favor of a multilateral, developmental-statist, reformist, democratic approach (as opposed to a bilateral, private capital–driven, conservative, and militarized arrangement)."[85] Consistent with these views, American business leaders asserted that they were "excluded from participating in the alliance."[86]

Yet some in the administration actively tried to appease the investor community. As newly appointed Assistant Secretary of State Thomas Mann, a business-friendly Latin American expert, told a group of the region's leaders:

> I do venture to suggest, however, that if our respective governments are to provide all of the facilities which will be needed to take care of present and future populations—such things as schools, sanitation facilities and roads which only governments can provide—the resources of governments will be hard-pressed to meet the need. *It is for this practical reason that my delegation suggests that the main burden of providing jobs for an ever-increasing number of breadwinners must fall heavily on private enterprise which alone has resources adequate to the need.*[87]

Griffith-Jones deftly squares this circle by pointing out that by the early 1960s, American business leaders had become ardent supporters of foreign aid. In their view, aid would improve the investment climate by targeting government policy reform, infrastructure development, and education; those investments would make recipients more attractive to foreign investment. As she points out, "big business was not as absent in the birth of the Alliance as the 'liberals' claim. [Douglas] Dillon, who headed the U.S. mission to Punta del Este [the site of the Alliance for Progress negotiations], was an international banker. One of the strongest defenders of the Alliance in the U.S. Congress was the international banker David Rockefeller who, during that whole decade, headed the lobby of U.S. business interests in Latin America. There had been a significant shift since the late 1950s; North American big business, and in particular the multinationals, were clearly shifting to favor and support increases in U.S. foreign aid."[88]

Further, the Kennedy administration had adopted the earlier ECLA estimate for annual investment needs in the region of $1 billion, with $300 million coming from foreign investment—a number that the business community now deemed unrealistic in light of the scare caused by the Cuban Revolution. Still, members of the administration tried to make the case that the Alliance for Progress was fundamentally an effort to make Latin America safe for private investment. Assistant Secretary of State Richard Goodwin said that the overriding purpose of the program was to "keep the conditions of political stability which make it possible for a company to go in without fear of expropriations."[89] But it was hard to reconcile this view with the president's emphasis on "long-term development loans" as the "instrument of primary emphasis."[90]

In any case, the administration would pay a political cost for gaining business support of the Alliance. In particular, some American business leaders—notably International Telephone & Telegraph's (ITT) CEO, Harold Geneen, who of course became infamous in the context of that company's role in the downfall of Salvador Allende in Chile (see Chapter 4)—lobbied Congress to pass what would become the "Hickenlooper Amendment" (named after Congressman Bourke Hickenlooper (R-IA)), which required the US government to stop providing economic assistance to any country that expropriated American property without speedy and adequate compensation.[91] Geneen in particular had pressed for the amendment following the expropriation of some ITT assets in the Brazilian state of Rio Grande do Sul in 1959 (more on US policy towards these expropriations in Chapter 4). While the Kennedy administration initially tried to block the amendment, believing that the proper response to a particular expropriation had to be in the context of the whole spectrum of US policy objectives in a given country, the president eventually caved in due to overwhelming congressional support. But for all the debate it caused, surveys indicated that business leaders ultimately did not find the amendment productive and were supportive of President Nixon's efforts to overturn it (more on this in Chapter 4).[92]

As it turned out, Congress would ensure that the voices of American big business would be heard when it came to the Alliance for Progress—not just for ideological reasons, but because of the underlying economics. For many in Congress, the Alliance's "turn" toward more government-to-government assistance and less reliance on private investment was troubling. In Hearings held by the Joint Economic Committee in 1964, Senator

John Sparkman (D-Al) made the point (perhaps incorrect, though undoubtedly reflecting his own beliefs) that "when this Alliance for Progress was originally set up, it was contemplated that private enterprise would play a very important part."[93] A number of congressmen worried that official aid programs might displace private investment, and in so doing lend support to those in Latin America who sought development through state-owned enterprises. Indeed, business witnesses before Congress expressed their concern that loans from the US Agency for International Development (USAID) and the EXIM Bank were being used on behalf of state-owned enterprises.

The failure of US FDI toward Latin America to increase by a substantial amount in the early 1960s raised further concerns among these politicians that the region's development goals were not being met, helping fuel the communist fires that seemed to be burning hot in the wake of the Cuban Revolution. A 1963 report on private investment in Latin America commissioned by the Commerce Department stated that "Latin America is a continent in political and social ferment and this is just as truly a deterrent to private investment as are the purely economic and financial obstacles."[94] During the first two years of the Alliance for Progress, regional economic growth was barely 1 percent per year, less than half the amount the region's leaders had anticipated.[95]

Even worse in the eyes of some business leaders active in Latin America, the Alliance was lending support to the region's statist elements. In a letter to Chairman Peter Grace of the Commerce Committee for the Alliance for Progress (COMAP), David Rockefeller and two colleagues emphasized that Alliance funding was not being accompanied by

> efforts to push through economic reforms which would encourage private initiative and enterprise . . . we urge that U.S. policies be reoriented to place far greater emphasis on the encouragement of private enterprise and investment . . . foreign aid should be used as an inducement to nations to adopt policies which will improve the business climate. . . . The United States should concentrate its economic aid programs in countries that show the greatest inclination to adopt measures to improve the investment climate, and withhold aid from others until satisfactory performance is demonstrated.[96]

The COMAP report and the Rockefeller letter caused heartache for the Kennedy administration. In an interdepartmental meeting held on 20 March 1963 on "Problems Related to Private Participation in the Alliance for Progress," one official called the Report "the worst blow yet for the alliance." Still, Under Secretary of State McGhee insisted that "we should not be talked out of our basic philosophy on the Alliance for Progress by Mr. Grace . . . we are going forward with social measures at the same time

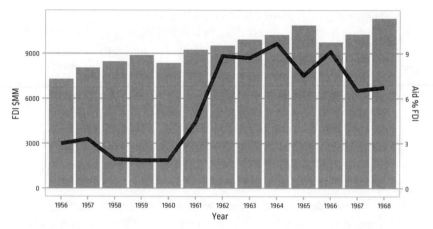

Data source: World Bank, "World Development Indicators," https://datacatalog.worldbank.org/dataset/world
-development-indicators.

FIGURE 3.2   Latin America: FDI in Millions of Dollars ($MM, left axis) vs.
Foreign Aid (Percent of FDI, right axis), 1956–1968

as with the private sector . . . [but] we have to consider how far to press."
As McGhee put it when it came to private investment, "the Latin American countries themselves have much to do. We have limited means to induce them."[97]

To a certain extent, the Alliance for Progress provides a test case for the "crowding in/crowding out" debate regarding the relationship between foreign aid and private enterprise. During the 1960s, aid, trade, and investment to Latin America all grew, with investment continuing even after a brief Cuban Revolution "setback." While this investment remained heavily concentrated in a few countries and sectors (e.g., oil in Venezuela), it nonetheless rose from $8.2 billion in 1961 to over $11 billion in 1968. Further, this period achieved economic growth of 2.8 percent per annum, a figure that sadly would not be sustained in following decades (and one that was much lower than levels found, for example, in the East Asian "tigers"). These investment flows were accompanied by a significant increase in foreign aid to the region via the Alliance for Progress. Why this mix of aid and investment was not more complementary in Latin America is a fascinating question that deserves more research. Figure 3.2 provides data on FDI and aid inflows during the period from 1956 to 1968.

But despite—or because of—these inflows from the northern "colossus," Latin America would find the search for political stability elusive. During the time of the Alliance, many democratic regimes were overturned, and the military once again rose to power in such countries as Brazil. In 1971 an election would take Chile in a socialist direction, troubling the United States to the point of supporting a coup against the new leader, Salvador Allende. The troubled relationship between ITT in Chile and the CIA would prompt congressional investigations into the role of multinational corporations in US foreign policy; more on this in Chapter 4. Yet rather than roll back the private enterprise thrust, the Nixon administration would try to advance it with the creation of a new agency, the Overseas Private Investment Corporation. This continuing belief in the power of foreign investment—despite the backlash against it in many countries—would continue to animate US foreign aid policy.

Conclusions

No region within the developing world has been deemed more hostile to foreign investment than Latin America. Many books have been written about the continent's embrace of economic nationalism and its antipathy to Yankee enterprise. The more Washington hammered the continent about improving the investment climate, the worse that climate seemed to become. Hopefully, if nothing else, this chapter has revealed that story line to be a caricature that masks a much more complex reality.

For one thing, Latin American leaders had more agency in shaping economic policy than is often suggested by accounts that emphasize American (neo) colonialism. Indeed, Washington changed its foreign economic policy over time to meet Latin American demands. During the late 1940s and early 1950s, the United States believed that foreign investment alone would be sufficient to catalyze the region's economic growth. But by the end of the Eisenhower administration, officials recognized that they would have to step up their foreign aid programs. This policy shift reached its apogee with President Kennedy's "Alliance for Progress," an ambitious reform program rooted in ideas that first germinated in Latin America itself. While that program may have failed to achieve many of its lofty objectives, its emphasis on inclusive growth is one that perhaps has had a lasting legacy effect on the aid community.

Despite the policy shift towards official aid, it would be misleading to discount the role that direct investment played in Latin America's industrialization and the spillover effects to local firms generated by the accompanying "linkages" that followed. At the same time, there was considerable heterogeneity in those linkage effects across sectors, regions, and countries. Firms that extracted natural resources tended to have fewer linkages than those in manufacturing, and multinationals in Brazil (particularly in São

Paulo) seemed to build more extensive linkages with the local economy than those, say, in Mexico. Firms that were export oriented had higher linkages than those that were producing for domestic consumption, while countries with more highly developed capital markets enabled local firms to get the credit they needed to forge working relationships with foreign capital.[98]

These facts suggest some important lessons for contemporary policy makers. First, economic structure and the related preferences of local elites matters for private sector development. Despite its decades of effort, Latin America has found it difficult to diversify away from commodity-dependent economies. But, second, local institutions matter as well. In regions—like São Paulo, Brazil—which worked hard to develop an industrial base and which generally welcomed FDI, efforts were also made to increase the human capital stock and the technical capacity of domestic firms (in 2012, Sao Paulo's GDP per capita was twice that of Brazil overall).[99] It is not enough to attract FDI through, say, low taxes or "cheap" labor if the economy is to benefit fully from that injection; complementary investments are also needed. It is interesting to consider how the trajectory of Latin American economic history may have been different, had greater investments been made in universal education and technical training at an earlier date.

Over time, Latin America would come to open itself increasingly to multinational firms, as leaders there recognized the contributions multinationals made to local economies through technology transfer and organizational know-how. This trend became especially apparent in the 1980s and 1990s, following the devastating debt crisis that began in August 1982. But before that shift occurred, Latin American countries would continue to wrestle with the role of FDI in national economies, and many governments would first engage in expropriations that led to conflict with the United States. This tumultuous period from the late 1960s to the mid-1980s is covered in the following chapter.

4

"Storm over the Multinationals"

Foreign Investment from Nixon to Reagan

A heated debate is now underway over American trade and investment policy. At the center of this debate is the multinational
corporation.

—SENATOR FRANK CHURCH, 1973[1]

SPEAKING AT A 1973 congressional hearing on the role of the CIA and
International Telephone & Telegraph (ITT) in plotting the overthrow of
President Salvador Allende of Chile, Senator Clifford Case (R-NJ) asked

> whether it is normal for U.S. multinational corporations to attempt to make
> the foreign policy of this country, and we have to ask whether it is normal for
> the CIA to ask favors of international U.S. companies. If so, what are the con-
> sequences of this activity? What is the line between proper and improper ac-
> tivities by U.S. multinational corporations in foreign countries and by foreign
> multinational corporations in the United States?

More generally, Case sought to understand the "link between private investment and U.S. foreign policy in the developing world."[2]

In the process of answering such questions, scholars during the 1970s
produced some of the most important books on the economics and politics of the multinational enterprise, including Raymond Vernon's *Sovereignty at Bay* (1971), Richard Barnet and Ronald Muller's *Global Reach:
The Power of the Multinational Corporation* (1974), and Robert Gilpin's
U.S. Power and the Multinational Corporation (1975). For his part, Vernon
generally extolled the spread of these firms from an economic perspective
while recognizing the challenges they posed to home and host countries

alike. In contrast, Barnet and Muller saw the rise of the multinational corporations (MNCs) in a less benevolent light, stressing that the main beneficiaries from foreign direct investment (FDI) were the great firms themselves and the executives who ran them. Coming from a completely different perspective, Gilpin saw these firms as instruments of US policy, doing the government's bidding, rather than vice versa. Everyone seemed to agree that multinational firms needed more regulation—but pinning down exactly how and for what purpose remained contested.[3]

The issues raised by the Senate hearings on the relationship between MNCs and the US government reverberated far beyond the Beltway. During the 1970s, tensions between developing world governments and American-based companies grew more heated, with an increasing number of expropriations. More generally, developing countries called for a "New International Economic Order" at the United Nations, under which they sought to "regain effective control over their natural resources and economic activities."[4] Washington, in turn, was drawn into the disputes between firms and foreign countries, in part because it had provided either aid to the expropriating governments and/or investment insurance to the companies. In any case, the American taxpayer was on the hook.

As Vernon pointed out in 1977, these tensions between firms and governments arose owing to the peculiar nature of the multinational enterprise. Hosting these firms was unlike other forms of international engagement, such as trade or finance. Multinational operations, Vernon wrote, "differ . . . in one critical respect: their involvement in the internal economy."[5] And it wasn't just their involvement in the domestic economy that was troublesome; it was their efforts to influence domestic politics as well.

This chapter covers a particularly tumultuous period in the history of US efforts to promote FDI and private sector development. It begins with the efforts of the Nixon administration to weather what Vernon called the "storm over the multinationals," and the policy and organizational innovations that the administration, along with Congress, elaborated, especially in the face of growing economic nationalism. Looming in the background of US development policy during this period was the legacy of the Vietnam War, and upon becoming the nation's thirty-seventh president, Richard Nixon confronted a United States that was tired of international engagements. "This isolationism is a troublesome trend," the president told his cabinet in the spring of 1969. Nixon thought that Americans saw their nation's foreign policy as fundamentally misguided, noting that "there's Vietnam, there are the obvious failures in foreign aid."[6] As a consequence, restoring the credibility of the United States in world affairs and respect for its preeminent military and economic power became his overriding foreign policy priority.

The chapter devotes less attention to the Carter presidency, as that one-term administration did not emphasize private enterprise for development, but rather "pro-poor" policies with an emphasis on increasing the foreign aid budget for that purpose. The Carter administration did, however, take quite seriously the issue of bribery by MNCs around the world, leading to passage of the Foreign Corrupt Practices Act of 1977.[7]

We then turn to the Reagan administration and its handling of the debt crisis of 1982. As I will show, that crisis had a profound effect on developing countries and their attitudes toward FDI, forcing many governments to change their stance toward FDI as other sources of capital dried up. That, in turn, gave Reagan an unprecedented opportunity to bolster his preferred, market-oriented approach to economic growth. Facing a variety of violent insurgencies in Central America, the Reagan administration would also meld its economic and security policies in such initiatives as the Caribbean Basin Initiative (CBI). Reagan would reinvigorate a private enterprise thrust that carried through to US policies toward the postcommunist transition, as detailed in Chapter 5.

The Nixon Years

Toward the end of Lyndon Johnson's presidency, in 1968, a number of factors had combined to lead Congress to question America's role in "third world" development, and in so doing to reduce foreign aid expenditures. The United States had poured billions into Vietnam, but that country's elite still refused to adopt the economic reforms—like land reform—that might counter and undermine the communist insurgency there. Elsewhere, foreign aid was associated with any number of "white elephants," or inefficient projects that had no apparent development impact.[8] Even senators once sympathetic to foreign aid—like the powerful J. William Fulbright (D-AR), who chaired the Senate Foreign Relations Committee—were turning against the president's aid requests in retaliation for his continuing the war in Vietnam. Johnson's FY67 aid budget request of $3.3 billion had been slashed to $2.9 billion; in FY68, he had only bothered to request $2.5 billion.[9]

The nation's ongoing balance-of-payments crisis, itself exacerbated by the Vietnam War, had caused the president to place further limits on FDI, including to developing countries. This group, however, would be subject to less stringent limitations than those facing investors who sought to launch greenfield operations or expand existing ones in the industrial world. Some US officials worried that if developing countries could obtain neither aid nor investment, then falling levels of economic growth would translate into rising political instability.[10] An interagency task force reported to Johnson: "Major U.S. foreign policy interests would be seriously threatened if the AID appropriation is not significantly higher for FY 1969 than FY 1968."[11]

During the 1960s, the developing world was seemingly becoming more hostile toward the "liberal" international economy. Between 1960 and 1969, some 455 expropriations and nationalizations of multinational companies took place—not just in raw materials, but in sectors across the board, including manufacturing.[12] These expropriations necessarily pitted the US government against the leaders of countries in which Washington had multiple interests, as political risk insurance was often provided by the US Agency for International Development (USAID). With the growth in expropriations, many in Washington also grew concerned about access to raw materials, and officials sought new policy instruments that could encourage American firms to invest in resource-rich developing countries despite the obvious risks.

These multiple factors caused members of Congress, led by Senator Jacob Javits (R-NY, who had long been at the forefront of those calling for more active government promotion of private enterprise) to consider what could be done to encourage US investment in the world's poorest nations. As they were not seeing much appetite among their colleagues for large increases in foreign aid, they focused on private enterprise to fill investment gaps. They called for an end to the balance-of-payments restrictions placed on FDI in the developing world. More important, they also backed an idea floated some months earlier by the International Private Investment Advisory Council—an independent body of multinational executives who consulted the administration on ways to incentivize private investment—to create a new, quasi-public corporation devoted to promoting private enterprise, largely by assuming the insurance function held by USAID.[13] As Senator Javits told a congressional committee, "we as a nation have turned more toward development through private investment because it has a higher multiplier . . . and since publicly financed development programs have faced increasingly severe difficulties in the U.S. Congress."[14]

This idea resonated with the new administration. President Nixon, of course, had extensive experience with foreign aid from his time in Congress and then as vice president (more on this below). He was skeptical about the value of government-to-government aid programs, as indicated in this note to Secretary of State William Rogers, which is worth citing at length:

I believe we need to give very serious and careful thought to our relation to countries in the developing world. I do not believe we understand very clearly how our aid programs and our policies, in general, actually affect the political and economic development of these countries and their orientation on foreign policy matters of concern to us. . . . I do not believe we should put ourselves in the position of being blackmailed by countries which threaten to go Communist. . . . I am also concerned about the tendency of our aid programs and, indeed, of the activities of our personnel overseas, in general, to draw us into a deep involvement in the domestic politics of developing countries. Our concern, I believe, should be primarily with their foreign policies, insofar as they affect our own interests.[15]

Nixon's reflection on "deep involvement in . . . domestic politics" is particularly telling, given Washington's "deep involvement" in Vietnam and many other countries where the United States tried, often in vain, to shape foreign regimes and their policies, and where it had also, of course, used covert action to engineer preferred outcomes.

On 28 May 1969, President Nixon addressed Congress on the topic of foreign aid. He knew that Congress was losing its appetite for these outlays; as already mentioned, it had drastically cut the aid proposals of the Johnson administration, and there was no reason to anticipate a change of heart. But despite his doubts regarding aid, the president did not wish to cede this particular ground to the Soviet Union, which was building up its presence in the developing world through an "economic offensive." He therefore called for a "fresh start"—but one that had a familiar refrain.

Specifically, Nixon told Congress: "*We must enlist the energies of private enterprise,* here and abroad, in the cause of economic development. We must do so by stimulating additional investment through businesslike channels, rather than offering ringing exhortations." The president also called for more technical assistance to developing countries.[16] To carry out this plan, he would establish a new Overseas Private Investment Corporation (OPIC). Overall, he requested $2.7 billion in aid spending—some $900 million over current levels.[17]

Nixon, of course, was a seasoned politician who had first been elected to Congress shortly after World War II. He was aware of the Marshall Plan (he had gone on a congressional junket to study Marshall Plan recipients) and the Point Four program, and as vice president he had been engaged in Eisenhower administration debates over foreign aid. His proposal drew on elements of all these past experiences. Just as Congress had demanded that a new, "businesslike" agency be established to administer Marshall Plan funds, so too would his private enterprise thrust be removed

from USAID and placed in a new agency. Just as Point Four had emphasized technical assistance, so too would this new foreign aid program.
Finally, placing private enterprise at the center of international development was consistent with both his ideology and political understanding
of what Congress would accept. Nixon's proposal exemplified the ways
in which ideology interacted with fiscal realities in American foreign economic policy during the Cold War era.

But it must be emphasized that OPIC was mainly created for political
reasons—part of the administration's effort to mollify those in Congress
who sought to reinvigorate the US foreign aid program. As National Security Advisor Henry Kissinger wrote in a memo to the president:

> A public corporation could be created to promote U.S. private investments
> in the LDCs [less-developed countries] and take over all AID programs in
> this area. It would do so primarily through expanded use of specific and
> extended risk guarantees but would also lend to U.S. firms and carry out
> some promotional activities. Such a proposal is widely expected on the Hill
> and would reflect a decision to give greater emphasis to private sector partici-
> pation in our aid effort. However, there is no assurance that it will, even over
> time, increase the flow of private resources or provide any other concrete
> benefits.
>
> *Issue for Decision:* Creation of a public Private Investment Corporation.
> (Propose such a corporation, essentially for cosmetic reasons.)[18]

In fact, Kissinger described most of the new aid proposals he and his colleagues had dreamed up as "cosmetic"—aimed mostly at getting Congress
to accept higher levels of aid funding.

If that was the purpose, the gambit worked—at least partially. With
strong support from Javits and other business-minded members of Congress, OPIC was approved as part of the Foreign Assistance Act of 1969,
along with an overall aid budget of nearly $2.2 billion. This was the amount
Kissinger had already deemed "the highest possible," presumably based on
his regular telephone conversations and meetings with senior members of
Congress (including Javits), so although it fell short of Nixon's request (and
the $2.9 billion Johnson had received in FY67), the outcome could not be
viewed as a disappointment for the administration.[19]

Overall, the House report on the bill highlighted how Congress expected
foreign assistance to operate in the future, laying "new stress on AID's role
as a stimulant to private enterprise abroad," thus providing support to
OPIC's mission.[20] In fact, the Congressional Research Service has said that
OPIC "was created as a first step in the eventual overhaul of the entire
U.S. aid program."[21] Still, because of doubts about its purpose on the part of
some in Congress—led by Senator Frank Church (D-ID)—the Corporation

was only capitalized for two years of operations, instead of the five years the White House had recommended.[22]

In subsequent congressional hearings on OPIC in 1973, Senator Javits made a subtle point regarding the corporation's development impact and why it should be continued:

> OPIC has the effect of allowing the U.S. investor to take a longer-term view of his Investment. Without Investment Insurance, an Investor would either attempt to obtain an unreasonably high rate of return on his Investment, or would make his investment in a "safer" country. For instance, the alternative to American investment in Jamaican bauxite would probably be investment in Australia.[23]

Here Javits reflects a point that "institutional" economists have made in more recent years: that development requires lengthening the "shadow of the future." Countries that take a short-term perspective on investment are unlikely to have good developmental outcomes, which require a commitment to "good" institutions like property rights and impartial judiciaries. From this perspective, the essence of development policy is to incentivize long-term investments by encouraging governments to credibly commit to such institutions.[24]

OPIC, of course, is the forerunner of what is now the recapitalized International Development Finance Corporation (DFC), and these agencies reflect long-held American beliefs about economic development and the role of private investment in encouraging it. The DFC, which among other purposes is supposed to "challenge China" in the developing world, by promoting private enterprise, will be treated in greater detail in Chapter 7. In its early years, however, OPIC had a relatively slow start, in part because it was under constant threat of being eliminated by members of Congress who were growing tired of US taxpayer support of developing countries. Measuring OPIC's influence during its lifetime (1971–2019) is also difficult, owing to the lack of data it generated about its impact. It is telling, in this regard, that OPIC's self-published history of its operations contains virtually no data.[25] Still, at the time of its creation, there were few alternatives to OPIC for political risk insurance, which was its main product.

As Nixon had hoped, during the late 1960s and early 1970s, US FDI to the developing world continued on an upward trend (see Figure 4.1). The New International Economic Order may have sought to "reclaim" developing world control over national economies, but many of these countries still saw FDI as an important vehicle for meeting their requirements. The fact of growing FDI at a time of economic nationalism reminds us of the importance of always looking beyond the rhetoric to the data.

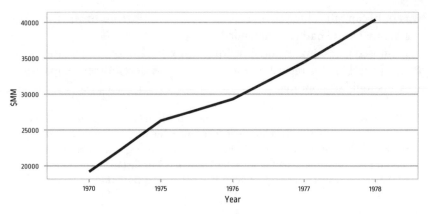

Data source: Bureau of Economic Affairs, US Department of Commerce.

FIGURE 4.1   US FDI to Developing Countries, 1970–1978, in Millions of Dollars ($MM)

Expropriation and Intervention

During the Nixon years, the pace of expropriations against US firms began to increase, even as FDI was rising.[26] Whereas the 1960s had witnessed 455 forced ownership changes, the 1970s would see 914, more than double that number (see Figure 4.2).[27] As Stephen Krasner has written, "The early 1970s proved to be the most propitious moment for the developing world to launch a major attack on the liberal international order."[28] The United States was being vilified overseas for its Vietnam imbroglio, and countries around the world were beginning to ask questions about the US-led international order and whose interests it served. Normative debates in academic and policy circles about how that order should be structured gave renewed attention to issues of international development.[29]

The Latin American nations alone undertook some twenty-two expropriations of US property during Nixon's presidency. The question of how best to respond to these expropriations divided the administration, and even the president himself was torn. As historian Hal Brands has written: "The Nixon administration viewed the expropriation problem as central to US–Latin American relations, and devoted considerable attention and effort to addressing the issue. Expropriation threatened US interests on economic, diplomatic, and ideological grounds, holding the potential to undermine Washington's position in Latin America and damage its relations with the region."[30] On the one hand, Nixon was a strong advocate of private investment who recognized the need to protect the property rights of inves-

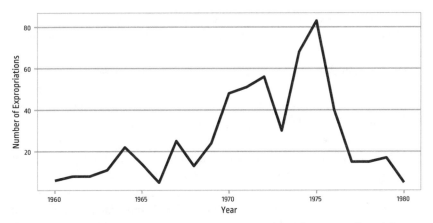

Data source: Michael Minor, "The Demise of Expropriation as an Instrument of LDC Policy, 1980–1992," Journal of International Business Studies 25, no. 1 (First Quarter 1994): 177–188.

FIGURE 4.2 Expropriations by Year, 1960–1980

tors. On the other hand, he was a "realist" when it came to world politics, always attentive to the international security environment, and he was careful to consider whether his actions would strengthen or weaken the United States at a time of growing doubt—within the country and abroad—about its power and purpose.[31]

Peru's nationalization of the International Petroleum Corporation in October 1968 presented a paradigmatic case for the Nixon administration just months before it took office. Despite the "Hickenlooper Amendment"—a congressionally imposed requirement under which the United States would cease all foreign aid to countries that had engaged in nationalizations without prompt and adequate compensation—the Johnson administration had tried to forestall any actions against the government of Peru and instead had sought mediation.[32] Similarly, Nixon initially sought both to avoid confrontation with the Peruvian government and to find ways around the Hickenlooper Amendment.

Nixon therefore engaged Robert McNamara—who had left the Department of Defense to become president of the World Bank, in one of the most ironic career changes in history—to reach out to Lima to see whether mediation was possible. Nixon was further motivated to resolve the crisis, given the amount that OPIC, and thus the American taxpayer, was on the hook for in terms of political risk insurance—not just in Peru, but across Latin America. He feared that if America mishandled the conflict in Peru, it would motivate other Latin governments to nationalize US holdings.

Indeed, while the conflict with Peru was ongoing, President Eduardo Frei of Chile notified Nixon of his intention to nationalize the copper holdings of US firms operating there.[33]

All these developments spurred the administration to develop an expropriations policy. As an input for that policy, the CIA provided a National Intelligence Estimate (NIE) in June 1971 on the problem of growing economic nationalism in the developing world. The CIA believed that economic nationalism was the product of several factors, including domestic problems within those countries that led governments to seek convenient scapegoats; growing technical and managerial competence, which now enabled countries to run these Western firms; balance-of-payments difficulties that led governments to seek ways to reduce payment outflows; and reduced amounts of foreign aid, which meant that any American sanctions would have less bite.[34]

Yet the CIA was remarkably nonplussed about the effects of such nationalizations on the economies of the industrial world. "Even if many LDCs [less-developed countries] nationalize the bulk of foreign investments . . . the effects on investor countries will not be very great." The simple fact was that, even counting petroleum and minerals, investments in the developing world constituted less than half of overall FDI. Much of this was concentrated in natural resources and in only a few countries. If countries nationalized, many states would still seek management contracts with Western firms despite growing technical competence in several of these countries. Furthermore, firms based in the industrial world, including those that concentrated on raw materials production, still had bright prospects in such developed countries as Australia and Canada.[35]

At the end of July, the National Security Council (NSC) presented a paper on "The U.S. Response to Expropriations of U.S. Private Investment in Developing Countries."[36] There, it presented a somewhat less optimistic view than the one put forth by the CIA. The paper stressed America's dependence on raw materials, the need for export markets, the importance of foreign-derived income for the U.S. balance of payments, and the risk of losses to OPIC insurance among the factors to be considered in crafting an expropriations policy. Yet it also recognized the myriad interests the United States had in many developing countries. Accordingly, it provided five alternative policy stances in response to expropriation of American property: first, respond strongly by cutting off foreign assistance; second, threaten to cut off foreign assistance if prompt and just payment wasn't received within a certain time frame; third, state that a determination will be made as to whether and which types of aid should be cut; fourth, cut only certain types of assistance; and finally, make diplomatic representations but avoid applying economic pressure.

The NSC recognized that Washington's ability to influence expropriations was rather limited, especially in light of falling aid levels. Still, it believed that a strong and clear policy stance was required, if only for its possible deterrence effect. Further, there were voices within and outside the administration (including in the business community and Congress) that demanded such a policy.[37]

Interacting with these statements of general policy were specific problems on the ground, none of which were greater than the 1971 election of the socialist Salvador Allende as president of Chile and the economic threat he posed to American interests in that country. For years, the CIA, working closely with American corporate interests, had run covert operations aimed at keeping conservative politicians in power who, among other things, respected the property rights of American firms. As it turned out, several of these firms—notably, Pepsi-Cola and ITT—were clients of Richard Nixon's former law firm. Further deepening the connections between government and industry, John McCone, a former CIA director, had joined the ITT board of directors after leaving the agency, where he served as a go-between; indeed, McCone remained on the books as a consultant to the CIA and made a host of contacts between the agency and ITT executives, including its chairman, Harold Geneen (who, as we saw in the previous chapter, had been a major proponent on the Hickenlooper Amendment). While scholars continue to debate the extent to which corporate interests drove US policy in Chile, there is little doubt that they were a contributing factor—part of the coalition of interests that wanted to see Allende's election reversed.[38]

However, one important element in the Chile story that has been little reported is the fact that OPIC was on the hook for over $100 million in political risk insurance, specifically for ITT's investment there. Following the 1973 coup and Senate investigations that revealed the depth of ITT and CIA meddling in that country's politics, OPIC refused to pay out its insurance claim.[39] This claim would only be settled later by Chile. At the time, it revealed the incoherence of US policy and of how government agencies could work at cross-purposes.

The proximate cause of the controversy surrounding the CIA-ITT-Chile story was an explosive article published by syndicated columnist Jack Anderson in March 1972. There he claimed that a CIA official (William Broe, who was then operating in South America but would later become the agency's Inspector General—once again reminding us of Marx's dictum that history begins as tragedy and repeats as farce) "is reported to have personally visited ITT Vice President E. J. Gerrity Jr. in his New York office to urge ITT to join in a scheme to plunge the Chilean economy into chaos and thus bring about a military uprising that would keep Allende out of power."[40]

Following the publication of Anderson's allegations, the Senate undertook an investigation of the relations between MNCs and US foreign policy that would lead to a multivolume study, which indeed created a "storm" over the operations of these firms. During the investigation, both ITT and the CIA dissembled regarding their respective roles, a fact that only came out later and still has not been widely publicized (more on this when we discuss the Senate hearings below). It has since been largely forgotten that Anderson's initial story was about a *purported* coup attempt in 1970; of course, ITT and CIA continued to foment instability in Chile after that date, ultimately leading to the ousting of the Allende government and takeover by General Augusto Pinochet in September 1973.[41]

While the Chilean story was unfolding, Nixon delivered a major address on expropriations policy in January 1972. As context for his audience—which was mainly Congress and, more indirectly, the American people and its business community—he reiterated his view that FDI was crucial to development and that foreign aid was only effective when it created the conditions under which more capital would flow to recipient nations. He stated that foreign investors who operated in developing countries did so based on contracts that had been negotiated with governments, and that these should be respected. Nixon also suggested that expropriations in one country could harm the prospects of other developing nations that sought foreign investment—a sort of policy contagion.

With this as background, the president said that the United States would withhold any "new" assistance from the expropriating country until adequate compensation had been paid. He also stated the United States would "withhold its support" for any multilateral loans. Finally, he urged developing countries to use international mechanisms for matters of dispute resolution.[42]

According to Brands, Nixon's speech did not meet with the reception he had hoped for, either at home or overseas. At home, the "legalese" in which the speech was couched moved Congress to amend the Hickenlooper Amendment with even tougher language, creating the new "Gonzalez Amendment," which sought to prevent expropriating countries from receiving loans from multilateral development banks until any outstanding claims were settled. Abroad, developing country governments painted the speech as another manifestation of Yankee imperialism, an infringement on their sovereignty. Even other industrial world governments, with important foreign investments of their own to consider, refused to offer support.[43] In any event, if Nixon had been hoping to deter nationalizations, the policy seems to have failed. In 1972, a spate of new nationalizations took place in Latin America, despite (or perhaps because of) US threats to withhold aid.

To the Nixon administration, the gravest threats came from Allende's Chile, where the government had nationalized or was on the road to nationalizing important American copper and telecommunications firms—the latter run by ITT, which seemed to have an inordinate amount of influence in the White House. Still, scholars continue to debate what led to American support for the 1973 coup that brought Pinochet to power.[44] Leading up to the election and then during the Allende presidency, the CIA had issued relatively benign NIEs about the regime, downplaying its ability to consolidate and then export communism. The NIEs generally stated that Allende was struggling to consolidate power and had stayed within the lanes provided by the Chilean constitution.[45] This contrasted markedly with the view of the national security adviser, Henry Kissinger, who told the press in 1970:

> Now, it is fairly easy for one to predict that if Allende wins, there is a good chance that he will establish over a period of years some sort of Communist government. In that case you would have one not on an island off the coast which has not a traditional relationship and impact on Latin America, but in a major Latin American country you would have a Communist government, joining, for example, Argentina, which is already deeply divided, along a long frontier, joining Peru, which has already been heading in directions that have been difficult to deal with, and joining Bolivia, which has also gone in a more leftist, anti-U.S. direction, even without any of these developments. So I don't think we should delude ourselves that an Allende take-over in Chile would not present massive problems for us, and for democratic forces and for pro-U.S. forces in Latin America, and indeed to the whole Western Hemisphere.[46]

In short, Kissinger was applying the domino theory to the region. The United States would try to stop that process by supporting (and perhaps fomenting) a coup against Allende—though ironically, his US-backed successor, Pinochet, would continue with the nationalization process. As in Guatemala, US efforts to overthrow a regime didn't always produce the expected policy changes. But why should it? After all, these new leaders also had to survive within their country's political-economic structures. While perhaps they could rely on new coalitions in order to hold on to power, it proved difficult to overturn completely those elements in the structure that had cast doubt on the benefits of FDI in the first place. In sum, new leaders often had to make their peace with old policies.

Indeed, developing countries around the world began to make a grab for industries that had previously been controlled by foreign firms, most notably in the petroleum and mineral sectors. And no grab would be more dramatic than the Arab oil embargo announced in the midst of the Yom

Kippur War of 1973. While initially only focused on the United States, Israel, and the Netherlands, the impact of the "oil crisis" soon became globalized. That embargo, in turn, served to stimulate developing world demands for a "New International Economic Order" under which they would gain greater control over their natural resources through a series of nationalizations.[47]

There would be another longer-term effect of the 1973–1974 oil price shock (and a subsequent shock in 1978–1979, associated with the Iranian revolution): a tremendous transfer of dollars from oil importers to oil exporters. During the 1970s and early 1980s, the exporters decided to "recycle" these holdings to the oil-importing countries, including in the developing world, by placing funds in international banks that in turn engaged in making commercial and sovereign loans. Developing world indebtedness would balloon during these years. In 1982, it finally burst—as we will discuss in the section below on the presidency of Ronald Reagan.[48]

To summarize, the 1960s and 1970s witnessed a "storm over the multinationals." In fact, there were several separate storms, including the rise of economic nationalism and expropriations; US covert involvement in foreign elections, undertaken in cooperation with multinational firms; and an oil shock that sent the global economy reeling and generated a new wave of nationalizations. This period suggested that developing countries were dissatisfied with the "liberal" postwar order and—with higher commodity prices during the late 1960s and early 1970s—were prepared to exercise their economic muscle. Yet in order to fuel their ambitions, they borrowed heavily from international commercial banks, setting them up for a debt crisis that would radically change their economic policies. Developing countries sought greater independence from the constraints posed by the international division of labor and their place within that scheme, but their agency, while significant, was hardly unlimited.

Reagan and the Magic of the Marketplace

> The American dream of human progress through freedom and equality of opportunity in competitive enterprise is still the most revolutionary idea in the world today.
>
> —RONALD REAGAN, SPEECH TO THE US CHAMBER
> OF COMMERCE, 26 APRIL 1982[49]

During the administration of Jimmy Carter, multinational firms were not at the core of the president's policies for international development. North–South tensions over such issues as debt and commodity prices tended to grab policy attention, and the Carter administration wrestled with where to focus its foreign aid. Should it emphasize "global problems" like hunger or health, or more targeted interventions aimed at providing for the basic needs of the world's "poor"?[50] The available archival records tell the tale of an administration that struggled throughout its single term in office to elaborate a policy that would satisfy the developing world, its Western allies seeking greater US engagement, and a Congress that was firmly focused on domestic economic problems in light of the sluggish economy that followed upon the heels of the Arab oil embargo and the consequent hike in petroleum prices.[51]

These continuing economic problems were the overriding concern of the newly elected president, Ronald Reagan. But even without the Carter hangover of "stagflation," Reagan would undoubtedly have left his stamp on the American—and global—economy. Few presidents have entered office with such a well-defined economic vision as Ronald Reagan. Called "Reaganomics" by its advocates, it included, in the president's own words, the following key elements: "Reducing the growth of [government] spending, cutting marginal tax rates, providing relief from overregulation, and following a noninflationary and predictable monetary policy."[52]

In terms of foreign economic policy, the Harvard economist Richard Cooper said that "Ronald Reagan was the first American president to espouse free trade openly."[53] Reagan's grand objectives, both at home and abroad, were to reduce government's role in the economy and promote private initiative. Even when it came to such vexing problems as dealing with the racist regime in South Africa, Reagan believed in market-oriented solutions, saying, "Our own history teaches us that capitalism is the natural enemy of such feudal institutions as apartheid."[54]

But when Reagan entered the Oval Office in January 1980, the American economy was in dire shape. The Iranian Revolution had sparked another round of rising oil prices, and high levels of inflation and unemployment had dragged the economy back into stagflation. Federal Reserve Chairman Paul Volcker, determined to slay the inflation dragon once and for all, did so by raising interest rates. From 1980 to 1982, the United States suffered a deep recession.[55]

Volcker's policy would also have profound international implications. For the previous generation, many developing countries had sought to fuel their growth on the back of international bank loans. These loans were offered at floating interest rates (normally the London Inter-Bank Offer Rate, or LIBOR), meaning that the cost of the loan repayment fluctuated with rate changes. As interest rates rose sharply, borrowing countries faced higher repayment costs.

In the wake of these heightened rates following the Volcker shock, Mexico announced in August 1982 that it would be unable to make the next round of payments on its outstanding debt. That announcement signaled the beginning of what would become known as the "debt crisis," which would plunge much of the developing world into a prolonged economic tailspin. The International Monetary Fund (IMF) would emerge as crisis manager, providing emergency assistance at the cost of hard-to-swallow advice. Countries would have to cut domestic spending and engage in numerous reforms that ultimately went under the banner of "neoliberalism" (also called the "Washington Consensus" policies). These reforms, which emphasized opening national economies to trade, investment, and competition, very much reflected the economic philosophy of President Reagan.[56]

Even prior to the debt crisis, in a 1981 speech to the World Bank and the IMF, Reagan had already suggested his theory of economic development, uttering in the process one of his most famous phrases: "The societies which have achieved the most spectacular, broad-based economic progress in the shortest period of time are not the most tightly controlled, nor necessarily the biggest in size, or the wealthiest in natural resources. No, what unites them all is their willingness to believe in the magic of the market place." Accordingly, he called on the World Bank and the IMF to encourage private investment and international capital flows, and he offered the view that the role of the International Finance Corporation should be "enhanced."[57]

This speech was followed up in early 1982 with a careful analysis of the multilateral development banks (MDBs), carried out by the US Treasury. As this report emphasized, the Reagan administration believed that its participation in the MDBs "should fully reflect its economy philosophy as to how economic development can be most efficiently promoted."[58] Not surprisingly, the report emphasized in part the role the MDBs should play in private sector development. In particular, the Treasury argued that the MDBs ought to become more selective with respect to the recipients of their loans, working with market-oriented economies. It argued that *the willingness of borrowing countries to adopt and implement appropriate policies should be a prime consideration in the country allocation of MDB lending.*[59] Nonetheless, Treasury admitted that if the United States was to influence the MDBs, it needed allies among other donor countries.

The accompanying data presented in the report highlighted one trend in international capital flows to developing countries that apparently did not merit further analysis at the time, but that would become headline news within a few months: namely, the rapid increase in sovereign borrowing from multinational commercial banks. Whereas in 1970 FDI flows were higher than bank loans, that situation was reversed the following year, and by 1973 bank loans were more than twice the level of FDI—$10.3 billion vs. $4.7 billion. By 1978, bank loans reached nearly $26 billion while FDI flows had climbed to $11 billion.[60] These loans, of course, would be at the heart of the debt crisis.

As the crisis raged, Reagan turned to the private sector for ideas about how to get capital flowing to the developing world. In 1982, he created the Task Force on International Private Enterprise, composed of business leaders, which issued its report in December 1984. Predictably, the Task Force emphasized that US foreign assistance programs on one hand and developing world governments on the other must act to "increase private investment and improve the investment climate."[61] But unlike the Treasury, which argued that the MDBs should focus on those countries which were willing to adopt a market-orientation, the Task Force said that the US "owes it . . . to the people of the developing countries, to try to persuade their governments . . . that the key to development lies in a vigorous private sector." Again, the United States itself provided the model: "Our own record of economic development gives us a credential that we should use far more boldly."[62]

Interestingly, the Task Force also emphasized the role that American institutions—including private enterprise and universities—could play in bolstering the human capital of developing countries through training programs, as the United States had done in such countries as Taiwan during the 1960s. The report noted that most training programs were currently aimed at the public sector; according to the Task Force, they should be reoriented toward entrepreneurship. The members stated: "A major objective of the Reagan administration is to help developing countries rely less on their public sector and more on their private sector."[63]

The Reagan administration would further address international investment in its 1983 policy statement on that topic, the first issued since the Carter administration in 1977. While Carter advocated "neutrality" with respect to international investment, meaning that the US government should neither promote nor discourage it. Reagan adopted quite a different stance, saying that "the United States will pursue an active international investment policy aimed at reducing foreign government actions that impede or distort investment flows."[64]

The debt crisis, of course, gave new urgency to mobilizing FDI—with bank loans drying up and limited Congressional appetite for increases in foreign spending, developing countries now had little choice but to attract more investment—the gist of this new policy reflected the Reagan philosophy and had already been presented to Congress in earlier hearings on aspects of the president's foreign economic policy. It is worth citing at some length a witness from the Office of the US Trade Representative, who provides an excellent summary of Reagan administration policy:

> A major goal of U.S. investment policy is the encouragement of flows of private direct investment into developing countries. . . . Our private direct investment in LDC's represents, however, only 20 percent of our total foreign investment; furthermore, the large majority of the increase in U.S. Investment in LDC's since 1970 has been concentrated in relatively few countries. . . . The Administration is working to draw greater private sector resources of the United States, of other developed countries, and of the developing countries themselves into the pursuit of economic growth in the LDC's. Appropriate measures encompass unilateral, bilateral and multilateral approaches. . . . Unilaterally, the United States is supporting foreign investment in developing countries by: (1) acting to strengthen the U.S. economy in order to maintain a prosperous and open market for the products of new investment projects in LDC's . . . (2) expanding the range of the operations of OPIC to reduce the political and expropriation risks facing U.S. investors in developing countries; (3) channeling more AID assistance activities into greater support for the creation of greater management and technical skills necessary to attract investors in LDC's; (4) lessening the burden of disincentives to U.S. business activities in LDC's, including modification of the Foreign Corrupt Practices Act to more clearly define illegal activities under the Act. Bilaterally the Administration is working to support U.S. investors in developing countries by initiating a series of bilateral investment treaties (BIT's). . . . By agreeing to a bilateral Investment treaty, a country which desires to attract U.S. investment will agree to general and specific commitments which will be welcomed by U.S. investors. Multilaterally, the Administration is working to support foreign investment in developing countries by (1) encouraging developing countries . . . to pursue economic reform, including the relaxation of economic controls placed on activities of the private sector; (2) promoting greater use of investment syndicating facilities such as the International Finance Corporation (IFC) . . . and (3) encouraging the study of a new multilateral insurance program . . . it deserves serious attention as a facilitator of foreign investment and economic development in the poorer LDC's.[65]

Ironically, the debt crisis gave a fillip to these policies. Moreover, the strong dollar—a product of the rising interest rates used to stifle inflation—negatively affected US exporters and caused the trade deficit to skyrocket as demand rose for "cheap" imports (facilitated further by currency devaluations in many developing countries). Though FDI was much less affected than, say, new bank loans, its flow to Latin America nonetheless fell after 1982; according to Lipsey, flows dropped by 25 percent and only recovered to near-1981 levels toward the end of the decade. Remaining FDI was increasingly geared toward exports rather than servicing local markets. In part, these investments were facilitated by "debt-equity swaps," in which investors turned country debt into equity shares of local companies. Outright privatization would further motivate foreign investment.[66] Indeed, this period saw many developing countries reconsider their commitment to state-owned enterprises, as fiscal pressures generated the necessity of selling them off to private investors, either foreign or domestic.

Throughout the 1980s, the overall geographic distribution of FDI also changed dramatically—not necessarily to the economic benefit of developing countries. Whereas somewhere between one-quarter and one-third of all FDI had flowed to developing countries in the decade prior to the debt crisis, that number plummeted thereafter; by the end of the 1980s, only one-eighth of all FDI went to the developing world. Poor economic performance and a bleak outlook curbed the risk appetite of many direct investors, despite the promise of using these countries as export platforms. That development would have to wait for the 1990s, when the postcommunist transition would make those countries inviting sites for European FDI in particular, and when other developing regions would become export-oriented hubs (recall that the World Trade Organization, an institutional manifestation of the increasingly globalized economy, was founded in 1994). As Figure 4.3 shows, FDI as a share of GDP exploded during the period from 1990 to 2000, especially after 1995. Recent economic analysis suggests that the Reagan administration's insistence on emphasizing liberalization and openness, especially to FDI—what these authors call "the Baker Hypothesis,"

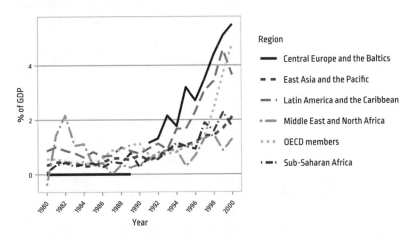

Data source: World Bank, "World Development Indicators," https://datacatalog.worldbank.org/dataset/world-development-indicators.

FIGURE 4.3   FDI as Percent of GDP in the Developing World, 1980–2000

after Secretary of the Treasury James Baker—has contributed, on average, to the long-run growth of recipient economies.[67]

Reagan also used ongoing security threats, particularly in Central America, as a rationale for advancing his market-oriented policies; for the president, economics and security were inextricably linked. One of the strategic issues the Reagan administration confronted upon taking office was the rising tide of leftist insurgencies and civil war in that region; of course, Reagan had come to office with a strong anticommunist ideology.[68] At this time, Guatemala, Nicaragua, and El Salvador were all riddled by violence. In the eyes of administration officials, the economic situation in these countries and the grievances they were generating only served to compound the degrading security environment. The president addressed leaders from the Organization of American States in launching what would become known as the Caribbean Basin Initiative (CBI):

> At the moment . . . these [Central American] countries are under economic siege. In 1977, 1 barrel of oil was worth 5 pounds of coffee or 155 pounds of sugar. Well, to buy that same barrel of oil today, these small countries must provide 5 times as much coffee—nearly 26 pounds—or almost twice as much sugar—283 pounds. This economic disaster is consuming our neighbors' money, reserves, and credit, forcing thousands of people to leave for other countries, for the United States, often illegally, and shaking even the most established democracies. *And economic disaster has provided a fresh opening to the enemies of freedom, national independence, and peaceful development.*[69]

Among the countries affected by civil war, few had known more violence than El Salvador. From the late 1970s until a settlement was finally reached in 1992, an estimated 30,000 to 70,000 people lost their lives.[70] The Reagan administration would spend over $4 billion on this small country alone.

The conflict in El Salvador was deeply rooted in what the State Department described as "decades of misgovernment during which a small oligarchy, allied with a corrupt military, exploited the nation."[71] In particular, extreme inequality in land holdings and household incomes, coupled with widespread poverty, created an explosive situation that was exploited by insurgent groups supported by Cuba and Nicaragua. Further, the number of landless peasants grew during the 1970s as they were continually displaced from the plots of land they had worked. Extreme violence on the part of El Salvador's military added fuel to what was already a raging flame.

Yet despite these unpromising conditions, El Salvador was slowly undergoing economic change, with opportunities for land reform opening up as the nation's elites began to look for fresh opportunities in industry and banking. According to a RAND Corporation study, the land reform program was "designed by American experts, financed by American economic aid, and largely implemented by American organizers and technicians."[72] American officials recognized that their program would only succeed in quelling the insurgency if it was accompanied by growth in the new economic opportunities that were gradually emerging for capital and labor alike. In some respects, the El Salvador land reform program seemed to take a page from the Taiwanese case, in which landlords would be encouraged to move assets from agriculture to industry, promoting productivity and income growth in the process—and hopefully undermining one cornerstone of the insurgency.[73]

The CBI was to play a key role in accelerating that process of structural change in El Salvador's economy. It gave Central America and the nearby islands (among other regional states) unfettered access to the American market, leading export-oriented industries to set up shop in these countries. Between 1979 and 1990, agriculture's share in El Salvador's GDP would fall from 27.5 percent to 17.4 percent, while industry climbed from 17.5 percent to 22 percent.[74]

In presenting the CBI to Congress, Reagan again emphasized the interplay of economics and security:

> The economic, political and security challenges in the Caribbean Basin are formidable. Our neighbors need time to develop representative and responsive institutions, which are the guarantors of the democracy and justice that freedom's foes seek to stamp out. . . . The alternative is further expansion of political violence . . . resulting in the imposition of dictatorships and—inevitably— more economic decline, and more human suffering and dislocation. . . . Today, I seek from the Congress the means to address the economic aspect of the challenge in the Caribbean Basin—the underlying economic crisis which provides the opportunities which extremist and violent minorities exploit.[75]

He emphasized, however, that the CBI was not just another foreign aid program. The president told Congress: "It builds on the principles of integrating aid, self-help and participation in trade and investment. . . . It is a different kind of assistance program for developing countries, based on principles and practices which are uniquely American and which we know have worked in the past."[76] We again see how the themes of self-help and private investment re-emerge throughout the history of US foreign economic policy.

The crux of the CBI was unconstrained access to the American market, free of tariffs, with the main exceptions being in textiles (where an international system of textile quotas already existed) and sugar (which was tightly controlled by Congress under a quota system). Special tax credits would be available to firms that invested in the region, so long as they respected

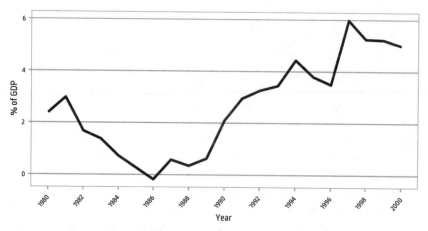

Data source: World Bank, "World Development Indicators," https://datacatalog.worldbank.org/dataset/world
-development-indicators.

FIGURE 4.4   FDI as Percent of GDP in Caribbean Small States, 1980–2000

a local content requirement of 25 percent value added. This would be
supplemented by foreign aid, with El Salvador being by far the single
largest beneficiary.[77]

The CBI has received surprisingly little scholarly attention since its prom-
ulgation. But the few economic studies that have been performed agree that
it has had a modest but measurable impact on trade and investment.[78] As
shown in Figure 4.4, by the mid-1980s, FDI as a percentage of GDP was
skyrocketing in the Caribbean region—a marked contrast to the region's economic free-fall prior to the CBI announcement.

For the purposes of our study, the CBI is noteworthy in a number of respects. First, it exemplified the linkages between economics and security
drawn by American leaders, showing how trade and investment were used
for strategic purposes in the developing world. Second, as Reagan himself
said, it exemplified the American philosophy of economic development,
with its emphasis on "self-help" and private enterprise. Third, it was a relatively coherent program, combining land reform, trade, and investment in
a way that gave firms high-powered incentives to build export-oriented platforms, in the process attracting capital and labor away from agriculture
(where they had violent conflicts) and into industry. The new DFC could
profitably learn from the CBI example as it contemplates how to advance
American influence in the developing world.

Conclusions

The Nixon administration saw a true "storm over the multinationals." Controversy over the economic and political roles these firms played at home and abroad led to a major study of their behaviors by the US Senate—and several of its findings were less than kind. Unlike previous textbook views that conceptualized these firms as efficient transmitters of new technologies and industrial processes and generators of good jobs, they came to be viewed instead as monopolists who used the power of the American state to advance their interests (at least when corruption failed). In short, they had power that they wielded to the detriment of host countries.

They also had economic power. They could use transfer pricing to hide profits while targeting their ongoing operations to stifle domestic competition. Their bargaining power enabled them to extract rents from host countries that were never recycled back into the economy.

Developing countries, of course, were not mere victims of the MNCs. During the 1960s and 1970s, they began to expropriate these firms at an accelerated rate, especially in the area of natural resources. Their growing power over commodity pricing would be demonstrated most dramatically during the Arab oil embargo of 1973–1974. Increasingly, it seemed, the postwar vision of a harmonious world economy was being torn asunder— not so much by the East-West conflict, as expected, but by North-South divisions.

With the inauguration of Jimmy Carter as president, the new administration sought to heal some of these wounds. It focused its foreign assistance policies not on direct investment, but rather on poverty reduction and "basic human needs." But by the end of his term, Carter faced a US economy that was reeling from stagflation, and coping with that challenge took much of the president's attention.

As Ronald Reagan assumed the presidency, the United States was diving into the deepest recession it had experienced since the end of World War II. Federal Reserve chairman Paul Volcker was dedicated to slaying the scourge of inflation through high interest rates, while Reagan continued to press for more market-oriented economic policies at home and abroad. This combination of actions and ideology would have extraordinary international implications.

In 1982, faced with rising interest payments on their debt but reduced demand for their exports—brought on by the now-generalized industrial world recession—developing countries, led by Mexico, began to halt payments on their outstanding loans. The debt crisis overtook most of Latin

America and many countries beyond, forcing them to accept IMF "neo-liberal" prescriptions in return for structural adjustment loans. As the developing world struggled to reorient its economies toward more market-oriented institutions, many countries began to reconsider their long-held skepticism toward FDI.[79] FDI, it seemed, was less risky than portfolio investment—and while it posed many challenges, it was also a potential vehicle for industrialization, modernization, and export growth.

Alongside the debt crisis, no global event would shape flows of FDI so much as the end of the Cold War. By the 1990s, the FDI floodgates would open—not just in countries that had a history of accepting (and occasionally rebuffing) such investment, but across much of the former Soviet bloc as well. Communist China, which had already begun to open up new export processing zones in the 1980s, would continue its opening to the global economy. A "new world order" was being created, with economic globalization providing its centerpiece. It is to this history that we now turn.

5

Capitalism Triumphant

Private Enterprise and the New World Order

The [Support for East European Democracies] legislation is directed toward an unprecedented goal: that of helping new or evolving governments in Eastern Europe build successful free-market democracies on the rubble of failed communism.

—SENATOR CLAIBORNE PELL, 3 AUGUST 1990[1]

DURING THE EARLY 1990S, I served as a principal administrator at the Organisation for Economic Co-Operation and Development (OECD) in Paris. My mandate was to work with officials in the former Soviet Union on their plans for defense conversion, or how to transform defense-related industries into innovative private sector firms.

One experience I had at that time was particularly suggestive of the difficulties Soviet-era enterprises faced in achieving their market-oriented objectives. While visiting Krasnoyarsk, a Siberian city that housed important defense-industrial plants, I was accompanied to one such enterprise by a newly minted MBA working for a major consulting firm. After the tour—which included visits to company-run schools, cafeterias, and apartment buildings—the consultant began to harangue the old "hero of the Soviet Union" (you could tell by all the medals he proudly wore!) who managed the facility.

"You need to reduce your workforce and spin off the non-core activities," he lectured. "You can only attract foreign investors by focusing on the technologies you can transfer to the commercial sector." He continued on in this vein, providing ideas for dismantling the company's social welfare programs and extolling a lean corporate infrastructure.

Finally, the manager turned to the consultant and said, "I'm sure you're right, young man. But where can my workers go? They can't get residency permits to live in Moscow or St. Petersburg. Where would their children go to school if we closed ours? Where would they live if we shut down our apartments? We can't make these changes overnight."

Witnessing this exchange, along with many others like it, would inspire me to research the post-Soviet transition (both solo and in collaboration with such outstanding scholars as Branko Milanović and Michael Mandelbaum)[2] and eventually led me to examine in depth the promises and pitfalls of private sector development in "emerging" economies, both as an academic and as an adviser to multinational corporations (MNCs) and development agencies. This book, of course, is reflective of that effort.

With the collapse of communism in Central and Eastern Europe (CEE) and in the Soviet Union during the late 1980s and early 1990s, the United States was in a unique position to export capitalism and democracy to political economies built on entirely different foundations. The former Soviet Union and its "allied" states seemingly presented Washington with a tabula rasa upon which it could experiment with untried models of economic and political reform, and the new governments of these states—if not all the citizens they represented—generally welcomed the introduction of market economies after years of communist-era shortages and deprivations. The "transition" from communism thus presented a unique opportunity to demonstrate the material, and perhaps even moral, upsides of adopting Western-style institutions and policies, offering the people the right to choose the goods and services, jobs, and elected representatives they desired.[3]

The US government's response to the post-Soviet transition was characterized by an impressive degree of innovation and speed, unseen in normally sluggish Washington since the New Deal or the end of World War II.[4] Legislation creating new policies, programs, and institutions was hurriedly passed through Congress in the wake of the surprisingly rapid collapse of the Soviet bloc, which had caught most public officials and Kremlinologists off guard. These responses included an array of new grants, loans, and credits, as well as an extension of the services of such agencies as the Export-Import (EXIM) Bank and the Overseas Private Investment Corporation (OPIC)—initially to Poland and Hungary, but soon thereafter to other Central and Eastern European countries as well. After the USSR disintegrated, Russia and the new post-Soviet states also qualified for many American assistance programs.[5]

In addition, White House action and subsequent congressional legislation led to the creation of a batch of enterprise funds whose purpose was to invest in small and medium-sized enterprises (SMEs), as well as backing for US participation in a new European Bank for Reconstruction and Development (EBRD), which had an explicit mandate to promote private enterprise and democracy in the region. For its part, the European Union (EU) held out the promise of membership in its community of liberal and democratic states and provided substantial funding to help countries clear the hurdles that membership required. Even more than the United States, it was Western Europe—with its combination of market-oriented economies and robust social welfare systems—that provided the political and economic "model" that most of the transition countries aspired to adopt.[6]

Despite a great deal of collaboration between Congress and the administration of President George H. W. Bush in responding to the postcommunist transition, some scholars have suggested that the collapse of the Soviet bloc introduced new dynamics into the process of creating and funding US foreign policy. These new dynamics included the end of foreign policy bipartisanship and, more generally, a newfound lack of congressional respect for presidential prerogatives beyond the water's edge.[7] With the demise of the Soviet Union and the communist threat, some members of Congress began to express the view that defense budgets and foreign policy engagements could and should be sharply reduced.

That viewpoint also spilled over to foreign assistance policy, leading to debates within Congress about the American role in the post-Soviet transition. As Zeuli and Ruttan have written, "When the Soviet Union disintegrated, the common thread of foreign aid goals, the threat of Soviet expansion, also disappeared."[8] Given these differing opinions over the role of the United States in what President Bush famously called the "new world order," it was hardly a foregone conclusion that Washington would seize the opportunities for exporting capitalism offered by the post-Soviet transition.[9]

While debates ensued up and down Pennsylvania Avenue over the appropriate levels of policy engagement and expenditures to support this transition, economists warned that the overwhelming challenge of reforming the Central and Eastern European (and eventually the Soviet/Russian) economies could not be met by official development resources in any case; in fact, these resources would hardly make a dent. They calculated that the cost of "rebuilding these economies may be $3 trillion . . . if the aim were to rebuild the Soviet Union as well, the cost would be even higher. . . . But worldwide official development assistance . . . was just $48 billion in 1988."[10] The gap between official resources and projected requirements was not merely in the billions of dollars; it was in the trillions.

The "neoliberal" ideological climate of the period—which, after all, followed two terms of a Reagan presidency in the United States alongside the long reign of conservative Prime Minister Margaret Thatcher in Britain (who served until 1990)—also pointed toward a relatively limited role for foreign assistance and an emphasis on free markets and private enterprise in supporting economic renewal and growth. As one Harvard economist asserted in an early paper: "Restructuring the Soviet Union and Eastern Europe is primarily a job of the private sector."[11] Note that this assertion was made without any reference to the myriad institutions that the private sector requires in order to thrive, including, inter alia, the provision of credit; property rights; independent judiciaries; and labor markets; these are all institutions that depend upon a capable state to function properly.

American business leaders warned Congress that until these institutions were put into place, and incomes started growing, it would be difficult for them to invest in Central and Eastern Europe. As the head of the National Association of Manufacturers said in a 1990 US Senate hearing,

> I am concerned that too many people, both in the administration and in the Congress, are taking it for granted that American business, the private sector, in fact can be the major transportation vehicle for U.S. policy in this area . . . to put the American business community at the point of the spear is to get things a little bit off balance.[12]

There were, of course important debates among economists concerning how the transition to a market economy should proceed. Should the new governments of these nations adopt "shock therapy"—meaning the rapid privatization of state-owned enterprises along with the acceptance of price signals for allocating goods and services—or should a more gradualist approach be adopted? Should governments focus on creating a favorable investment climate for the emergence of new businesses, or should they emphasize restructuring the state-owned enterprises that employed a large share of workers in many transition economies? The answers to these questions, of course, also had important political implications concerning who would control the transition process and who would benefit from it.[13]

As we will see, Washington looked to the private sector to play a leading role in driving economic growth and the transition in the Central and Eastern European countries, and it even expressed skepticism about the need to fund the transition countries' public sectors in that process.[14] But this absence of strong, supporting institutions would come back to haunt the transitions of many countries of the former Soviet bloc. The great variance in post-transition outcomes is powerfully suggestive of the role that the domestic political economy plays in shaping a nation's economic trajectory, even in the presence of overwhelming systemic forces.

At the same time, as the data will show, the extent to which the private sector has taken root across the region cannot be denied (some of it with close, kleptocratic ties to the state). Private enterprise is responsible for an increasing share of economic activity and employment, and such countries as Poland have developed strong entrepreneurial cultures. After thirty years, the political-economic consequences of these developments are still unfolding, with the ultimate destination still unknown.

This chapter outlines the American response to the post-Soviet transition. It also discusses—albeit in somewhat less detail—the EU's important work to steer the Central and Eastern European countries toward community membership. In so doing, it examines the response of the White House and Congress to the collapse of the communist bloc, with a focus on the foreign assistance programs legislated during the early years of transition. It then turns specifically to the emergence of the enterprise funds and the EBRD, and the role that policy makers hoped American private enterprise would play in the process of creating market-based economies, including support for the privatization of state-owned enterprises across the Central and Eastern European countries. The chapter also offers an assessment of how successful these various activities have been.

It begins, however, by providing some context regarding the world economy the post-Soviet states were expected to enter. After all, the end of the bipolar competition between the United States and the Soviet Union heralded the arrival of a truly global economy, with new opportunities for trade and investment available to firms and entrepreneurs. And given the inevitable shortfall of official resources to help countries plug into this new world order, that job would fall largely on MNCs, which had the experience of operating across many different regime types and economic environments. Countries now scrambled to attract these firms in the search for capital, technology, and modern management techniques. The large-scale privatization of previously state-owned enterprises provided a further opportunity for drawing in foreign capital. In many important respects, the 1990s represented a heyday for foreign direct investment (FDI).

Neoliberal Globalization and the New World Order

With the debt crisis of 1982, the West was handed unprecedented economic leverage over those developing countries (including some in Eastern Europe, such as Poland) that sought structural adjustment loans from bilateral and multilateral donors. Faced with unsustainable financial burdens and the need to raise cash, countries had to engage in a major effort to curb domestic spending, privatize assets, liberalize markets, and open themselves to the international economy, even at the cost of rising unemployment and cuts to social welfare programs. These prescriptions became known as the "Washington Consensus," but they also went under the banner of "neo-liberalism," a phrase used with disdain by those critics who were more concerned with equity and social justice than economic efficiency.[15] Such policies, of course, characterized the Reagan-Thatcher era of economic policy in the industrial world, with its turn to free markets and smaller governments—even if these were respected more, to quote Hamlet, in the "breach than in the observance."

By the early 1990s, the new emphasis on opening economies to trade and investment and the progressive "globalization" of the world economy—perhaps best exemplified by the founding of the World Trade Organization (WTO) in 1994, which formalized and expanded the remit of its predecessor, the General Agreement on Tariffs and Trade—had changed the developing world's attitude toward FDI. Countries were working to attract FDI through debt-equity swaps where available, chiefly in Latin America. In such cases, foreign investors bought up debt in return for equity stakes in companies—often state-owned enterprises that were being privatized. The ongoing privatization of state-owned enterprises around the world (a phenomenon that began in Britain but spread globally) and the possibility of grabbing assets on the cheap also provided a crucial opening for foreign investors who wished to enter the former Soviet bloc, as we will see in the following sections. Finally (as suggested by the reference to the WTO), countries also attracted FDI by offering the possibility of creating new export platforms, given the reduction in trade barriers the WTO was meant to encourage (currency devaluations in many developing countries also made this attractive). In an era of globalization, trade and investment would truly become the drivers of sustained growth. To put this more starkly, countries that sought to isolate themselves from the globalization process did so at their economic peril.[16]

In an important sense, developing countries no longer had the luxury of limiting FDI inflows if they sought capital for investment purposes. With official development assistance, portfolio investment, and bank loans all falling off during the early 1980s, FDI became their leading source of fresh capital (see Figure 5.1 on FDI flows during the 1980s). Political scientist Stephen Brooks notes that states responded to the trend by quickly tearing down barriers to investment; during the 1990s; for example, 95 percent of all investment-related policies were aimed at creating a more favorable climate for MNCs, rather than placing new restrictions on them.[17] In fact, states were now throwing all kinds of investment subsidies at these firms, including tax breaks and free land—some of which were arguably too generous. As further evidence of the new climate for FDI, Brooks finds no

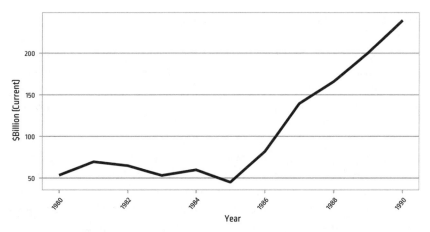

Data source: World Bank, "World Development Indicators," https://datacatalog.worldbank.org/dataset/world
-development-indicators.

FIGURE 5.1   FDI Flows, 1980–1990, in Current Billions of Dollars

cases of developing world expropriations between 1987 and 1992, a remarkable shift from prior decades.[18]

But it was not just for macroeconomic purposes—that is, to augment domestic savings—that FDI became so important, even if that was the initial
driver. Brooks notes that during the 1990s, MNCs increasingly became
sources of proprietary technologies, including in the rapidly changing sector
of information and communications technology. If developing world governments sought to "plug in" to this technological revolution, they had no
choice but to invite these firms to invest. That desire, of course, would only
grow stronger as the internet became a crucial means for conducting business
transactions during the 1990s. Only by working with MNCs could periph-
eral countries enjoy the benefits of the innovation being generated in the core
industrial economies (or more accurately, the postindustrial economies).

Brooks notes yet another economic trend of great importance during
the 1990s: the move toward regional trade agreements. One example was
Mercosur in Latin America, which was founded in 1994 and combines
Argentina, Brazil, Paraguay, and Uruguay (note that the North American
Free Trade Agreement also went into effect in 1994). Washington had advocated for Latin American economic integration since the Eisenhower
administration, in part because it believed that a larger trading bloc would
attract more FDI. The events of the 1980s and early 1990s finally pushed at
least that small group of states to do so, in the hope that a larger economic
bloc would attract more foreign investment.[19] Indeed, Mercosur's website

highlights the economic size of this grouping, including its combined population and GDP.[20]

Finally, Brooks stresses the changing nature of FDI. Whereas investments were previously more or less self-contained, they were now becoming integrated parts of "global supply chains."[21] Firms were slicing and dicing their operations for a combination of economic and political reasons. On the economic side, firms were seeking arbitrage opportunities in different countries; in the words of Narayan Murthy of Infosys, "Globalization is about producing where it is most cost effective, sourcing capital where it's cheapest, and selling where it's most profitable."[22] On the political side, countries were bargaining with firms for production opportunities, based largely on their market size. This was particularly important for multinationals producing expensive capital goods, such as aircraft, that had to be sold in large quantities on the global market in order to be profitable, given the upfront capital costs associated with development and production. If, say, Turkey was likely to buy some significant share of their end product, it would have a stake in getting contracts to supply the intermediate goods.[23]

Thus, the post-Soviet transition coincided with a set of significant developments in the global economy that would influence policy making in the East and West alike. A strong preference toward liberalization, privatization, and openness marked Western prescriptions, while a desire to break out of the grim, decades-long autarky imposed by the Soviet Union colored the aspirations of many "transition" leaders, alongside a desire to join the world's foremost regional economic bloc, the EU. President George H. W. Bush's "new world order" of democratic capitalism indeed seemed imminent (although it is sometimes forgotten that Bush invoked this phrase in the context of Iraq's 1990 invasion of Kuwait, a bitter harbinger of the disorder the new millennium would bring).

But somehow, despite these seemingly convergent preferences in the East and West for democratic capitalism, the transition did not work out as planned. Once again we will see that the particular circumstances of the domestic political economies of the recipient countries would prove just as decisive as systemic international forces in shaping their trajectories. Despite these pressures from "above," and even in the midst of an economic shock of Great Depression proportions, the countries of the former Soviet bloc retained, for better and for worse, considerable agency in shaping their future.

Certain countries, such as Hungary and Poland, joined the EU—but then after an initial period of enthusiasm about their democratic trajectory, veered off in a populist or even authoritarian direction. Others, like the Central Asian "Stans," remained firmly autocratic (and kleptocratic), both economically and politically. Since the collapse of the Soviet Union, Russia has developed its own strange mixture of authoritarianism and kleptocracy, which may or may not outlast its current leader, Vladimir Putin (Russia may need to reconsider its heavy dependence on energy exports as the key driver of its economy should global climate change initiatives continue to erode the value of those distressed assets).The wide variety of post-Soviet experiences speaks to how powerful the stickiness of domestic arrangements can be, even when states are most vulnerable to adopting international dictates. Having said that, we will see that elements of the market economy have become fixtures across the postcommunist world; as a recent survey in Russia concludes, "market principles have become ingrained in mass consciousness."[24] That alone is no small achievement.

Political Economy of the Postcommunist Transition

Following the collapse of communism across Eastern Europe and, eventually, the Soviet Union itself, the region faced the immense and unprecedented task of constructing, simultaneously, democratic and capitalist institutions. As an American official involved in the process recalled, "In prior cases of transition from authoritarian rule, at least some elements of a market economy or liberal democracy were already in place. . . . Among the post-communist countries, everything had to be changed . . . and everything was related to everything else. New elections had to be held even while constitutions were being revised and wholesale economic restructuring undertaken."[25]

Echoing this policy maker's comment, the political economist Allan Drazen has argued that a defining feature of the postcommunist transition was its sheer magnitude. By "magnitude," he was referring to three distinct aspects of change: the *number* of new policies that had to be implemented by the new Central and Eastern European governments, which were manned in many cases by relatively inexperienced officials; the *scope* of those changes, which spanned the political, economic, and social; and the *uncertainty* surrounding the effects of the various changes on society and the economy, which naturally made emerging interest groups cautious about investing, lest they lose out.[26]

Specialists on the communist economies, and in the field of international development more generally, were also uncertain about what recommendations to give—or worse, recommended applying a set of neoclassical economic theories that most policy makers felt were irrelevant under the circumstances. Thus, experts had little empirically grounded guidance to offer to public officials as they confronted the rapidly changing situation. As former US National Security Council (NSC) official Robert Hutchings has written, there seemed to be a disconnect between the "expert advisers" who traveled to the region with their theoretical neoclassical toolkit in hand and the immediate problems that local government officials had to resolve with the limited policy instruments and finances at their disposal.[27]

In particular, many of the theoretical frameworks that were meant to provide officials with some guidance on how to *improve* markets that were already functioning (for example, introducing more competition, which is thought to remedy a fair number of economic ills) seemed to have little relevance to the problem of how to *build* market economies in the first place. These countries generally lacked the underlying social and legal foundations that markets demanded, and their state-owned enterprises were often inefficient. Indeed, one weakness of most economic theory was that it tends to assume the presence of such cornerstone market institutions as property rights, the rule of law, stable monetary policies, and contractual enforcement mechanisms. What guidance could neoclassical models provide in those cases where the necessary market institutions were weak or absent? How could foreign advisers help build free markets in places where at least some influential elements in society were either hostile to that economic form or sought to capture it in the interest of rent extraction? We will see these problems re-emerge when we tackle private sector development in fragile and conflict-affected states in the following chapter.

As noted in the previous section, during this time the Washington Consensus on the priorities for economic reform emerged to provide a blueprint for policy making. However, this too assumed the existence of the institutional underpinnings that these reforms required.[28] The Consensus reflected mainstream economic thought about what constituted the foundations of economic reform, including, as already noted, such cornerstones as fiscal and monetary stabilization, trade liberalization, tax reform, deregulation, privatization, and the adoption of competitive exchange rates. If one were to boil down the Washington Consensus to two crucial words, they would probably be *stabilization* and *efficiency* (as opposed, say, to the couplet of *equity* and *opportunity*). Macroeconomic stabilization was critical, because if inflation went wild, there would be no investment. Efficiency was no less important, as state-owned "white elephants" were a drag on national budgets that desperately needed to cut outlays and generate tax revenues.

Yet some economists also feared that the Consensus would create as many problems as it solved. Price liberalization was necessary in order to bring goods to market, but if inflation reached levels that called for draconian stabilization measures, these would inevitably reduce growth, increase unemployment, and undercut popular support for the transition process. In fact, inflation would explode in Poland in 1990 as prices reflected the sudden scarcity of all manner of goods and services. If inflation had been hidden by shortages during the communist era, it now burst into the open.[29]

Regarding efficiency, economists hoped that with the unwinding of state-owned enterprises, a more competitive and productive economy would emerge over time, boosting long-run economic growth. But in the short run, this was likely to be achieved at the cost of higher levels of unemployment as enterprises shed unnecessary labor—an unfortunate side effect that did come to pass.

For its part, the US government expressed some wishful thinking when it came to the difficulties associated with building up the institutional foundations of economic growth. In Washington's view, it was "the new private sector" that would generate "economic growth and . . . new jobs." According to NSC official Hutchings, "It would be imperative to nurture this sector, so that fledgling small business could prosper and expand. . . . Improved access to Western markets was essential both for private sector growth and the attraction of foreign investment."[30]

But building up "small business" would not happen overnight. As Lipton and Sachs pointed out in a seminal paper on the transition, the Central and Eastern European countries, especially Poland, were heavily invested in large industrial plants that employed many thousands of workers. These plants had been tightly integrated into the Warsaw Pact economies, with their exports mainly heading toward the Soviet Union. Restructuring these industrial behemoths, creating new enterprises, and reorienting them toward trade with local and Western consumers was a massive undertaking that would likely take years to accomplish.[31] Sadly, the transition governments felt that they did not have the luxury of several years to get their houses in order. Economic instability could spur on political instability and perhaps even a return to communism; this, too, was a fear shared by President Bush.[32]

Indeed, the Bush administration was wont to recognize the long-term nature of this transition. Reflecting on its response to the events of 1989, NSC official Hutchings wrote, "The essential task for Western policies was to consolidate the gains of the 1989 revolutions. . . . We could . . . provide *emergency assistance* where needed so as to avert a chaotic breakdown of order and assist with the transition . . . toward market-based economies."[33] A member of the congressional staff who was intimately involved in related legislation, William Scheurch, has emphasized the administration's refusal to accept that the transition would likely take many years; instead, it commonly spoke of the process lasting three to five years at most.[34]

The Bush administration recognized that Washington Consensus–type policies faced potentially sharp political opposition in the Central and Eastern European countries, given their distributive outcomes, or the fact that they would generate "winners" and "losers." As Drazen has emphasized, "for a program of reform and transition to succeed, it must have the necessary political support at crucial decision stages."[35] Pervasive uncertainty among agents over outcomes (or certainty for some agents, such as workers at state-owned enterprises who knew they would be axed following the privatization of their firms) provided the basis for counterattacks on government policy prescriptions. In fact, the Bush administration mobilized "emergency assistance" in the hope that it would make the crucial difference in preventing a political backlash against the transition.[36]

But as the postcommunist transition got underway, the initial period of elation soon gave way to harsh economic realities. Instead of witnessing the rapid emergence of European-style political economies, in which markets were coupled with social safety nets, the ground truth seemed closer to chaos and an "everyone-for-themselves" mentality. Industrial production plummeted between 15 and 40 percent across the Central and Eastern European countries as they lost their former captive Warsaw Pact markets before establishing their capability to make the products Western consumers demanded. Further, slowing global economic growth in the early 1990s reduced the demand for tradable goods.[37]

As a consequence, unemployment—which was virtually unknown under communism—jumped to 30 percent or more of the active population, and poverty levels rose to new heights.[38] Inflation skyrocketed in many countries, with excess demand for available goods causing prices to rise once price liberalization had been implemented. As previously noted, President Bush worried over the possibility that some Central and Eastern European countries might even experience a counter-revolution if the United States failed to support the transition process.[39]

Clearly, these countries, and later the Soviet Union (which collapsed in late December 1991), would need outside economic assistance to navigate this treacherous period of transition. But how would the West, and the United States in particular, respond? How would newly elected President George H. W. Bush navigate between his campaign promise of fiscal rectitude ("Read my lips: no new taxes") and growing demands for US foreign aid? Would Congress be supportive of higher levels of foreign assistance as the Cold War came to an end? These are among the questions that shaped Washington policy debates and that I address in the following section.

Supporting the Transition:
The Politics of the SEED Act

In many respects, the US government *was* working with a blank slate when it came to foreign aid for Eastern Europe. This is not to say that the recipient countries themselves were "blank slates"—each had its own societies and institutions that would shape the postcommunist political economy regardless of foreign assistance. But from an aid perspective, there was little precedent in place. While some assistance had been given to Poland and Hungary at various points during the Cold War, and while the Soviet Union was granted permission during the 1970s to import American foodstuffs in return for a relaxation of its strict policy against Jewish emigration, these transfers were largely transactional and not part of any comprehensive foreign aid and economic development scheme for the region.[40]

The sudden collapse of communism in Poland and Hungary in 1989 caught the Bush administration largely off guard, and its initial response to engagement was cautious (as many inside and beyond the Beltway would criticize, overly cautious), for reasons I examine in more detail below. For one thing, the US Agency for International Development (USAID) had virtually no experience building market economies from scratch; in fact, a number of innovative new programs and institutions were ultimately created by the US government, reflecting the novelty of the situation. For another, while Congress yielded to the president and his regional strategy during the early days of the transition, over time members became frustrated with what they perceived as foot dragging at a time when, in the view of many elected officials (including those from districts with heavy concentrations of voters with Eastern European roots), bold American action was needed.[41] Congress would thus also play an active role in the policy process.

The assistance package that ultimately resulted from this process of "pulling and hauling" between the president and Congress was the Support for East European Democracy (SEED) Act of November 1989.[42] As already noted, and as will be further elaborated in what follows, several domestic and international factors shaped its legislation, including a divided government (the Democrats had strong majorities in both chambers); concerns over budget deficits; caution over the Soviet Union's presence in the region (recall that it continued to exist until late December 1991, and that Eastern Europe had been in its sphere of influence since at least the late 1940s); and Bush's concerns about attacks from the right wing of his own party if he appeared too generous.[43] Together, these factors, along with an ideological propensity that favored private sector–led solutions to economic problems, shaped US policy toward the region.

Despite these constraints on Washington, the post-Soviet transition process offered an enticing range of possibilities for the extension of American power into the former Warsaw Pact, one of those rare moments of political vacuum that great powers cannot ignore. As Steven Weber has written:

> Reform in Eastern Europe held important opportunities to advance U.S. interests in a number of different ways. CEE seemed the ideal place for the Bush Administration to champion its economic ideology by stressing the philosophy of open markets, private control of enterprises, and the reduction of state intervention in reforming economies—all of which would also be good for U.S. business prospects in the region.
>
> There were also substantial geopolitical stakes, as successful reform in CEE would consolidate the overthrow of Soviet power in Europe and would also provide new chances for Washington to nudge the EC [European Community] further away from an insular "fortress Europe" orientation toward the preferred U.S. vision of the EC as a more outward-looking foreign policy actor.[44]

Yet specific policies had to be developed in order to advance these preferences, and those policies had to be paid for at a time of growing debate over how to reduce federal budget deficits.

As Weber has also argued and as the data show, it would be misleading to look at the United States as the financial champion and thought leader when it came to the post-Soviet transition. By dint of history, geography, and immediate political-economic interests, Europe had a more pressing stake in developments in the East—and within Europe, Germany was literally on the front line. Between 1990 and 1993, Germany provided far more assistance to CEE than did the United States. Naturally, East German reunification alone occupied Bonn and Berlin for many years; that process cost upward of $2 trillion, making light of early economic estimates of transition costs. Thus, while this chapter focuses on American foreign economic policy, any complete analysis of transition-era assistance policies (something that still remains to be written) would feature European policies and programs as well.

Returning to the scene in Washington, the Bush administration's initial reaction to the events of 1989 was mainly shaped not by economic interests (which in any case were hardly overwhelming in the former Soviet bloc, again casting doubt on neo-Marxian assessments of the capitalist "need" to expand markets), but more by its geostrategic view of how Moscow would react to these regime changes. At this time, the administration still believed that Moscow's "perestroika" might work, and thus there was no reason to believe that the Soviet Union faced imminent collapse. To the contrary, Bush feared that Moscow might consider invading the Central and Eastern European countries if their revolutions proved threatening to its interests.[45] In any event, he had to appear tough on Moscow to avoid criticism by the right wing of the Republican Party.

Bush therefore sought to achieve a balance between his desire to support the Central and Eastern European transition on the one hand without antagonizing Moscow—or conservative Republicans who remained wary of Chairman Mikhail Gorbachev—on the other. One way to achieve this was to call for only a modest program of US foreign assistance to the region, which had the added benefit of being congruent with his conservative fiscal policy stance. In pursuing this option, the president was trying to thread the needle between the foreign and domestic pressures he faced.

This cautious approach, however, "which characterized the Bush administration's attitude toward economic assistance for the CEECs[Central and Eastern European countries] throughout its tenure, prompted severe criticism, especially from congressional Democrats, as well as from some Republicans and foreign policy experts, who looked upon the disintegration of the Soviet empire as an unprecedented foreign policy opportunity."[46] If Bush felt constrained by the pressures driving his decisions at the outset, Congress became progressively less handcuffed as the year 1989 progressed. A Congressional Research Service report is worth citing at length:

> The 101st Congress' approach to Eastern Europe in its first session changed over time and can be seen in two distinct phases. From January until after President Bush's trip to Poland and Hungary in July [1989], congressional attention to developments in Eastern Europe was limited mainly to human rights. On other issues Congress largely deferred to and supported the administration's lead. After Solidarity established the first non-Communist led government in Eastern Europe [in Poland in October 1989, following its electoral sweep in June], the House and Senate took a much more active role in formulating policy, often different from that of the administration.[47]

Zeuli and Ruttan further argue that,

> While the Bush administration chose to play a defensive . . . role, Congress erupted with both verbal and monetary shows of support for the emerging democracies of Eastern Europe, especially Poland and Hungary. . . . Congressional Democrats harshly criticized Bush's aid proposals for Poland and Hungary as inadequate. . . . Each party and each chamber tried to outdo the other in its generosity; each wanted the credit for having given the most aid to Poland and Hungary, especially after the installation of the Solidarity government.[48]

On 17 April 1989, following the signing of the Polish "Round Table Agreement" between the Warsaw government and the country's Solidarity trade union, President Bush proposed an assistance package focused mainly on US support for international financial institutions to assist Poland with restructuring its debt and achieving macroeconomic stability.[49] Even at this early stage of US involvement, some in Congress already wanted to see a newer, bolder approach—but the majority "seemed satisfied the Administration was properly engaged."[50] Their opinion of the administration's actions, however, became increasingly critical over time, as a growing number in Congress came to the view that Washington could and should do more.[51] One staff member who was active in the relevant legislation complained that Congress was capable of responding "rapidly to the changes in the region while the executive branch, torn by greater internal debate, was incrementally adjusting policies."[52]

In June 1989, Congressman Lee Hamilton (D-IN) introduced the "Democracy in Eastern Europe Act" (HR 2550), which authorized some modest assistance programs for Poland and Hungary.[53] In presenting this proposal to the House, Hamilton explained that "President Bush will be making an historic visit to Poland and Hungary in mid-July . . . it is important for him and for the Congress that he be able to present these countries with concrete evidence of US support for their political and economic initiative."[54] Notably, this legislation had a private sector tilt, in that it required the "Overseas Private Investment Corporation to support projects in Poland and Hungary to enhance the nongovernmental sector and reduce state involvement in the economy."[55] That same month, Representative Dante Fascell (D-FL), then chairman of the House Committee on Foreign Affairs, introduced another major foreign aid reform bill (HR 2655), which included a modest $15 million for assistance to those two countries.[56] Both the House and Senate also held hearings during this period related to foreign assistance programming.[57]

President Bush's July 1989 visit to Poland and Hungary was a pivotal moment in US foreign policy toward the region. During his visit, Bush pledged to seek congressional support for a number of more ambitious assistance programs, including $100 million for the initiation of a novel Polish-American Enterprise Fund, whose objective would be to grow the private sector.[58] State Department official Ralph Johnson told a subsequent congressional hearing that the president "hoped to signal strong support for the reform efforts underway," while underscoring that the United States could "only help Poland and Hungary help themselves."[59] As we might have predicted, the theme of "self-help" reemerged as the transition process got underway.

In light of his various political and economic concerns, Bush favored a "fiscally responsible" approach to assistance that emphasized foreign investment and private sector development. He was therefore hoping to attract American firms to the region with support from the OPIC, the EXIM

Bank, and new enterprise funds aimed initially at Poland and, soon thereafter, Hungary. (These funds, discussed below in greater detail, would operate as independent organizations.) While US business leaders welcomed government assistance to the transition economies, they also warned that foreign investment would not pour in overnight. As the vice president of the US Chamber of Commerce stated in Senate hearings, "a precondition for U.S. private sector initiatives in Eastern Europe, as elsewhere in the world, is to create a climate in which free enterprise can flourish. In Eastern Europe, this will require overcoming some unique obstacles."[60]

Ambassador Matlock in Moscow also sought to encourage foreign investment to the Soviet Union, recognizing that foreign aid to that country would certainly be limited by congressional opposition so long as it remained a communist superpower.[61] Yet Matlock was circumspect. As late as 1989, many officials in Washington believed that Gorbachev could still save the Soviet Union from collapse if he implemented dramatic political and economic reforms. But in observing Gorbachev, Matlock was reminded of the many legends "of the curse carried by ill-gotten property." Just as in legend, the Bolsheviks had stolen the nation's property from its owners. Now that there was no possibility of returning it (since most of the previous owners were dead or held no legitimate title to their land), that property was cursing the present regime. "Unless the state could find a way to divest itself of control over . . . property," Matlock writes, "reform could not take hold," as there would be no assets to provide the foundation and collateral for market exchange.[62]

Those in Congress who were critical of Bush's policies shared a belief that effective and timely assistance to the region would serve an array of US economic and security interests.[63] While hotly contested, foreign aid was viewed by many in Congress as an effective instrument for advancing those broad interests, and some also felt compelled by their constituents of Eastern European heritage to signal US support for the dramatic changes in the region with greater levels of economic assistance.[64] Given domestic politics in the United States, both parties and chambers had their own incentives to demonstrate generosity to the region. Lech Walesa's dramatic visit to Washington in mid-November 1989, and his emotional pleas for substantial financial assistance to a joint session of Congress, certainly helped boost support for Polish aid—though even at its most generous, Congress would never appropriate close to the $10 billion that Walesa sought.[65]

Ultimately, the most significant achievement in assistance policy during 1989 was the SEED Act (P.L. 10 1-179). It authorized a total of up to $938 million in aid to Central and Eastern European countries over a three-year period—more than twice the amount proposed by the president. FY1990 funding for the SEED Act was designated at $285 million. SEED funding would mainly be for new enterprise funds for Hungary and Poland—funds meant to accelerate private sector development in those countries (later to be expanded across the post-Soviet states). The SEED Act was suggestive of increasing congressional involvement in the transition process.[66]

As this history suggests, the executive branch did not operate in a vacuum in shaping its policies toward CEE; it had to contend with a Congress that wanted to flex its muscles on this particular issue. Following its November passage, SEED was soon expanded to other Central and Eastern European countries beyond Hungary and Poland, while additional funds were allocated for US membership in the newly founded European Bank for Reconstruction and Development (EBRD; more on this in a following section). Thus, within a compressed and tumultuous period of a few months in 1989, the main thrust of US economic policy, emphasizing self-help and private sector development, toward the region was established.

As noted, at the core of SEED programming was the creation of enterprise funds for the Central and Eastern European countries. The idea of creating these enterprise funds was first raised in discussions between senior State Department officers and then National Security Advisor (and Russia expert) Condoleeza Rice. As Daniel Fried, then Assistant Secretary for the Bureau of European and Eurasian Affairs, recalled,

> The Funds were an outgrowth of discussions about radical new opportunities for U.S. development assistance in the former Soviet Bloc. . . . It was Condoleezza Rice who raised the question with me and John Cloud [former US ambassador to Lithuania]. She said "What if we had $100 million for the Poles, what would you do? How do you take advantage of this?" John and I brainstormed the idea of a fund. . . . The concept was to provide a wide charter, but without the standard development bureaucracy. Give it to people who know about free markets—nobody in government. Give it an independent board. Give it a charter. And get out of its way.

President George H. W. Bush announced the new program in a speech in Poland, promising $100 million for the enterprise fund for that country, but "Congress ultimately thought $100 million was awfully paltry and raised it to $240 million, and that's how the concept was born."[67]

After the passage of the SEED Act, no one anticipated the need for immediate additional assistance to the Central and Eastern European countries. The following year, however, geopolitical developments were seen by many in Congress as offering fresh opportunities to influence outcomes in Europe.[68] The Bush administration's enthusiasm regarding aid to Eastern Europe was, however, "characteristically as restrained in 1990 as it was in 1989, and it continued to receive criticism regarding its reluctance to support large aid programs for Eastern Europe."[69] The idea of deploying foreign aid to Eastern Europe retained its popularity with Congress throughout 1990, despite growing concerns over budget deficits.[70]

The gap between the administration and Congress is revealed by their respective budget requests. Bush requested only $230 million for FY1991 for aid to Eastern Europe, while the House approved $419 million and the Senate $320 million. In the end, $369.7 million was appropriated for SEED funds, $44 million for Polish debt restructuring, and $70 million for the EBRD.[71]

If foreign aid to Eastern Europe generated controversy between the president and Congress, the situation was even more fraught when it came to the Soviet Union. (It should also be emphasized that by the time serious consideration was being given to assistance to the Soviet Union in 1990, the administration was largely occupied with Saddam Hussein's invasion of Kuwait and the eventual military response to it, called Operation Desert Storm.) Throughout 1990, Gorbachev had pleaded with the West for foreign assistance, eventually winning a large package from Germany.[72]

But Gorbachev also sought assistance specifically from the United States, including foreign aid and agricultural credits. A debate ensued in Washington over the terms of such an agreement, and Secretary of State James Baker demanded "a Soviet economic plan that would demonstrate practical results."[73] Eventually a package of trade and agricultural credits, along with some support for technical assistance, was approved, but it fell far short of what Gorbachev had requested. President Bush also sent a delegation of business leaders, led by Commerce Secretary Robert Mosbacher, to Moscow in September 1990—again signaling that FDI would drive the US approach to assistance programming.[74] Little more would be done to "save" the Soviet Union; instead, the administration looked to Western Europe and the Arab oil producers to provide Gorbachev with funding. (On a personal note, I was part of a small group from Harvard University that former president Richard Nixon invited to his home for dinner during this time. Nixon was trying to impress upon "opinion leaders" the importance of trying to preserve the Soviet Union, and he thought the Bush administration needed to provide more assistance. Nixon was fearful that the collapse of the Soviet Union and end of the bipolar order would issue in a new era of global instability; needless to say, he was prescient.)

Once the Soviet Union ceased to exist, and with a fragile democracy emerging in Moscow, the United States felt compelled to assume a leadership role in mobilizing the international community. A multilateral gathering of major donors occurred in January 1992, while various legislative proposals went up and down Pennsylvania Avenue soon thereafter. These culminated in the FREEDOM Support Act of 1992, which provided $505 million for various assistance programs, including yet another enterprise fund. As a director of that fund put it, "The [US-Russia Investment] Fund really becomes a champion, if you will, of Western and American values."[75] Ultimately, assistance to the former Soviet Union would dwarf the funds allocated to Eastern Europe; during the 1990s, for example, Russia received over $1 billion in USAID funding, while Poland received less than one-quarter of that amount.[76] But no amount of public money would be sufficient to meet the demands of the transition, especially now that funds also had to be mobilized for Russia. The only path forward was to promote foreign investment and private sector development.

The Role of Private Enterprise

As seen in the previous country cases we have examined, Washington looked to the private sector to take the lead in growing the postcommunist economies for reasons both pragmatic and ideological. On the pragmatic side, international assistance funds would certainly be inadequate to fuel the economic transition. Ideologically, the United States believed that the private sector was the cornerstone institution in market economies; as a key part of civil society, it would underpin democratic politics as well. For all these reasons, the central policy thrust had to be aimed at unleashing private enterprise.

In order to advance private sector solutions to the economic challenges posed by the transition, the United States looked to several possible vehicles, including FDI, enterprise funds (mainly for catalyzing SMEs), and the EBRD. All of these could also contribute to the growth of entrepreneurship and the related privatization of state-owned enterprises.

Private sector development would also shape the programming of USAID. According to a report from that agency,

> The overarching objective of USAID's private enterprise development strategy was to help rapidly grow a business sector that would reduce increasing unemployment resulting from privatization and disintegration of integrated state-owned enterprises. . . . The strategy was also predicated on the belief that with greater economic freedom, the political trends that led to the collapse of the Communist system could not be reversed. Helping to jump start growth in private sector activity would result in good jobs, promote economic prosperity and reduce growing poverty in the region, thus stifling any desire of the population and politicians to slip back into the past and return to the supposed "good old days of Communism." Growing economic instability and

high inflation throughout the region were viewed as serious threats to the nascent democracies.[77]

But how could a private sector be grown from scratch? According to
American officials and those who advised them, the private sector could be
grown organically within the Central and Eastern European economies
themselves (including the Soviet Union after 1991), through privatization
and by igniting the entrepreneurial spirit with enterprise funds—or exter-
nally, through FDI, which would then spur the creation of private firms
through their supply chains. This latter view, of course, had animated US
development thought since the late 1940s.

Thus, at a conference held by the RAND Corporation in 1991, an economist proclaimed that foreign capital had an "unprecedentedly crucial role
to play" in the post-Soviet transition.[78] A State Department official who
attended this meeting echoed that remark by asserting that

> we must accord a high priority to the role of the American private sector in
> the transformation and recovery of the Central and Eastern European econo-
> mies . . . it is through American and Western private investment that the re-
> gion will obtain the capital needed to create jobs and self-sustaining economic
> growth. . . . I can assure you that the U.S. government is doing everything it
> can to make Central and Eastern Europe . . . an attractive place for American
> investment.[79]

While a few American companies had been operating in Eastern Europe
even during the Cold War—Coca-Cola, for example, started selling its concentrate in Hungary as early as 1968—these operations were usually in
the form of joint ventures with state-owned companies. Now, Washington
hoped that foreign investors would flood into the region given the seemingly infinite opportunities it presented in the face of so many unmet needs,
spurring the growth of local private enterprise. How could this region present anything but a golden opportunity for foreign investors?

Accordingly, the government devised a range of policies aimed at private sector development. At home, the OPIC was authorized to extend its
political risk products to the postcommunist countries; by the early 1990s,
it was already providing such insurance to American companies that had
invested in Russia. For its part, the EXIM Bank, which had financed trade
with the Soviet Union as early as 1973, was now authorized to finance US
exports across the postcommunist region. The Commerce Department established a "BIZNIS" office with the express purpose of linking US firms
to local companies.[80]

Within the former Soviet bloc, USAID took the lead in trying to create an
inviting investment climate. This included technical assistance for improving

the legal and regulatory regimes for business—which, of course, would benefit local firms as well. In addition, efforts to ensure macroeconomic stability were deemed essential to create a sound platform for investment.

The data suggest that US firms did respond to the opportunities made possible by the post-Soviet transition, even if not at the game-changing level the region needed. Indeed, in 1991 economist Peter Murrell lamented that "the most important single fact to be noted in discussing the present role of multinational corporations in Eastern Europe (in which I include the Soviet Union) is the insignificance of the activities of these corporations."[81]

Perhaps Murrell was a bit impatient, however, given the recent occurrence of the transition and all the uncertainties surrounding it. From a starting point of basically zero investment in 1990, FDI flows to the region climbed to a total of $1.12 billion in 1995 and $1.8 billion in 1998. The total stock (or book value) of US FDI in Eastern Europe in 1998 stood at $8.2 billion, or about the same amount US firms had invested in Sweden and Denmark combined; by way of comparison, USAID allocated $3.6 billion to the region during the entire period of 1990–1998.[82] However, European firms invested significantly more, reflecting in part their geographic proximity; indeed, over 90 percent of the investment in most Central and Eastern European countries came from Europe. Still, FDI had begun to flow from the United States to the Central and Eastern European countries, creating linkages with local economies in the process.

Not surprisingly, the extent of these linkages has generated debate within the relevant academic literature.[83] But perhaps the most sensible conclusion comes from a 2009 paper put out by economists at the European Central Bank. They found that overall, FDI has made a major contribution to closing the productivity gap between the countries of Central and Eastern Europe and the EU through their linkages with local firms, but that this impact varies by country and sector. In particular, manufacturing has shown the greatest increases in productivity, services less so. Further, the extent of the increase in productivity has also been a function of a country's stock of human capital. Countries with greater supplies of human capital are better able to seize upon the economic opportunities offered by FDI.[84] This reminds us once again of the critical importance of the domestic institutional setting in capturing the benefits of foreign capital injections.

But how could an entrepreneurial culture be created in the transition economies, which would motivate individuals to acquire skills and build new businesses that could service both multinational firms and local needs? Clearly, one shortfall was in the area of credit to the SME sector. If finance was unavailable, it would be impossible to launch a firm in the first place, discouraging the type of human capital formation needed to drive the transition process (by analogy, consider that an individual might not be very motivated to do well in her high school studies if she had no hope of receiving grants and loans to finance her higher education). This gap motivated the idea of the enterprise funds that were rolled out in each transition country.

In considering how best to organize and implement these funds, there was a fear among some government officials in both branches of government that the nation's primary aid agency, USAID, did not have the capability to administer this type of assistance. As Jonathan Koppell put it, on the basis of interviews he held in Washington, "Bush administration officials and Republicans in Congress did not have faith in [US]AID'S ability to develop the private-sector institutions seen as the key to economic and political development in Eastern Europe."[85] It will be recalled that this skepticism about the ability of foreign aid officials to operate in a business-like manner is also a transcendent theme in American assistance policy.

Thus, a new organization was created to implement the Marshall Plan (the Economic Cooperation administration, run by a businessman); a new OPIC was created by President Nixon to run international guarantee programs (removing these programs from USAID); and more recently, as we will see in a later chapter, a new International Development Finance Corporation (DFC) was started by President Trump to challenge China's "state-led" assistance programs (DFC also took over some private sector functions from USAID). Similarly, the enterprise funds were created to operate independently of USAID.

As noted in a previous section, the State Department initially generated the enterprise fund idea, and the first two funds for Poland and Hungary were legislated in the SEED Act of 1989 at levels of funding higher than those requested by the president. Under that act, the funds were given two broad objectives: first, "to promote the development of the Polish and Hungarian private sectors," and second, "to promote policies and practices conducive to private sector development." The bulk of funds were allocated toward the first objective, but in each case, about $10 million was dedicated to technical assistance. In short, the funds were intended to both directly support firms and help create a fertile business environment.[86]

The design of these first funds for Poland and Hungary—a design that was eventually applied to funds for other Central and Eastern European economies as they shed their communist governments—was similar. An "independent" board of directors was formed, along with a chief executive officer and investment advisors. (I place "independent" in quotation marks here because in some cases, friends of the president or other leading officials were appointed; still, there is no evidence of Washington "influence-peddling" on

TABLE 5.1   Enterprise Funds with Dates of Organization and Initial Funding

Fund Title	Founding Date	Funding ($MM)
EUROPEAN FUNDS		
Polish-American Enterprise Fund	1990	264
Hungarian American Enterprise Fund	1990	70
Czech and Slovak Enterprise Fund	1991	65
Bulgarian American Enterprise Fund	1992	55
Baltic American Enterprise Fund	1994	50
Romanian American Enterprise Fund	1994	50
Subtotal		554
NIS FUNDS		
US Russia Investment Fund	1995	440
Central Asian American Enterprise Fund	1995	150
Western NIS Enterprise Fund	1994	150
Subtotal		740
TOTAL		1,294

Data source: USAID.

the board or efforts to steer investment opportunities to particular companies.) Funds often had offices in both the United States (usually New York City) and the capital city of the recipient country; in some cases, they had field offices as well. The objective of the funds was to make equity investments and loans "to a wide-range of private enterprises" and to introduce such innovative financial instruments as mortgage lending, leasing, and an array of consumer and business financial services.[87] USAID made initial grants to each fund, which were expected to become self-sustaining after a short (though unspecified) period of time. The funds were also expected to liquidate their investments after a period of time and return any profits to the American taxpayer, although in several cases, fund assets have been turned over to "legacy foundations," whose objective is to continue supporting private sector development. Table 5.1 provides information on each of the enterprise funds approved for the Central and Eastern European countries and the former Soviet Union countries as of 1996.

The funds met with controversy nearly from the start. They were criticized for being slow to allocate funding, for spending too much on salaries and office space, and for devoting insufficient attention to their dual mission of securing private investment and cultivating business environment. From a more ideological standpoint, some questioned whether the US government should even be in the business of providing funds to private firms in the first place; shouldn't venture capitalists be the ones taking on such investments? In a few cases the firms were tainted by corruption or conflicts of interest, which didn't help matters at all.[88]

Yet despite the difficulties they faced in rolling out their activities, the funds were hardly idle. By 2013, they had invested nearly $3 billion directly and leveraged an additional $7 billion in "debt, equity capital and co-investment." They had financed nearly $80 million in technical assistance projects. Further, they had rolled out numerous financial innovations across their target countries. Upon liquidation, they received more in proceeds ($1.7 billion) than they had in initial USAID grant outlays ($1.18 billion), meaning they actually returned money to the American taxpayer.[89]

According to the former chairman of the Polish-American Enterprise Fund, investment banker John Birkelund, "Taken together, the funds have created or supported thousands of small and medium-sized businesses employing a total of 150,000 people, created or finance 24 free-standing financial institutions with more than 100 branches, made more than 50,000 small business loans with a default rate averaging less than 4 percent, and leveraged their government grants by more than 100 percent."[90]

For its part, the US-Russia Investment Fund injected capital into a number of Russian companies and Russian joint-ventures with American firms; some of these investments also received OPIC guarantees. Examples of recipients included a clothing retailer, a chicken producer, and a joint venture with Xerox. Many of these investments were subsequently sold at a profit, which was returned to the American taxpayer upon the fund's liquidation.[91]

Such was their success that the enterprise fund idea has spread beyond the transition economies. The United States, for example, has started such funds for Egypt and Tunisia as well. Some other donor countries, like the United Kingdom, have created dedicated venture capital firms (such as CDC) outside their foreign aid agencies, and multilaterals like the International Finance Corporation (IFC) and the EBRD are similarly invested in such funds. We will turn to the case of the EBRD in the following section.

Still, in recent years the number of new business start-ups seems to have stabilized in much of the region, as shown in Figure 5.2. This appears to be a reflection of several factors, including slower economic growth, higher labor and capital costs, and relatively low increases in productivity. Consulting firms have argued that the Central and Eastern European countries need to make a big push into digitalization and high-tech, which would be natural developments in those countries with the requisite supplies of human capital.[92] We will return to the future of private enterprise in the transition economies in the concluding section.

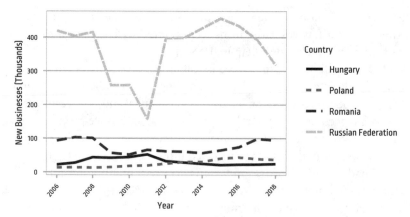

Data source: World Bank, "World Development Indicators," https://datacatalog.worldbank.org/dataset/world
-development-indicators.

FIGURE 5.2   New Business Registrations in Selected CEE Economies,
2006–2018

Eastern Europe's Business Bank: The EBRD

Soon after the collapse of several communist regimes in the last quarter of
1989, French President François Mitterrand brought forth a bold proposal
to supplemental bilateral assistance initiatives with the creation of a new
international development bank to help finance Eastern Europe's transition.[93] According to Weber, the EBRD proposal was initially received with
skepticism in Washington (not to mention in Bonn as well).[94] In particular,
he notes that a number of top Treasury Department officials were concerned
by the "poor track record" of other regional development banks in their
efforts to support private sector development.

The White House, in contrast, was more amenable to the concept of such
an institution. While the Bush administration had serious concerns about
Soviet participation—it did not want to see the EBRD become a Trojan
horse that facilitated Soviet entry into other international institutions—it
ultimately took the view that it "should not seem disinterested in this pan-
European project in the first months of the post–Cold War world."[95] President Bush thus accepted Mitterrand's invitation to join the negotiations,
although he made no commitments about formal US participation.

During the EBRD negotiations, the main objective of the United States
was to ensure that it would concentrate its activities on loans to the private sector (and, as noted above, to ensure that Soviet participation was
limited, especially in terms of the amount of borrowing allowed). Congress

also had something to say when it came to this new institution. It wanted the EBRD to focus its lending on SMEs. Representative LaFalce of New York, for example, made this point to Treasury Undersecretary David Mulford during the EBRD hearings: "But I feel strongly that we can make the most significant gains with the populace of these countries if' we can assist them to start their own small little mom-and-pop shops, and then grow. What is your perception of the charter in this regard, and then, most importantly, if there is going to be some major effort to help potential entrepreneurs in these countries, what type of delivery system do we envision coming from this European Bank, because it is so difficult for small entrepreneurs to deal with a World Bank, an Inter-American Development Bank, an Asian Development Bank."[96] For his part, Mulford refused to commit beyond saying that "by charter, at least 60 percent of the bank's [the EBRD] aggregate annual lending must be to the private sector."[97]

In emphasizing the role of private enterprise, the EBRD reflected lessons the US government had learned in the past. As Representative Jim Leach (D-IA) put it, "It has been 45 years since the establishment of the first multilateral development bank, the World Bank. One of the valued lessons of development learned during this time is that true development comes from private energies, not governmental enterprises."[98] Accordingly, like the enterprise funds, the EBRD was expected to foster privatization of state-owned companies and promote the creation of new firms. Note that Leach had little to say about what the United States might have learned about *how* to motivate private sector development in the first place!

The EBRD had a further mission that also differed from that of any other development bank. Again in the words of Representative LaFalce, "The EBRD will be the first development bank to have an overt political context within its charter that explicitly commits the bank to the development of multi-party democracies."[99] According to US thought, at least, promoting the private sector—particularly SMEs—and developing multiparty democracy went hand in hand. SMEs were the industrial equivalent of that bulwark of democracy, the Jeffersonian small-hold farmer.[100]

Fundamental to American support for the EBRD was the view that it would leverage its relatively small amount of capital—$12 billion, which would generate approximately $2.5 billion in annual lending—by attracting many times that amount in private investment. In the words of Representative LaFalce, it would do that by demonstrating Western "commitment" to the "people of Eastern Europe."[101] In essence, the fundamental purpose of the EBRD was to provide an additional level of comfort to investors beyond that offered by the World Bank, the IFC, and other official development agencies operating in the region.

Like the enterprise funds, the EBRD was dogged nearly from the start by allegations of mismanagement; in later years, numerous reports of corruption would also emerge (leading in one instance to the resignation of the Russian executive director). Its first president, Jacques Attai of France (who had been handpicked by Mitterrand), would be hounded from office within two years of arriving for his lavish travel expenses. However, his successor, the widely respected Jacques de Larosiere (who had served as executive director of the International Monetary Fund [IMF] during the 1980s and played a central role in managing the debt crisis) would bring stability to the organization during his tenure (1993–1998). By 1995, in fact, the *International Herald Tribune* was calling the EBRD the "very model of a [development] bank."[102]

While that may be true, it is challenging to evaluate the EBRD's performance at the project or programmatic level, as is true of the enterprise funds; it is very hard to determine, for example, how many new private sector firms can be attributed to an EBRD intervention. As critically noted by the US Treasury, the EBRD carries out relatively few monitoring and evaluation projects compared to its peer development banks, and its evaluations tend to lack methodological rigor.[103] In short, organizational performance remains opaque in many important respects. While the EBRD produces useful annual reports of its activities, these do not replace an experimental approach to evaluation that explores the efficacy of the EBRD "treatment effect" compared to other possible interventions. Academics, too, have failed to analyze the EBRD since its founding; the most informative piece remains Weber's 1994 article on its origins. A complimentary analysis of its operations is well overdue. This question of evaluating PSD interventions will be taken up again in Chapter 8.

The best that can be done for now is to assess the transition process as a whole in terms of private sector development. Here we do that primarily in terms of the two pathways that foreign assistance officials believed would lead to a free market economy: (1) support for entrepreneurship and business start-ups and (2) the privatization of state-owned industries, which will be covered in the following section.

As we will see, there has been considerable variance across transition economies in terms of private enterprise creation. Figure 5.3 provides data on credit to the private sector across several Central and Eastern European economies over time. According to a Federal Reserve Bank study, the private sector shot up from negligible communist-era levels to assume the majority of economic activity by the late 1990s. While to some extent that is not surprising—after all, "privatization" could quickly shift assets from

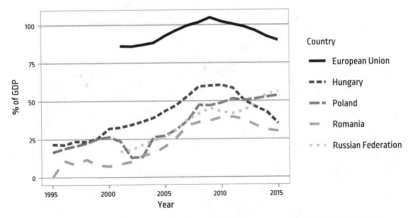

Data source: World Bank, "World Development Indicators," https://datacatalog.worldbank.org/dataset/world
-development-indicators.

FIGURE 5.3   Credit to the Private Sector as Share of GDP: Russia and Selected
Eastern European Countries, 1995–2015

state to private ownership, even if those firms were still being subsidized
by the state—it is indicative of the large-scale economic transformation that
was underway.[104] Figure 5.4 looks at rates of GDP growth; we see that after
a period of rapid increase, those rates have stabilized, just as we saw rates
of new business registration stabilizing in Figure 5.2.

As previously noted, both the enterprise funds and the EBRD were expected to devote a significant share of their resources to the SME sector.
This was for several political-economic reasons: First, SMEs would deliver
new goods and services to consumers; second, SMEs would create jobs; and
third, they would contribute to democracy promotion. These three were
interrelated to the extent that one causally identified democratic stabilization with satisfied consumers and workers.

But as McMillan and Woodruff pointed out in an early survey, "Some
governments actively made it hard for entrepreneurs to operate."[105] Again,
there were several reasons for such (bad) behavior on the part of state officials. First, entrepreneurs were targets of corruption. Second, SMEs in
some sectors might threaten state monopolies or private monopolies being
created through "crony capitalism." Third, entrepreneurs as a class might
seek political voice, threatening those who controlled power. If the uncertainty surrounding the future of transition countries wasn't enough, political and economic rent-seeking by government elites could further serve
to discourage would-be entrepreneurs from taking on risk.

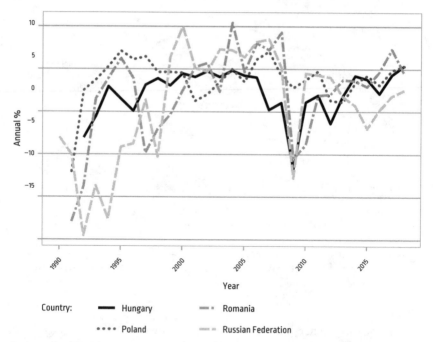

Data source: World Bank, "World Development Indicators," https://datacatalog.worldbank.org/dataset/world
-development-indicators.

FIGURE 5.4   GDP Growth in Hungary, Poland, Romania, and Russia,
1990–2018

However, as McMillan and Woodruff further emphasize, and as later
studies have borne out, there has been a fair amount of heterogeneity across
countries in terms of entrepreneurial behavior. This was evident from the
earliest days. In Poland, for example, there seemed to be a greater willingness among entrepreneurs to seize new economic opportunities than in Romania or Russia. While the level of self-employment in Poland "increased
from 6 percent of the labor force in 1988 to 12 percent in 1993," for example, during the same period in Russia, self-employment rose from just
2 to 3 percent.[106] Of course, part of this might have been due to the Russian
state's ability to maintain public sector employment, and such employment
may have been preferable across the transition economies had it been available. In this sense, entrepreneurship sometimes emerges because it is imposed upon people rather than chosen by them.

More recent research has highlighted continuing divergence in entrepreneurship across transition economies, for reasons that econometric analysis
does not fully uncover. In a study prepared for the EBRD, for example,

Nikolova and colleagues demonstrate the variation in start-up activity across the transition economies. At first glance, it appears that much of the divergence is explained by GDP per capita—but once controls are introduced, that no longer seems significant. Instead, the authors highlight credit availability as a driving factor; but since credit availability is usually linked to GDP, it is unclear from their analysis what explains the differential.[107]

Writing a decade earlier, McMillan and Woodruff highlighted the role of government in these differences. They and others suggest that early in the transition, some US policy makers believed that the role of public officials (and foreign aid) was to get the government "out" of the economy and that, left to its own devices, the market would naturally evolve.[108] While there was some truth to that—markets *did* eventually develop for all manner of goods and services—they have taken very different forms, with market capture by "insiders" prominent in many of the post-Soviet economies. As Joel Hellmann brilliantly argued, these insiders advocated for "partial reforms"; that is, they promoted reform up to the point where they could fully capture its benefits, then put a halt to further opening of the economy.[109]

Governments also differed in their willingness and ability to provide public goods, like legal frameworks and macroeconomic stabilization, that only government could provide. Why governments differ along this dimension is, of course, a key question in the political economy of reform. One factor may have been the pull exercised by potential EU membership, which many Central and Eastern European countries craved. Further, the EU provided substantial financial assistance to most of the Central and Eastern European economies. But the data don't seem to indicate that (future) EU members have had higher start-up rates than non-EU members.

That being said, among the nations that have enjoyed sufficient economic growth to reach the "advanced" class of nations (as classified by the IMF) in recent decades, six are found in among the Central and Eastern European countries: the Czech and Slovak republics, Lithuania, Latvia, Estonia, and Slovenia, with Poland and Hungary just under that threshold. According to economic analyst Ruchir Sharma, one of the main drivers of that growth has been the region's "manufacturing prowess. Because it can generate regular export income . . . manufacturing can become a self-sustaining growth engine." Taking the case of Poland, Sharma says that it "stands out . . . for the capitalist energy of a nation producing world-class companies."[110]

The extent to which private enterprise has promoted democracy, however, remains an open question. After all, countries like Poland and Hungary were in the vanguard of creating new firms and joining the EU; however, recent years have seen these countries backslide toward illiberal forms of democracy. The future of democratic institutions in these (among other) countries remains unclear. This should call into question any purported causal relationship between private enterprise and democratization.

The Politics of Privatization

If PSD was the key to a successful economic transition, then the privatization of state-owned enterprises was essential—and the sooner and more complete the process, the better. As the World Bank's John Nellis recalled of this rush to privatize,

> The primary reason was one of political economy: the fear that delaying change of ownership would provide opportunities for the return of the communists. . . . The idea gained credence that one way to increase quickly support for the reintroduction of capitalism was to create more capitalists; that is, through privatization, to build up rapidly and dramatically the number of private owners of productive entities. This . . . would create a group of people with a stake in and commitment to the market reforms.[111]

But it was not just a fear of a communist backlash that caused Western assistance programs to urge privatization upon the transition economies. Even in those cases where the return of the communist threat seemed less pronounced, delaying privatization might raise concerns about a government's commitment to entrepreneurship and the profit motive, causing investors to put their money elsewhere.

Further, if privatization was only partial—meaning that if only a few state-owned enterprises were privatized—then the gains from that privatization might never be realized. For example, if a state-owned company provided critical inputs to a privatized firm, then those inputs had to be made to a certain standard and delivered on time and within budget. Could the state-owned firm be trusted to meet these requirements, given the fact that it lacked the necessary economic incentives to perform?

While these technical issues were important, perhaps even more important was the symbolism surrounding privatization. As Aslund has written, "Nothing aroused more passion than privatization. . . . It was the fundamental dividing line between a socialist and a capitalist society."[112] He rightly notes that while Thatcher put into place a relatively "leisurely" privatization scheme, with fewer than a dozen firms per year put up for sale, the drive for new ownership within the Central and Eastern European countries was of an altogether different magnitude. Indeed, the transfer of ownership from state to private hands would prove "unprecedented. In one incredible decade, more than 150,000 large and medium-sized enterprises, hundreds of thousands of small firms, and millions of apartments and houses" were privatized.[113] For many observers, transition *was* privatization.

Privatization was also a rich arena for the battle of ideas. Unlike Britain, which had a long experience of private enterprise, the transition countries had been socialized since the end of World War II—or much earlier, of course, in the case of Russia. Therefore, even fundamental questions of how privatization should proceed and what form it should take were up for debate.[114] The international community would contribute to that debate by funding consultants, many of whom came from universities, to contribute their own ideas about how and why to privatize.

Similarly, privatization posed a confounding set of dilemmas for economic reformers. For example, while foreign investment was viewed by nearly all officials as being essential to a successful transition—how else could the transition countries receive needed capital injections?—and while privatization was also viewed as the most obvious method for attracting such investment, it was not obvious that selling state-owned enterprises to foreigners was politically astute. Instead, many reformers called for "voucher privatization," in which citizens would receive the equivalent of shares in these firms; after all, weren't the citizens the true owners of state-run enterprises? Resolving dilemmas such as these in a way that satisfied both political and economic demands proved difficult, to say the least.

This section provides a brief overview of Western efforts to promote privatization across the transition countries. For donors, privatization was the key that unlocked PSD and underpinned democracy—and for many Western officials, the two were inextricably linked. As USAID summarized its efforts:

> USAID supported privatization as essential to open, competitive markets, believing that the key to living in a democracy was valuing private, not state, ownership. In each of the 29 countries that received economic assistance, support to some form of privatization sought to reach the goal of having more than 50% of the economy under private ownership. Speed and the creation of a shareholder class, even if the process was imperfect, were viewed as necessary to achieve private ownership.[115]

Throughout the Central and Eastern European countries and the former Soviet bloc, two forms of privatization emerged. The first was mass privatization, or the selling off of large numbers of state-owned enterprises through the distribution of "vouchers" that could be redeemed as shares in newly privatized companies. This approach was most famously—or infamously—used in Russia, where vouchers were artificially cheapened and bought up by those with inside information about the true value of the firms, including enterprise managers and future "oligarchs." USAID and the World Bank, among other donors, provided assistance that facilitated the implementation of mass privatization by helping finance the infrastructure necessary to distribute millions of vouchers.

In its second form, privatization was carried out on a "case-by-case" basis. In this approach, utilized by several countries, governments selected firms for their inclusion in the program. Western donors funded technical experts and investment bankers to conduct valuations of these enterprises and help sell them off, including to foreign buyers. For its part, USAID claims that it did not determine which firms should or should not be sold; again, it simply funded implementers who assisted with the technical dimensions of these processes.[116]

These approaches to privatization were accompanied by strong political and intellectual arguments regarding how privatizations should proceed in practice. Should companies be rapidly sold off? If so, to whom—insiders, the public, or outside and foreign investors? Or should companies be "prepared" for market and ownership change through reforms, implemented gradually if necessary? Indeed, should transition economies focus on building private enterprise from the ground up—meaning through the creation of property rights and credit markets that would enable entrepreneurs to launch new businesses? Or through top-down PSD that depended first and foremost on the privatization of state-owned enterprise?[117]

The World Bank, for its part, urged the transition countries to engage in massive and speedy privatization. This was motivated to a large extent by its long and ultimately frustrating experience with trying to motivate the reform of state-owned enterprises and the tightening of the soft budget constraint that allowed them to make massive losses, an experience that led World Bank officials to believe that reform was simply impossible without a change in ownership.[118]

Overall, however, privatization accomplished much—if not all—of what it promised. It lessened political control over enterprises, at least in some countries; afforded myriad opportunities to local entrepreneurs; and catalyzed both foreign and domestic investment. At the same time, in such countries as Russia, the privatization process was captured by a small group of individuals who rose to become "oligarchs," creating privileged relations with the state. This process then fueled the creation of a kleptocracy, or corrupt political-economic class, which casts doubt on the separation of public and private sectors, and the very meaning of "private" property (it should be recalled that the former Soviet states were also kleptocratic, with small rent-seeking elites). That, in turn, has created widespread skepticism among Russians about big business and whether it's even possible to be an "honest" business person.[119] In the concluding section I will also present some data that suggest, across the transition economies, that people are dissatisfied with the outcomes of the privatization process, despite its "objective" fiscal benefits.

At the same time, privatization probably had less *political* impact than anticipated. It may have created entrepreneurs, but they have not provided the bulwark against authoritarianism and populism that American officials had hoped for. Instead, many of them spent their precious political capital on rent-seeking behavior.[120] The neat separation that Americans like to draw between the public and private sectors is not, for better or worse, one that is found and accepted everywhere. That, too, is an important lesson for contemporary policy makers who seek to promote PSD around the world.

Conclusions

The postcommunist transition offered the United States an unprecedented opportunity to shape the political economies of a region that had hardly known either democracy or capitalism for many decades. It was a mission that celebrated the American victory in the Cold War, seemingly demonstrating the superiority of its political economy and ideology. With the collapse of the Soviet Union, the world could truly march toward globalization; the borderless economy seemed finally to be within sight!

But that grandiose vision proved to be a mirage. While some of the post-Soviet economies would thrive, becoming democratic nations in their own right—such states as Estonia and Slovenia come to mind—others, like most of the Central Asian "Stans," would never fully embrace the way of democratic capitalism, becoming full-fledged kleptocracies instead. Then there was Russia under Putin, determined to restore its great power status, even as its economy was based on fossil fuels, a resource increasingly viewed by the financial community as "distressed" given concerns with climate change, and its population was plummeting in the face of grim future prospects. When coupled with an increasingly authoritarian regime, these developments undermined the prospects for long-run growth.

Overall, the EBRD has found that "large parts of the population in the transition region remain unsatisfied with their life today." In surveys, only one-third of the population felt that life was better now (the survey was conducted in 2016) than before 1989 (interestingly, a similar percentage felt the same way about the political environment). Over half believe that privatization should be reversed. The EBRD notes that these perceptions are in contrast to the generally higher incomes (accompanied, it must be emphasized, by greater inequality, which may be a source of the discontent) found across the transition economies.[121]

The varieties of transition experience are powerfully suggestive of the limits of international systemic pressures in shaping the trajectories of nation-states, even those that seem to be relatively powerless to resist the polar attraction of great powers. It cannot be denied that the United States and Western Europe helped unleash private enterprise across the former Soviet bloc, and in most of those states it has taken root. To that extent, capitalism has surely triumphed.

But the "varieties of capitalism" that have emerged are no less impressive—from productive versions to kleptocratic ones to everything in between. Perhaps the only commonality across countries is that a small group of elites has managed to capture most of the rewards, as inequality has increased everywhere across the region.[122] Perhaps we in the West should take the experiences of these transition countries as a warning sign, as we ourselves may now be confronting similar problems of kleptocratic or "winner take all" rule.

For today's policy makers seeking to promote PSD, the transition experience offers many important lessons. First, *building* new, free market-oriented institutions in regions with little experience of that economic form is different from *reforming* market economies. It requires investing in complementary institutions, like judicial systems, contracting, and property rights, that may also have little prior history in such places. It means that vigilance is needed to ensure that the process isn't captured by a small group of insiders to the detriment of other groups in society. Succeeding in these efforts is only possible if foreign donors locate the moving parts (usually some element within the elite) in recipient nations that share similar political-economic objectives, and can also provide a coherent set of policy measures that provides high-powered incentives for that group to adopt market-oriented policies. As this book has shown, the cases in which local elite interests and those of the international community are fully aligned when it comes to political-economic reform are rare.

Second, and related, foreign interventions can only have strong multiplier effects when the domestic setting is supportive. Foreign investment, for example, generates its strongest linkage effects in localities with high levels of human capital and access to finance. Sharma makes the point that the most successful Central and Eastern European countries benefited from their lack of natural resources, forcing them to depend on their highly educated workers to drive growth instead.[123] This, too, speaks to the importance of "opening" up societies to all groups so that those with ideas and initiative can flourish.

Third, while investment funds and similar interventions can promote entrepreneurship, policy makers need to be mindful of the "fallacy of composition." This is the idea that a number of micro interventions will lead to systemic, political-economic change. I have little doubt that the range of Western interventions in postcommunist economies contributed to creating a private sector that is more or less robust in most of those countries. But in too many places, there is little to distinguish the public and private sectors. The western vision of separate spheres of economic activity has rarely been realized. One finds, instead, just one big sphere defined by rent-seeking.

Finally, Western officials need to be modest in their expectations. Building on the previous point, for example, the EU did have a macro-strategy in mind when it extended membership to several of the postcommunist nations. That was supposed to "lock-in" democratic-capitalist institutions as these states converged politically and economically with their European neighbors. That has happened to some extent, but recent developments in Hungary and Poland have suggested the limits to what even regional integration can accomplish. Recalling the limits of foreign assistance in promoting systemic change is a lesson we will see play out once again in the following chapter on fragile and conflict-affected states.

6

Exporting Capitalism
to Fragile States

Positive economic growth is highly correlated with the likelihood
that a country does not slip back into conflict and instability.

—JOHN PODESTA AND JOHN NORRIS, 2013[1]

DURING A RESEARCH TRIP to Afghanistan in 2010, I wrote an upbeat
note to Thomas Ricks, my colleague at the Center for a New American
Security (CNAS, where I was a visiting fellow) and a great student of
military affairs. While critical and fearful of the troop withdrawal President Obama had just announced, I was optimistic that if security could
be achieved, the economy would blossom. Afghanistan, I told Tom, "is
ready for an economic take-off; after so many decades of conflict, there's
pent-up demand for almost every good and service imaginable. As a result, many different sectors of the economy are booming, including
construction, finance, and transportation." I also noted that "foreign investors are . . . discovering the Afghan economy. Some 150 firms regis-
tered in Kabul last year, with estimated employment of more than 6000
workers."

I was excited, in short, about Afghanistan's economic potential—writing
that "when Afghans feel secure, they invest in their economy. The United
States and its coalition partners should not depart before they are confident
that this economic momentum can be maintained, since it is growth which
provides the surest foundations for a more peaceful future."[2] I am embar-
rassed to admit how much these comments echo those of Graham Greene's
Quiet American, who was "impregnably armored by his good intentions
and his ignorance."[3] Even more, they now have a pathetic ring to them in
light of America's flight from that country in August 2021, leaving behind
an economy in shambles.[4]

Policy makers and pundits will debate the lessons that should be drawn from the Afghanistan intervention for many years to come. Some of those lessons will concern the use and misuse of military power, while others will focus on the role of foreign assistance in conflict-affected states. Under what conditions can foreign aid help promote peace? In particular, should the United States seek to develop capitalist institutions in war-torn economies, in the interest of both economic growth and social harmony?

The belief that free enterprise promotes not just wealth but comity has deep roots in both political-economic thought and American foreign policy. Adam Smith famously taught that "the establishment of commerce and manufactures . . . is the best police for preventing crimes,"[5] while Franklin D. Roosevelt's Secretary of State,, Cordell Hull, no less famously said that "if we could increase commercial exchanges among nations . . . we would go a long way toward eliminating war itself."[6] During the height of the Vietnam War, Senator Jacob Javits (R-NY) introduced a bill to create a "Peace by Investment Corporation" for the developing world, proclaiming that the encouragement of foreign direct investment (FDI) in developing countries was "in the interest of world peace through mutual economic progress."[7]

As I will show in this chapter, the idea that private investment could be a force for peace has been central to US development policy, including in such countries as Iraq and Afghanistan. In brief, officials and at least some academics posit that, among other benefits, private enterprise creates jobs and opportunities, thereby reducing the pool of would-be insurgents; in the words of one former US defense official, "people without hope—people with no prospects—will act out."[8] Through taxation, private firms also generate revenues for the state, increasing its ability to provide public goods and security, thereby establishing its legitimacy with the population.

Further, the promotion of private enterprise has important political and social ramifications in fragile states. As the Special Inspector General for Afghanistan Reconstruction (SIGAR) has written, "the choice of a private-sector, open-market economy was seen [by American officials] as reinforcing electoral democracy, individual freedoms, women's rights, a free media, and other Western values. Free enterprise was seen as transformational."[9]

This chapter reviews these ongoing efforts to spur private sector development, with a focus on US programs in Iraq and Afghanistan and the lessons they generate for other fragile settings. In both cases, the United States Agency for International Development (USAID) and the Department of Defense (DoD) launched multiple programs aimed at bolstering foreign investment and the growth of indigenous firms (note that I do not cover here the work of the "Provincial Reconstruction Teams" in Iraq and Afghanistan, which did not focus on growing private enterprise). One of these new organizations was the DoD-created "Task Force of Business and Stability Operations" (TFBSO) in Iraq, which would later be exported to Afghanistan; it was shuttered in 2015 following numerous allegations of mis-spending, but its legacy remains mixed, with proponents citing its multiple achievements even today.[10]

One might think that war-torn economies present an ideal setting for the creation of new political and economic institutions that support democracy and free enterprise. Consider the incredible success of postwar Germany and Japan, which rose to prosperity and have maintained stable democracies in large part thanks to generous American economic and security assistance after 1945. The challenging search for the "moving parts" among the elite that are amenable to US policy manipulation seems less salient in states where the United States has intervened militarily; after all, Washington should be in a position to impose its will in such places. For their part, local elites should be motivated to work closely with the US government as their country's new power broker.

Thus, places like Afghanistan and Iraq appeared to offer something of a blank slate for foreign advisers and policy makers—even more so than did the post-Soviet world, whose industrial societies had remained largely intact and included well-organized groups that either resisted political and economic change or sought to capture it for personal benefit. Americans came to Afghanistan and Iraq promoting the idea that economic assistance and private sector development would generate growth, assuming in the process that growth was an objective that any reasonable person should welcome and agree upon, transcending any differences fueling the conflict in the first place. As one DoD official involved in private sector development in both countries put it, "If we could . . . demonstrate we were working for the long-term economic benefit of the people in the area, we could become a potent tool for reducing support to violent actors."[11]

This idea that economic growth could offset social conflict is one that is deeply embedded within the American political economy. As Charles Maier has described it, the promise of sustained growth—of an ever-expanding pie—has been central to domestic peace *within* the United States itself since the beginning of the Republic. For Americans, its economy has never been a "zero-sum" game, but rather a cooperative enterprise in which everyone who works hard can access opportunity—and this type of economy is something that can be exported and applied anywhere. Maier writes: "American opinion generally viewed the transition to a society of abundance as a problem of engineering, not of politics."[12] Contra the skepticism of Louis Hartz, American exceptionalism really was exportable.

Tragically, the experiences in Iraq and Afghanistan would show that such transitions are hardly inevitable or straightforward in deeply torn societies.

As Berman, Felter, and Shapiro put it, the political economy of fragile states may "turn an economist's usual intuition on its head. In settings where people and property are not safe enough to support markets, increasing economic activity can just as easily stoke predatory violence as it can alleviate deprivation by increasing incomes." This is because economic activity is viewed as a rent that warring factions seek to capture, rather than as the source of sustainable and inclusive growth.[13]

This chapter is about the limitations of US policy in countries that are experiencing violent conflict. It begins with an overview of the relevant academic and policy work on building private enterprise in fragile and conflict-affected states. The chapter then examines US policies in Iraq and Afghanistan. It closes with lessons for policy makers.

Private Enterprise, Political Instability, and Peace

So-called fragile and conflict-affected states, or FCS, are of increasing concern to the international development community. These states are characterized by: "(i) deep governance issues and state institutional weakness; (ii) situations of active conflict; and (iii) high levels of interpersonal and / or gang violence."[14] In our interconnected world, these problems can generate severe externalities on a global basis. As USAID writes, "Low-income countries that fail to grow can pose serious problems for the United States and the world. They are more likely to experience political crises, including failed-state status, violent conflicts, and civil wars."[15]

If that is the case, how can the donor community most effectively promote economic growth in these settings? How can we build a market economy where security and property rights are largely taken for granted? What role can private enterprise and foreign investment play in the economies of fragile states? These are among the questions we take up in this chapter.

The relevant economics literature provides useful insights into these questions. Most prominently, the foundational work of Douglass North on the role of institutions in promoting or stifling economic growth—particularly his emphasis on the establishment of secure property rights regimes—has motivated a growing body of research on how businesses operate in insecure settings. North's Nobel Prize–winning studies began with an effort to locate the root cause of varying growth rates in the quality of different nations' institutions.[16] Unlike an earlier generation of development economists, who emphasized differences in savings (and thus investment), North instead posited that the foundations of growth are derived from a government's willingness and ability to enforce a strong property rights regime.

During periods of political instability and violent conflict, governments may find it too costly to enforce property rights, especially in regions beyond their military control. Governments may also actively erode a firm's property rights and profits through their own corrupt and predatory practices. In some cases, the conflict itself may be, at least in part, about which group gets to define and enforce the property rights regime, and to extract rents from it.[17] While we in the West have come to think of property rights as a "public good" protected by governments, in many parts of the world it is a private good, available to those with power. Property rights are allocated on the basis of proximity to those in power, and outsiders may rightfully fear that their property can be taken from them at any moment.

Following North, a number of studies have examined the relationship between political instability and policy uncertainty on investment and growth. In one of the most important contributions in this tradition, Svensson modeled and then tested the effects of political instability and weak property rights on private sector investment. He showed that these country characteristics were strongly associated with lower rates of investment and that the results were specifically driven by the quality of the property rights regime.

From a political economy perspective, Svensson posited that when property rights are essentially privatized, only the group capable of providing this good can profit from it; thus, powerful elite "in-groups" keep these rights for themselves.[18] This work is also consistent with findings that ethnic fractionalization (or situations where the difference between "insiders" and "outsiders" is most powerfully delineated) is associated with lower rates of growth and public good provision.[19] Svensson's argument has important policy implications in its suggestion that efforts (e.g., by international donors) to strengthen local property rights may not be welcomed in places where certain groups derive a rent from them.

In this chapter, I argue that the property rights channel is of crucial importance to the political economy of conflict-affected states, and that it deserves a great deal more attention from policy makers. For example, as we will see below, much of the development community's private sector work to date has focused on capital market failures, with foreign assistance programs aimed at "deepening" capital markets by assisting the banking sector and venture capital investments (the Enterprise Funds discussed in Chapter 5 provide just one example of this type of programming). While this may be appropriate in some settings, the underlying problem facing capital markets, especially in conflict-affected states, may in fact be nonexistent or weakly enforced property rights. If firms lack secure collateral in the first place, then they will be unable to obtain credit irrespective of its availability;

the policy issue, then, is not the lack of credit, but rather the lack of property rights.

Importantly, American officials in Iraq and Afghanistan were slow to understand that some groups in a society may wish to prevent others from gaining market access through secure property rights. If the question of who gets market access is ultimately about power, then it is a political decision as much as an economic one. Gaining access to markets in FCS might require engaging in corruption or violence; it is not simply a matter of having a good idea and getting the capital to finance it. The situation is somewhat analogous to that found in cities where the Mafia once controlled the food delivered to restaurants. Consider, for example, the restaurants in New York City that in the past had to "make payoffs" at Fulton Fish Market in order to acquire their seafood. Now imagine an entire economy that runs on this basis; that is the economic world found in all-too-many places (but perhaps it's even worse, in that you might not have any access at all to certain goods and services, either public or private, if you come from the "outside" group).[20]

It is thus useful to remember that entrepreneurs everywhere face the "irreversible" nature of their investment decisions when starting a business. Once an entrepreneur builds, say, a factory, the money spent is a sunk cost that can only be recouped through its profitable operation. As David Stasavage has written, "when one assumes that investments are irreversible, firms can be prompted to delay or forego investments out of the fear that the economic environment might change for the worse."[21] In short, when property rights are insecure, firms and households are less likely to make productive investments.

The threat of conflict and instability can influence not only decisions around whether to invest, but also the type of investments that are made (and it should be emphasized that reasons other than conflict could stymie or influence investment, such as poverty, weak infrastructure, macroeconomic instability, and an absence of good business opportunities—all of which could be exacerbated by violence). Firms operating in fragile states, for example, might choose to reduce their *levels* of investment if entrepreneurs are wary of putting too much capital at risk. We might therefore fail to observe the kinds of "lumpy" or capital-intensive projects we might otherwise expect given the underlying consumer demand.

Related to levels, political instability and violence might also influence the *type* of investments made. As Fielding points out, "In risky environments the demand for non-traded capital goods (buildings and other construction works) may be particularly low, because these are not geographically mobile and cannot be shipped out to another area if there is a major breakdown in civil society. Some . . . goods . . . are more mobile, and there-fore less of a risk." Thus, entrepreneurs may invest more in sectors like trading and less in manufacturing in fragile contexts.[22] Taking the case of Israel, Fielding finds that violence (in this case, the Palestinian uprisings, or intifada) affected both levels of aggregate investment and types of in-vestment; overall, he concludes that "violence . . . depresses investment demand."[23]

Subsequent research has also found that political instability in the form of violence discourages private investment. As Le summarizes the empir-ical findings, "SPI [socio-political instability] destroys physical capital and displaces human capital . . . disrupting personal savings, hence lowering in-vestment." Le further notes that SPI "leads investors to shift their assets from fixed capital stocks to more liquid . . . forms." Overall, his analysis of a panel of developing countries shows that violent conflict in particular (as opposed to instability that takes the form of nonviolent protest) "has a large, negative impact on private investment."[24]

In turn, violence can also be expected to affect the size of firms. Large, productive firms, for example, are most likely to be targets of predation (by government and rebel forces alike, not to mention bandits), but are also most likely to be capable of having enough resources to devote to their own protection. Small firms, in contrast, lack resources but could strive to stay below the predators' radar screen; this could be a reason behind the wide-spread informality common to FCS. Given this possibility of a bimodal dis-tribution of firms, one could hypothesize that the entrepreneurs most likely to suffer are those who seek to build a small or medium-sized enter-prise (SME). Caught in the middle, they would be too large to evade pre-dation, but too small to protect themselves.[25]

In short, the "missing middle" problem that has been so frequently ob-served and given policy attention across the developing world might be par-ticularly intractable in FCS because of this predatory setting.[26] Again, this line of argument suggests to policy makers that donor efforts to promote SMEs in conflict settings may flounder in the absence of security. It also suggests that capital may not solve the problem; indeed, it could conceiv-ably exacerbate it, as those who do manage to get capital become the tar-gets of "shakedowns" by government or insurgent forces (or both).

Conflict may also influence the locations within a country where firms operate. In nearly all countries, even the most violent ones, some regions tend to be safer than others. The distribution of violence in Afghanistan and Iraq, for example, was not evenly spread across the country; it tended to be concentrated in particular regions or even districts.[27] We can hypoth-esize that firms are less likely to be present in violent areas (or that if present, they would leave when violence erupts), and we would expect them to employ fewer workers in such regions.

This finding raises an interesting issue for donors in terms of PSD programming. Should they focus their attention on peaceful areas that already enjoy private sector activity, or should they invest in more violent regions in the hope that economic development and job creation will mitigate at least some of the underlying drivers of conflict? I will return to this question in the concluding section and final chapter.

Finally, firms in conflict-affected countries may need to reallocate labor from production to protection, resulting in a loss of productivity and output. In a paper that makes use of the World Bank Enterprise Surveys, Besley and Mueller focus on firms' protection costs in insecure environments and their consequences. Because these firms face the risk of predation, they tend to reduce investment and (mis)allocate labor to the provision of security, suffering output losses as a result.[28]

Overall, then, FCS do not provide a promising setting for putting capital at risk. A World Bank study found that firms in these countries were more likely to be small and informal, and less likely to invest in innovation. A lack of trust leads to reliance of "who you know" supply chains, further shrinking the scope of business and its potential for growth. By acting as kleptocrats, government officials, of course, may only exacerbate the problems entrepreneurs face. In the event, the poor quality of infrastructure, alongside pervasive insecurity, in many fragile states makes it difficult to move goods to markets.[29]

While much of the relevant academic and policy literature has (unsurprisingly) focused on conflict's negative impacts on the economy, some agents are more capable than others of surviving or even thriving in such environments. If a firm is able to protect itself enough to ride out the storm, it may actually profit, either due to the lack of competition or its ability to channel the violence to profitable ends (an analogy is provided by organized crime syndicates and gangs operating in urban settings). As noted above, large, established firms tend to have more resources to hire security guards to protect their plants and workers. Mines, oil wells, and other capital-intensive operations, which are often managed by multinational enterprises, have also demonstrated time and again the ability to establish protected "zones of peace" around the firm. In short, firms that are able to protect themselves in conflict zones can earn rents from their unique ability to manage in such environments.[30]

To conclude this review, a few words might be said about how we study the private sector in conflict-affected countries. The usual survey instruments are likely to be less valuable if enumerators cannot travel safely throughout a country; further, the governments of these countries are less likely to carry out the regularly scheduled industrial, labor market, and household surveys found in more stable developing countries. The lack of data makes studying the private sector (and therefore coming up with appropriate policy interventions) a tremendous challenge.

As a consequence, scholars have made great progress in recent years in integrating new sources of large-scale digital data in empirical social science research. Nightlights and cell phone metadata, for example, are increasingly being used by scholars as proxy measures of economic activity. In Afghanistan, for example, colleagues and I used cell phone data to explore the private sector there (it turns out that the number of cell phone lines a company has is a good proxy measure for the size of its workforce, while the locations of calling activity are a good proxy for where it conducts business). We are interacting these data with the available data on violence to assess how violent activity influenced firm behavior (not surprisingly, business activity falls following violent attacks).[31] This line of research holds out promise for providing input into policy making in places where the development community has little insight into economic activity on the ground.

Rebuilding Iraq

Following the invasion of Iraq, the United States faced the task of rebuilding and restructuring that nation's shattered economy. What were the priorities of the American occupiers when confronting that war-torn economy, one that had already suffered from decades of misrule and international economic sanctions? Should the United States focus on humanitarian assistance, job creation, macroeconomic stability, or rebuilding infrastructure and critical industries (like oil, in the case of Iraq)? During the Marshall Plan, for example, Washington's priority was on helping Western Europe's recipient nations overcome their "dollar shortage," which limited the continent's ability to import needed commodities like food and fuel.[32]

In Iraq, US policy makers wanted to introduce systemic change, both politically and economically. The initial economic director of the Coalition Provisional Authority (CPA, the multinational body entrusted with preparing Iraq for its turnover to civilian leadership), Peter McPherson, was told by CPA director Paul Bremer that his mission in Iraq "was to bring capitalism."[33] Economic adviser Keith Crane testified in a 2005 Senate hearing: "The key economic policy task in Iraq is to create an economic environment conducive to private sector activity."[34] It was the private sector that would rebuild Iraq and lead it on the path of sustained growth.

In order to carry out this market-oriented mandate, the CPA focused on three inter-related missions: creating new financial institutions, including an independent Central Bank (and, related, a new currency), commercial banks, microfinance lenders, and even a stock exchange; private sector development through new legislation (including legislation regarding FDI) and the provision of credit; and the restructuring of Iraq's state-owned enterprises. According to the Special Inspector General for Iraq Reconstruction (SIGIR), the US government spent $1.82 billion on these activities between 2004 and 2012, equal to about 4 percent of total reconstruction spending. These initiatives were expected to "create conditions for growth."[35]

The United States would soon discover that creating a private sector required more than throwing money at the problem. From a cultural perspective, the World Bank stated in 2004: "Antipathy to private and particularly foreign investment is strong in Iraq," which was hardly surprising given the association that many Iraqis drew between private enterprise and state corruption, a legacy of Saddam's iron-fisted economic rule.[36] Even without such antipathy, the structure of the Iraq economy was horribly distorted. According to another World Bank study:

> The economic wreckage of wars and sanctions, combined with the dissolution of the country's key institutions, meant that growing oil revenues in the post-2003 period reinforced the status quo rather than becoming an impetus for reform. The central government alone has expanded to 44 percent of GDP . . . and the public sector is by far the largest formal sector employer . . . the dominance of SOEs was strengthened as the state had no incentives to restructure them. Aside from their value as means of economic control, they provided jobs for many Iraqis. State dominance of the financial sector continued as the insolvency of the system made reform difficult, and banks expanded as their government business grew.[37]

Thus, the American "liberators" were confronted with a crucial issue. Should the state-dominated economy be preserved in the interest of stability—or should it be dismantled and a new privatized economy created in the interest of long-run growth? This fundamental question would come to divide the American officials in Baghdad and Washington who were leading the rebuilding process.[38]

On the one hand, according to Baghdad-based *Washington Post* reporter Rajiv Chandresakaran, "the neoconservative architects of the war . . . regarded wholesale economic change in Iraq as an integral part of the American mission to remake the country. To them, a free economy and a free society went hand in hand."[39] As Robert Looney of the Naval Postgraduate School wrote in 2003, "for many in the Bush Administration Iraq is now the test case for whether the United States can create, within the Arab world, a system of American style free market capitalism."[40] For McPherson, this meant rapid privatization of Iraq's many state-owned enterprises, which employed millions of workers. In McPherson's words, "we need to shrink government employment, not increase it."[41]

On the other hand, those officials of the Department of Defense who were on the ground in Iraq and who had a hand in its economic reconstruction were less enamored of this free market ideology. From a security standpoint, they feared the mass unemployment that privatization might bring in its train, creating a new cadre of potential insurgents (this view, of course, is based on the idea that unemployment and a lack of economic prospects are critical drivers of insurgency). They believed, at least during a transition period, that it would be preferable to invest in those state-owned enterprises that could maintain their operations through government (including US government) contracts.[42]

No matter one's ideological position, the occupiers did not really confront a tabula rasa when it came to Iraq's economy. As a quartet of advisers to the CPA put it: "Although the . . . CPA enjoyed sweeping powers to make economic policy, policymakers were not free to pull out their textbooks and recast Iraq's economy as they saw fit. They faced three constraints in reforming Iraq's economy: one legal, one political and one logistical."[43]

The legal constraint came from the international laws and norms governing the behavior of occupation authorities. In particular, occupiers are not supposed to make "irreversible changes" to a country's economy that a future freely elected government could not alter if it so chose. Thus, the idea of privatizing state-owned enterprises (SOEs) on a large scale, as had happened in some of the transition economies, raised a basic question in Iraq: even if privatization were desirable (which, as we will see, the DoD disputed), was it legal?

The second constraint revolved around Iraqi politics and what would be not only feasible in this context but acceptable to the Iraqi people and their new leaders. Would they embrace market-oriented solutions to their economic challenges, or did they prefer that the state (or occupiers) maintain control? Could Iraq build the institutions that markets required? Was it possible to create a new economic society out of one formerly based on insider information and access to well-placed government officials?

The third constraint was the rapidly degrading security situation in light of the growing post-invasion insurgency (which was in part a product of the CPA's rash decision to disband the Iraqi Army). This made it effectively impossible for the occupation's advisers to move around the country and learn first-hand about the economy. What was actually going on in terms of production and employment? Which sectors were still operating, and which were starved for inputs? While satellite imagery and other technologies might help answer some of these questions (e.g., with respect to electricity production), too many remained unanswered; with basic data about firms and households nearly impossible to collect, policy making was happening in the dark. Here, as we will see, DoD's eventual economic wing, the TFBSO, would have a decided advantage over other development actors, given its ability to travel around the country while other advisers rarely ventured outside Baghdad's Green Zone, the heavily guarded area where the CPA was based.

Still, when data are missing and the situation on the ground is foggy or uncertain, more space is given to ideas and ideologies to shape policy making. Policy makers grasp at analogies and their understanding of the past in order to provide context for the current challenges they face.[44] In terms of the ideas and experiences that influenced the general direction of economic policy in Iraq, "the biggest . . . was the experience of the transition economies of eastern Europe and central Asia during the 1990s."[45]

This was also due to the personnel then working in Iraq. In 2003, the CPA's Office of Economic Policy was placed under the direction of Marek Belka, an economist from Poland who had served as a consultant to the government during the crucial transition years of 1990–1996 (he had also served as Poland's finance minister in 1997 and again in 2001–2002). His instincts were strongly supported by senior CPA official Peter McPherson, who had extensive experience in the foreign aid community (including a long stint as USAID administrator under Ronald Reagan). As previously noted, McPherson believed "that Iraq must move to a market system as quickly as possible by encouraging the growth of private firms."[46]

Along those lines, a CPA strategy document stated that US policy "is intended to provide the future Government of Iraq with the opportunity to transition the SOEs toward a market-based environment . . . seamlessly transitioning workers from non-performing SOEs to the private sector."[47] This is an incredible statement, given the difficulty that even workers in advanced industrial states face when economic circumstances force them to "transition" to new jobs; such transitions are rarely "seamless," as they may entail moving to new locations and accepting jobs at lower wages. Nonetheless, several CPA officials expressed the view that Iraq's transition would be relatively easy compared to that of Central and Eastern Europe, as suggested by the following statement: "Iraq is actually fortunate that its non-energy SOEs comprise no more than 5% of its workforce and probably a smaller proportion of its GDP. Certainly, some countries in the former Soviet bloc had it worse."[48]

In fairness to CPA, however, many of its policy makers *did* recognize the political sensitivities surrounding SOE reform. In particular, CPA did not wish to further degrade the already precarious employment situation among Iraqis, which they feared would widen the pool of potential insurgents, and they kept state workers on payroll even when they no longer had jobs. The CPA thus pursued the general idea of putting companies on a "glide path to reform"—meaning a strategy by which they would eventually become profitable, self-sustaining companies within a reasonable time horizon (hopefully by finding foreign business partners who could inject capital and technology into their operations)—or be forced to shutter their operations.[49]

Yet beyond its high levels of violence, there was another crucial distinction between Iraq and most of the early transition economies like Poland and Hungary: the overwhelming dominance of oil in its economy. But as I have discussed elsewhere in this book, countries that rely heavily on natural resources may have less motivation to develop an entrepreneurial environment; this is one facet of the "natural resources curse." Prior to the war, oil was responsible for about two-thirds of Iraq's GDP.[50] As the extent of Iraq's economic damage became more apparent, getting oil facilities back online and channeling oil export revenues into public goods became the CPA's priority; the importance of restructuring of state-owned industrial enterprises became secondary (though as we will see below, the DoD took a somewhat different perspective on that issue, launching its own economic response to the problems it believed the country confronted). As Foote and colleagues put it, "Iraq needs every oil dollar it can get to rebuild its infrastructure."[51]

Despite the preoccupation with getting the oil sector back up and running, building a vibrant private sector remained an objective of CPA and those in Washington. Thus, the CPA (with support from the White House) sought congressional funding to create an "American-Iraqi Enterprise Fund," modeled after those rolled out in Eastern Europe during the early transition years; Congress, however, was in no mood to support such a fund and killed it in committee.[52] A particularly vociferous critic of the fund was Rep. (later Chicago Mayor) Rahm Emanuel (D-IL), who said in congressional hearings: "Let me point to one thing: $353 million for an American Iraqi enterprise fund. . . . Yet, the President's budget cut $316 million in the vocational education program [in the United States]." More generally, Emanuel was incensed that the United States was generously funding health, education, and economic programs in Iraq while reducing them at home.[53]

As in all the other country cases we have studied, the United States also urged Iraq to open up to FDI. According to Chandresakaran, getting the

Iraqis to pass a new foreign investment law was "the centerpiece" of McPherson's agenda. He believed that "foreign investment was the key to economic recovery. The way to create jobs . . . was to lure multinational firms into Iraq."[54]

Under Saddam, Iraq had severe restrictions on FDI that the CPA now sought to liberalize, asserting "that facilitating foreign investment will help to develop infrastructure, foster the growth of Iraqi business, create jobs, raise capital, result in the introduction of new technology into Iraq and promote the transfer of knowledge and skills to Iraqis." In short, US officials expressed confidence that FDI would create deep linkages with the local economy. To encourage such investment, CPA Order 39 of September 2003 specified the rights of foreign investors in Iraq, stating that a "foreign investor shall be entitled to make foreign investments in Iraq on terms no less favorable than those applicable to an Iraqi investor" and that the "amount of foreign participation in newly formed or existing business entities in Iraq shall not be limited."[55] In essence, foreign investors could feel comfortable that they would receive national treatment in Iraq.

This turned out to be a contentious issue with the new Iraq Governing Council, whose members feared a Western takeover of Iraqi resources and real estate.[56] As a team of economic advisors recounted:

> After the war, many Iraqis feared that allowing better funded and more productive foreign firms into Iraq would destroy domestic businesses. Economists from the Coalition and from international financial institutions responded to these concerns with three arguments. First, they noted that Iraq was starved for capital. If foreigners could supply some of the capital that Iraq needed, so much the better. Second, they argued that foreign investment would dilute the power of rich domestic investors who had amassed their fortunes through corrupt connections with the previous regime. Third, they cited studies and presented data showing that in other countries, foreign investment has been a prime source of technology transfer and downstream demand for domestically produced goods.[57]

Eventually the Council relented, agreeing to open up the country to foreign investors outside of some key sectors, such as oil, where Iraq would retain ownership of the underlying resource. However, the CPA's push on FDI cost it precious political capital that most observers believe was misspent, given how unlikely it was that Iraq would become a major destination for foreign investment anyway, in light of its poor security environment and shaky governance arrangements.[58] Figure 6.1 provides the sad story of FDI inflows to Iraq as a share of GDP since 2004; as we can see, it's more a picture of disinvestment.

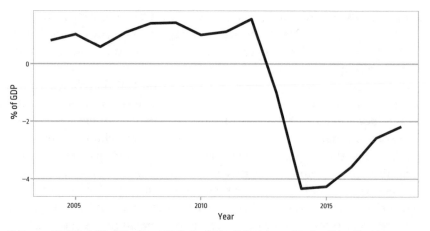

Data source: World Bank, "World Development Indicators," https://datacatalog.worldbank.org/dataset/world
-development-indicators.

FIGURE 6.1   FDI Inflows as a Share of GDP in Iraq, 2004–2018

Complicating Iraqi reconstruction was tension between the CPA and
DoD regarding how best to proceed. As noted, the DoD had set up the
TFBSO with the purpose of "revitalizing Iraq's economy and creating jobs
for Iraqis."[59] TFBSO officials traveled around the country (something most
CPA officials could not do, limited as they were to Baghdad's Green Zone),
assessing the viability of numerous industries, including SOEs, with the specific objective of determining which could provide the goods demanded by
the US military in Iraq (the Task Force averaged about $150 million per
year in funding between FY07 and FY11). This mission put it at odds with
the CPA economics team, who did not believe firms should be allowed to
survive if they were not of interest to private investors. As the head of the
TFBSO, Paul Brinkley, reported, one of these CPA officials told him that
Iraq "was a Baathist, socialist state. We learned in eastern Europe how to
handle post-socialist economies. You shut them down, and get the old inefficient companies out of the way so the free market can emerge." According to Brinkley, the CPA was "advocating an economic model known
as shock therapy."[60]

The CPA and DoD were operating with two separate missions informed
by different sets of beliefs. The CPA's mission was to rebuild and recon-
struct Iraq's economy, and its methodology was largely guided by neoliberal prescriptions. In contrast, the TFBSO was primarily concerned with
the security of American forces; it was guided by the hypothesis that if more

Iraqis were gainfully employed, fewer would be willing to take up arms and become insurgents.

This difference powerfully illustrates how long-run economic and short-term security objectives do not necessarily converge on the ground. Indeed, the United States would never really resolve the tension between these two efforts—and of course, the sectarian insurgency in Iraq would continue to gain traction, eventually generating groups like the Islamic State. One painful lesson that Iraq teaches policy makers is that economics does not necessarily overcome political differences, especially when these are grounded in (or exacerbated by) sectarian conflict.[61] No matter what the United States did on the economic front, it couldn't make up for the fact that the former Sunni rulers of Iraq had lost out both politically and economically as a result of the US invasion—and that they were willing to fight to regain some of their lost status.

Private Sector Development in Iraq

Despite being classified as an upper-middle-income economy by the World Bank (thanks to its oil revenues), Iraq is also rated as one of the most difficult countries in the world in which to do business. Across the Middle East and North Africa (MENA) region—which contains some tough neighborhoods—it ranks below only three other countries in the Bank's Doing Business surveys, all also conflict-affected: Libya, Yemen, and Syria. While the World Bank's Doing Business rankings do not explicitly ask firms about such impediments to growth as violence and corruption, problems in the institutional environment can be inferred from their responses to carefully worded enumerator questions. For example, Doing Business asks entrepreneurs about such factors as the quality of property rights and the judiciary; in both areas Iraq ranks quite low. Indeed, political instability was second to a lack of electricity as the most frequently cited "obstacle to business" by entrepreneurs responding to the World Bank's most recent Enterprise Survey (which, unfortunately, dates back to 2011; a smaller phone survey was carried out in 2018).[62]

Building up private enterprise in Iraq was never going to be an easy task. Not only had the nation suffered years of conflict, it had toiled even longer under a state-dominated economy. Further, the presence of rich oil rents "cursed" the economy, in that resources flowed to that sector while there were few incentives for productive investment elsewhere. In the event, to the extent that private firms were permitted to operate, they usually had close ties to Saddam's region.

Where, in this environment, should the development community focus its efforts? In 2004, USAID launched its three-year, $140 million "Izdihar" (Arabic for "prosperity) private sector development program, with the following planned activities: "direct assistance to would-be entrepreneurs in the form of microgrants, business development services, and training; targeted reform of an administrative environment that under three decades of Saddam's control had made it deliberately difficult for businesses to function; support to revive the banking sector as an efficient provider of capital to fuel the growth of private business; [and] promotion of free trade."[63] In its final report on Izdihar, USAID focused on the establishment of a microfinance industry as its chief accomplishment. As USAID reported, Izdihar

> assisted in the establishment of a nation-wide microfinance industry that now comprises 3 large international NGOs and 9 indigenous institutions operating throughout the country. These partner institutions now have a combined loan portfolio of over $33.3 million extended to over 24,000 active clients, and almost 70,000 loans worth over $150 million having been disbursed by the industry since Izdihar started.[64]

This program was embedded in broader USAID efforts to revive Iraq's economy through a variety of interventions, including economic reforms (e.g., of tax policy) and training interventions (e.g., of government officials and entrepreneurs). Writing in 2008 after its review of the "economic growth" program carried out by contractor Bearing Point, the USAID inspector general (IG) came to a scathing conclusion: the program "has not been successful in achieving its intended results—to help provide the foundation for an open, modern, mixed-market economy—and it has not made a significant impact upon the economic environment in Iraq."[65] In particular, the IG faulted USAID for failing to monitor the contractor and hold it accountable; more generally, the program lacked any meaningful monitoring and evaluation (M&E). That finding provides a crucial take-away for the development community today: projects need to be well-designed, including a justifiable "theory of change," and M&E must be "baked in" to the project design to ensure it is on track to deliver what is expected of it (or, if not, the assumptions that underlie project effectiveness can be highlighted should they ultimately prove unfounded).

Tragically, the security situation in Iraq would continue to deteriorate for many years following the American invasion, taking a horrific turn with the rise of the Islamic State, which took over significant parts of the country. A 2018 damage assessment of the seven most directly affected governorates estimated "overall damages to be $45.7 billion and reconstruction and recovery needs to be $88.2 billion." At the same time, the development community saw one potential bright spot in this terrible story: the possibility of using the reconstruction process to promote private sector activity. Indeed, the World Bank launched a "Bring Business Back" in Iraq project to contribute to that effort.[66]

As part of that effort, the World Bank conducted a phone survey of a sample of firms in Iraq in 2018. It found that few firms had access to finance or even have a bank account and that widespread insecurity and corruption have discouraged business investment. Sadly, it found that "the total number of employees reported by firms fell by 52 percent between 2014 and 2018." Consistent with Fielding's findings about the effects of conflict on investment in Israel, the Bank similarly reports that many firms (particularly in the construction industry) had cancelled "planned investment due to the conflict."[67]

Prolonged insecurity may also help to explain the sectoral distribution of economic activity in Iraq. Outside of oil, government remains by far the largest sector, with wholesale and retail activities next in terms of business. Clearly, incentives to invest in private enterprise are still elusive in Iraq. And despite efforts by the development community to deepen financial markets, including through the creation of microfinance facilities to SMEs, credit to the private sector and private investment are very low, as shown in Figure 6.2.

The Iraq data, of course, should be treated with caution. There is a paucity of recent data, and the websites of relevant government offices (e.g., the

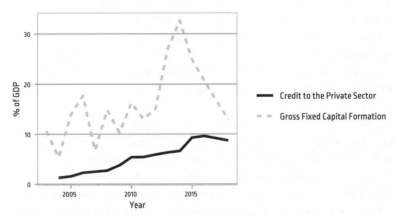

Data source: World Bank, "World Development Indicators," https://datacatalog.worldbank.org/dataset/world-development-indicators.

FIGURE 6.2   Credit to the Private Sector and Gross Fixed Capital Formation as Percent of GDP in Iraq, 2003–2018

Central Statistics Office) and private sector organizations (e.g., the Iraqi Federation of Industries) tend to be unhelpful or nonfunctional. For example, recent data on employment are lacking; a 2004 survey by the International Labor Organization showed that nearly 80 percent of the workforce was employed by government or state-owned enterprises. Private companies constituted just 3 percent of the workforce.

According to the Government of Iraq, its private sector today is composed mainly of small firms operating

> in retail and trade, construction and transportation services as well as in light industry. The majority of businesses are owned by sole proprietors, with most of the remainder being family partnerships. Iraq possesses few large, typically family-owned and run multi-industry conglomerates, active in retail, domestic trade and construction. However, large private businesses are emerging in Iraq in ICT [information and communications technology], particularly mobile communications, in technical services for oil and gas, and in manufacturing.[68]

As evidenced by the small percentage shown in the 2004 data, Iraq's manufacturing sector is still tiny in comparison to other countries in the region. A 2012 survey of 950 SMEs provides some potentially useful information on the sectoral distribution of small firms. These were found in agriculture (5.6 percent of firms), manufacturing (8.6 percent), construction (19.2 percent), trade and retail (54.6 percent), and other services (12 percent). A government-sponsored study concludes from this review that "activity-wise, the private sector dominates in agriculture, wholesale and retail trade, hotels and tourism, ownership of dwellings and personal and social services."[69] In terms of "new" business development—recognizing the outdated numbers—the report states that "In the period 2008–2010, the Ministry of Industry and Minerals (MoIM) licensed about 1,400 new industrial projects (with a peak of 500 reached in 2010). Actual performance is not monitored or recorded, but it is estimated that not more than 20–25% of the private manufacturing industry firms are still operating or in business."[70]

Costantini has highlighted a number of ongoing structural and political-economic issues that deter business development in Iraq, despite the donor community's efforts to catalyze PSD in the wake of an invasion intended to "liberate" the country from the clenched fist of Saddam Hussein. From a structural perspective, she notes that Iraq remains an oil-based economy and suffers from many of the symptoms of the "natural resources curse" (recall that one of our hypotheses concerns the relationship between natural resource exports and private sector development). This means that oil interest groups and the public officials who represent them focus on controlling the spigot rather than investing in the real economy. This leads the bulk of capital (both financial and human) to flow to the oil sector—modeling the "Dutch disease," in which a large amount of capital (including human capital) flows to the resource sector, undermining other industries in the process.[71]

From a political-economic perspective, Costantini notes that entrepreneurs face many other impediments as well. During Saddam's reign, the business sector was largely populated by those friendly to the regime, who were given special opportunities to profit, especially during the sanctions era. This fostered a negative image of entrepreneurs among the country's population, lowering the motivation to launch new businesses. She claims that a hangover of distrust of business executives lingers to the present day.

Further, the private sector has proved unable to create anything resembling a united front when it comes to advocating for certain government policies. To cite Costantini again, "business organizations have not only suffered from poor internal representation, they have also been hindered by the lack of a common agenda. After 2003, the entry of a number of new representative entities in competition with the existing professional organizations and trade unions contributed to the fragmentation of business representation."[72] From this description, it appears that firms and their associations are competing for rents rather than trying to establish a "common agenda."

Costantini's analysis raises several important points about donor efforts to promote business in postconflict settings. First, an economy's structure will set the background conditions against which private sector development is carried out. Economies that are essentially monocultures, for example, will have different opportunities and constraints for PSD than more diversified ones. Second, the prewar "reputation" of business is important. If the private sector is associated with the former (unpopular) regime or high levels of rent seeking and corruption, then efforts to rebuild it—much less subsidize it—may not be met with popular acclaim; people are likely to simply view it as a new form of crony capitalism. Finally, businesses themselves might see donor efforts toward PSD as a potential rent, and they will invest in capturing that rent as opposed to investing in the real sector.

On top of the "natural resource curse" of oil, which already tends to discourage private investment in other sectors for both political and economic reasons (economic activity tends to gravitate toward the pump, while policy makers are focused on rent maximization as opposed to long-term institutional investments), Iraq has suffered from political fragmentation which compounds a sense of political instability and "short-termism" (and this will only worsen to the extent that oil is increasingly considered a "distressed asset" by the international financial community). In fact, the oil curse and the political structure interact to discourage property rights and private investment even more than either of these factors might do on their own. A recent World Bank report states that "The availability of oil rents . . . reinforces the reluctance of the Iraqi government to foster the development of an autonomous private sector, consigning the private sector to be an arena for political influence rather than a potentially transformative force in the country's economy." Although it is hard to gauge the current size of Iraq's private sector, one relevant data point is that it has much lower non-oil tax revenue than most other oil-producing states.[73]

Overall, the story of private enterprise in Iraq has not been a happy one. Despite a massive invasion and occupation, the country has proved impressively resistant to outside influence. Its dependence on oil and state-owned enterprise effectively limits the space in which the private sector can operate, while instability and insecurity further constrain investment. Iraq is a case study of America's inability to locate the "moving parts" within developing countries' political economies that align with Washington's preferences.

Private Sector Development in Afghanistan

Perhaps even more so than Iraq, Afghanistan is the very definition of a "deeply fragile and conflict-affected state."[74] This is all the more so since the Taliban recaptured the country in the summer of 2021. After a brief period of political stability and economic development in the 1950s and 1960s, when the country saw a burst of modernization (fueled in part by foreign aid from the United States and Soviet Union), a political coup in 1973 launched the country into the generations of violence that it continues to endure. These upheavals, of course, attracted the superpowers to the country, culminating in the Soviet invasion of Afghanistan in December 1979 and then the US intervention after the terrorist attacks of September 11, 2001.[75]

Tragically, after an apparent lull in fighting in 2010–2011, violence went on to reach new heights, as the Government of the Islamic Republic of Afghanistan and the Taliban jockeyed for power even while negotiating a possible peace settlement. These attacks may have been widely unpopular, but they represented a Taliban effort to telegraph the ineptitude of the government and its security forces. Over the decade since 2010, civilian casualties rose from 7,156 to over 10,000 in 2019. If nothing else, it may be hoped that the Taliban victory leads to reduced civilian deaths (though, tragically, starvation may now take the place of war as a leading cause of death).

Yet it must also be emphasized that the violence in Afghanistan tended to be fairly concentrated in a few provinces and even districts, like Helmand,

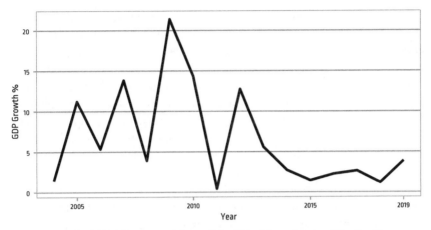

Data source: World Bank, "World Development Indicators," https://datacatalog.worldbank.org/dataset/world
-development-indicators.

FIGURE 6.3   Annual Changes in GDP in Afghanistan, 2004–2019

infamous for the battles Western troops fought there against the Taliban.[76] This concentration of violence raises important questions for donors and entrepreneurs alike. Should donors target their programming at a country's safest or most dangerous regions? Similarly, for entrepreneurs, it raises issues of where and in what to invest.

Economic growth in Afghanistan was, according to the World Bank, "rapid and volatile" over the past ten years, owing to changes in inflows of official development assistance (ODA), agriculture (including opium) prices, and military spending. For a decade or more following the 2001 military actions undertaken by the United States and its allies to remove the Taliban from power and eliminate Al Qaeda as a terrorist threat, growth averaged levels of 9 percent per annum. More recently, however, growth was muted, perhaps as the American withdrawal deprived the nation of both security and resources. Figure 6.3 provides data on recent changes to Afghanistan's GDP.

Unfortunately, Afghanistan's firms were unable to find an escape valve from local instability in global markets. Trade as a share of GDP fell ever since 2003, due to an overvalued exchange rate and Afghan firms' lack of international competitiveness. Further, Afghan companies with enough resources to service the needs of the foreign aid and military sectors focused their activities on these markets, rather than on serving consumers at home and abroad. Only three economic sectors (outside of opium) were active in exporting their products: mining, carpets, and dry fruits. According to the 2014 World Bank Enterprise Survey in Afghanistan, 98 percent of formal firms reported no exports at all.[77]

Yet we must not overlook the fact that there were many bright spots in the Afghan picture; tremendous economic progress was being made on several fronts during the period of Western intervention. According to a 2015 report by the Stockholm International Peace Research Institute, for example, "vehicles on the road have increased from under 200,000 in 2003 to nearly one million. The telecom and media sectors, led by private corporations, have seen tremendous growth. From two telephones for every 1000 Afghans in 2002, there were over 20 million mobile subscriptions in 2012."[78] These are indicators of modernization and better economic conditions for many thousands of people.

From a sectoral perspective, the *CIA World Factbook* estimates that agriculture (including illegal opium production) constitutes 24 percent of GDP (but 50 percent of employment), industry equals 21 percent, and services dominate with 55 percent.[79] According to Ghiasy, Zhou, and Hallgren, the vast majority of firms are small and informal: "The Federation of Afghanistan Craftsmen and Traders for instance, has 75,000 members, many of them . . . informal businesses, organized in some 1000 *senfs* [guilds]."[80]

In sum, the Afghan economy during the period of Western intervention represented something of a puzzle, if not a paradox. Despite (or perhaps because of) massive inflows of foreign aid and military expenditure, the country was unable to find a sustainable growth path. Continuing political uncertainty, made manifest in ongoing violence and corruption, were among the factors impeding Afghanistan from achieving sustainable growth and private sector development. High levels of poverty provided a further deterrent to business creation, given the lack of consumers with purchasing power. Nonetheless, efforts to develop a private sector in Afghanistan were ongoing, and we review them in the following section.

American Efforts to Promote the Private Sector in Afghanistan

By any measure, Afghanistan presented a challenging environment for business even during the Allied occupation, and we can only imagine it worsening under the Taliban regime. In 2018 it ranked 177 out of 180 countries in the "corruptions perception index" and 183 out of 190 in the "Doing Business" rankings.[81] From an economic perspective, "GDP per capita is among the lowest in the world, poverty is deep and widespread, and social indicators are still at very low levels." In 2016, the World Bank estimated that GDP per capita in Afghanistan amounted to $1,802. This despite the fact that Afghanistan was for many years the world's single largest recipient of ODA, receiving $3.4 billion in 2016 alone.[82]

Upon its occupation of Afghanistan (alongside, of course, numerous allied forces gathered as the International Security Assistance Force), Washington set about trying to "stabilize" the country. Stabilization required numerous economic and security interventions, and indeed the economic interventions were viewed by many officials in Washington as a counterinsurgency tool; in fact, the Defense Department published a document called "money as a weapons system," which guided officers on how best to spend contingency funds to "stabilize" their areas of operation.[83]

At a more macro level, the United States sought to create monetary and financial stability through reform of the Central Bank, maintenance of a "strong" local currency, and modernization of the banking system (one of these banks, Kabul Bank, would nearly collapse in late 2010 after the discovery that $1 billion in deposits had been embezzled).[84] New legislation aimed at streamlining business registration was created, and a new institution, the Afghanistan Investment Support Agency (AISA, launched in 2003) was created to provide "one-stop" shopping for investors (on a personal note, I was very impressed by AISA staff in my interactions with them while conducting research in Kabul beginning in 2010).

For its part, "U.S. government support for private sector development and economic growth from 2001 through 2017 can be classified into five main areas of intervention," as follows:[85]

1. "Creating an Enabling Environment": This entails creating the stable macroeconomic policies and legal institutions that most investors seek. Interestingly, "security" was not mentioned as a priority task for foreign assistance in this regard, although corruption did feature as a barrier.
2. "Providing Access to Finance": Here, the emphasis of US efforts has been on strengthening Afghanistan's Central Bank (DAB) and its commercial banking system. In addition to these, the United States "also supported the establishment of non-bank, sector-specific financial institutions to offer loans that were attractive to micro and small enterprises."
3. "Promoting Investment": American policy in this area has focused on attracting local and FDI through privatizing Afghan SOEs, creating industrial parks, and encouraging the exploitation of Afghanistan's mining deposits. The United States also encouraged the creation of an Afghan Investment Agency to provide a "one-stop shop" for those seeking opportunities in the country. (I can personally attest to the kindness of those who work for the agency, at least on the data side!)
4. "Promoting Regional and International Trade": The policy effort in this domain focused on bringing Afghanistan into the World Trade

Organization, where it ultimately gained membership in 2016. Trade with regional partners proved more challenging, as Pakistan frowned on Kabul's dealings with India. Ultimately, in 2016, Afghanistan, India, and Iran reached a trade pact of their own (a point not noted by SIGAR). Remarkably, the United States never signed a free trade agreement with Kabul—which, while it might have had little substantive meaning, would provide a useful signal to investors within and outside of Afghanistan.

5. "Providing Direct Support to Enterprises": While an enterprise fund was never created for Afghanistan, a number of programs were designed to provide firms with technical assistance, grants, and seed funding. Beyond the programs supported by such agencies as USAID and the Department of Agriculture, the DoD undertook several initiatives in different forms, including operating its TFBSO in Afghanistan, similar to its work in Iraq. More on this in what follows.

But American policy in Afghanistan confronted several challenges from the outset.[86] First, when the United States invaded the country, it did not intend to engage in "nation-building"; instead, it invaded with a "light footprint," with the mission of overthrowing the Taliban regime and rid the country of Al Qaeda terrorists. But the United States soon became "entrapped" in the country, eventually leading to the necessity of creating an array of policies aimed at state-building, including economic policies.

Second, the United States based its policies on a number of questionable assumptions regarding its relationship to the government in Kabul. Chief among them was that the interests of Washington and Kabul were in close alignment, and that Afghan leaders shared the priorities and preferences of the Americans. This, of course, proved not to be the case.

Third, and related, the United States threw billions of dollars at this poor country in the hope that these funds would somehow prove "stabilizing." But in many instances, development assistance became another "rent" worth fighting over among those the country's various factions. Further, the United States found it difficult to reconcile meeting the short-run needs of the Afghan people with longer-run developmental priorities, and as a result there was policy incoherence. Over the short run, for example, an overvalued exchange rate of the local currency (the Afghani) meant that imports were relatively inexpensive, but over the longer run, it disincentivized domestic entrepreneurs from entering import-competing industries. Indeed, even some of Afghanistan's traditional handicraft trade would suffer as imports (from such countries as Iran and Pakistan) came in on the cheap.

Finally, the United States had decided to coordinate its policies with those of a number of its allies (not to mention the multitude of nongovernment organizations that implemented official development projects, perhaps weakening the Government of the Islamic Republic of Afghanistan's internal capacity in the process). While perhaps a political necessity, this added a layer of complexity for planning, programming, and project delivery and execution. The allies contributed immense resources to reconstruction, but they also contributed their own ideas and priorities, for better or for worse. While there were undoubted benefits to having an international mandate in Afghanistan, the costs should not be overlooked.

Among the many assistance agencies, both public and nongovernmental, operating in Afghanistan, perhaps the one with the sharpest private sector focus was the one we have already met in Iraq: the DoD's Task Force on Business and Stability Operations. The TFBSO expanded to Afghanistan at the military's urging and was funded to operate there in the FY2011 National Defense Appropriations Act, which stated that its mission was to "reduce violence, enhance stability, and support economic normalcy in Afghanistan through strategic business and economic activities." As in Iraq, "One operating assumption often made by the military in Afghanistan was that unemployment contributes to insurgency, and TFBSO was thus seen as an operational enabling capability. This implied that TFBSO efforts should be nested within military campaign plans."[87]

While TFBSO officials accepted that role, they had other objectives as well, including building up the Afghan economy over the long term so that it could be self-sustaining and therefore less reliant on international donors for funding. This meant that the TFBSO sought to invest in sectors where Afghanistan might attract foreign investors and earn windfall rents from royalty payments (like mining), while building up local firms operating in other promising, export-oriented sectors (like carpets) through technical assistance and networking. Further, the TFBSO (controversially) supported at least one state-owned enterprise, Ariana Airlines, with full-time consulting services. As we have already seen, the United States—as a general rule—tended to avoid giving support to state-owned enterprises lest they undermine private initiative.

As emphasized in a RAND Corporation report, the TFBSO confronted a very different economic environment in Afghanistan from what it had in Iraq.[88] For better or worse, Afghanistan did not have the legacy of heavy industrial SOEs that provided employment for millions of people. Afghanistan was primarily agricultural, and its industries were primarily artisanal, operating on a small scale. However, some American and local officials thought that multinational firms might wish to develop and exploit its promising mineral deposits. The TFBSO also rightly believed the Afghan people to be highly entrepreneurial. Accordingly, its three lines of effort—to enhance small firms with export potential, ignite the mining sector, and promote a start-up culture—followed from these perceptions about the country's economy. As I show in the next section, Afghanistan did build up its private sector, but it was one that probably depended for its existence on the influx of foreign resources. Now we will see which if any of these companies survive under Taliban rule.

Afghanistan's Private Sector

During my trips to Afghanistan, I used to visit the modern Coca-Cola bottling plant on the outskirts of Kabul. I marveled at the modern machinery and the little red trucks that delivered Coke and other drinks; it looked like a Coca-Cola bottler anywhere in the world. The managers hailed from Pakistan (the owner was an Afghan national) and while they were confident in their ability to operate in Afghanistan, they noted that the firm could not expand as they wished, as ownership of the land next door to them was disputed. This seemed like a metaphor for the opportunities and constraints on doing business in that country.

Despite the large influx of military and foreign aid spending into Afghanistan, the business environment was always exceedingly difficult. Beyond the ongoing (though concentrated) violence, poverty, and lack of purchasing power, a 2009 study prepared for USAID (and still relevant today) highlighted high levels of corruption, "a significant and growing problem across Afghanistan that undermines security, state and democracy building, and development . . . corruption has become pervasive, entrenched, systemic and by all accounts now unprecedented in scale and reach."[89] The country's abysmal international rankings, as previously noted, reflect the challenges facing would-be entrepreneurs and foreign investors. As a result, according to a 2017 Investment Climate Statement prepared by the US Department of State:

> Investment has declined in recent years, and what remains is largely financed by donors and the public sector. . . . New firm registrations tailed off dramatically in 2014, with half as many new firms registered in 2014 compared to 2013. That reduced level has remained relatively constant through 2016. Afghanistan has a small formal financial services sector and domestic credit remains tight. Challenges to business in Afghanistan center around a still-developing legal environment, security, varying interpretations of tax law, and the impact of corruption on administration.[90]

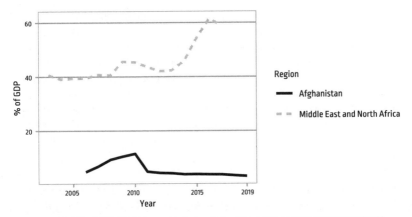

Data source: World Bank, "World Development Indicators," https://datacatalog.worldbank.org/dataset/world
-development-indicators.

FIGURE 6.4   Domestic Credit to the Private Sector, Afghanistan and Middle East
and North Africa, 2003–2019

These rankings and statements seem to be borne out by what Afghan entrepreneurs themselves were saying about their country's economic environment. The World Bank's 2014 Enterprise Survey of Afghanistan reported
that "political instability" was the most frequently cited "obstacle to business" among entrepreneurs. Other top obstacles included "corruption and
crime," "theft," and "disorder," strongly indicating an insecure investment
climate.

The fourth obstacle cited by the business community in this report was
"access to finance." Overall, 12 percent of Afghan firms cited access to finance as the largest obstacle to their operations, and funding from internal
sources provides the primary source of credit for 93 percent of firms. As
shown in Figure 6.4, credit to the private sector was low in Afghanistan
when compared to MENA countries overall. The Government of the Islamic Republic of Afghanistan also continued to play an active role in the
industrial sector, but the extent to which it crowded out private sector
opportunities, given the absence of domestic credit, remains unclear (competition between state-owned and private-owned telecommunications companies, for example, may not have been on a level playing field, as the
former may have relied on subsidies unavailable to the latter). Again, according to the US Department of State's Investment Climate Survey:

> The Government of Afghanistan operates over 30 active state-owned enter
> prises (SOEs), almost all of which are wholly-owned. About 11,000 people
> are employed, in sectors including public security, construction, transport, ag-

riculture, and extractives. Net income for all the SOEs is around USD 13M; few are profitable. All SOEs are overseen and regulated by the Ministry of Finance and directly operated by specific ministries depending on the nature of the operations. . . . The Afghan government is also a stakeholder in 13 state-owned corporations (SOCs), entities that have independent boards and are not operated or directly supervised by the government. SOEs and SOCs make up a small share of overall economic activity, although a few SOCs have significant market share in their sectors, including Afghan Telecom (Aftel), Ariana Afghan Airlines, and the electrical utility DABS (Da Afghanistan Breshna Sherkat).[91]

The World Bank Enterprise Survey (which, as noted, was last conducted for Afghanistan in 2014) reported that formal firms in Afghanistan were found mainly in manufacturing and construction, and the vast majority are "small," with fewer than 19 employees; of the 500 firms surveyed (out of a population estimate of 9,512 formal firms in the economy), about 70 percent are characterized as such. Most of these firms were active in the retail and trade sectors, or in manufacturing and construction. Women were not active in the workforce even before the Taliban regained power; less than 5 percent of firms reported having a "top female manager" (4.7 percent in 2014), a figure that is below the MENA and South Asian regional average.

An intriguing data point discovered by the Enterprise Survey was that, despite reporting that they are operating at or near full capacity, Afghan firms were much less likely than their counterparts elsewhere to invest in new fixed assets. In Afghanistan, only 28 percent of entrepreneurs reported investing in fixed assets, against an Enterprise Survey average of 38 percent. Again, this provides additional support for research which shows that firms operating in areas of violent conflict are less likely to make major investments.

Violence may also affect firms differently according to their size and sector. In Afghanistan, large firms are most likely to pay for security; these firms were also most likely, according to the Enterprise Survey, to be targeted by corrupt government officials and criminals. Large firms in Afghanistan paid the highest percentage of their annual sales—3.2 percent in 2014—to security costs. There were also sectoral differences in the types of firms that paid for security; manufacturing, for instance, seemed less affected than other sectors.

Additional insights into Afghanistan's private sector were provided by a pioneering study, in which I was involved, that made use of mobile phone data in combination with violence data at the district level. In this study, Blumenstock and colleagues used the mobile phone data of some 2,000 Afghan firms as a proxy for where they conducted business, how many employees they had, and how violent terrorist attacks and military actions near the firms influenced their decisions about where to operate. The results generated from this research point to the promise of using new sources of big data to track the private sector in countries where administrative data, including industrial censuses, are lacking; in the concluding section of the study, we discussed the implications of new sources of big data for donor programs.[92]

Blumenstock and colleagues generated three crucial findings from their research. First, fewer firms were active in more violent districts. They found a strong, negative relationship between the number of active firms in a district and the number of violent events per capita; specifically, each violent incident per 100,000 people led to a reduction of 0.56 active firms. Second, firms had fewer employees in violent districts. There was a strong, negative relationship between the number of active business subscribers in a district and violence per capita; each violent event per 100,000 people leads to 1.78 fewer subscribers. Third, firms reacted to violent incidents by changing their operations. Specifically, in cases where the violence was sustained—as was the case in Kunduz during the fall of 2015 (which the Taliban attacked and briefly held)—firms left the city and returned only when the situation had stabilized.[93]

Overall, the evidence from Afghanistan reveals a private sector that began to emerge during the Allied occupation but that probably was overly dependent on it for cash flow and security. Most of those private sector firms, however, are now likely moribund. It will be a major challenge for the Taliban, even should they so desire, to provide the kind of credibility that entrepreneurs require if they are to put scarce capital at risk.

Conclusions

Few cases more poignantly illustrate the American belief in the power of private enterprise than Iraq and Afghanistan. In these settings, private enterprise was meant to create jobs and incomes, reducing violence and generating sustainable growth in the process. Private enterprise would generate a virtuous cycle of wealth and peace, steamrolling anything that stood in its way. If "quiet Americans" were found anywhere, it was within the agencies of the U.S. government that came to these countries infused with belief in the healing power of free enterprise.

What the Americans failed to appreciate was that in certain places, economic life is a zero-sum game, a source of rents rather than of growth. Profound distrust limits the scope of markets, and there is a sharp distinction between insiders and outsiders that is not easily bridged by payoffs. Further, in violent settings, the time horizons of economic agents are drastically reduced. When safety is not a given, there is little concern for tomorrow; one must get as much as one possibly can *now* without regard for the future. Thus, rent extraction takes precedence over long-term investment.

The Americans likely compounded these problems by raining down billions of dollars on Iraq and Afghanistan. All that development assistance created a rent that people wanted to get their hands on and allocate to friends and family, creating or reinforcing networks of cronyism and corruption while reducing incentives for long-run business development. In essence, the United States helped to enrich kleptocratic systems of governance rather than market-oriented democracies.

But what were the alternatives? As Colin Powell famously put the "Pottery Barn rule" to President George W. Bush, "You break it, you own it."[94] Following the invasions of Afghanistan and Iraq, the United States found itself in control of two countries whose citizens now depended upon its guidance and largesse. It may not have *sought* to become an imperial power, at least in the formal sense—but it was now an occupier with a responsibility for picking up the pieces. Where should it begin?

As I have emphasized throughout this book, transforming the political economies of foreign lands means identifying the elites within them that are amenable to manipulation so that shared interests can be aligned. It also means designing and implementing an entire suite of internally coherent policies that ensure this incentive alignment over the long run. This is a heavy lift, and one that has only succeeded in a relatively few places. In both Iraq and Afghanistan, policies were based on flawed assumptions about the domestic political economy, and that proved fatal to US policy.

Structural issues have also interfered with American economic policy. Iraq was dependent on state-dominated oil production, crowding out private sector activity. Afghanistan was largely dependent on foreign aid and opium, and while these may encourage entrepreneurship in some respects, neither provides a solid foundation for long-run growth. These structural features were far different from those the United States confronted, say, in Central and Eastern Europe, which provided a "model" for economic reform, at least in Iraq.

Finally, in both cases the United States learned that security is paramount. Without security, economic activity will be stunted and resources misallocated. Yet in both places, insecurity was greater in some parts of the country than others. The United States might have considered focusing its economic efforts in the most secure regions, creating demonstration effects that might have, over time, created demands for conflict reduction in more violent areas. At a minimum, the issue of *where* to conduct economic programs in fragile states is one that deserves deeper thought on the part of academics and policy makers alike.

One country that seems to be giving serious thought about how to operate in fragile places is China. With its Belt and Road Initiative, it is making large-scale investments in some of the world's most unstable countries. In Chapter 7 I will examine how China is faring and what the United States is doing to counter its influence. I once saw this as a case of "dueling capitalisms," in which China's "state-led" model was pitted against the US preference for market-oriented economies, but perhaps the American economy too will become more state-led, particularly in an era when the combined forces of the COVID pandemic and concerns with climate change seem to be driving Washington toward greater state intervention.

7

Dueling Capitalisms?

Private Enterprise and the China Challenge

> The Development Finance Corporation . . . is one of the biggest changes in U.S. foreign policy this century.
>
> —ACTING DFC CEO DAVID BOHIGAN, 14 AUGUST 2019[1]

WHEN I WROTE the first drafts of this chapter, there was no question mark following its title. But as the Biden administration, with bipartisan support, adopts increasingly protectionist rhetoric alongside a bolder vision of government-led industrial policy, one wonders whether the gap in economic ideology between the United States and China is shrinking as both countries converge toward some form of state capitalism. The logic of a new Cold War is supplanting the logic of globalization, with the belief in markets and firms as drivers of innovation and growth falling victim to the grim primacy of national security.

The clash with China, of course, was already heating up under President Donald Trump. In 2020, then US Director of National Intelligence John Ratcliffe labeled China as America's "national security threat no. 1."[2] And reminiscent of the "Soviet economic offensive" of the 1950s, which I have referred to in earlier chapters, China is now engaged in expanding its influence around the world through its Belt and Road Initiative (BRI). Unlike the USSR, however, Beijing has enjoyed a dynamic economy alongside very deep pockets for financing such an undertaking. It remains to be seen, however, whether the internal politics of the Chinese Communist Party (CCP) and associated power grab of General Secretary Xi Jinping will derail the economic model that has brought the country such enormous success, to the extent that entrepreneurship is viewed as a threat to CCP primacy.

In labeling China as a national security threat, Ratcliffe argued that Chinese influence campaigns can be quite subtle in their design, reflecting Beijing's understanding of local political economies. Taking as his example a Chinese-owned manufacturing plant in the United States, Ratcliffe writes that in order to advance its policy preferences in Washington, the Chinese will lean on the plant's labor officials, suggesting they lobby their local members of Congress to adopt the policies that Beijing prefers. The implicit threat is that the plant's owners will lay off workers or even shut it down if the representative does not behave in the way that Beijing desires.[3] In sum, Beijing seeks to identify the "moving parts" within target nations that are amenable to its manipulation.

With the COVID pandemic, China has used its model of public health and its vaccine as new instruments of influence. Unlike the United States, which initially hoarded vaccines for its own population before making them available to other nations, Beijing has rolled out its jabs (e.g., CoronaVac) across the developing world, ineffective as they may be compared to those produced by Western pharmaceutical firms. According to the *Financial Times*, "In Pakistan, for example, China has . . . taken a leading role in supplying millions of vaccines."[4]

How should the United States respond to the China challenge? What can the new US Development Finance Corporation (DFC)—which is supposed to support private enterprise in developing countries in order to counter China's "state-led" model—learn from the history recounted in these pages as it develops its programming? To what extent does private sector development remain a compelling development strategy as we enter a postpandemic economic era? Will the United States continue to promote the global spread of private enterprise at a time when its own economic policies, along with those of other great industrial powers, seem to be turning increasingly inward and "nationalistic"? These are among the questions I will address in this chapter.

This last point about whether private sector development will even remain a central policy goal for the United States is worth some further emphasis. After years of being largely overlooked by the international development community (you will find few references to private enterprise in the leading textbooks in the field of development economics), growing the private sector has become a central preoccupation of foreign aid agencies, both bilateral and multilateral.[5] This new thrust reflected not just American influence over these institutions or the ideology of "neoliberalism" that allegedly permeates them,[6] but the pressing financial facts of life in the early twenty-first century. Whether it will survive a possibly more state-dominated and directed economic era remains to be seen.

But that does not diminish the developing world's need for private investment. Consider that in 2020, official development assistance flows to the developing world totaled some $160 billion (note that this figure does not count foreign aid from China or other donors that are not yet part of the Organisation for Economic Co-operation and Development's [OECD] Development Assistance Committee). By comparison, the infrastructure requirements alone of these countries were estimated by a Brookings Institution study at some $2.4 *trillion* per annum;[7] the OECD has placed that figure between $3.4 and $4.4 trillion.[8] Recognizing the enormity of this funding gap, the development community has come to believe that it can only be filled by mobilizing private financial resources.[9] Still more private funds and innovations will be needed to address such challenges as climate change. At the present time, however, the development finance institutions commit something on the order of $90 billion to private sector development.[10]

Yet that vision of private sector–led growth is now being challenged by China, with its $1 trillion state-directed Belt and Road Initiative. BRI relies heavily on China's policy banks and state-owned enterprises to finance and execute infrastructure projects across the developing world—projects that will presumably serve Beijing's political and economic interests. And BRI does not stand alone as a policy initiative, but is part of a broader effort on the part of the Chinese government, known as the "Going Out" or "Going Global" policy, which uses foreign direct investment (FDI), among other tools, as a resource for expanding the nation's influence and access to markets and raw materials (how coherent Chinese economic statecraft is in practice remains a topic of debate in the relevant literature, with some scholars arguing that Chinese policy is quite coherent, while others cast doubt on its internal consistency).[11] Like the United States during the early Cold War era, China now finds itself with ample reserves of capital that are ready for overseas deployment. How is China deploying that capital, and for what purposes?

As China "goes global," it brings with it a model of "political capitalism" that provides an alternative to the "liberal," free-enterprise model traditionally advocated by Western governments and the multilateral institutions they support. Under political capitalism, "private" enterprise still exists, as do markets for exchange, but the economy is actively guided by political elites whose primary allegiance is to the state and the Communist Party.[12] The apparent success of China's political capitalism, at least until recent times, has proved attractive to the world's authoritarian leaders who believe that controlling the economy gives them a source of rents to use for both personal and political payoffs.

But as economist Branko Milanović emphasizes, the successful guidance of political capitalism requires a technocratic policy elite that is pragmatic and skilled, which many developing countries are still in the process of grooming.[13] How state capitalism plays out in states that are still not very "capable" in the technocratic sense remains to be seen. In the event, technocrats may hold little sway in countries whose governments are bent on kleptocracy rather than inclusive growth.

Given China's rising prominence in the global economy, private sector development has again become an issue of geostrategic importance for the United States, as exemplified by the founding of the DFC. As the corporation describes its role, "DFC positions the United States to provide an alternative to the financing model offered by autocratic governments. The amount these governments have planned are staggering. . . . Fortunately, developing countries are searching for an alternative to investment capital that can often leave them worse off." DFC will play this role through its ability to "Drive Private Capital Toward US Foreign Policy Objectives: DFC serves as a critical tool of American foreign policy, mobilizing investment in regions, and industry sectors of strategic importance. . . . Leveraging private-sector resources to promote economic growth in developing countries helps extend American influence and reinforce American values, such as the rule of law, transparency, and fair business practices."[14] DFC is thus positioning itself to play a key role in the bipolar competition now playing out across the developing world.[15]

This chapter addresses that competition and its consequences for the distinct economic models that the United States and China have adopted to date. In the next section, I briefly describe China's BRI and then turn to the American institutional response to it, the DFC that was set up by the Trump administration. This chapter is admittedly more speculative than the others, in part because data are missing on the BRI on the one hand while, on the other, the DFC is a relatively new organization (even if it is a continuation of the Overseas Private Investment Corporation [OPIC] in important respects), having only been established in 2018. But given its combination of youth and ambition, perhaps the DFC is ripe for learning some key lessons from the past regarding private sector development.

China's Belt and Road Initiative: Political Capitalism in the Developing World

China's sustained growth over the past 30 years is one of the marvels of economic history, propelling it to a leading role in the global economy.

After only a generation of market-oriented reforms, it has become the world's leading exporter and has the second-highest GDP (although GDP per capita still lags); in so doing, it has amassed some $3 trillion in foreign exchange reserves, the highest level of any country.[16] These reserves give it plenty of ammunition for financing outward investment, both public and private. Some questions that should be raised by foreign policy analysts with respect to Chinese economic statecraft include: (1) whether China has developed a coherent strategy for such outward investment; (2) whether Beijing has the capability to execute that strategy; (3) the extent to which that strategy threatens Western interests; and (4) the extent to which that strategy is supportive of the developmental aspirations of recipient nations.

According to Princeton's Aaron Friedberg, China's overseas investment strategy "has three components." The first is to secure access to a "range of commodities, principally energy, minerals . . . and food"; this has taken the form of "buying equity stakes" in oilfields, mines, and farmland. The second component involves "buying, building and expanding port facilities" (along with container ships) in countries where it purchases these critical assets (Friedberg reports that "Chinese port operators now handle 39% of all container traffic worldwide"). The third and final piece is the BRI, whose objective is to "enable delivery of at least a portion of China's . . . critical commodities . . . via routes that run entirely overland from source to market."[17] In sum, China's economic statecraft regarding foreign investment consists of buying foreign assets; building ports for maritime shipping; and extending land-based infrastructure (e.g., road and railroads) that ties China to its trading partners.

Announced in 2013 by Xi Jinping, China's Belt and Road aims to create "a vast network of railways, energy pipelines, highways, and streamlined border crossings, both westward—through the mountainous former Soviet republics—and southward, to Pakistan, India, and the rest of Southeast Asia."[18] In fact, China's plans may be even more ambitious than this quote suggests, as recent investments in Western Europe, the Middle East, and Africa have also been tied to BRI.[19] While it is not easy to map the ever-changing BRI, it is now global in scope, with over seventy countries included in this scheme.

At the heart of these ambitions is the deeper political and economic integration of those countries that fall within what China considers its sphere of influence (which certainly includes countries bordering the South China Sea and China's neighboring nations). It generally does this through renminbi-denominated project finance loans that make intensive use of Chinese goods, services, and labor. In this sense, the BRI is as much a domestic initiative meant to address structural weaknesses in the Chinese economy as it is a grand foreign policy strategy. Given its combination of poor demographics, growing international hostility to its trade policies, and the specter of weakening domestic demand, Beijing cannot rely on homegrown supply and demand to solve current and future economic problems.[20] There is a neat irony in this, as some variants of Marxist theory predict that capitalist firms must spread overseas as domestic markets become saturated; it appears that the same fate may befall Chinese state capitalism as well![21]

While data on BRI are hard to parse, a study by the Brookings Institution estimates that China is spending upwards of $40 billion annually on infrastructure investments alone; it is unclear to what extent this funding comes in the form of grants versus loans or how much of the lending is subsidized. (There are also frequent allegations of Chinese lending being extortionist, in which recipient nations end up handing over access to ports and other infrastructure when loans go unpaid. Of course, the terms of any given loan could vary dramatically by project and borrower.)[22] By way of contrast, the combined request of the US State Department and the US Agency for International Development for all their worldwide operations was precisely that same amount, $40 billion, for FY20.[23]

In Washington, there has been a great deal of hand wringing about the BRI's implications for recipient nations (in the following section, we will examine the US response, particularly by the DFC). Less attention has been paid to possible benefits of Chinese lending and investments, a topic we take up in more detail below. Analysts at a Washington think tank, the Center for a New American Security (CNAS), have argued that BRI poses seven challenges in particular:

1. **Erosion of National Sovereignty:** Beijing has obtained control over select infrastructure projects through equity arrangements, long-term leases, or multidecade operating contracts.
2. **Lack of Transparency:** Many projects feature opaque bidding processes for contracts and financial terms that are not subject to public scrutiny.
3. **Unsustainable Financial Burdens:** Chinese lending to some countries has increased their risk of debt default or repayment difficulties, while certain completed projects have not generated sufficient revenue to justify the cost.
4. **Disengagement from Local Economic Needs:** Belt and Road projects often involve the use of Chinese firms and labor for construction, which does little to transfer skills to local workers, and sometimes involve inequitable profit-sharing arrangements.
5. **Geopolitical Risks:** Some infrastructure projects financed, built, or operated by China can compromise the recipient state's telecommunications

infrastructure or place the country at the center of strategic competition between Beijing and other great powers.

6. **Negative Environmental Impacts:** Belt and Road projects have in some instances proceeded without adequate environmental assessments or have already caused severe environmental damage.

7. **Significant Potential for Corruption:** In countries that already have a high level of kleptocracy, Belt and Road projects have involved payouts to politicians and bureaucrats.[24]

The seventh item on this list is perhaps of greatest potential import to the arguments in this book. By definition, private sector development requires empowering entrepreneurs to translate their ideas into profitable businesses. That requires access to markets on a "what you know" rather than "who you know" basis. In kleptocracies, however, access to markets, along with fundamental property rights, are doled out by rulers in return for political favors. If China is actively supporting kleptocratic forms of government, that obviously poses a problem for those world leaders who wish to strengthen and spread democratic capitalism.

But China, of course, has adapted itself to work with many different regime types, some of which are more criminal than others. What explains the different instruments that China uses in its economic statecraft? According to political scientist Audrye Wong, China uses bribes in states where the institutional setting is weak, and more sophisticated influence attempts where the legal system is more robust.[25]

And before worrying too much about China's ability to buy off corrupt governments in the developing world, one should think deeper about what it is that Beijing is getting (or hoping to receive) in return, as well as the potential consequences of basing a relationship on bribery. After all, bribes are transactional, a quid pro quo. Bribing a government minister to win a particular contract, odious as it might be, is not the same as buying off an entire government's foreign policy orientation; it is likely that the benefits do not extend far beyond that particular transaction. Further, the minister who accepted the bribe today may be gone tomorrow, and with it possibly the contractual arrangement that was in place. In other words, bribes may not deliver as promised, and certainly not over time.

This is not meant to diminish in any way the effects of corruption on many of the political and economic outcomes that concern the development community. Corruption can amplify insider/outsider problems within a society; diminish trust in economic relationships; lead to profound inefficiencies in an economy; subvert efforts at "good governance"; and more generally, undermine the prospects for inclusive growth. Shining a light on it is generally a good thing.[26] But whether bribery is an effective tool of statecraft is a question worthy of deeper study.

At the same time, it must be acknowledged that BRI projects may improve welfare in recipient countries. The World Bank, for example, estimates that the new transportation networks associated with BRI could significantly reduce the time of getting goods to market (and, of course, it may bring new economic agents to market as well—to the extent that the infrastructure reaches previously isolated places). These welfare gains are estimated at 2–4 percent of GDP in participating countries, which represents a considerable economic boost.[27]

Further, China may be primarily lending to countries that cannot otherwise access international capital markets. Many fragile states, for example, lack access to such funding, and to the extent they receive official development assistance from OECD donors, the amounts may be insufficient to provide for investment needs. Countries like South Sudan and the Central African Republic are among those that have received Chinese aid. In this sense, Chinese transfers via foreign aid and BRI are providing additional resources to countries that desperately need such inflows. All this suggests that a balanced assessment of the costs and benefits of China's investment activities in the developing world is sorely needed. Of course, China itself could help such an assessment by being more transparent.[28]

In addition to BRI, China has also become a net exporter of outward FDI to a growing number of countries; it remains a topic of debate as to whether the BRI is a major contributor to that development. On the one hand, FDI might be flowing to BRI recipients simply because, in addition to providing needed infrastructure, the presence of Beijing-supported projects in those places provides "comfort" to investors who might be fearful of political risk. Alternatively, the flag might be following trade in this case. Preliminary analysis suggests that several BRI countries were significant recipients of Chinese FDI *before* that initiative was launched.[29] If this is true, China may be providing public funds in support of the country's enterprises that have already made investments and that are now demanding infrastructure to make them profitable. On the other hand, research to date shows that, overall, the BRI has not had any statistically significant effect on Chinese outward foreign direct investment (OFDI).[30]

Thus, the jury remains out on whether BRI has generated the positive externality effect of attracting FDI (either from China or elsewhere). But this is an important, ongoing issue that deserves close observation. After all, few beliefs are more long-standing in economic development than the positive effects of good infrastructure on private investment and growth.

In the event, Chinese OFDI rose from virtually nothing in 2000 to more than $100 billion per annum in recent years. As shown in Figure 7.1, China is now approaching the United States as a major supplier of global capital needs. Again, this is unsurprising from a macroeconomic perspective; it simply reflects the building up of Chinese surpluses and their recycling into foreign assets. The extent to which these deals are driven by economics or politics (or some complex melding of the two), however, remains an issue that is debated in the relevant literature. According to a US congressional body, China has acted in a relatively strategic fashion, arguing that "foreign direct investment deals indicate that government encourages Chinese enterprises to invest overseas in order to gain access to raw materials and advanced technology from abroad, increase foreign exchange earnings, and promote China's exports."[31]

The increasing importance of China's OFDI has promoted a nascent research agenda studying issues around its impact on China itself and recipient states.[32] In some respects, this mirrors the research on US FDI that appeared in the 1970s, as various scholars debated its merits for home and host countries alike. There are, of course, significant differences between these agendas. First, because of the novelty of OFDI in China, scholarship on the subject is very much in the early stages; serious empirical research

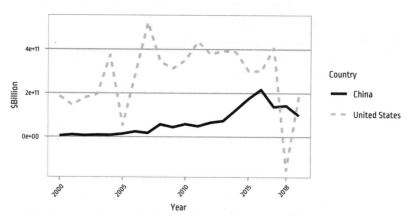

Data source: World Bank, "World Development Indicators," https://datacatalog.worldbank.org/dataset/world
-development-indicators.

FIGURE 7.1   China and the United States, Net Outward FDI, 2000–2019, in Billions of Dollars

is hampered by the lack of data. Second, it is difficult for an outsider to understand the extent to which scholars can conduct open debates about the costs and benefits of OFDI within China; the political climate there may play a powerful role in shaping research programs and findings.[33] Despite these limitations, both Chinese and foreign scholars are beginning to conduct some impressive work.[34]

As previously noted, in 2001 China began to encourage its firms to "go global" by loosening restrictions on FDI (though all OFDI must still be vetted by the central government). In 2004, this policy was accelerated through China's granting of various financial subsidies to foreign investors; these seem to mirror the kinds of tax breaks the United States offered its firms beginning in the late 1940s, although China does not yet offer its firms political risk insurance (apparently there are discussions along these lines).[35] At the same time, the Chinese government began incorporating FDI into broader diplomatic relations, taking measures to promote Chinese firms during official state visits abroad.[36]

Chinese overseas investments are tied to its domestic economy in at least three ways. First, as China has become more dependent on energy and raw materials to fuel its own growth, the government has encouraged firms (often state-owned enterprises) to seek those resources abroad. Second, recognizing that Chinese wage costs were rising and the country was losing its competitive advantage in "cheap" labor, the government began encouraging Chinese firms that rely on that particular factor to move to other Asian markets (e.g., Vietnam and Cambodia) that could serve as export hubs.[37] Third, and related, economists have found that trade increases with countries that host Chinese FDI; in this sense, trade and FDI are complimentary.[38]

What effects does Chinese investment have on recipient economies? Here, too, the evidence is mixed. Overall, studies find that Chinese firms boost local employment but have done little by way of technology transfer.[39] From a micro perspective, a study in Ethiopia shows that Chinese investment crowds out competing local enterprises but facilitates the emergence and growth of firms that provide needed inputs and services; thus, Chinese firms may create linkages in specific cases. While these two economic effects of crowding out on the one hand and creating linkages on the other cancel out over the short run, it appears that Chinese investment contributes to economic growth over the longer term.[40]

In terms of politics and policy, as previously noted, some observers have expressed concern that Chinese investments promote corruption and degrade institutional quality in recipient countries. Yet other studies have found that institutional quality in BRI nations has *improved* following Chinese investment.[41] These effects on governance will be of crucial interest to the international development community as it asks, in what direction is China taking the global economy? Is China "racing to the top" or to the "bottom" when it comes to governance arrangements? If Beijing is driving a race to the bottom, how should the United States respond?

To summarize, Beijing has been "going global" since the dawn of the new millennium. It has done so in large part by participating (after its own fashion) in the multilateral regimes established during the postwar era, such as the World Bank and World Trade Organization, which have done much to promote its domestic reform process. But more recently it has begun to launch a new suite of foreign economic policies, programs, and institutions, notably the BRI and organizations built to support it (most notably the Asian Infrastructure Investment Bank). Further, Chinese companies have been encouraged to engage in outward FDI, echoing in some respects US policy when it actively sought to push American firms overseas. More research is needed to determine the effects of these policies on recipient nations.

For the administration of Donald J. Trump, these developments posed an existential threat to American economic and foreign policy interests—enough to merit a response in the form of the newly created DFC. His successor, Joe Biden, seems to be continuing the policy of economic confrontation with China. The next section reviews the DFC and its role in providing Beijing with strategic competition in the developing world.

The US Response to the China Challenge

Is the developing world falling under China's sway? If so, how is the United States responding? How *should* it respond? This section provides a framework for thinking about these questions, which are of particular import in Washington today. Of course, in analyzing and writing about contemporary policy making, it is essential to recognize that scholars lack access to the interagency debates that help shape US policy formulation; for now we must rely on the public record, which is sadly rather thin on this topic. Related, as of this writing, the Biden administration had yet to appoint a CEO for the DFC. That does not bode well for the president's promise to "Build Back Better World" (B3W), his as-of-yet ill-defined program of private sector–led infrastructure development, which would make intensive use of DFC financing. Oftentimes, congressional hearings on senior appointments can provide key insights into administration priorities, but these had not yet occurred in this particular case.

I should also say that this section does not attempt to survey US policy toward the developing world in general in recent years. But this is not because the United States has been inactive. In 2015, for example, the Africa Growth and Opportunity Act was renewed for 10 years, encouraging trade and investment with the continent.[42] And despite efforts by the Trump administration to cut foreign aid spending, it was restored by Congress and in 2019 totaled some $39 billion, which makes the United States the world's largest contributor in absolute terms (though not as a share of GDP).

However, with the rise of China and its increasing global reach, the goals of foreign aid may be changing. Just as it had a predominant anti-communist and anti-Soviet focus during the Cold War, now aid may be repurposed away from such goals as poverty reduction and humanitarian assistance and more toward countering China. As Daniel Runde of the Center for Strategic and International Studies has recently stated, "the developing world still needs U.S. foreign assistance, but where and how the United States invests its money and expertise will require a strategic repositioning."[43]

How, then, does contemporary Washington conceptualize China's role in the international system? According to the 2017 National Security Strategy developed during the early days of the Trump administration (a document, incidentally, that many observers found to be valuable, including Trump critics),[44] China is deemed a "revisionist power" that wants "to shape a world antithetical to U.S. values and interests. China seeks to displace the United States in the Indo-Pacific region, expand the reaches of its state-driven economic model, and reorder the region in its favor."[45] Thus far the Biden administration has maintained a similarly hostile tone toward China, partly for legitimate security reasons but also because it sells politically at home. Less obvious is whether the rest of the-world has any interest in making decisive "US or China" decisions, especially at a time when the American economy may be turning inward.[46]

As a revisionist power, China presumably rejects the "rules of the game" established by the United States and its allies after World War II, and as its global power grows it poses even more of a threat to those rules. Ultimately, it may seek to overturn them altogether and establish its own Beijing playbook, which would include regulations and standards that are in its interest rather than those of Washington. As then–Vice President Mike Pence remarked, "Beijing is . . . taking steps to exploit its economic leverage, and the allure of their large marketplace, to advance its influence over American businesses."[47] His mention of "American business" is notable, reminding us that Washington continues to view business as a strategic asset. (One of the more interesting elements in this speech is Pence's depiction of Beijing as actively trying to manipulate American business interests and voters, or its theory of how to influence American policy. In the introduction to this chapter I cited John Ratcliffe's similar claims along these lines).

How should the United States respond to the China challenge? At least three possibilities suggest themselves. First, it could do nothing, passively accepting that Beijing has a sphere of influence in East Asia that the United States cannot reasonably counter, just as it accepted Moscow's domination over Central and Eastern Europe during the Cold War (recall, in this regard, the muted US policy response to such events as the Hungarian uprising of 1956 and the Czech uprising of 1968). Second, it could cooperate with China, recognizing that BRI might provide a useful supplement to current development funding, especially given its focus on infrastructure. Third, it could seek to counter or challenge China directly by trying to provide BRI countries a "better deal."[48]

Note that there is some confusion in Washington as to the precise policy implications of a rising China. A Republican member of Congress from Wisconsin, for example, called upon the Trump administration—and the American people—to recognize China's relationship with the United States as a new "Cold War." He therefore argued for more investments in "hard power" to ensure that the United States possesses a credible military deterrent, while further arguing that America "must also compete in the 'gray zone,' leveraging allies and liberal values to . . . ensure countries don't embrace the Communist Party's authoritarian model."[49] But where, precisely, is that "gray zone"? What policies should be enacted there? Can the United States compete with China throughout the gray zone? Should it?

At present, it seems that Washington is taking the view that it should seek to challenge China along the Belt and Road by offering countries a different economic model of development. Under that strategy, the DFC would become a key instrument of US foreign policy. When he was Vice President, Pence certainly seemed to frame it in such terms: "I'm . . . pleased to report that we're streamlining international development and finance programs. We'll be giving foreign nations a just and transparent alternative to China's debt-trap diplomacy."[50]

In principle, this new institution could help Washington to align its commercial and developmental assets with its foreign policy objectives. But the DFC begins its operations at a significant disadvantage to China: relative poverty. As previously mentioned, the new DFC will have about $60 billion in capital—whereas the BRI is a $1 trillion effort. To date, Pakistan alone has already received more cash commitments from China than the value of the entire DFC budget.[51]

Further, as I have emphasized throughout this book, the ability of Washington to steer the investments of its multinational firms to countries along the Belt and Road may be doubted. This is a crucial point, because at least some analysts around the Beltway are hoping that DFC will unleash such investments. As Daniel Kleiman of CNAS writes, "To compete with China, the USDFC will have to incentivize American companies to play a more active role in countries with weaker regulatory environments and greater political instability."[52] Yet while investment guarantees and other subsidies may be welcomed by executives in places where they already had thought to invest, these instruments are very unlikely to change C-suite decisions in any fundamental way, as this book has shown time and again.

On that note, however, it should be emphasized that DFC—unlike OPIC—is empowered to invest directly in local private sector firms. In that important sense, it can promote private sector development without relying upon multinational firms to do that job via their linkages strategies. How successful that effort will be, of course, remains to be determined.

In deciding which investments to make, the DFC has adopted a metric it calls the "Impact Quotient" (IQ). The IQ is composed of the following elements: first, whether the project contributes to economic growth; second, inclusion, or whether a given project provides goods and services to "underrepresented groups"; and third, "innovation," which seems to be a catch-all phrase for project novelty.[53] While the DFC admits to the difficulties associated with quantifying these factors, especially *ex ante*, it does represent a good-faith effort to specify what it is looking for in a project proposal.

Note that missing from this list, however, is "contribution to U.S. foreign policy goals." To be sure, by promoting growth, inclusion, and innovation, a given project may advance American interests, if only indirectly. But if the United States is to challenge China, doesn't the DFC need to be more strategic regarding *where* it invests and in *which* sectors?

In particular, the DFC needs to be mindful of the "fallacy of composition" problem, by which policy makers believe that a number of micro interventions *in* a country will somehow lead to systemic change *of* a country— this is a problem we have already confronted in previous chapters. To date, DFC is emphasizing six sectors of activity: technology and infrastructure; energy; financial inclusion; food security and agriculture; health; and water, sanitation, and hygiene. Across each sector it has established goals of investing a certain percentage of funds in low-income countries and fragile states. A map of DFC projects shows a smattering of activity in countries across the globe.[54] But how do these interventions "add up" as a foreign assistance strategy?

In fact, in its 2020 annual report, the DFC does not even mention China in its chapter on "advancing American foreign policy."[55] Instead, it mentions three projects in Eastern Europe (one on trade promotion in Georgia, one on energy diversification in Ukraine, and one on economic development in Kosovo) the first two of which are directed against expanding Russian influence. Other projects mentioned in this chapter concern promoting economic growth in Central America and oil development in Iraq. None of these directly challenge China along the Belt and Road. Certainly, the DFC is investing in projects within BRI countries and in Africa. But whether these are sufficient to counter Chinese expansion may be doubted, especially if they are not accompanied by large-scale FDI that creates local linkages.

More generally, the DFC can only succeed if its projects are nested within a coherent set of foreign economic policies and programs. Policies for trade, aid, and investment must work together if DFC's relatively paltry funds are to have anything like a systemic impact. Specifically, that means giving local entrepreneurs the incentive to go global by striking trade deals with host governments, and providing the foreign aid needed, say in infrastructure, to facilitate the ability of firms to get to markets and ports. Only in this way can the United States provide a compelling alternative package to what the Chinese have on offer.

Again, what is certain is that DFC lacks the funds to confront China directly by offering similar levels of project funding. By 2025, for example, DFC hopes to invest $25 billion around the world, while mobilizing an additional $50 billion; again, this is less than China is investing in Pakistan alone.[56] The financial shortfall raises the question of what the United States can actually do, beyond trying to develop the coherent policies stressed previously, to derail the juggernaut—or, to mix metaphors, how it can play David to China's Goliath (and the idea that the United States is a "David" in the developing world may, admittedly, strike the reader as somewhat far-fetched).

One answer is to use a version of what economists have called the "judo strategy," a method small firms deploy to compete against larger companies. Judo strategies involve turning what is supposedly one's competitor's key asset—in this case, its size—against it. For example, smaller retail firms can outcompete bigger chains by providing products and services that cater more to the tastes of local clients.[57]

When it comes to US–China competition, a successful US judo strategy should consist of four building blocks. First, Washington should leverage the fact that China may be violating well-established international norms with its lending policies by ensuring that the publics in recipient nations are aware of any harmful agreements their leaders are striking. Second, and related, the United States should draw attention to corruption associated with the BRI. Third, US officials should creatively use DFC resources to liberate countries that find themselves unhappily trapped in Beijing's financial clutches. (In that respect, the recent G-20 initiative to reduce the debt burdens of developing countries that are reliant on Chinese lending is of particular interest; it also suggests a growing sensitivity within the Chinese government to the costs associated with some of their lending practices to date.) Finally, the United States should work to help friends and allies promote best practices in development finance (e.g., making project finance transparent), as it does with the "Blue Dot Network" of countries, while continuing to promote the use of private firms in related infrastructure projects.[58] Of course, none of these initiatives will succeed if the United States itself continues to eschew international norms (e.g., "Buy American" policies which may be at odds with the spirit if not the law of WTO disciplines).

Indeed, these international norms—as articulated by such multilateral institutions as the World Bank, the International Monetary Fund (IMF), and the OECD—should not be overlooked as instruments for constraining China's predatory lending practices and sources of political leverage. For example, the OECD has established norms against the use of tied aid, or funds that require recipients to use that foreign aid to purchase goods and services from the donor, because it forces recipient countries to spend their money inefficiently. And even if BRI funding—which primarily takes the form of loans—does not formally constitute foreign aid, Beijing often violates the spirit of this principle by mandating that the infrastructure projects it pays for use Chinese contractors.[59]

Washington should leverage these and other established norms of international development to isolate Beijing. China and the OECD's Development Assistance Committee (DAC), for example, have formed a study group that analyzes whether China is adopting best practices in foreign assistance. If China continues to neglect such practices, then the OECD (with US encouragement) should halt China's participation in the DAC in a very public fashion. The World Bank and the IMF should also put the spotlight on China's lending activities much more vigorously than they have done to date—something that should be encouraged by the United States, which has tremendous influence with both organizations by dint of its voting power—not to mention the fact that the current head of the World Bank, David Malpass, is an American citizen.

The second part of Washington's judo strategy should be to highlight corrupt BRI payments, as noted earlier in this chapter. While the extent of this corruption may be disputed, there is little doubt that Beijing has at times been willing to engage in corrupt practices abroad to further its economic and political agendas. A January 2019 investigation by the *Wall Street Journal*, for example, revealed how the Chinese offered to bail out a troubled Malaysian investment fund in return for infrastructure projects that would give their firms "above market profitability."[60] More generally, many BRI partners, including Kazakhstan and Laos, suffer from endemic corruption.[61]

Third, the DFC should work closely with Wall Street and development finance institutions such as the International Finance Corporation to help BRI countries elaborate alternatives to China's "debt diplomacy." The success of this strategy depends in part on how bankable the BRI's projects really are. Are countries turning to Beijing to finance projects that simply wouldn't qualify for financing elsewhere, or are at least some of these projects sound enough that, with some restructuring, they could create credible capital structures? America should make use of its competitive global advantage to unleash development finance on BRI. As noted earlier, a G-20 initiative to help reduce the debt burden on countries that took on Chinese loans represents a promising multilateral approach to that issue—and one that has even induced Chinese cooperation!

Finally, the United States should continue to promote the Blue Dot Network (BDN) and its "best practices" in development finance; sadly, from all I can tell as of this writing, these BDN efforts seems rather moribund.[62] The Network, which currently has Japan and Australia as members, aims to encourage competitive bidding, sound environmental management, and transparency in infrastructure projects. It should add private sector development to that menu of objectives and make it a core part of network strategy. After all, infrastructure projects offer potentially great opportunities to local firms and workers—possibly in partnership with multinationals—to scale up and develop their capabilities. It would be a missed opportunity if private enterprise was not placed at the center of this global infrastructure thrust.

All this being said, there is one other policy that Washington should consider with respect to China's growing role in the developing world: cooperation. In the midst of the increasingly heated Beltway discussions over China, which raise the specter of a new Cold War, it should not be forgotten that developing countries require billions, if not trillions, of dollars of assistance in infrastructure alone. These demands may be even higher as we consider the transition to a "net zero" carbon future. The United States and China should strive to find areas of cooperation to meet these pressing needs.

Conclusions

What could be more ironic than a future in which Washington passes the global economy leadership baton to Beijing? And yet, that future is beginning to seem not so far-fetched. As recent polling suggests, Americans have become skeptical about the value of international trade to their economy, and we have already seen that both the Trump and Biden administrations have advanced more protectionist ideas and policies than their predecessors. Ironically, citizens of the developing world are more confident in the value of globalization than are Americans (or Europeans, for that matter).[63] That, alone, may be an important commonality that China shares with those countries that it seeks to influence: a convergent view of the benefits of trade and investment for economic well-being.

The irony, of course, is particularly deep when one thinks of the postwar trajectories of each country. Building upon its ideology, material position, and the lessons its leaders had learned from war and depression, the United States was able to ignite a new era of globalization from the ashes of World War II. Communist China, in contrast, strove for relative autarky (although it did, of course, receive substantial aid from the Soviet Union in the 1950s)— even at the cost of millions of lives that might have been saved had Mao adopted market dictates sooner.

Globalization, however, rested upon the implicit bargain that a rising tide would lift all boats. During the Cold War, it was politically essential to sustain that domestic bargain. After all, the capitalist system needed its workers to serve in the armed forces, and they would only be willing to do so if the system offered them in return the promise of social mobility through education and relatively meritocratic career structures.[64] While that system never completely fulfilled its pledge—particularly to African Americans, among other minority groups—somehow, its mythical power has been sufficient to allow it to survive for an extensive period of time.[65] Now, however, the global economy model of inclusive growth is under threat.

What does all this have to do with the American response to the China challenge? First, it suggests that Americans may simply be growing tired of assuming international burdens (which have included seemingly endless wars and their costs in terms of human life and suffering, and the misallocation of government financial resources away from productive uses). And when one gets tired, one can easily overlook the benefits of a given arrangement—such as those associated with being part of a rules-based multilateral order. The belief that these old arrangements no longer serve the American people, in turn, can fuel demands for economic nationalism, whether labeled as "America First" or, in Joe Biden's terminology, "Build Back Better."

Lest we believe that these more inward foreign economic policies belong only to the Republican Party, as championed by Donald Trump, that would be a mistake. Numerous leading Democrats—most notably Bernie Sanders, but also Joe Biden and Elizabeth Warren—have also criticized American trade policies as being anti-labor. As Senator Warren (D-MA) put it, "our trade policy in America has been broken for decades, and it has been broken because it works for giant multinational corporations and not for much of anyone else."[66] Sadly, one would be hard-pressed at the present time to find a politician on either side of the aisle who espouses the benefits of free trade, as Ronald Reagan once did.

Statements like Warren's make it difficult to believe that contemporary Washington will devote much political capital to foreign economic policy or, more specifically, to private sector development, even under the shadow of the so-called China threat. And while initiatives like the DFC should be applauded and strengthened, they will not make much of a mark unless they are part of a broader and coherent strategic vision—a grand strategic vision that incorporates trade, aid, and investment policy. Will the United States continue to "export capitalism" in the years ahead, learning from the past so that its policies can be even more effective in future? That is the big question that will inform the final chapter.

8

The Future of Private Sector Development

> I see the economic instincts of man . . . reaching out across artifi-
> cially created political and ideological boundaries to join in a
> common cause: the promotion of peaceful commerce and industry.
> This development has enormous potential for the welfare and well-
> being of all humanity. Once peoples and governments become in-
> extricably tied to one another by economic self-interest, the spectre
> of instability and war begins to recede.
>
> —SAMUEL PISAR, 1973[1]

THIS CONCLUDING CHAPTER is being written at a particularly fraught
moment for modern global capitalism. Far from the cosmopolitan vision
expressed by Samuel Pisar in the epigraph, many of today's global leaders
seem to be adopting some local variant of the "America First" nationalism
espoused by Donald Trump during his administration, and that is now continuing, and perhaps even expanding, under his successor. Even the economically "liberal"[2] president of France, Emmanuel Macron, was forced
to change his stripes during the COVID-19 pandemic, stating that "certain
drugs were no longer manufactured in France or even in Europe. . . . We
must draw lessons from that . . . and the state is ready to invest in such reshoring projects."[3]

Similarly, during his campaign for the presidency, Joe Biden stated
that "We've seen the importance of bringing home critical supply chains
so that we aren't dependent on other countries in future crises." His
promise to "build back better" focuses on restoring American manufacturing and innovation.[4] In fact, nowhere on the "build back better"
website can one find any mention of US foreign economic policy, much

less foreign assistance.[5] Upon becoming president, Biden proclaimed his interest in bringing supply chains back to the United States, in part by making more active use of "Buy American" provisions in federal legislation.

In the meantime, China is continuing to expand its global economic footprint. It is notable that, even during the heat of the pandemic, the Asian economies went ahead to negotiate a Regional Comprehensive Economic Partnership (RCEP), which includes Australia, China, India, Japan, New Zealand, and the Republic of Korea, in addition to the smaller economies in the Association of Southeast Asian Nations. Notably missing, of course, is the United States.[6] In December 2020, China also signed a new investment treaty with the European Union.[7]

What, then, is the future of private sector development as a vehicle for promoting economic growth in an era of rising economic nationalism? Readers might conclude that a less engaged Washington would make little difference to most developing countries, since one lesson from this book is that US efforts to promote private enterprise have had only mixed success. They might say that the research presented here gives proof of Louis Hartz's contention that America had exported "the wrong thing" in trying to bring democratic capitalism to the world. To Hartz, American exceptionalism was precisely that: a system that had arisen and evolved in a very particular environment, and not one that could take root just anywhere.[8]

This suggests an important task for our final chapter: to synthesize the lessons learned from the history recounted here for the current generation of development scholars and policy makers. For even beyond the geopolitics of the China challenge, there will be myriad reasons for the United States to support the process of international economic development, ranging from concerns with climate change and the environment; to the search for new market opportunities for American firms and entrepreneurs; to humanitarian impulses and a desire for conflict resolution in war-torn states. Each of these concerns is represented by a deep web of interest groups in Washington (and other industrial world capitals) that is likely to remain of sufficient political power to form a winning coalition on behalf of continued, if not expanded, development programming. In that context, what role should private enterprise be expected to play? Assuming that the world needs to mobilize private capital to meet an array of pressing needs, what actions should policy makers take, and which pitfalls must they avoid? These are among the key questions that I will now address.

Examining the Findings

I have covered a lot of ground throughout this book, both temporally and geographically. I confess that huge gaps in coverage still remain: An entire chapter could have been devoted to Sub-Saharan Africa, for example, where I have worked on issues related to private sector development for many years, and where China, of course, is extremely active economically.[9] But despite the rich history and diverse places covered, the devoted reader will recognize that certain themes have reappeared in each chapter. In what follows, I highlight several of the most prominent findings uncovered during the research process.

To recapitulate, this book has been framed around some core ideas of American officials regarding private sector development that have seemingly transcended time and space.[10] They were present during the Cold War and, for the most part, have endured to the present day. This reflects their resonance with the nation's ideology and historical experience.

The first core idea is that the roots of economic growth are found within countries themselves and thus only "self-help" makes development possible. The second is that private enterprise in general and foreign investment in particular could, and should, serve as the main drivers of growth—though I recognize that there may be increasing hostility to this idea within the United States and around the world. The third and related idea is that nations need to develop suitable "investment climates" that provide the fertile soil in which businesses can grow.

While these ideas have shaped American policy, public officials were not, for the most part, strident ideologues. They made their peace with state-owned enterprises when it was expedient to do so, and eventually they came to recognize the necessity for a permanent foreign aid program, given the shortfalls in private investment and its failure to provide many of the public goods that developing countries required. Nonetheless, Washington's desire to promote private enterprise is an enduring feature of its approach to foreign assistance, as made manifest in recent years by the creation of the Development Finance Corporation (DFC).

So how have these ideas performed in practice?

First, despite the availability of various subsidies, US-based multinationals have proved hesitant to invest in the developing world. In fact, as a recent study by the Bureau of Economic Analysis (based on 2018 data) summarizes, the activities of these firms remain heavily concentrated in the United States. By almost any measure of corporate performance—whether it be in terms of revenue, net income, research spending, or employment—the contribution of the world's poorest countries is relatively small. Only about 20 percent of overall value added is generated overseas, and about 60 percent of that comes from Canada and Western Europe; in contrast, Latin America generates 11 percent and Sub-Saharan Africa only 1 percent.[11] This hardly makes a compelling case that the US government has been overwhelmingly effective in pushing its firms to invest beyond the industrial world or, conversely, that American capitalism has "needed" the developing world in order to survive.

But it does not follow that these investments have been unimportant to recipient firms and nations. As seen from the other end of the telescope, foreign direct investment (FDI) has been a significant input for the economies of many developing regions. In Central and Eastern Europe, for example, FDI inflows (much of which comes from EU-based firms) comprise nearly 5 percent of GDP. Again, foreign investment is probably of greater significance to recipient nations in the developing world and transition economies than it is to the home country. From a macroeconomic standpoint that is not surprising, given the shortage of savings and thus investment capital in poorer nations.

And in those cases where multinationals have ventured into the developing world, they often succeeded in generating a deep set of linkages with *local* firms (with important caveats, some of which are highlighted below), promoting employment and income growth. In that sense, the intuition of American policy makers that FDI could serve to promote economic development finds support in the relevant academic literature.[12] Despite those who decry FDI as an instrument of a metropole or imperial power bent on creating "third world" dependencies, multinational investments have probably meant more to recipient economies than to that of the United States. Foreign firms have provided technology and organizational know-how to local suppliers, increasing their productivity and output.[13]

In recent years, this topic of linkages has commanded increasing attention from economists. As Havranek and Irsova noted in their meta-analysis of the linkages literature, "Few topics in international economics have been examined as extensively as productivity spillovers from foreign affiliates to domestic firms."[14] Taking into account the various biases in the literature (economics journals, for example, tend to publish more studies that report statistically significant findings than those that don't), these two scholars conclude that foreign firms make a robust contribution to the performance of their local suppliers. In particular, "Greater spillovers seem to be received by countries that are open to international trade."[15]

This is because firms in open economies tend to learn from their experiences working with a wider range of foreign firms, enabling them to extract the most value from their linkages. When firms are exposed to trade, they receive constant feedback about how they are faring compared to potential competitors, driving them to become even more productive.[16] This may be one reason why those Latin American countries that adopted relatively protectionist economic policies may have enjoyed fewer benefits from FDI than they might otherwise have expected.[17]

We have seen in earlier chapters that factors beyond openness also seem to have an impact on the extent of linkages between foreign and domestic firms. The quality and abundance of human capital, for example, has been found to be important, which of course makes intuitive sense. The more capable that local managers and engineers are, the more likely it is they can benefit from foreign investment. That fact also has implications for foreign assistance programming, as discussed later in the chapter.

The data on productivity spillovers thus lends qualified support to one of Washington's fundamental beliefs: that FDI has contributed to local private sector development. This suggests that multinational firms, in promoting their own interests, may also promote local economic development by contributing to domestic firms' productivity—a neat example of Adam Smith's invisible hand at work. Again, this is a broad generalization, and we will examine below some of the structural factors that may be influential as well.

Structural Barriers to Private Sector Development

Identifying the underlying structural factors that shape a nation's political economy is a crucial exercise because they will suggest the constraints surrounding a given policy effort. An obvious place to start such a structural analysis is with the famous (or infamous) "natural resource curse," especially since so many developing world economies are commodity exporters. Academic research has long observed that resource-rich economies often tend to underperform in terms of economic growth. This happens for a host of political and economic reasons that have been carefully described and analyzed in the relevant literature.[18]

For our purposes, one channel is that investment in commodity-dependent economies is focused on resource extraction, with relatively few spillover effects or linkages to the broader economy. As a consequence, economic elites, who are often political insiders, gravitate to the spigot rather than to other sectors of activity. Writing many years ago, Albert Hirschman warned that foreign investment in natural resources could lead to the destruction "of local industry," the depletion of "soil and subsoil," and the corruption of "local elites."[19]

Findings from a recent study by the United Nations Conference on Trade and Development (UNCTAD) on the relationship between commodity dependence and per capita incomes are suggestive of the so-called resource curse, or the failure of resource-dependent economies to enjoy sustainable growth. The study shows that most commodity-dependent developing countries are below the median of income for all countries in that grouping; the few commodity-dependent countries that are wealthy include a handful of oil-exporting states like Saudi Arabia and members of the Organisation for Economic Co-operation and Development (OECD) like Australia and New Zealand. Among developing countries, Brazil and Argentina are among a small number that are commodity-dependent and above the median of income. Further research might examine the extent to which economic-diversification strategies in those countries have contributed to national income growth (much of the work to date has emphasized the growth of income inequality in Latin America, as opposed to absolute income growth). Still, both of those countries have experienced tremendous economic volatility over the years, due in part to their continuing reliance on commodity exports. That volatility, in turn, can undermine the incentive to make long-term investments.[20]

UNCTAD further emphasizes that many of these commodity-dependent economies have attracted relatively high levels of FDI over the years. But has this FDI promoted local entrepreneurship in resource-rich economies? What are the linkage effects?

Sadly, the evidence—such as it is—does not demonstrate the existence of strong ties between the extractives sector and local industry. While the limited data admittedly do not make a "slam-dunk" case, the relationship between mineral rents and new business registration is striking. In Figure 8.1 I compare new business registration in Latin America and the Caribbean and East and Central Europe. As we can see, the former has relatively low business registration compared to the latter. This association is again suggestive of the "resource curse" that seemingly plagues many commodity-dependent economies, at least in terms of business development.

But even here, caveats are warranted. In research I undertook with Rene Kim in Ghana, for example, we found that the Newmont Mining Corporation, working in cooperation with the International Finance Corporation (IFC), had developed an impressive program of local sourcing. Similarly, in Uganda, the South African Brewing Company has made intensive use of local farmers by using ingredients grown in that country rather than relying on imports.[21] As Hirschman also stated many years ago, commodity dependence need not lead to underdevelopment if investments are made that promote linkages, raise productivity, and bring products to market.

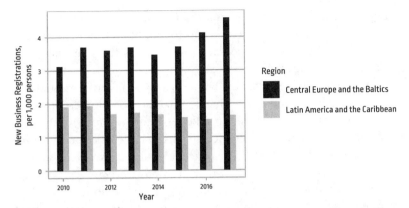

Data source: World Bank, "World Development Indicators," https://datacatalog.worldbank.org/dataset/world
-development-indicators.

FIGURE 8.1   New Business Registrations in Central Europe and the Balkans and Latin America and the Caribbean (per 1,000 Persons Ages 15–64), 2010–2017

Investments in food processing, for example, create such linkages in agricultural economies. Sadly, it must be emphasized that "tariff escalation" in the industrial world, by which higher tariffs are placed on more refined products—such as juice vs. fruits—has served to discourage such investments.[22] The overall lesson, however, is that policy makers who wish to promote foreign investment in resource-rich economies need to think long and hard about how best to promote linkages with the local economy.

Before leaving the commodity exporters, one additional point should be made. Should fossil fuels become "distressed assets" in light of global climate policies that subsidize a shift to renewable resources, oil-dependent countries will have little choice but to diversify their economies. That could be a blessing in disguise for many of them, fueling (literally!) a renewed interest in private sector development on the part of governments. Should that prove to be the case, the international community must be prepared to provide the technical assistance needed to help oil exporters make this energy transition—but that also means that the leading industrial states will need to keep their markets open to the new products that the firms in these countries may develop. This reminds us of the crucial importance of policy coherence—of bringing trade, aid, and investment together in a mutually supportive package—when it comes to promoting private sector development.

Yet another structural condition I have highlighted in this book is violent conflict. In fragile and conflict-affected states, the challenges of private sector development are perhaps greater than anywhere else. As an evaluation of such programming in these settings found, "fewer than 50 percent [of private sector development programs] were successful in reaching and exceeding planned outcomes and impact . . . in job creation or investment generation. " Notably, "Successful PSD projects . . . involved training of entrepreneurs for livelihood development, rehabilitation of micro or small businesses, and improving access to markets." Efforts to improve the "investment climate" and access to finance, in contrast, were deemed effective in only 30 percent of the cases.[23] This particular study also found no evidence of a capitalist peace—the idea that promoting private sector development contributed to peace and stability in recipient nations.

Violent conflict discourages investment for many reasons, not the least of which is the insecurity of property rights. Fragile states also tend to depend relatively heavily on mineral rents for their economic activity, so in these places the natural resources curse is multiplied. Even in such cases, however, caution is warranted when it comes to sweeping generalizations. In most conflict-affected countries, the violence tends to be concentrated in a relatively few provinces or even districts, making it possible for development to proceed in more peaceful regions.[24]

For policy makers, this leads to the argument that private enterprise is most effectively encouraged in those places that are more secure. In short, the governance environment, even at the local level, must be supportive of private enterprise and its role in the economy. If local leaders act more like crime bosses, extorting whatever the private sector earns, then it is unlikely that business creation can succeed. On the other hand, regions that incentivize entrepreneurship and private activity may create a "demonstration effect" for more insecure parts of the country, particularly if these private investments help fuel local economic growth and opportunity. Still, as we have seen tragically in Afghanistan, it was not enough for some regions to make economic progress (e.g., the northern province of Balkh) to prevent the Taliban's ultimate victory over the entire country.

A further structural condition that may influence private sector development is the extent to which a country is aid dependent; one prominent concern that critics of foreign aid have expressed over the years is that foreign aid can undermine growth by "crowding out" local industry.[25] If foreign aid provides officials with large rents, why should they bother to promote private enterprise? While we cannot do justice to these debates in full here, the question is worth deep consideration by the policy community.

Unfortunately, the available econometric studies that explore the relationship between aid and the competitiveness of local industries does not, in general, provide support for complementarity. Rajan and Subramanian, for example, find that aid inflows lead to exchange rate appreciation, which makes export-oriented firms less competitive. They assert that this may be an important pathway through which aid reduces the growth of recipient economies.[26] Parenthetically, the United States has also encouraged over-valued exchange rates in conflict-affected settings in order to reduce the prices of imports; this lessens the effects of the conflict on consumers but may have important negative ramifications on growth in the long run.[27]

Beyond this exchange-rate issue, aid can contribute to a number of other problems in recipient countries. In fragile states, for example, aid represents another resource worth fighting over; pouring billions into a violent setting may literally be akin to pouring fuel on the fire.[28] Aid can also favor cronyism when contracts are given to "insiders." This may in turn exacerbate local conflict, which often occurs because of these very distinctions between insiders and outsiders.

At the same time, we have seen several cases in this book where foreign aid contributed positively to private sector development. From Taiwan to Central and Eastern Europe, donors created programs that provided powerful incentives for local elites to invest in industry, further helped in some places by the forging of linkages with foreign direct investors. These programs were also relatively successful because the United States, among other industrial nations, advanced complimentary policies with respect to trade.

One structural factor I have not emphasized in this book is whether democratic or authoritarian countries are more likely to provide hospitable climates to private sector development in general and FDI in particular. This has been the topic of much debate in the scholarly literature, and it is indeed ongoing.[29] Are property rights more secure in democracies than under authoritarian regimes? Do foreign investors prefer authoritarian regimes because they tend to suppress labor? These are among the questions that researchers continue to raise.

For their part, American officials have also debated this topic over the years. During the Eisenhower administration, for example, Secretary of the Treasury Humphrey expressed the view that authoritarian regimes provided investors with more stability, while the president thought that the United States should promote democratization, at least over the long run. In any event, I found no evidence that the question of whether a regime was democratic or authoritarian was decisive in terms of American policy regarding whether or not to promote private enterprise. Many Latin American countries during the period we have covered, for example, were led by military regimes (in some cases installed with the help of the CIA), and FDI flowed to these countries, with US encouragement. We have also seen that in authoritarian regimes like Taiwan and South Korea, the United States insisted on private sector development as part of foreign aid packages, despite recalcitrance on the part of local governments. The lesson for policy makers is that the interests and capabilities of the regime seem to matter more than its type. Relatedly, there is relatively little evidence to support the view that private sector development will necessarily lead to democratization, as the case of China makes painfully clear.

Perhaps the key determinant of private sector development is the nature of domestic economic elites. Where elites are economically diversified, as in much of East Asia, with interests in different sectors of the economy, private sector development is more likely to appear as an attractive policy option. Indeed, the data reported in the Introduction to this book show that, among all regions of the developing world, East Asia has the highest level of credit to the private sector, and it is also where FDI seems to have contributed most strongly to that result; further, it has relatively low mineral rents compared to other regions. Of course, East Asia is now known as a major site of manufacturing activity and the heart of global supply chains, the result of linkages formed with multinational corporations. In short, the interaction of economic structure and elite preferences is decisive for private sector development.

These lessons lead us to another important question: How can foreign aid agencies and development finance institutions most effectively encourage domestic enterprise? What programs "work" and which fail? We address these issues in the following section.

Programming for Private Sector Development

As noted in the Introduction, private sector development is now a big business in its own right, with annual commitments by the major development finance institutions of some $90 billion dedicated to this type of programming. Unfortunately, there is a paucity of solid evaluations of the related private sector development projects, limiting our confidence in the robustness of any takeaways that we may wish to put forward. Rigorous evaluations (e.g., based on randomized controlled trials) are costly and time consuming, and must be built into projects from the start in order to establish the appropriate baseline against which the "treatment" (i.e., the effects of a private sector development program on a population) can be measured. Since there are few high-powered incentives within the development community to invest in such evaluations (after all, who wants to be evaluated?), few of them are carried out.

As a general matter, aid agencies have adopted either "macro" or "micro" approaches to private sector development (or some combination of the two). Macro approaches focus on improving "the investment climate" (e.g., interventions which make it easier for businesses to start-up and operate) while micro approaches target firms either directly, through such interventions as capital injections from dedicated venture capital funds (or, as we saw in Eastern Europe, "enterprise" funds), or indirectly, through support to local financial institutions. Macro interventions rely on the assumption that government will act to maximize social welfare—an idea surprisingly resilient in the development community, in light of the decades of kleptocratic governance that those in the field have consistently observed. In any case, a recent report to the Swedish International Development Agency finds that "there is good evidence to suggest that a better investment climate results in higher levels of private investment. However, identifying which of the many factors that make up the investment climate should be prioritized is not straightforward."[30]

Even if it were possible to identify these factors correctly, the underlying political economy of investment climate interventions might be problematic. If there are barriers to business, they may be present because they are of benefit to someone or some group. While economists, for example, often think of property rights as a public good, in many countries they may be considered a private good, of tremendous value for the kleptocratic governments in charge, which can dole them out for a fee. Similarly, access to finance may be a private good whose value can be allocated through authoritative rather than market measures.[31] In short, kleptocrats may use their control over security and financial markets to allocate property rights and scarce capital to friends and insiders, making it impossible for outsiders to launch or grow businesses.

A few examples illustrate the problem at hand. The US Department of State has written of Azerbaijan that "government bureaucracy, weak legal institutions and predatory behavior by politically connected monopoly interests continue to hinder investment."[32] Similarly, in Rwanda—often considered a darling of the development agencies due to its impressive economic rebound from decades of brutal conflict—a report finds that "a small inner circle of . . . leaders takes the important decisions . . . [and] a clientilistic network referred to as the *akazu* accumulates wealth and privileges."[33] In such settings, entrepreneurship by "outsiders"—anyone outside the established circle of power—may represent an unwanted challenge, not a welcome opportunity.

Can these problems be avoided or mitigated if donors take the micro approach, funneling capital straight to firms or working to develop local financial institutions? One issue must be highlighted from the outset: what economists call the "fallacy of composition." Many micro interventions, as successful as each might be individually, do not necessarily add up to systemic change in the business climate; imagine a pointillist painting where each dot is perfectly composed, yet the canvas as a whole fails to convey a larger meaning or emotion. As a study on private sector development from the World Bank's Independent Evaluation Group (IEG) put it, "interventions may individually be successful, but they do not automatically foster synergies or an integrated system."[34] In this context, think of US development interventions in Afghanistan, many of which were effective at a tactical level (e.g., the expansion of schooling to girls) but that failed from a strategic perspective (e.g., preventing the country's takeover by the Taliban).

Many World Bank programs, and foreign assistance programs more generally, use a micro approach to target the small and medium-sized enterprises sector in recipient nations. Such programs include equity and investment funds; increasing access to finance through programs for local banks and financial institutions (often through some combination of technical assistance and capital injections); and removing obstacles to business development, either by supporting new infrastructure (e.g., power and roads) or identifying local practices that make it difficult to start a new firm, such as cumbersome regulations. Again in these cases, the IEG has identified the domestic political economy as a fundamental barrier that donors need to address. If governments feel threatened by such programs, or seek to capture them, then their spillover effects to the local economy are likely to be small.

Having said that, there have been notable successes in private sector development programming, particularly with respect to technical assistance and advice provided to firms and governments. The IFC's legal advice to China on how to open its economy to foreign investment, provided through its Foreign Investment Advisory Service, provides a powerful case in point regarding the kind of support the development community can offer to a willing governmental client (the fact that contemporary China may be turning its back on that history does not negate its economic impact).[35] On a micro or firm level, Nicholas Bloom and colleagues have powerfully shown that modern management techniques are a "technology" that greatly boosts firm productivity in developing countries; technical assistance that makes available this technology should therefore be high on the private sector development agenda.[36] Technical assistance generally does not get the blood racing, but it does seem to be one of the more effective interventions, especially when it complements other interventions, such as access to finance.

In that regard, technical assistance provided directly to firms has been shown to make their operations more productive—and it should be emphasized that such technical assistance need not be provided by development agencies; multinational firms may also provide technical assistance to their suppliers in order to improve productivity and output quality. Indeed, Bloom and colleagues find that linkages with multinationals contribute to generating these benefits for local firms.[37] This approach to private sector development goes back to the Marshall Plan, when the United States created its Technical Assistance and Productivity Program. As we saw in Chapter 1, President Harry Truman's Point Four program was also grounded on the promise of technical assistance. James Silberman, one of the American officials who designed the Marshall Plan program, wrote, "At the core of the productivity assistance program, 1500 productivity study tours brought about 24,000 Europeans and several thousand Japanese, Koreans and Taiwan Chinese to the United States, where they observed at first hand the multiple requirements for a competitive industry: new concepts of marketing, business organization, and organization of the work place; new products, designs, and engineering functions; and new equipment."[38]

Silberman insists upon a crucial difference between these postwar programs of productivity assistance and those rolled out during, for example, the post-Soviet transition. The former brought managers and workers to the United States to observe manufacturing processes and facilities—as opposed to sending management consultants, who often had little knowledge of the industries or regions to which they were assigned, to recipient countries.

On one level, these technical assistance programs were generous, in that their avowed objective was to raise foreign productivity levels to those found in the United States. And subsequent analyses have found them to be successful in achieving that objective. In one remarkable study, Giorcelli finds that Italian enterprises that sent employees to the United States as part of the program showed enduring increases in productivity.[39]

Yet on another level these programs were also reflections of the Cold War. Following World War II, officials in Europe and Asia were fearful of the growing flirtation between the working class in their countries and local communist parties. They were concerned that capitalists would reap all the benefits of reconstruction without adequately sharing the gains with their workers, creating a source of grievance that the communists would readily exploit. The productivity programs were thus designed to include managers and employees who would jointly decide upon which measures to take in the interest of improving manufacturing operations; it was, in essence, a model of a corporatist approach to business.[40]

At a time of rising income inequality around the world, with corporate executives earning many multiples of what their workers bring home, this history is worthy of deep reflection. For one thing, it points to the pervasive importance of the Cold War as a structural condition that shaped not just geopolitics but domestic socioeconomic arrangements as well. How one recaptures a more equitable political economy in the absence of an existential threat (and it is unlikely that China will simply replace the Soviet Union in that role, given its much higher degree of interdependence with the industrial world) is a question that scholars, activists, and at least some policy makers are grappling with. Perhaps the history of technical assistance programs yields some useful lessons for addressing these issues.

The Future of Private Sector Development

I now turn to some concluding thoughts on the future of private sector development. For despite assertions by scholars such as Branko Milanović that capitalism has won a "global victory," we have reasons to be circumspect along these lines, at least for those among us who continue to believe in the virtues of the free enterprise system, as compared to more authoritarian alternatives.[41] As Henry Kaufman wrote in 2020 in sharp contrast to Milanović, "American capitalism is rapidly disappearing."

One source of concern for those who care about the future of private enterprise is the rising share of government spending as a share of GDP in the member states of the OECD, which was already a significant long-run trend *prior* to the outbreak of COVID-19. Governments now command upwards of 50 percent of GDP in some countries, and with the economic fallout of the pandemic, including the introduction of large-scale stimulus packages, these numbers are exploding.[42] While there are undoubtedly sound reasons for this trend, including voter preferences for public goods (including medical treatments and vaccines), it signals an era of increasing state control over the economy.

In fact, recent economics research reminds us "that government spending produces important crowding-out effects, by negatively affecting both private consumption and investment," even in those high-spending countries or regions where private entrepreneurship remains at high levels (e.g., Scandinavia).[43] No less worrying, there are signs that the private enterprise that remains in the industrial world is becoming increasingly monopolistic, choking off the growth of smaller firms—just think of the so-called FAANG companies (Facebook, Amazon, Apple, Netflix, and Alphabet (formerly Google) in that regard.[44] In short, the future of private enterprise may face its gravest threat in the very countries that once worked to espouse and promote it.

If the spirit of global private enterprise diminishes within the industrial countries as big and nationalistic governments, coupled with monopolistic firms, dominate the economy, it will inevitably spill over into their foreign economic policies. During his tenure as head of the DFC, Adam Boehler stated that one of the most important elements of US foreign policy is "ensuring competitive private markets that are transparent [and] follow rule of law."[45] But what happens to those noble objectives when they are no longer prioritized at home?

Further, the evidence suggests that global trade—a leading indicator of economic globalization—may have reached its plateau. While the reasons for this stalling of trade are unclear—it could, for example, simply be a hangover effect from the Great Recession of 2008–2010—it could also reflect changing demographics. As the world's population ages, there will be more demand for medical services and other nontradable goods (notwithstanding the fact that many countries rely on immigrants to staff their medical facilities) and less demand for manufactures.[46]

Accompanying these trends is a policy shift toward deglobalization, as expressed recently in the United States among other nations as a concern with supply chain vulnerabilities. In signing a new executive order in February 2021 to address these vulnerabilities, President Joe Biden said, "We shouldn't have to rely on a foreign country—especially one that doesn't share our interests or our values—in order to protect and provide our people during a national emergency."[47] While the global economic consequences of this policy of "reshoring" remain to be seen—after all, the costs of bringing back manufacturing to a country which no longer has a comparative advantage in such production could be astronomical—it does not bode well for spreading the doctrine of free enterprise.

Despite the doom and gloom suggested by these opening paragraphs, however, there are many reasons to remain optimistic that the process of market-oriented globalization will continue to advance. There is also reason to believe that it will continue to encourage the emergence of new firms, which will respond to changing business and consumer demands, many of which we don't even yet recognize.

First, the state capitalist model that China offers, with its hazy distinction between the government and private sector, is inherently problematic. There is a reason why the public and private sectors splintered into relatively distinctive spheres over time across most of the capitalist world: because models of state capitalism tended to fail in delivering either wealth or security. Instead, sovereigns became entrapped in the costly ventures of capitalists, while elsewhere capitalists became entrapped in the costly ventures of rulers.[48]

The Chinese, in fact, may be discovering this currently along the Belt and Road as they are faced with the task of renegotiating the unsustainable loans they arranged with recipient nations.[49] At home, the Chinese Communist Party is also trying to figure out the balance between state power and private enterprise, as suggested by its recent efforts to rein in its most successful entrepreneurs.[50] Just as the West has grown more fearful than ever of the China model, it may be reaching the apex of its power, as occurred with the Japan "threat" of the 1980s that ebbed soon thereafter.

Second, and related, science and technology remain global undertakings, as the coronavirus crisis has made clear. Through its Operation Warp Speed, for example, the Trump administration provided up to $2.1 billion in COVID-19 vaccine funding to the French pharmaceutical firm Sanofi and the Swedish-British firm AstraZeneca, which in turn worked in collaboration with the University of Oxford in England.[51] The fact that these two companies are among the world's largest vaccine manufacturers means that the United States—no matter President Trump's espoused policy of "America First"—could not afford to go it alone.

Further, the US share of global R&D spending has been falling over time, suggesting that it will become increasingly dependent on sourcing foreign technology in the years ahead. According to the Congressional Research Service, the United States was responsible for 70 percent of global R&D spending in 1960; by 2018 that percentage had fallen to less than 30 percent.[52] Turning inward to a state of scientific autarky would doom the United States to second-class economic status.

Third, capital flows continue to go global, even to the world's poorest countries. Indeed, a recent study by the Center for Global Development concludes that "external private capital is an important and growing source of finance" for low-income countries.[53] While the COVID-19 crisis undoubtedly took "risk off" from emerging markets, with significant capital inflows rerouted to "safe-haven" instruments like US Treasury Bonds, the overall post-2010 data suggest that in periods of low returns in the industrial world, investors will seek more aggressive opportunities elsewhere. And from a political economy perspective, it may be assumed that these investors will use part of their earnings to lobby for policies that are favorable to global capital flows.

Related, these developing world markets could become leading centers of growth in their own right, due in part to the fact that they are among the few places left with growing populations. Hard as it may be to believe, both incomes and living conditions have greatly improved for millions of people in the developing world over the past generation, thanks in part to the positive effects of globalization. (China is of course the poster child for this phenomenon, but India should also not be overlooked.) In fact, polling data from the Pew Research Center suggests that, overall, people in the developing world have a more positive view of globalization than do those in the industrial world.[54] Further, as the international community promotes the Sustainable Development Goals aimed at such objectives as reducing poverty and promoting universal education, and as it moves toward a "carbon neutral" future, the private sector will need to play a prominent role given its capacity for innovation.

Even in Sub-Saharan Africa, which has often been the subject of much economic despair, there are reasons for optimism. In a recent paper, for example, Henn and Robinson highlight Africa's entrepreneurial culture, something that those who seek to implement private sector development programs should leverage to the extent possible.[55] Indeed, as I wrote many years ago, Africa may surprise its economic naysayers and lead the world's next capitalist revolution.[56] The world's poorest countries still have a long road before they attain economic or income "convergence" with the (post)industrial economies, but for many, the road ahead is more promising than it has ever been. It would be tragic if the global door gets shut at this crucial time in development history.

Along these lines, the role of the multinational enterprise as a "development agency" should again be highlighted. For a combination of economic and political reasons, multinational firms often help grow the economies where they are embedded, by promoting linkages and creating local supply chains. The recent attempts by the Biden administration to encourage more FDI in Central America exemplify a continuing belief in this theory of change.

As we saw earlier in the chapter, research continues to explore these linkages and the conditions under which they are most effective. That body of work should be more closely integrated with foreign assistance programming to ensure that there are synergies between the two. Aid agencies, for example, might consider targeting their capital-deepening programs in areas where multinational firms are trying to develop linkages with local firms, which would help these firms get the resources they need to become attractive suppliers.

What, then, should public officials keep in mind as they confront future development challenges? One place to start would be by reconsidering, and perhaps amending, the doctrines that Robert Packenham long ago summarized as fundamental American beliefs about the process of economic growth, based on his work with the foreign aid community (though it should be emphasized that other distinguished scholars have disputed the accuracy of Packenham's list as a reflection of policy beliefs; nonetheless, it's probably fair to say that policy makers have sometimes made it sound *as if* they believed these things).[57] They are as follows:

1. Change and Development Are Easy
2. All Good Things Go Together
3. Radicalism and Revolution Are Bad
4. Distributing Power Is More Important than Accumulating Power[58]

If indeed public officials ever asserted Packenham's first point, they have long since recognized that change and development are *not* easy, often requiring major shifts in the political economy of recipient governments. Some of these shifts may be motivated by foreign economic policy and the provision of appropriate economic carrots, but that requires uncovering the incentive system of local elites and what might motivate them to adopt certain reforms. After all, economic reforms often come at the price of distributing political power—a principle that elites in foreign nations may fundamentally oppose, and that strikes at the heart of Packenham's fourth point about US policy.

How to promote reform and the related distribution of power are among the hardest nuts to crack in political economy. Previously I have argued that these problems may be particularly acute in those countries whose economies rely heavily upon natural resources and in conflict-affected states (where the conflict may be about the very distribution of political power!). In contrast, when economies are more diversified, it is easier to move elite interests toward new sectors of activity with the appropriate package of incentives. Foreign aid programming must be reflective of the differing structural conditions and elite preferences it confronts and adapt accordingly.

Even under the best of circumstances in recipient nations, the United States has often been unable to bring all "good things together" when it comes to foreign economic policy, owing to internal incoherence. But it makes little sense to promote private sector development on the one hand, for example, while discouraging the exports of the very firms that Washington has supported (directly or indirectly) on the other. Recent US trade policies are particularly worrisome in that regard, as they signal to foreign investors that the country is becoming less and less open for business.

Policy coherence is undoubtedly a big ask for any government of a liberal polity with myriad interest groups, but one place to begin is by becoming more transparent about the package of policies that would likely be needed in order for a particular intervention abroad to be most effective. Congress, for example, could mandate that the US assistance agencies undertake such reviews as they formulate their private sector development programs (although it's admittedly hard to imagine that individual representatives would have much incentive to call for such a policy, given that they are the source of at least some of the incoherence!). The various bilateral and multilateral development agencies, along with the relevant think tanks, could also do more to cast a spotlight on the hypocrisy and the contradictions often found in foreign assistance policy.

To the extent that the United States and the world's various development agencies continue to promote private enterprise, they should take a more experimental approach to programming. This means using randomized control trials or quasi-experimental methods to assess the effectiveness of a given treatment, along with ongoing monitoring and evaluation (M&E) of programs that are actually fielded. That type of analytic approach should, in fact, be baked into any "theory of change" that a development agency is proffering. While experiments and M&E are costly endeavors, wasting money on ineffective projects is even harder on taxpayers and, of course, on would-be recipients. Field experiments in private sector development have found, for example, that combining credit programs with management training makes both interventions more effective than either one would be on its own.[59]

At the same time, policy makers need to be aware of the "fallacy of composition." As effective as many single projects might be, they may not add up to systemic change; a private sector initiative that works, say, in different parts of Iraq might not lead to fundamental changes in economic policy in Baghdad. Further, the replicability (or "external validity") of a project must be considered: what works in place A may not do so in place B. This means that modesty about expectations for a given intervention are generally appropriate.

These comments, however, should not detract from America's historical project of exporting capitalism across the developing world. Although Washington's efforts to promote private enterprise have not always been successful, the move toward more market-oriented economies has improved the lives of millions of people. As economist Martin Ravaillon has recently concluded, the opening up of national economies to trade and foreign investment is among the policies that has led to "massive absolute poverty reduction."[60]

That point must be kept at the forefront as we continue to debate the effects of globalization, for good and for ill, within the United States and the industrial world. But as we continue that debate and make needed policy adjustments, we must not overlook the fate of the developing world. Recalling America's commitment to international development through trade and private enterprise is of invaluable importance at a time when it may be imperiled.

Notes

Index

Notes

Preface

Epigraph: Cited in C. Fred Bergsten, Thomas Horst, and Theodore Moran, *American Multinationals and American Interests* (Washington, DC: Brookings Institution, 1978), 310.

1. For an overview of some of these projects, see Ethan B. Kapstein and Rene Kim, "Sourcing Locally for Impact," *Stanford Social Innovation Review* (Fall 2011): 48–53.

Introduction

1. Dwight D. Eisenhower, "Special Message to Congress on Foreign Economic Policy," 6 January 1955, in *Public Papers of the Presidents of the United States: Dwight D. Eisenhower, 1955*, 32–39, at 36, https://quod.lib.umich.edu/p /ppotpus/4728407.1955.001/78?page=root;rgn=full+text;size=100;view =image;q1=foreign+economic+policy.

2. Full name: the Better Utilization of Investments Leading to Development Act.

3. Congressional Research Service, *BUILD Act: Frequently Asked Questions about the New U.S. International Development Finance Corporation*, 15 January 2019, 3, https://fas.org/sgp/crs/misc/R45461.pdf.

4. "Remarks by Vice President Pence on the Administration's Policy toward China," 4 October 2018, https://www.whitehouse.gov/briefings-statements /remarks-vice-president-pence-administrations-policy-toward-china/.

5. "OPIC CEO Washburne Statement as President Signs BUILD Act into Law," 5 October 2018, https://www.opic.gov/press-releases/2018/opic-president-and -ceo-washburne-statement-president-signs-build-act-law.

6. Mark Green, Statement on the Creation of the U.S. International Development Finance Corporation, 3 October 2018, https://www.usaid.gov/news-information /press-releases/oct-3-2018-administrator-green-statement-creation-usidfc. USAID is the United States Agency for International Development.

7. Bob Corker, "Corker, Coons BUILD Act to Modernize U.S. Development Finance Passes Committee," 26 June 2018, https://www.coons.senate.gov/news room/press-releases/corker-coons-build-act-to-modernize-us-development -finance-passes-committee.

8. Myron Brilliant, letter to Sen. Bob Corker and Sen. Bob Menendez, 8 May 2018, https://www.uschamber.com/sites/default/files/180508_s2463_build_corker _menendez.pdf.

9. David Baldwin, *Economic Development and American Foreign Policy: 1943– 1962* (Chicago: University of Chicago Press, 1966); Raymond Mikesell, *Promoting United States Private Investment Abroad* (Washington, DC: National Planning Association, 1957).

10. Dwight D. Eisenhower, "Foreign Economic Policy," Message to Congress, 10 January 1955, in *Public Papers of the Presidents: Dwight D. Eisenhower, 1955,* 32, https://quod.lib.umich.edu/p/ppotpus/4728407.1955.001/74?rgn =full+text;view=image;q1=foreign+economic+policy.

11. Theodore Moran, Edward Graham, and Magnus Blomstrom, eds., *Does Foreign Direct Investment Promote Development?* (Washington, DC: Institute for International Economics, 2005).

12. On the policy relevance of modernization theory, see David Ekbladh, *The Great American Mission: Modernization and the Construction of an American World Order* (Princeton, NJ: Princeton University Press, 2011); Nils Gilman, *Mandarins of the Future: Modernization Theory in Cold War America* (Baltimore, MD: Johns Hopkins University Press, 2003).

13. Richard N. Cooper, "Economic Aspects of the Cold War, 1962–1975," in *Cambridge History of the Cold War,* ed. Melvyn Leffler and Odd Arne Westad (New York: Cambridge University Press, 2010), 44. See also Robert Pollard, *Economic Security and the Origins of the Cold War, 1945–1950* (New York: Columbia University Press, 1985).

14. Baldwin, *Economic Development and American Foreign Policy,* 19.

15. Robert Gilpin, *US Power and the Multinational Corporation: The Political Economy of Foreign Direct Investment* (New York: Basic Books, 1975).

16. Raymond Mikesell, *Promoting United States Private Investment Abroad* (Washington, DC: National Planning Association, 1957).

17. Gilpin, *US Power and the Multinational Corporation,* 139.

18. See, for example, Stephan Haggard, *Developmental States* (New York: Cambridge University Press, 2018); Stephan Haggard, *Pathways from the Periphery: The Politics of Growth in the Newly Industrializing States* (Ithaca, NY: Cornell University Press, 1990); and James Lee, who emphasizes the importance of the Cold War in US development policy in "US Grand Strategy and the Origins of the Developmental State," *Journal of Strategic Studies* 43, no. 5 (2019): 737–761, https://www.tandfonline.com/doi/full/10.1080/01402390 .2019.1579713. On economic divergence, see Lant Pritchett, "Divergence, Big Time," *Journal of Economic Perspectives* 11, no. 3 (1997): 3–17.

19. Ruth Gold, "Position Paper on General Assembly Resolution to Establish Grant Fund for Economic Development," 2 May 1952, in U.S. Department of State, *Foreign Relations of the United States, 1952–1954*, Vol. I, p. 232.

20. Stephen G. Rabe, *Eisenhower and Latin America: The Foreign Policy of Anti-Communism* (Chapel Hill: University of North Carolina Press, 1988).

21. Daniel Runde and Aaron Milner, *Development Finance Institutions: Plateaued Growth, Increasing Needs* (Washington, DC: Center for Strategic and International Studies, February 2019).

22. The definition of credit to the private sector may be found at "Domestic Credit to Private Sector By Banks (% Of GDP)," World Bank, https://datacatalog .worldbank.org/domestic-credit-private-sector-banks-gdp#:~:text=Domestic %20credit%20to%20private%20sector%20by%20banks%20refers%20to %20financial,receivable%2C%20that%20establish%20a%20claim, accessed 23 November 2020.

23. I thank a reviewer for emphasizing this point.

24. USAID, *Private Sector Engagement Policy* (Washington, DC: USAID, n.d.), 46, https://www.usaid.gov/sites/default/files/documents/1865/usaid_psepolicy _final.pdf. It must be noted that these definitional statements raise numerous issues, including for data collection and analysis. The World Bank, for example, seems to include SOEs in some of its proxy measures of private investment (e.g., gross fixed capital formation), which would be consistent with USAID so long as they are "for profit." That, however, is not the case for all such firms, whose executives may have objective functions other than profitability (e.g., job creation, receipt of bribes, and so forth). And from a policy standpoint, Washington sometimes ended up supporting SOEs during the Cold War when it made strategic sense to do so, even if it discouraged this business model as a general rule. More recently, USAID has been explicitly prohibited from financing SOEs, as was the case in postwar Iraq.

25. Tarini Parti, "Biden Administration Taps Private Sector to Invest in Central America," *Wall Street Journal*, 27 May 2021, https://www.wsj.com/articles /biden-administration-taps-private-sector-to-invest-in-central-america-11622 113201.

26. Alex Counts, "Reimagining Microfinance," *Stanford Social Innovation Review*, Summer 2008, 46–53, at 51, https://ssir.org/articles/entry/reimagining _microfinance#:~:text=ALEX%20COUNTS%20is%20the%20president,of %20partners%20in%2025%20countries.

27. For a brief literature review, see Jason Hickel, "The Microfinance Delusion: Who Really Wins?," *The Guardian*, 10 June 2015, https://www.theguardian .com/global-development-professionals-network/2015/jun/10/the-microfinance -delusion-who-really-wins.

28. Note that I will also use the term "free enterprise" as a synonym, although "free" suggests an absence of government meddling in or control over firm decision-making, which may not be the case, even where firms are "private").

29. Cited in Nick Cullather, "Food for the Hungry Dragon: The U.S. and Industrial Policy in Taiwan, 1950–1965," *Diplomatic History* 20, no. 1 (Winter 1996): 1–25, at 16.

30. A group of economists, who apparently conducted only limited historical research, have recently called this "The Baker Hypothesis," after Reagan's secretary of the treasury (1985–1988), James Baker, who advocated for economic liberalization in the developing world and specifically more openness to foreign investment. See Chari Anusha, Peter Blair Henry, and Hector Reyes, "The Baker Hypothesis" (NBER Working Paper No. 27708, August 2020).

31. See, for example, Laura Alfaro, "Foreign Direct Investment and Growth: Does the Sector Matter?" (Harvard Business School Working Paper, April 2003).

32. *Report to the President on Foreign Economic Policies* (Grey Report) (Washington, DC, Government Printing Office, 1950), 13.

33. Albert Hirschman, *The Strategy of Economic Development* (New Haven, CT: Yale University Press, 1958), 100.

34. Albert Hirschman, *How to Divest in Latin America, and Why* (Princeton, NJ: International Finance Section, Department of Economics, Princeton University, 1969).

35. Baldwin, *Economic Development and American Foreign Policy.*

36. See, for example, USAID, *Private Sector Engagement Policy.*

37. Baldwin, *Economic Development and American Foreign Policy,* 16–19.

38. Scott Bowman, *The Modern Corporation and American Political Thought: Law, Power and Ideology* (University Park: Pennsylvania State University Press, 1996), 2.

39. Lawrence B. Glickman, *Free Enterprise: An American History* (New Haven, CT: Yale University Press, 2019), 2.

40. Eisenhower cited in Bevan Sewell, *The U.S. and Latin America: Eisenhower, Kennedy and Economic Diplomacy in the Cold War* (New York: I. B. Taurus, 2015), 22.

41. USAID, *Private Enterprise Development* (Washington, DC: USAID, March 1985), 1.

42. See Glickman, *Free Enterprise,* for an analysis of the relationship between free enterprise and American democracy.

43. Louis Hartz, *The Liberal Tradition in America* (New York: Harcourt, Brace, 1955), 305.

44. Robert Stone, *A Flag for Sunrise* (New York: Vintage Books, 1977), 267.

45. Nancy Bermeo, "Conclusion: Is Democracy Exportable?," in *Is Democracy Exportable?,* ed. Zoltan Barany and Robert Moser (New York: Cambridge University Press, 2009), 242–264, at 242.

46. Vincent Arel-Bundock, Clint Peinhardt, and Amy Pond, "Political Risk Insurance: A New Firm-Level Data Set," *Journal of Conflict Resolution* 64, no. 5 (2020): 987–1006.

47. Cited in Ethan B. Kapstein, *Seeds of Stability: Land Reform and U.S. Foreign Policy* (New York: Cambridge University Press, 2017), 42.

48. Charles S. Maier, "The Politics of Productivity: Foundations of American International Economic Policy after World War II," in *Between Power and Plenty: Foreign Economic Policies of Advanced Industrial States,* ed. Peter J. Katzenstein (Madison: University of Wisconsin Press, 1978), 23–49, 25.

49. Milton Friedman, "Capitalism and Freedom," *The New Individualist Review* 1, no. 1 (1961), oll.libertyfund.org/title/2136/195245.
50. USAID, *Private Enterprise Development*, 1–2.
51. The data are available from the author, but they derive from the World Development Indicators. See World Bank, "World Development Indicators," https://datatopics.worldbank.org/world-development-indicators/, accessed 20 June 2021.

1. Private Enterprise, International Development, and the Cold War

1. Stephen Macekura, "The Point Four Program and U.S. International Development Policy," *Political Science Quarterly* 128, no. 1 (Spring 2013): 127–160.
2. The text of Truman's inaugural address can be found at https://avalon.law.yale.edu/20th_century/truman.asp, accessed 23 November 2020.
3. Lloyd Gardner, "FDR and the Colonial Question," in *FDR's World: War, Peace, and Legacies,* ed. David B. Woolner, Warren F. Kimball, and David Reynolds (New York: Palgrave Macmillan, 2008), 123–144.
4. For a relatively recent study, see Bevan Sewell, "A Perfect (Free-Market) World? Economics, the Eisenhower Administration, and the Soviet Economic Offensive in Latin America," *Diplomatic History* 32, no. 5 (November 2008): 841–868.
5. These points are brilliantly elaborated in David Baldwin, *Economic Development and American Foreign Policy: 1943–1962* (Chicago: University of Chicago Press, 1966).
6. The text of NSC-68 can be found at https://digitalarchive.wilsoncenter.org/document/116191.pdf?v=2699956db534c1821edefa61b8c13ffe, accessed 20 April 2020.
7. Baldwin, *Economic Development,* 19.
8. On the long-run effects of wartime destruction, see David Cook, "World War II and Convergence," *Review of Economics and Statistics* 84, no. 1 (February 2002): 131–138.
9. Robert Wood, *From Marshall Plan to Debt Crisis: Foreign Aid and Development Choices in the World Economy* (Berkeley: University of California Press, 1986).
10. Cited in Ethan B. Kapstein, *Seeds of Stability: Land Reform and U.S. Foreign Policy* (New York: Cambridge University Press, 2017), 30.
11. The World Bank's Articles of Agreement may be found at http://pubdocs.worldbank.org/en/722361541184234501/IBRDArticlesOfAgreement-English.pdf, accessed 22 April 2020.
12. See Devesh Kapur, John P. Lewis, and Richard C. Webb. *The World Bank: Its First Half-Century* (Washington, DC: Brookings Institution, 2011).
13. Cited in Kenneth Vandevelde, *The First Bilateral Investment Treaties: U.S. Postwar Friendship, Commerce and Navigation Treaties* (New York: Oxford University Press, 2017), 38.

14. Vandevelde, *The First Bilateral Investment Treaties*, 39.
15. Vandevelde, *The First Bilateral Investment Treaties*, 43.
16. Vandevelde, *The First Bilateral Investment Treaties*, 43.
17. Vandevelde, *The First Bilateral Investment Treaties*, 56.
18. Harry S. Truman, "Inaugural Address," 20 January 1949, https://www
    .trumanlibrary.org/whistlestop/50yr_archive/inagural20jan1949.htm.
19. Secretary of State to President Truman, "Progress Report on Point IV," 14
    March 1949, in U.S. Department of State, *Foreign Relations of the United
    States*, 1949, Vol. I, 779 (hereafter referred to as *FRUS*, with the appropriate
    year, volume, and page numbers).
20. Cited in Baldwin, *Economic Development*, 78.
21. Dean Acheson, Department of State Press Release no. 58, 26 January 1949,
    in *FRUS*, 1949, Vol. I, 759.
22. A point also emphasized throughout Baldwin, *Economic Development*.
23. David McLellan and Charles Woodhouse, "The Business Elite and Foreign
    Policy," *Western Political Quarterly* 13, no. 1 (March 1960): 172–190.
24. Thomas Zeiler, *Free Trade, Free World: The Advent of GATT* (Chapel Hill:
    University of North Carolina Press, 1999).
25. Burton Kaufman, *Trade and Aid: Eisenhower's Foreign Economic Policy,
    1953–1961* (Baltimore: Johns Hopkins University Press, 1982), 2–3; Johan
    Norberg, "American and European Protectionism Is Killing Poor Countries
    and Their People," *Investor's Business Daily*, 25 August 2003.
26. Bela Balass, "Tariff Protection in Industrial Nations and Its Effects on the Ex-
    ports of Processed Goods of Developing Nations," *Canadian Journal of Eco-
    nomics* 1, no. 3 (August 1968): 583–594.
27. Robert Pollard, *Economic Security and the Origins of the Cold War, 1945–
    1950* (New York: Columbia University Press, 1985), 205.
28. H. W. Singer, "The Distribution of Gains between Investing and Borrowing
    Countries," *American Economic Review* 40, no. 2, Papers and Proceedings
    of the Sixty-Second Annual Meeting of the American Economic Association,
    May 1950, 473–485; Raul Prebisch, "Commercial Policy in the Underdevel-
    oped Countries," *American Economic Review* 49, no. 2, Papers and Proceed-
    ings of the Seventy-First Annual Meeting of the American Economic Asso-
    ciation, May 1959, 251–273.
29. A point emphasized by William Adams Brown and Redvers Opie, *American
    Foreign Assistance* (Washington, DC: Brookings Institution, 1953). See also
    Charles P. Kindleberger, *The Dollar Shortage* (Cambridge, MA: MIT Press,
    1950).
30. Kaufman, *Trade and Aid*.
31. W. W. Rostow, *Eisenhower, Kennedy and Foreign Aid* (Austin: University of
    Texas Press, 1985), 34.
32. United Nations, Department of Economic Affairs, "Measures for the Eco-
    nomic Development of Under-Developed Nations" (New York: United Na-
    tions, Department of Economic Affairs, May 1951), https://digitallibrary.un
    .org/record/708544?ln=en. For a discussion of the investment gap and its
    influence in the development community, see William Easterly, *The Elusive
    Quest for Growth* (Cambridge, MA: MIT Press, 2001).

33. Minutes of Meeting of the National Advisory Council, 14 April 1949, in *FRUS, 1949*, Vol. I, 784–786.

34. Marina Von Neumann Whitman, *Government Risk-Sharing in Foreign Investment* (Princeton, NJ: Princeton University Press, 1965), 50.

35. Thomas DiBacco, "American Business and Foreign Aid: The Eisenhower Years," *Business History Review* 41, no. 1 (Spring 1967): 21–35; McLellan and Woodhouse, "The Business Elite and Foreign Policy."

36. Whitman, *Government Risk-Sharing*, 60.

37. Gardiner Patterson, *Survey of U.S. International Finance, 1949* (Princeton, NJ: Princeton University Press, 1950), 202.

38. Gardiner Patterson and Jack N. Behrman, *Survey of U.S. International Finance, 1951* (Princeton, NJ: Princeton University Press, 1951), 85.

39. Raymond Mikesell, *Promoting United States Private Investment Abroad* (Washington, DC: National Planning Association, 1957), 49.

40. See Zachary Karabell, *Architects of Intervention: The United States, the Third World, and the Cold War, 1946–1962* (Baton Rouge: Louisiana State University Press, 1999).

41. Minutes of Meeting of the National Advisory Council, 14 April 1949, in *FRUS, 1949*, Vol. I, 785.

42. Minutes of Meeting of the National Advisory Council, 14 April 1949, in *FRUS, 1949*, Vol. I, 785.

43. Richard N. Cooper, "Economic Aspects of the Cold War," in *Cambridge History of the Cold War*, ed. Melvyn Leffler and Odd Arne Westad (New York: Cambridge University Press, 2010); see also Bevan Sewell, *The US and Latin America Eisenhower, Kennedy and Economic Diplomacy in the Cold War* (New York: I. B. Taurus, 2015).

44. Robert Pollard, *Economic Security and the Origins of the Cold War, 1945–1950* (New York: Columbia University Press, 1985), 204.

45. Patterson and Behrman, *Survey of U.S. International Finance, 1951*, 88.

46. Patterson and Behrman, *Survey of U.S. International Finance, 1951*, 89.

47. Patterson and Behrman, *Survey of U.S. International Finance, 1951*, 82.

48. Kaufman, *Trade and Aid*, 7.

49. Stephen D. Krasner, *Defending the National Interest: Raw Materials Investments and U.S. Foreign Policy* (Princeton, NJ: Princeton University Press, 1978).

50. Rostow, *Eisenhower, Kennedy and Foreign Aid*, 15–21.

51. Kaufman, *Trade and Aid*, 7.

52. Dwight D. Eisenhower, "Inaugural Address," 20 January 1953, The American Presidency Project, https://www.presidency.ucsb.edu/documents/inaugural-address-3.

53. Kaufman, *Trade and Aid*, 17. On trade policy during the Eisenhower administration, see Douglas Irwin, *Clashing over Commerce: A History of US Trade Policy* (Chicago: University of Chicago Press), 513–519.

54. Commission on Foreign Economic Policy, *Report to the President and Congress* (Washington, DC: Government Printing Office, 1954), 8.

55. Commission on Foreign Economic Policy, *Report to the President and Congress*, 44.

56. Commission on Foreign Economic Policy, *Report to the President and Congress,* 18.

57. For background on the address, see Memorandum by the Deputy Assistant Secretary of State for Economic Affairs to the Secretary of State, 18 March 1954, in *FRUS, 1952–1954,* Vol. I, 57–53; "Minutes of a Cabinet Meeting Held at the White House," 19 March 1954, in *FRUS, 1952–1954,* Vol. I, 63–65. The text of Eisenhower's Message to the Congress is in *Department of State Bulletin,* 19 April 1954, 602–607.

58. The text of Eisenhower's Message to the Congress is in *Department of State Bulletin,* 19 April 1954, 602–607.

59. Harold Stassen, "The Case for Private Investment Abroad," *Foreign Affairs* 32, no. 3 (April 1954): 402–415.

60. Rostow, *Eisenhower, Kennedy and Foreign Aid,* 92.

61. U.S. Department of Commerce, *Selected Data on U.S. Direct Investment Abroad, 1950–76* (Washington, DC: Bureau of Economic Analysis, 1982), table 1.

62. Memorandum of Conversation, 1 September 1954, in *FRUS, 1952–1954,* Vol. I, 89. The conversation occurred among members of a new "Randall Committee" on foreign economic policy.

63. There is some dispute over who actually originated the idea of an IFC. An alternative theory is that it arose during the deliberations of a postwar committee headed by Nelson Rockefeller, which issued a 1951 report, *Partners for Progress,* where an IFC was indeed proposed. But one scholar has found that the staff work for the IFC proposal was really done at the World Bank, and Rockefeller had drawn on its research. For the historical background, see B. E. Matecki, *Establishment of the International Finance Corporation and United States Policy: A Case Study in International Organization* (New York: Praeger, 1957).

64. Memorandum for the Assistant Secretary of State for Economic Affairs to the Under Secretary of State, 2 May 1952, in *FRUS, 1952–1954,* Vol. I, 231.

65. International Development Advisory Board, *Partners for Progress* (Washington, DC: Government Printing Office, 1951).

66. Kaufman, *Trade and Aid,* 47.

67. Patterson and Behrman, *Survey of U.S. International Finance, 1951,* 91.

68. Memorandum for the Assistant Secretary of State for Economic Affairs to the Under Secretary of State, 2 May 1952, in *FRUS, 1952–1954,* Vol. I, 230.

69. Draft Position Paper Concerning the IFC, 17 June 1953, in *FRUS, 1952–1954,* Vol. I, 272.

70. Cited in McLellan and Woodhouse, "The Business Elite and Foreign Policy," 184.

71. Paper Presented by the Staff Committee for the National Advisory Council on International Monetary and Financial Problems, 1 July 1954, in *FRUS, 1952–1954,* Vol. I, 288.

72. *Special Report of the United States Delegation to the Sixteenth Session of the Economic and Social Council,* 5 August 1953, in *FRUS, 1952–1954,* Vol. I, 277.

73. United States Representative to the United Nations to the Department of State, 8 October 1954, in *FRUS, 1952–1954,* Vol. I, 295.

74. Minutes of the 218th Meeting of the National Advisory Council, 3 November 1954, in *FRUS, 1952–1954*, Vol. I, 302.

75. McLellan and Woodhouse, "The Business Elite and Foreign Policy," 185.

76. George Humphrey, "Remarks by Secretary of the Treasury Humphrey," 23 November 1954, at the meeting of Ministers of Finance and Economy, Rio de Janeiro, Brazil, in *Annual Report of the Secretary of Treasury for the Year Ended 30 June 1955* (Washington, DC: Department of the Treasury, 1955), 250.

77. Message by President Eisenhower to the Congress, "Foreign Economic Policy," 10 January 1955 (Washington, DC: Department of State), 1955.

78. Kaufman, *Trade and Aid*, 48.

79. Uner Kirdar, *The Structure of United Nations Economic Aid to Underdeveloped Countries* (The Hague: Springer, 1966).

80. U.S. Department of Commerce, *Selected Data on U.S. Direct Investment Abroad, 1950–76* (Washington, DC: Bureau of Economic Analysis, 1982), table 1.

81. International Finance Corporation, *Annual Report: 1960–1961* (Washington, DC: International Finance Corporation, 1961), 17.

82. "Memorandum by the Senior Adviser to the United States Delegation to the United Nations," 2 September 1954, in *FRUS, 1952–1954*, Vol. I, 98.

83. Albert Hirschman, "The Political Economy of Import Substituting Industrialization in Latin America," *Quarterly Journal of Economics* 82, no. 1 (February 1968): 1–32. The thesis that developing countries faced declining terms of trade was made famous by UN economist Raul Prebisch.

84. Samuel A. Morley and Gordon W. Smith, "Import Substitution and Foreign Investment in Brazil," *Oxford Economic Papers* n.s., 23, no. 1 (March 1971): 120–135.

85. For a discussion of export pessimism, see Bo Sodersten and Geoffrey Reed, *International Economics* (London: Palgrave, 1994), chap. 19.

86. Kaufman, *Trade and Aid*, chap. 6.

87. Kaufman, *Trade and Aid*, 106.

88. USAID, *Terminal Report of the Development Loan Fund* (Washington, DC: USAID, January 1962), 3. As we will see in the following chapter on East Asia, however, it may have had somewhat greater success in stimulating local private enterprise.

89. Kaufman, *Trade and Aid*, 110.

90. Kaufman, *Trade and Aid*, 111.

91. Norman Girvan, "Economic Nationalism," *Daedalus* 104, no. 4 (Fall 1975): 145–158.

2. Private Sector Development in the Shadow of War

1. Cited in Nick Cullather, "Fuel for the Good Dragon: The United States and Industrial Policy in Taiwan, 1950–1965," *Diplomatic History* 20, no. 1 (Winter 1996): 1–25.

2. Dwight D. Eisenhower, "Special Message to the Congress on Increased Aid to South Korea," 27 July 1953, The American Presidency Project, https://www

.presidency.ucsb.edu/documents/special-message-the-congress-concerning
-increased-aid-for-the-republic-korea.

3. The Charge in the Republic of China to the Department of State, "Discussion of Budget Policy and Military Program with President Chiang Kai-shek," 19 September 1952, in U.S. Department of State, *Foreign Relations of the United States, 1952–1954*, Vol. XIV (hereafter referred to as *FRUS*, with the appropriate year and volume numbers).

4. U.S. Department of State, Acting Officer in Charge of Economic Affairs, Office of Chinese Affairs, "Memorandum of Conversation," 1 June 1953, in *FRUS, 1952–1954*, Vol. XIV.

5. Yongping Wu, *A Political Explanation of Economic Growth: State Survival, Bureaucratic Politics, and Private Enterprises in the Making of Taiwan's Economy, 1950–1985* (Cambridge, MA: Harvard University Asia Center, 2005).

6. Hun Joo Park, "Small Business in Korea, Japan, and Taiwan," *Asian Survey* 41, no. 5 (2001): 846–864, at 856. On *dirigisme* in East Asia, see Stephan Haggard and Tun-jen Cheng, "State and Foreign Capital in the East Asian NICs, in *The Political Economy of the New Asian Industrialism*, ed. Frederic Deyo (Ithaca, NY: Cornell University Press, 1987).

7. For reviews of the literature on the East Asian Miracle, see Michael Sarel, *Economic Growth in East Asia: What We Can and What We Cannot Infer* (Washington, DC: International Monetary Fund, 1996); and Stephan Haggard, *Pathways from the Periphery* (Ithaca, NY: Cornell University Press, 1990). On the role of economic ideas in Taiwan, see Douglas Irwin, "How Economic Ideas Led to Taiwan's Shift to Export Promotion in the 1950s" (NBER Working Paper No. 29298, September 2021).

8. James Lee, "US Grand Strategy and the Origins of the Developmental State," *Journal of Strategic Studies*, 43, no. 5 (2020): 737–761, https://doi.org/10 .1080/01402390.2019.1579713.

9. U.S. Senate, *Aid to Formosa* (Washington, DC: Government Printing Office, 1951), 5.

10. George Aseniero, "South Korean and Taiwanese Development: The Transnational Context," *Review* (Fernand Braudel Center) 17, no. 3 (Summer 1994): 275–336, at 280.

11. Pan-Long Tsai, "Explaining Taiwan's Economic Miracle: Are the Revisionists Right?," *Agenda* 6, no. 1 (1999): 69–82, at 75.

12. Cullather, "Fuel for the Good Dragon."

13. Taekyoon Kim, "Translating Foreign Aid Policy Locally: South Korea's Modernization Process Revisited," *Asian Perspective* 37, no. 3 (July–September 2013): 409–436, at 410.

14. Bruce Cumings, "The Origins and Development of the Northeast Asian Political Economy: Industrial Sectors, Product Cycles, and Political Consequences," *International Organization* 38, no. 1 (Winter 1984): 1–40, at 25.

15. USAID considers its technical assistance to Taiwan as one of its great successes. See USAID, *Principles from East Asia: The Case of Taiwan* (Wash-

ington, DC: USAID, 2003). On US support of Korean research institutes, see Kim, "Translating Foreign Aid Policy Locally."

16. Samuel Ho, "Economic Bureaucracy and Taiwan's Economic Development," *Pacific Affairs* 60, no. 2 (Summer 1987): 226–247. The $220 is measured in 1973 dollars.

17. Frank and Mei-Chu Hsiao, *Economic Development of Emerging East Asia: Catching Up of Taiwan and South Korea* (New York: Anthem Books. 2017).

18. Identifying and distinguishing among the different groups that inhabited Taiwan is a fraught exercise. In this chapter I refer to the "established Taiwanese" and those who occupied the island before the mainlanders arrived from China. However, when speaking of the population overall, I refer to the "Taiwanese." I thank Ian Malcolm of Harvard University Press for guidance along these lines.

19. On relations between the Nationalists and Taiwanese, see Steven E. Phillips, *Between Assimilation and Independence: The Taiwanese Encounter Nationalist China, 1945–1950* (Stanford, CA: Stanford University Press, 2003).

20. This history is reviewed in Nancy Tucker, *Taiwan, Hong Kong, and the United States: 1945–1992* (New York: Twayne, 1994).

21. Charge in China (Strong) to Secretary of State, 17 May 1950, in *FRUS,* 1950, Vol. VI.

22. President Harry S. Truman, "Statement Issued by the President," 27 June 1950, in *FRUS,* 1950, Vol. VII. 39.

23. Wu, *A Political Explanation of Economic Growth,* 39.

24. U.S. Senate, *Aid to Formosa,* 6.

25. A. James Gregor and Maria Chang, "Essays on Sun Yat-Sen and the Economic Development of Taiwan," *Occasional Papers/Reprint Series in Contemporary Asian Studies,* no. 1 (1983), University of Maryland School of Law.

26. See Park, "Small Business in Korea, Japan and Taiwan."

27. Wu, *A Political Explanation of Economic Growth,* 41.

28. Wu, *A Political Explanation of Economic Growth,* 47.

29. See C. X. George Wei, "The Economic Cooperation Administration, the State Department, and the American Presence in China, 1948–1949," *Pacific Historical Review* 70, no. 1 (February 2001): 21–53.

30. "Who's Who in Free China," *Taiwan Today,* 1 April 1951, https://taiwantoday .tw/news.php?unit=4&post=6617.

31. A point emphasized by Haggard in *Pathways from the Periphery.*

32. United Nations, *World Economic Survey: 1950–1951* (New York: United Nations, 1951), 50.

33. Cullather, "Fuel for the Good Dragon," 4.

34. U.S. Senate, *Aid to Formosa,* 6.

35. A point emphasized by Cullather, "Fuel for the Good Dragon."

36. This section draws from Ethan B. Kapstein, *Seeds of Stability: Land Reform and U.S. Foreign Policy* (New York: Cambridge University Press, 2017), chap. 4.

37. Ho, "Economic Bureaucracy and Taiwan's Economic Development," 233–234.
38. Ho, "Economic Bureaucracy and Taiwan's Economic Development," 236.
39. International Cooperation Administration, *Economic Progress of Free China, 1951–1958* (Taipei: International Cooperation Administration, November 1958).
40. David Chang, "U.S. Aid and Economic Progress in Taiwan," *Asian Survey* 5, no. 3 (March 1965): 152–160, at 156.
41. Kevin Gray, "The United States and Uneven Development in East Asia," *Annals of the American Academy of Political and Social Science* 656 (November 2014): 41–58, at 51.
42. Ho, "Economic Bureaucracy and Taiwan's Economic Development," 233–234.
43. For a recent estimate, see Chad Bown and Douglas Irwin, "The GATT'S Starting Point: Tariff Levels circa 1947" (NBER Working Paper No. 21782, December 2015).
44. Robert Baldwin and Douglas Nelson, "The Political Economy of U.S.-Taiwanese Trade and Other International Economic Relations," in *Trade and Protectionism*, ed. Takatoshi Ito and Anne O. Krueger (Chicago: University of Chicago Press, 1993), 307–337, at 312.
45. U.S. Department of Commerce, *Overseas Business Report*, January 1963 (Washington, DC: Department of Commerce, 1963). On the change to the foreign exchange regime, see Irwin, "How Economic Ideas Led to Taiwan's Shift to Export Promotion in the 1950s."
46. Vei-Lin Chan, "Foreign Direct Investment and Economic Growth in Taiwan's Manufacturing Industries," in *The Role of Foreign Direct Investment in East Asian Economic Development*, ed. Takatoshi Ito and Anne Krueger (Chicago: University of Chicago Press, 2000), table 12.3.
47. In this regard compare the previously cited works by Ho and Cullather.
48. Neil Jacoby, "Evaluation of U.S. Economic Aid to Free China, 1951–1965" (Agency for International Development Discussion Paper no. 11, January 1966).
49. Tucker, *Taiwan, Hong Kong, and the United States*, 15.
50. Neil Jacoby, *Evaluation of U.S. Economic Aid to Free China, 1951–1965* (Washington, DC: USAID, January 1962), 41. It should be noted that Jacoby wrote this report as a contractor to USAID.
51. Tucker, *Taiwan, Hong Kong, and the United States*, 54.
52. Jacoby, *Evaluation of U.S. Economic Aid to Free China*, 42.
53. International Cooperation Administration, *Economic Progress of Free China*, 33.
54. Cullather, "Fuel for the Good Dragon," 17.
55. USAID, *Terminal Report on the Development Loan Fund*, 2.
56. Gary Hamilton and Cheng-Shu Kao, *Making Money: How Taiwanese Industrialists Embraced the Global Economy* (Stanford, CA: Stanford University Press, 2018), 35.
57. "Free Enterprise for Prosperity," *Taiwan Review*, 1 June 1964, https://taiwantoday.tw/print.php?unit=4&post=7127.

58. Hamilton and Kao, *Making Money,* 35.
59. International Cooperation Administration, *Economic Progress of Free China,* 32.
60. International Cooperation Administration, *Economic Progress of Free China,* 32.
61. International Cooperation Administration, *Economic Progress of Free China,* 32.
62. Kuei-Lin Chang and Hsueh-Liang Wu, "Policy Design and Implementation of Taiwan's Privatization," n.d., https://www.oecd.org/daf/ca/corporategover nanceofstate-ownedenterprises/2482165.pdf, accessed 26 April 2020, 3.
63. International Cooperation Administration, *Economic Progress of Free China,* 17.
64. K.T. Li, *The Evolution of Taiwan's Development Success* (New Haven, CT: Yale University Press, 1988), 58.
65. International Cooperation Administration, *Economic Progress of Free China,* 35.
66. Michela Giorcelli, "The Long-Term Effects of Management and Technical Transfers," *American Economic Review* 109, no. 1 (2019): 121–152.
67. International Cooperation Administration, *Economic Progress of Free China,* 35.
68. Haggard, *Pathways from the Periphery,* 89.
69. Haggard, *Pathways from the Periphery,* 86.
70. Haggard, *Pathways from the Periphery,* 88–89.
71. David Chang, "U.S. Aid and Economic Progress in Taiwan," *Asian Survey* 5, no. 3 (March 1965): 152–160, at 154.
72. Cullather, "Fuel for the Good Dragon," 22.
73. Jordan Schreiber, *U.S. Corporate Investment in Taiwan* (New York: Dunellen Press, 1970), 31.
74. K.T. Li, *The Evolution of Policy behind Taiwan's Development Success* (New Haven, CT: Yale University Press, 1988), 95–96.
75. Yu Zheng, *Governance and Foreign Investment in China, India, and Taiwan* (Ann Arbor: University of Michigan Press, 2014), 164.
76. Stephen Haggard and Yu Zheng, "Institutional Innovation and Investment in Taiwan: The Micro-foundations of the Developmental State," *Business and Politics* 15, no. 4 (December 2013): 435–466, at 446.
77. Schreiber, *U.S. Corporate Investment in Taiwan,* 95.
78. Chi Schive, *The Foreign Factor: The Multinational Corporation's Contribution to the Economic Modernization of the Republic of China* (Stanford, CA: Hoover Institution Press, 1999), 99; Nichola Lowe and Martin Kenney, "To Create an Industry: The Growth of Consumer Electronics Manufacturing in Mexico and Taiwan," *Science, Technology and Society* 3, no. 1 (March 1998): 49–73; Chan, "Foreign Direct Investment."
79. Parts of this section are drawn from Kapstein, *Seeds of Stability.*
80. Stephen H. Lee, "Military Occupation and Empire Building in Cold War Asia: The United States and Korea, 1945–1955," in *The Cold War in East Asia:*

1945–1991, ed. Tsuyoshi Hasegawa (Washington, DC: Woodrow Wilson International Center for Scholars, 2011), 98–121.

81. Ronald Spector, *In the Ruins of Empire: The Japanese Surrender and the Battle for Postwar Asia* (New York: Random House Trade Paperbacks, 2007).

82. A. J. Grajdanzev, "Korea in the Postwar World," *Foreign Affairs* 22, no. 3 (April 1944): 479–483.

83. Spector, *In the Ruins of Empire*, 268–275.

84. William Adams Brown and Redvers Opie, *American Foreign Assistance* (Washington, DC: Brookings Institution, 1953).

85. Lee, "Military Occupation and Empire Building."

86. Memorandum by the Director of the Policy Planning Staff (Kennan), September 24, 1947, in *FRUS*, 1947, Vol. VI, Doc. 620; Memorandum by the Secretary of Defense (Forrestal), September 29, 1947, in *FRUS*, 1947, Vol. VI, Doc. 624.

87. Haggard, *Pathways from the Periphery*, 54.

88. See Suk Tai Suh, "Foreign Aid, Foreign Capital Inflows, and Industrialization in Korea, 1945–1975" (Korea Development Institute Working Paper No. 7712, October 1977), 1–5.

89. C. Clyde Mitchell, "Land Reform in South Korea," *Pacific Affairs* 22, no. 2 (June 1949): 144–154.

90. Spector, *In the Ruins of Empire*, 269.

91. Spector, *In the Ruins of Empire*, 268.

92. Gary L. Olson, *U.S. Foreign Policy and the Third World Peasant: Land Reform in Asia and Latin America* (New York: Praeger, 1974), 40.

93. Spector, *In the Ruins of Empire*, 268.

94. Kristen Looney, "The Rural Developmental State: Modernization Campaigns and Peasant Politics in China, Taiwan and South Korea" (PhD diss., Harvard University, 2012), https://dash.harvard.edu/handle/1/9807308, 163; General of the Army Douglas Macarthur to Secretary of State, February 24, 1946, in *FRUS*, 1946, Vol. VIII, Doc. 480.

95. David Ekbladh, *The Great American Mission: Modernization and the Construction of an American World Order* (Princeton, NJ: Princeton University Press, 2011), 128–129.

96. Looney, "The Rural Developmental State," 163.

97. Yong-Ha Shin, "Land Reform in Korea, 1950," *Bulletin of the Population and Development Studies Center* 5 (1976): 14–31.

98. K. S. Bo, "South Korea's Land Reform and Democracy," *Seoul Journal of Korean Studies* 26, no. 1 (June 2013): 60.

99. Bo, "South Korea's Land Reform and Democracy," 69.

100. Looney, "The Rural Developmental State."

101. Shin, "Land Reform in Korea, 1950," 21.

102. Edward S. Mason, et al., *The Economic and Social Modernization of the Republic of Korea* (Cambridge, MA: Harvard University Asia Center, 1980), 171.

103. David Steinberg, *Foreign Aid and the Development of the Republic of Korea: The Effectiveness of Concessional Assistance*, Aid Special Study no. 42 (Washington, DC: Agency for International Development, December 1985), 23.

104. Haggard, *Pathways from the Periphery*, 55.

105. Steinberg, *Foreign Aid*, 24.

106. Mason et al., *The Economic and Social Modernization of the Republic of Korea*, 45.

107. B. C. Koh, "The War's Impact on the Korean Peninsula," *Journal of American–East Asian Relations* 2, no. 1, special issue: The Impact of the Korean War (Spring 1993): 57–76, at 59.

108. The report of the Tasca Mission may be found in National Security Council (NSC 156), *Strengthening the Korean Economy*, 23 June 1953, in *FRUS*, 1952–1954, Vol. XV, Part II.

109. Mason et al., *The Economic and Social Modernization of the Republic of Korea*, 185.

110. The report of the Tasca Mission may be found in National Security Council (NSC 156), *Strengthening the Korean Economy*, 23 June 1953, in *FRUS*, 1952–1954, vol. XV, Part II.

111. Wonhyuk Lim, "The Emergence of the Chaebol and the Chaebol Problem," in *Economic Crisis and Corporate Restructuring in Korea*, ed. Stephan Haggard, Wonhyuk Lim, and Euysung Kim (New York: Cambridge University Press, 2014), 42.

112. Lim, "The Emergence of the Chaebol," 43.

113. Haggard, *Pathways from the Periphery*, 55.

114. Wan-Chun Liu and Chen-Min Hsu, "The Role of Financial Development in Economic Growth: The Experiences of Taiwan, Korea and Japan," *Journal of Asian Economics* 17, no. 4 (October 2006): 667–690, at 678.

115. Steinberg, *Foreign Aid*, 53.

116. USAID, *Terminal Report of the Development Loan Fund*.

117. "OCI Company, Ltd.," https://www.industrialchemicalblog.com/industry/oci-company-ltd/, accessed 25 June 2021.

118. Stephan Haggard and Tun-jen Cheng, "State and Foreign Capital in the East Asian NICs," in *The Political Economy of the New Asian Industrialism*, ed. Frederic C. Deyo (Ithaca, NY: Cornell University Press, 1990), 84–135, at 110.

119. Kim, "Translating Foreign Aid Policy Locally," 425.

120. See Kim, "Translating Foreign Aid Policy Locally."

121. June-Dong Kim and Sang-In Hwang, "The Role of Foreign Direct Investment in Korea's Economic Development: Productivity Effects and Implications for the Currency Crisis," in Ito and Krueger, *The Role of Foreign Direct Investment in East Asian Economic Development*, 267–294. On the role of the United States in promoting economic policy change, see Douglas Irwin, "From Hermit Kingdom to Miracle on the Han: Policy Decisions that Transformed South Korea into an Export Powerhouse" (NBER Working Paper No. 29299, September 2021).

122. Kim and Hwang, "The Role of Foreign Direct Investment in Korea's Economic Development."

123. The data come from World Bank, World Development Indicators, https://data.worldbank.org/indicator/BX.KLT.DINV.WD.GD.ZS?locations=KR, accessed 3 December 2020.

124. Kim and Hwang, "The Role of Foreign Direct Investment in Korea's Economic Development."

125. Memorandum of Conversation, Washington, DC, June 20, 1961, in *FRUS, 1961–1963*, Vol. XXII.

126. Steinberg, *Foreign Aid*, 25.

127. Haggard, *Pathways from the Periphery*, 51.

128. Haggard, *Pathways from the Periphery*.

129. Ralph Jennings, "Entrepreneurial Spirit Drives Taiwan," Reuters, 8 July 2008, https://www.reuters.com/article/us-taiwan-entrepreneurs/entrepreneurial -spirit-drives-taiwan-idUSTP31094120080709.

130. See Chan, "Foreign Direct Investment and Economic Growth in Taiwan's Manufacturing Industries," 369.

3. Capitalism, Colonialism, or Communism?

1. Memorandum of Discussion at the 366th Meeting of the National Security Council, Washington, May 22, 1958, in *Foreign Relations of the United States, 1958–1960*, Vol. V (hereinafter referred to as *FRUS*, with appropriate year and volume numbers).

2. Memorandum of Discussion at the 224th Meeting of the National Security Council, 15 November 1954, in *FRUS, 1952–1954*, Vol. IV.

3. Getulio Vargas, "Suicide Note," https://groups.google.com/forum/#!topic/soc .history.early-modern/yjoteOEAcqE, accessed 7 July 2020.

4. Cited in Eugene Staley, *War and the Private Investor* (New York: Doubleday, 1935), http://www.gwpda.org/wwi-www/investor/StaleyTC.html.

5. The literature on dependency is, of course, voluminous. For the concept's origins, see Joseph Love, "The Origins of Dependency Analysis," *Journal of Latin American Studies* 22, no. 1 (February 1990): 143–168. For a sophisticated analysis of "dependent development" with specific application to Brazil (and well worth reading—or rereading—after forty years), see Peter Evans, *Dependent Development: The Alliance of Multinational, State and Local Capital in Brazil* (Princeton, NJ: Princeton University Press, 1979).

6. For US policy toward ISI, see Sylvia Maxfield and James H. Nolt, "Protectionism and the Internationalization of Capital: U.S. Sponsorship of Import Substitution Industrialization in the Philippines, Turkey and Argentina," *International Studies Quarterly* 34, no. 1 (March 1990): 49–81.

7. Evans, *Dependent Development*.

8. For the contrast between Latin America and East Asia in light of dependency theory, see Peter Evans, "Class, State, and Dependence in East Asia: Lessons for Latin Americanists, in *The Political Economy of the New Asian Industrialism*, ed. Frederic C. Deyo (Ithaca, NY: Cornell University Press, 1990), 203–226.

9. For a brilliant (and wonderfully written) elaboration of this point, see Kathryn Sikkink, *Ideas and Institutions: Developmentalism in Brazil and Argentina* (Ithaca, NY: Cornell University Press, 1991).

10. For a critical review of Argentine policies, see Irene Brambilla, Sebastian Galiani, and Guido Porto, "Argentine Trade Policies in the XX Century: 60 Years of Solitude" (unpublished working paper, August 2010).

11. On expropriations, see Noel Maurer, *The Empire Trap: The Rise and Fall of U.S. Intervention to Protect American Property Overseas, 1893–2013* (Princeton, NJ: Princeton University Press, 2013).

12. National Security Council, "United States Objectives and Courses of Action with Respect to Latin America," 18 March 1953, in *FRUS, 1952–1954,* Vol. IV.

13. On the role of land reform in the Alliance for Progress, see Ethan B. Kapstein, *Seeds of Stability: Land Reform and U.S. Foreign Policy* (New York: Cambridge University Press, 2017).

14. For an overview of the history, see Alan M. Taylor, "Foreign Capital in Latin America in the Nineteenth and Twentieth Centuries" (NBER Working Paper No. 9580, March 2003).

15. Robert Swansbrough, *The Embattled Colossus: Economic Nationalism and United States Investors in Latin America* (Gainesville: University Presses of Florida, 1976), 22.

16. William Scroggs, "The American Investment in Latin America," *Foreign Affairs* 10, no. 1 (April 1932), https://www.foreignaffairs.com/articles/central-america-caribbean/1932-04-01/american-investment-latin-america.

17. Rosemary Thorp, "The Latin American Economies in the 1940s," in *Latin America in the 1940s: War and Postwar Traditions,* ed. David Rock (Berkeley: University of California Press, 1994), 41–58.

18. See Maurer, *The Empire Trap,* 259–260.

19. On the history of Volta Redonda, see Edward Rogers, "Brazilian Success Story: The Volta Redonda Iron and Steel Project," *Journal of Inter-American Studies* 10, no. 4 (October 1968): 637–652; on the visit by the American delegation, see Sidney Sherwood, "Mission to Brazil," 1946, William McChesney Martin Papers, https://fraser.stlouisfed.org/archival-collection/william-mcchesney-martin-jr-papers-1341/mission-brazil-456997.

20. Thorp, "The Latin American Economies in the 1940s."

21. Raymond Mikesell, *Foreign Investments in Latin America* (Washington, DC: Pan American Union, 1955), 14.

22. Mira Wilkins, *The Maturing of Multinational Enterprise: American Business Abroad from 1914 to 1970* (Cambridge, MA: Harvard University Press, 1974), 312.

23. Mikesell, *Foreign Investments in Latin America,* 17.

24. See, for example, "Charge in Argentina (Ray) to the Secretary of State, 1 August 1947," in *FRUS,* 1947, Vol. VIII, in which Argentine officials expressed the view "that Marshall Plan should be extended to Latin America."

25. Memorandum by Edgar McGinnis of the Division of North and West Coast Affairs, 3 September 1947, in *FRUS,* 1947, Vol. VIII.

26. Ambassador in the Soviet Union (Smith) to the Secretary of State, 17 September 1947, in *FRUS,* 1947, Vol. VIII.

27. Memorandum of Conversation by the Chairman of the United States Delegation (Marshall), 30 August 1947, in *FRUS, 1947*, Vol. VIII.

28. Cited in Stephen G. Rabe, *Eisenhower and Latin America: The Foreign Policy of Anti-Communism* (Chapel Hill: University of North Carolina Press, 1988), 15.

29. Roger Trask, "The Impact of the Cold War on United States–Latin American Relations, 1945–1949," *Diplomatic History* 1, no. 3 (July 1977): 271–284, 278–282.

30. Cited in Lawrence B. Glickman, *Free Enterprise: An American History* (New Haven, CT: Yale University Press, 2019), 37.

31. Rabe, *Eisenhower and Latin America*, 17.

32. Simon Hanson, "Latin America and Point Four," *Annals of the American Academy of Political and Social Science* 268, no. 1 (March 1950): 66–74.

33. Rabe, *Eisenhower and Latin America*, 17.

34. Trask, "The Impact of the Cold War," 283.

35. Bevan Sewell, "A Perfect (Free-Market) World? Economics, the Eisenhower Administration, and the Soviet Economic Offensive in Latin America," *Diplomatic History* 32, no. 5 (November 2008): 841–868, at 862.

36. Rabe, *Eisenhower and Latin America*, 27.

37. National Security Council, "United States Objectives and Courses of Action with Respect to Latin America," 18 March 1953, in *FRUS, 1952–1954*, Vol. IV.

38. Memorandum by the Under Secretary of State to the National Security Council, 23 July 1953, in *FRUS, 1952–1954*, Vol. IV.

39. National Security Council 144 / 1, United States Objectives and Courses of Action with Respect to Latin America, 18 March 1953, in *FRUS, 1952–1954*, Vol. IV.

40. See UN Economic Commission for Latin America, *International Co-Operation in a Latin American Development Policy* (New York: United Nations, 1954). The impact of this analysis on the Eisenhower administration is discussed in Rabe, *Eisenhower and Latin America*, 75.

41. See, for example, Memorandum by the Acting Regional Director of the Office of Latin American Operations to the Director of the Foreign Operations Administration, 19 July 1954, in *FRUS, 1952–1954*, Vol. IV.

42. Cited in Sewell, "A Perfect (Free-Market) World?," 850.

43. See UN Economic Commission for Latin America, *International Co-Operation in a Latin American Development Policy.*

44. Robert Pastor, *Exiting the Whirlpool: U.S. Foreign Policy toward Latin America and the Caribbean* (Boulder, CO: Westview Press, 2001), 207.

45. Memorandum of Discussion at the 224th Meeting of the National Security Council, 15 November 1954, in *FRUS, 1952–1954*, Vol. IV.

46. A recent study of the overthrow using new sources is found in Kapstein, *Seeds of Stability.*

47. See the discussion in Maurer, *The Empire Trap*, 306–307.

48. Isaiah Frank, "Comments on FOA Report for Rio Conference," 14 June 1954, in *FRUS, 1952–1954*, Vol. IV.

49. Minutes of a Meeting Held in the Executive Office Building, 21 June 1954, in *FRUS, 1952–1954*, Vol. IV.

50. Assistant Secretary of State to Under Secretary of State, 1 September 1954, in *FRUS, 1952–1954*, Vol. IV.

51. Rabe, *Eisenhower and Latin America*, 69.

52. See Richard Bernal, "Regional Trade Arrangements in the Western Hemisphere," *American University International Law Journal* 8, no. 4 (1993): 683–717.

53. Assistant Secretary of State to Under Secretary of State, 1 September 1954, in *FRUS, 1952–1954*, Vol. IV.

54. Rabe, *Eisenhower and Latin America*, 77.

55. Memorandum of Discussion at the 237th meeting of the National Security Council, 17 February 1955, in *FRUS, 1955–1957*, Vol. IV.

56. National Security Council, Statement of Policy on U.S. Policy toward Latin America, 25 September 1956, in *FRUS, 1955–1957*, Vol. IV.

57. Robert Woodward, cited in Sewell, "A Perfect (Free Market)," 852.

58. National Security Council, Statement of Policy on U.S. Policy toward Latin America, 25 September 1956.

59. National Security Council, Memorandum, 17 February 1954, in *FRUS, 1952–1954*, Vol. IV.

60. Cited in Maurer, *The Empire Trap*, 298.

61. Paul Gootenberg, "Hijos of Dr. Geschenkron: 'Latecomer' Conceptions in Latin American Economic History," in *The Other Mirror*, ed. Miguel Angel Centeno and Fernando López-Alves (Princeton, NJ: Princeton University Press, 2001), 55–80.

62. U.S. Department of State. Historian's Office, "Editorial Note," in *FRUS, 1958–1960*, Vol. V.

63. Pastor, *Exiting the Whirlpool*, 207.

64. Nixon report to NSC in Memorandum of Discussion at the 366th Meeting of the National Security Council, Washington, May 22, 1958, IN *FRUS, 1958–1960*, Vol. V.

65. Rabe, *Eisenhower and Latin America*, 110.

66. Sidney Dell, *The Inter-American Development Bank: A Study in Development Financing* (New York: Praeger, 1972), 28.

67. Richard Lindholm, "The New Imperialism: Latin American Public Utility Investment," *Southwestern Social Science Quarterly* 24, no. 2 (September 1943): 129–137. Lindholm labeled such investments as the "new imperialism" and urged the US government to step in to provide funding instead of the private sector. Disputes were bound to arise between profit-maximizing American firms and local governments whose public utility policies, such as rate-setting, were a matter of domestic politics, and such disputes could poison US–Latin American relations more generally.

68. Nader Nazmi, "The Impact of Foreign Capital on the Brazilian Economy," *Quarterly Review of Economics and Finance* 38, no. 3 (Fall 1998): 483–502.

69. Laura Alfaro, Andrés Rodríguez-Clare, Gordon H. Hanson, and Claudio Bravo Ortega, "Multinationals and Linkages: An Empirical Investigation," *Economía* 4, no. 2 (Spring 2004): 113–169.

70. See, for example, CIA, "National Intelligence Estimate: Probable Developments in Brazil," 15 March 1955, in *FRUS, 1955–1957*, Vol. VII.

71. Rabe, *Eisenhower and Latin America*, 141–144.
72. The citation from National Security advisor W. W. Rostow is found in Kimber Charles Pearce, *Rostow, Kennedy and the Rhetoric of Foreign Aid* (Lansing: Michigan State University Press, 2001), 88.
73. Jeffrey Taffet, *Foreign Aid as Foreign Policy: The Alliance for Progress in Latin America* (New York: Routledge, 2007), 26.
74. Stephen G. Rabe, *The Most Dangerous Area in the World: John F. Kennedy Confronts Communist Revolution in Latin America* (Chapel Hill: University of North Carolina Press, 1999).
75. Address by President Kennedy at a White House Reception for Latin American Diplomats and Members of Congress, 13 March 1961, legacy.fordham .edu/halsall/mod/1961kennedy-afp.1.html. The best single volume study remains Jeffrey Taffet, *Foreign Aid as Foreign Policy: The Alliance for Progress in Latin America* (New York: Routledge, 2007).
76. Douglas S. Blaufarb, *The Counterinsurgency Era: U.S. Doctrine and Performance, 1950 to the Present* (New York: Free Press, 1977), 282.
77. Papers of John F. Kennedy, Presidential Papers, National Security Files, Subjects, Foreign Economic Policy Task Force Reports, 31 December 1960, 11.
78. Felipe Pereira Loureirho, Feliciano de sá Guimarães, and Adriana Schor, "Public Opinion and Foreign Policy in João Goulart's Brazil (1961–1964): Coherence between National and Foreign Policy Perceptions?," *Revista Brasileira de Política Internacional* 58, no. 2 (2015): 98–118, 207–208.
79. W. W. Rostow, *The Stages of Economic Growth: A Non-Communist Manifesto* (New York: Cambridge University Press, 1960).
80. Memorandum from Rostow to President Kennedy, 28 February 1961, in *FRUS, 1961–1963*, Vol. IX.
81. Memorandum from Rostow to President Kennedy, 28 February 1961.
82. Christopher Darnton, "Asymmetry and Agenda-Setting in US–Latin American Relations," *Journal of Cold War Studies* 14, no. 4 (Fall 2012): 55–92; Stephany Griffith-Jones, "The Alliance for Progress: An Attempt at Interpretation," *Development and Change* 10, no. 3 (1979): 423–443.
83. Griffith-Jones, "The Alliance for Progress," 425.
84. Griffith-Jones, "The Alliance for Progress," 425.
85. Darnton, "Asymmetry and Agenda-Setting," 62.
86. Swansbrough, *The Embattled Colossus*, 110.
87. Darnton, "Asymmetry and Agenda-Setting," 82; emphasis added.
88. Griffith-Jones, "Alliance for Progress," 427.
89. Swansbrough, *The Embattled Colossus*, 116.
90. Swansbrough, *The Embattled Colossus*, 116–117.
91. Richard B. Lillich, "The Protection of Foreign Investment and the Hickenlooper Amendment," *University of Pennsylvania Law Review* 112 (1964): 1116–1131; Maurer, *The Empire Trap*.
92. Swansbrough, *The Embattled Colossus*, 211.
93. U.S. Congress, *Private Investment in Latin America: Hearings before the Subcommittee on Inter-American Economic Relationships of the United States,*

Eighty-Eighth Congress, Second Session, 14–16 January 1964 (Washington, DC: Government Printing Office, 1964), 50.

94. See "Proposals to Improve the Flow of U.S. Capital to Latin America, Report of the Commerce Committee for the Alliance for Progress," in U.S. Congress, *Private Investment in Latin America*, 56.

95. USAID, *Alliance for Progress: Program and Project Data* (Washington, DC: USAID, 1969), 2.

96. Cited in U.S. Congress, *Private Investment in Latin America*, 102.

97. Cited in *FRUS*, 1961–1963, Vol. XII, 20 March 1963.

98. Laura Alfaro, Andrés Rodríguez-Clare, Gordon H. Hanson, and Claudio Bravo Ortega, "Multinationals and Linkages: An Empirical Investigation," *Economía* 4, no. 2 (Spring 2004): 113–169.

99. See Herick Fernando Moralles and Rosina Moreno, "FDI Productivity Spillovers and Absorptive Capacity in Brazilian Firms: A Threshold Regression Analysis," *International Review of Economics and Finance* 70 (2020): 257–272.

4. "Storm over the Multinationals"

1. In U.S. Senate, Committee on Foreign Relations, *Hearings on Multinational Corporations and U.S. Foreign Policy, Part 2* (Washington, DC: Government Printing Office, 1974), 517. This chapter's title is taken from the book by Raymond Vernon, *Storm over the Multinationals: The Real Issues* (New York: Macmillan, 1977).

2. Cited in U.S. Senate, *Multinational Corporations and U.S. Foreign Policy*, part 1 (Washington, DC: Government Printing Office, 1973), 3.

3. For a review of the issues at the time (in a study that remains unsurpassed), see C. Fred Bergsten, Thomas Horst, and Theodore Moran, *American Multinationals and American Interests* (Washington, DC: Brookings Institution, 1978).

4. United Nations General Assembly Resolution 3201 (S-Vi): Declaration on the Establishment of a New International Economic Order, 1 May 1974.

5. Vernon, *Storm over the Multinationals*, 145.

6. Report of Meeting of the Cabinet Committee on Economic Policy, 10 April 1969, in *Foreign Relations of the United States*, 1969–1976, Vol. I (hereafter referred to as *FRUS*, with the appropriate year and volume numbers).

7. For an overview of foreign aid policies, see paper prepared by the National Security Staff, 11 October 1977, in *FRUS*, 1977–1980, Vol. III. On the Foreign Corrupt Practices Act, see Martin Biegelman and Daniel Biegelman, *Foreign Corrupt Practices Act* (New York: Wiley, 2010).

8. See William Easterly, *The Elusive Quest for Growth* (Cambridge, MA: MIT Press, 2001).

9. Memorandum from the Administrator of the Agency for International Development (Gaud) to President Johnson, 29 July 1967, in *FRUS*, 1964–1968, Vol. IX.

10. Stephen D. Krasner, *Structural Conflict: The Third World against Global Liberalism* (Berkeley: University of California Press, 1985), 24.

11. Report of the Task Force on Foreign Aid, undated but certainly 1968, in *FRUS, 1964–1968*, Vol. IX, Doc. 70.

12. Krasner, *Structural Conflict*, 184. For an analysis of the patterns of expropriation, see Stephen J. Kobrin, "Expropriation as an Attempt to Control Foreign Firms in LDCs: Trends from 1960 to 1979," *International Studies Quarterly* 28, no. 3 (September 1984): 329–348.

13. U.S. Congress, House, *The Involvement of U.S. Private Enterprise in Developing Countries* (Washington, DC: Government Printing Office, 1968).

14. Statement by Sen. Jacob Javits, U.S. Senate, in *Congressional Record*, 1 June 1961, p. 9228, in Committee on Foreign Relations, *Multinational Corporations and U.S. Foreign Policy*, part 3 (Washington, DC: Government Printing Office), 320.

15. Letter from President Nixon to Secretary of State Rogers, 12 April 1969, in *FRUS, 1969–1976*, Vol. IV.

16. Special Message from President Nixon to the Congress, 28 May 1969, in *FRUS, 1969–1976*, Vol. I; emphasis added.

17. For background on OPIC, see Charles Lipson, *Standing Guard: Protecting Foreign Capital in the Nineteenth and Twentieth Centuries* (Berkeley: University of California Press, 1985). Lipson's book remains a great source on US policy toward foreign direct investment, and expropriation policy in particular.

18. Action Memorandum from the President's Assistant for National Security Affairs (Kissinger) to President Nixon, undated (presumably March 1969), in *FRUS, 1969–1976*, Vol. I.

19. Action Memorandum from the President's Assistant for National Security Affairs (Kissinger) to President Nixon, undated (presumably March 1969), in *FRUS, 1969–1976*, Vol. I.

20. U.S. House, Committee on Foreign Affairs, *Report on the Foreign Assistance Act of 1969* (Washington, DC: Government Printing Office, 1969), 3.

21. Congressional Research Service, *Overseas Private Investment Corporation: Background and Legislative Issues* (Washington, DC: Library of Congress, 22 December 2016), 2.

22. See statement by Sen. Jacob Javits, U.S. Senate, in Committee on Foreign Relations, *Multinational Corporations and U.S. Foreign Policy*, part 3 (Washington, DC: Government Printing Office), 313.

23. Statement by Sen. Jacob Javits, U.S. Senate, in Committee on Foreign Relations, *Multinational Corporations and U.S. Foreign Policy*, part 3 (Washington, DC: Government Printing Office), 319.

24. Daron Acemoglu and James Robinson, *Why Nations Fail: The Origins of Power, Prosperity, and Poverty* (New York: Crown, 2012).

25. OPIC, *A History of OPIC: 1971–2019* (Washington, DC: OPIC, 2019).

26. For an excellent, recent history of US expropriation policy, see Noel Maurer, *The Empire Trap: The Rise and Fall of U.S. Intervention to Protect American Property Overseas, 1893–2013* (Princeton, NJ: Princeton University Press, 2013).

27. Krasner, *Structural Conflict*, 184

28. Krasner, *Structural Conflict*, 10.

29. For different perspectives on these normative debates, see Ethan B. Kapstein, *Economic Justice in an Unfair World: Towards a Level Playing Field* (Princeton, NJ: Princeton University Press, 2008).

30. Hal Brands, "Richard Nixon and Economic Nationalism in Latin America: The Problem of Expropriations, 1969–1974," *Diplomacy and Statecraft* 18, no. 1 (2007): 215–235, at 216.

31. The best discussion of these issues is found in Brands, "Richard Nixon and Economic Nationalism in Latin America," 215–235.

32. For background on the Hickenlooper Amendment, see Lipson, *Standing Guard*.

33. See the section on Expropriation Policies in *FRUS, 1969–1976*, Vol. IV.

34. CIA, *Implications of Economic Nationalism in the Poor Countries* (Washington, DC: CIA, 29 June 1971), https://www.cia.gov/readingroom/docs/CIA-RDP79R00967A000300030002-4.pdf.

35. CIA, *Implications of Economic Nationalism in the Poor Countries*, 26.

36. National Security Council, "The U.S. Response to Expropriations of U.S. Private Investment in Developing Countries," 31 July 1971, in *FRUS, 1969–1976*.

37. Both Lipson in *Standing Guard*, and Maurer in *The Empire Trap*, emphasize the business influence over US expropriations policy. It is worth emphasizing, however, that often this influence was exercised through Congress rather than the White House.

38. For a review of the historiography, see Zakia Shiraz, "CIA Intervention in Chile and the Fall of the Allende Government in 1973," *Journal of American Studies* 45, no. 3 (August 2011): 603–613. The report of the U.S. Senate, Committee on Foreign Relations, *The International Telephone and Telegraph Company and Chile, 1970–1971* (Washington, DC: Government Printing Office, 1973), provides useful background. For the classic account by a journalist who covered the story, see Seymour Hersh, "The Price of Power," *The Atlantic*, December 1982, https://www.theatlantic.com/magazine/archive/1982/12/the-price-of-power/376309.

39. CIA Deputy Director of Plans, "Proposed CIA Response to Request for Information from the Senate Foreign Relations Committee," 21 February 1973, https://www.cia.gov/readingroom/docs/CIA-RDP75B00380R000200060129-6.pdf.

40. "I.T.T. Said to Seek Chile Coup in '70," *New York Times*, 22 March 1972, https://www.nytimes.com/1972/03/22/archives/itt-said-to-seek-chile-coup-in-70-anderson-says-white-house-was.html.

41. U.S. Senate, Committee on Foreign Relations, *The International Telephone and Telegraph Company and Chile, 1970–1971*, 21 June 1973 (Washington, DC: Government Printing Office, 1973).

42. Richard Nixon, "Statement on U.S. Policy on Economic Assistance and Investment Security in Developing Nations," 19 January 1972, in *Public Papers of the Presidents: Richard Nixon, 1972*, https://quod.lib.umich.edu/p/ppotpus/4731812.1972.001/89?page=root;rgn=full+text;size=100;view=image.

43. Brands, "Richard Nixon and Economic Nationalism in Latin America."
44. See Shiraz, "CIA Intervention."
45. U.S. Senate, *Multinational Corporations and U.S. Foreign Policy,* part 1 (Washington, DC: Government Printing Office, 1973), 43.
46. Cited in U.S. House, *United States and Chile during the Allende Years, 1970–1973* (Washington, DC: Government Printing Office, 1975), 534.
47. Nazar Al-Khalaf, "OPEC Members and the New International Economic Order," *Journal of Energy and Development* 2, no. 2 (Spring 1977): 239–251.
48. For an excellent overview, see Michael Dooley, "A Retrospective on the Debt Crisis" (NBER Working Paper No. 4963, December 1994).
49. Ronald Reagan, "Remarks at the Annual Meeting of the United States Chamber of Commerce," 26 April 1992, Ronald Reagan Presidential Library and Museum, https://www.reaganlibrary.gov/research/speeches/42682a.
50. See paper prepared by the National Security Staff, 11 October 1977, in *FRUS, 1977–1980,* Vol. III.
51. See *FRUS, 1977–1980,* Vol. III.
52. Reagan, "Remarks at the Annual Meeting of the United States Chamber of Commerce."
53. Richard N. Cooper, "An Appraisal of Trade Policy during the Reagan Administration," *Harvard International Review* 11, no. 3 (1989): 90–94, at 90.
54. "Transcript of Talk by Reagan on South Africa and Apartheid," *New York Times,* 23 July 1986, https://www.nytimes.com/1986/07/23/world/transcript -of-talk-by-reagan-on-south-africa-and-apartheid.html.
55. For a review, see Martin Feldstein, ed., *American Economic Policy in the 1980s* (Chicago: University of Chicago Press, 1994). Feldstein's introduction to this volume provides his personal take on Reaganomics, based on his stint as chairman of the Council on Economic Advisors.
56. For a history of the debt crisis, see Ethan B. Kapstein, *Governing the Global Economy: International Finance and the State* (Cambridge, MA: Harvard University Press, 1994).
57. Ronald Reagan, "Address to the World Bank and International Monetary Fund," *New York Times,* 30 September 1981, https://www.nytimes.com/1981 /09/30/business/reagan-talk-to-world-bank-and-imf.html.
58. U.S. Department of the Treasury, *United States Participation in the Multilateral Development Banks in the 1980s* (Washington, DC: Department of the Treasury, February 1982), i.
59. U.S. Department of the Treasury, *United States Participation in the Multilateral Development Banks,* 68.
60. U.S. Department of the Treasury, *United States Participation in the Multilateral Development Banks,* 4.
61. Task Force on International Private Enterprise, *Report to the President,* December 1984, 4 (Washington, DC: Government Printing Office, 1984).
62. Task Force on International Private Enterprise, *Report to the President,* 45.
63. Task Force on International Private Enterprise, *Report to the President,* 109.
64. Ronald Reagan, "Statement on International Investment Policy," 9 September 1983, Ronald Reagan Presidential Library and Museum, https://www .reaganlibrary.gov/research/speeches/90983b.

65. Testimony of Harvey Bale, Office of U.S. Trade Representative, in U.S. Senate, Committee on Foreign Affairs, *U.S. Policy toward International Investment* (Washington, DC: Government Printing Office, 1981), 188–189.

66. Robert Lipsey, "Foreign Direct Investment in Three Financial Crises" (NBER Working Paper No. 8084, January 2001).

67. See Anusha Charis, Peter Blair Henry, and Hector Reyes, "The Baker Hypothesis" (NBER Working Paper No. 27708, August 2020).

68. Charles Hantz, "Ideology, Pragmatism and Ronald Reagan's World View," in "Intricacies of U.S. Foreign Policy," special issue, *Presidential Studies Quarterly* 26, no. 4 (Fall 1996): 942–949.

69. Ronald Reagan, "Remarks to the Permanent Council of the Organization of American States on the Caribbean Basin Initiative," 24 February 1982, Ronald Reagan Presidential Library and Museum, https://www.reaganlibrary.gov /archives/speech/remarks-permanent-council-organization-american-states -caribbean-basin-initiative; emphasis added.

70. See "Mass Atrocity Endings," https://sites.tufts.edu/atrocityendings/2015/08 /07/el-salvador/, accessed 1 June 2020.

71. Cited in Kapstein, *Seeds of Stability*, 187.

72. Cited in Kapstein, *Seeds of Stability*, 191.

73. It is interesting to note that one of the architects of El Salvador's land reform program, Roy Prosterman, had also been involved in land reform in Vietnam. He undoubtedly was well aware of earlier US efforts in East Asia. See Jeffrey M. Paige, "Land Reform and Agrarian Revolution in El Salvador: Comment on Seligson and Diskin," *Latin American Research Review* 31, no. 2 (1996): 127–139.

74. See Elaine Potoker and Richard H. Borgman, "The Economic Impact of the Caribbean Basin Initiative: Has It Delivered Its Promise?," *Canadian Journal of Latin American and Caribbean Studies* 32, no. 64 (2007): 79–119.

75. Ronald Reagan, "Message to the Congress Transmitting Proposed Caribbean Basin Initiative Legislation," 17 March 1982, https://www.reaganlibrary.gov /archives/speech/message-congress-transmitting-proposed-caribbean-basin -initiative-legislation.

76. Ronald Reagan, Message to the Congress, 17 March 1982.

77. See Congressional Research Service, "Congressional Basin Initiative: Information Pack" (Washington, DC: Library of Congress, n.d.).

78. See Potoker and Borgman, "The Economic Impact of the Caribbean Basin Initiative," 79–119.

79. See Edward Graham and Paul Krugman, "The Surge in Foreign Direct Investment in the 1980s," in *Foreign Direct Investment*, ed. Kenneth Froot (Chicago: University of Chicago Press, 1993), 13–36.

5. Capitalism Triumphant

1. 101 *Congressional Record*, part 16, 3 August 1990, S22820, https://www .congress.gov/bound-congressional-record/1990/08/03/senate-section. Special thanks are due to Princeton MPA student Michelle Nedashkovskaya for her fabulous research assistance and intellectual engagement on this chapter.

2. See Ethan B. Kapstein and Michael Mandelbaum, eds., *Sustaining the Transition: The Social Safety Net in Post-Communist Europe* (New York: Council on Foreign Relations, 1997); Ethan B. Kapstein and Branko Milanović, *Income and Influence: Social Policy in Emerging Market Economies* (Kalamazoo, MI: Upjohn Institute, 2003).

3. For a bitter critique of US policy toward Russia, see Stephen F. Cohen, *Failed Crusade: America and the Tragedy of Post-Communist Russia* (New York: Norton, 2000). For a balanced assessment from a former National Security Council staffer, see Robert Hutchings, *American Diplomacy and the End of the Cold War: An Insider's Account of U.S. Policy in Europe, 1989–1992* (Washington, DC: Woodrow Wilson Center Press, 1997).

4. Matlock, however, criticizes the Bush administration for responding sluggishly to Gorbachev's pleas for assistance; see Jack Matlock, *Autopsy of an Empire: The American Ambassador's Account of the Collapse of the Soviet Union* (New York: Random House, 1995), chap. 8.

5. For a review of American assistance, see USAID, *20 Years of USAID Economic Growth Assistance in Europe and Eurasia* (Washington, DC: USAID, 2013).

6. As Lipton and Sachs stress, there are of course many political-economy models within Western Europe, but most can be distinguished from, say, the United States in terms of their commitment to a particular mix of democracy, capitalism, and welfare state institutions like universal health care and access to higher education. See David Lipton and Jeffrey Sachs, "Creating a Market Economy in Eastern Europe: The Case of Poland," *Brookings Papers on Economic Activity* 1990, no. 1 (1990): 75–147.

7. Eugene Wittkopf and James McCormick, "Congress, the President, and the End of the Cold War: Has Anything Changed?," *Journal of Conflict Resolution* 42, no. 4 (August 1998): 440–466.

8. Kimberly Zeuli and Vernon Ruttan, "U.S. Assistance to the Former Soviet Empire: Toward a Rationale for Foreign Aid," *Journal of Developing Areas* 30, no. 4 (July 1996): 493–524, at 493.

9. George H.W. Bush, "Address before a Joint Session of Congress," 11 September 1990, Miller Center, University of Virginia, https://millercenter.org/the-presidency/presidential-speeches/september-11-1990-address-joint-session-congress.

10. Susan Collins, "U.S. Economic Policy toward the Soviet Union and Eastern Europe," *Journal of Economic Perspectives* 5, no. 4 (Fall 1991): 219–227, at 220.

11. Collins, "U.S. Economic Policy," 221.

12. Statement of Kempton Jenkins in U.S. Senate, Committee on Foreign Relations, *The Future of Europe, 21 March 1990* (Washington, DC: GPO, 1991), 369.

13. For a useful review of these debates, see Vladimir Popov, "Shock Therapy versus Gradualism Reconsidered: Lessons from Transition Economies after 15 Years of Reforms," *Comparative Economic Studies* 49 (2007): 1–31.

14. William E. Schuerch, "The Congressional Role in United States Assistance Policy in Central-East European Economies in Transition," in *East-Central European Economies in Transition,* ed. John P. Hardt and Richard F. Kaufman (Armonk, NY: M. E. Sharpe, 1995), 336–350, at 337.

15. For critical reviews of neoliberalism, see Jan Aart Schoulte, "The Sources of Neoliberal Globalization" (Geneva: United Nations Research Institute for Social Development, October 2005); and Quinn Slobodian, *Globalists: The End of Empire and the Birth of Neoliberalism* (Cambridge, MA: Harvard University Press, 2018).

16. For a good review of this early period of globalization, see Paul Krugman, "Globalization: What Did We Miss?" (unpublished manuscript, March 2018).

17. Stephen Brooks, *Producing Security: Multinational Corporations, Globalization, and the Changing Calculus of Conflict* (Princeton, NJ: Princeton University Press, 2005), 40–50.

18. Brooks, *Producing Security*, 41.

19. Brooks, *Producing Security*, 71.

20. Mercosur, https://www.mercosur.int/en/.

21. Brooks, *Producing Security*, chap. 2.

22. Cited in Pankaj Ghemawat, *Redefining Global Strategy: Crossing Borders in a World Where Differences Still Matter* (Boston: Harvard Business School Press, 2007), 169.

23. Consider, for example, the case of the F-35 jet fighter, in which foreign purchasers demanded a share of production. See Ethan B. Kapstein, "Capturing Fortress Europe: International Collaboration and the Joint Strike Fighter," *Survival* 46, no. 3 (September 2004): 137–159.

24. Andrei Koesnikov and Denis Volkov, "Pragmatic Paternalism: The Russian Public and the Private Sector" (Carnegie Moscow Center, 18 January 2019), https://carnegiemoscow.org/commentary/78155.

25. Hutchings, *American Diplomacy*, 185.

26. Allen Drazen, *Political Economy in Macroeconomics* (Princeton, NJ: Princeton University Press, 2000), 616.

27. On the ideas and policy debates shaping American assistance, see Hutchings, *American Diplomacy*, 196–212.

28. For a reflection on the Washington Consensus by the economist who penned that term, see John Williamson, "The Washington Consensus as Policy Prescription for Development," Lecture delivered at the World Bank, 13 January 2004, https://www.piie.com/publications/papers/williamson0204.pdf.

29. Lipton and Sachs, "Creating a Market Economy."

30. Hutchings, *American Diplomacy*, 188.

31. Lipton and Sachs, "Creating a Market Economy."

32. See George H. W. Bush, "Remarks to the American Society of Newspaper Editors," 9 April 1992, George H. W. Bush Presidential Library and Museum, https://bush41library.tamu.edu/archives/public-papers/4167. For a general overview of US policy during this period, see George Herring, *From Colony to Superpower: U.S. Foreign Relations since 1776* (New York: Oxford University Press, 2008), 906.

33. Hutchings, *American Diplomacy*, 190; emphasis added.

34. Schuerch, "The Congressional Role," 337.

35. Drazen, *Political Economy*, 624.

36. See Hutchings, *American Diplomacy*.

37. For a useful overview of the transition experience, see International Monetary Fund (IMF), *25 Years of Transition Post-Communist Europe and the IMF* (Washington, DC: IMF, October 2014).

38. See Ethan B. Kapstein and Nathan Converse, *The Fate of Young Democracies* (New York: Cambridge University Press, 2012), 84.

39. Bush, "Remarks to the American Society of Newspaper Editors."

40. Schuerch, "The Congressional Role," 337.

41. On the formulation of Bush administration policy, see Matlock, *Autopsy of an Empire*, chap. 8. Matlock emphasizes Bush's concerns with criticism from the right wing of the Republic Party as an explanation for the President's caution.

42. Sara Fritz, "Bush–Congress Relations Worsen Rapidly: Administration: The Capital Gains Fight Is Seen as the Main Cause of the Split: The Rancor Has Spread to Other Issues," *Los Angeles Times*, 9 November 1989, www.latimes.com/archives/la-xpm-1989-11-09-mn-1455-story.html.

43. See Steven Weber, "Origins of the European Bank for Reconstruction and Development," *International Organization* 48, no. 1 (1994): 11; Matlock, *Autopsy of an Empire*, chap. 8; and Hutchings, *American Diplomacy*, 196–212.

44. Weber, "Origins of the European Bank," 10.

45. See Matlock, *Autopsy of an Empire*, chap. 8.

46. Zeuli and Ruttan, "U.S. Assistance," 500.

47. Congressional Research Service, *Congress and the Transition of Eastern Europe in 1989* (Washington, DC: Library of Congress, 23 October 1990), 16.

48. Zeuli and Ruttan, "U.S. Assistance," 501.

49. Kimberly A. Zeuli and Vernon W. Ruttan, "Assisting the Former Soviet Empire: An Example of the Foreign Aid Crisis" (Staff Paper No. P96-01, Department of Applied Economics, College of Agriculture, University of Minnesota, 1996), https://ageconsearch.umn.edu/record/13716. See also "Excerpts from Speech by Bush on Polish Aid," *New York Times*, 18 April 1989, https://www.nytimes.com/1989/04/18/world/excerpts-from-speech-by-bush-on-polish-aid.html.

50. Francis Miko, "Congress and the Transformation of Eastern Europe in 1989," in Congressional Research Service, *Congress and Foreign Policy, 1989* (Washington, DC: Library of Congress, 1990), 26.

51. Schuerch, "The Congressional Role," 338. Eventually, Congress would be so involved in formulation of US foreign policy in this sphere that President Bush supposedly would veto legislation to signal that Congress was overstepping its authority in foreign affairs.

52. Scheurch, "The Congressional Role," 339.

53. H.R. 2550 proposed to "Give Poland generalized system of preference (GSPJ) eligibility; Give Poland and Hungary eligibility for OPIC guarantees; Authorize $1.5 million in fiscal year 1990 and $1.56 million in fiscal year 1991 to support the 1987 United States-Poland science and technology agreement; Authorize $2 million for fiscal year 1990 and another $2 million for fiscal year 1991 for medical supplies, hospital equipment, and training in Poland; Authorize $2 million for fiscal year 1990 and again for fiscal year 1991 for de-

veloping democratic institutions and activities in Poland and Hungary." This bill passed the House but stopped there, with many of its elements later incorporated into the SEED Act. See *Congressional Record* of the House of Representatives from 20 June 1989, 12442–12503, https://www.govinfo.gov /content/pkg/GPO-CRECB-1989-pt9/pdf/GPO-CRECB-1989-pt9-5-1.pdf.

54. *Congressional Record* of the House of Representatives from 20 June 1989, 12442.

55. See the text of HR 2550 at https://www.congress.gov/bill/101st-congress /house-bill/2550, accessed 22 July 2020.

56. H.R.2655, International Cooperation Act of 1989, https://www.congress.gov /bill/101st-congress/house-bill/2655.

57. Congressional Research Service, *Congress and the Transition*, 25.

58. Schuerch, "The Congressional Role," 339.

59. Transcript of Hearing before the Subcommittee on Europe and the Middle East of the Committee on Foreign Affairs, 26 July 1989, 5.

60. Statement of William Archey in U.S. Senate, *The Future of Europe*, 366.

61. Matlock, *Autopsy of an Empire*, 177–179.

62. Matlock, *Autopsy of an Empire*, 400.

63. Sara Fritz, "Bush–Congress Relations Worsen Rapidly: Administration: The Capital Gains Fight Is Seen as the Main Cause of the Split. The Rancor Has Spread to Other Issues," *Los Angeles Times*, 9 November 1989.

64. Zeuli and Ruttan, "U.S. Assistance," 501.

65. Zeuli and Ruttan, "U.S. Assistance," 501.

66. Zeuli and Ruttan, "U.S. Assistance," 501.

67. Byster Institute, *Building Entrepreneurial Economies: Lessons from the Enterprise Funds' Experience in Central and Eastern Europe and Central Asia 1990–2007* (San Diego: University of California at San Diego Rady School of Management, August 2007), 2.

68. LaFalce, for example, would remark "This past January, I had the pleasure of leading a delegation of 13 Members of Congress to Central Europe, and I was, like others, struck by the magnitude of the moment in history to which we were bearing witness." U.S. Congress, House of Representatives, *Proposed U.S. Participation in the European Bank for Reconstruction and Development (EBRD), and Update on Exchange Rate Report*, Hearing before the Subcommittee on International Development, Finance, Trade and Monetary Policy of the Committee on Banking, Finance, and Urban Affairs, 101st Congress, Second Session, May 9, 1990 (Washington, DC: Government Printing Office, 1990).

69. Zeuli and Ruttan, "U.S. Assistance," 501.

70. Zeuli and Ruttan, "U.S. Assistance," 501.

71. The text of the SEED Act can be found at https://www.congress.gov/bill/101st -congress/house-bill/3402, accessed 28 December 2020.

72. For a critical study of US policy at this time, see Diana Villiers Negroponte, "The Hesitant U.S. Rescue of the Soviet Economy," *The Washington Quarterly*, Fall 2016, https://www.wilsonquarterly.com/quarterly/the-lasting-legacy -of-the-cold-war/the-hesitant-us-rescue-of-the-soviet-economy/. Negroponte

emphasizes that Secretary of State James Baker "asked others to cough up" to save the Soviet economy.

73. See Negroponte, "The Hesitant U.S. Rescue."

74. See Matlock, *Autopsy of an Empire*, 412–415.

75. Byster Institute, *Building Entrepreneurial Economies: Lessons from the Enterprise Funds' Experience in Central and Eastern Europe and Central Asia 1990–2007* (San Diego: University of California at San Diego Rady School of Management, August 2007), 8.

76. USAID, *20 Years of USAID Economic Growth Assistance*, 122.

77. USAID, *20 Years of USAID Economic Growth Assistance*, 59.

78. Cited in Charles Wolf, Jr. ed., *Promoting Democracy and Free Markets in Eastern Europe* (Santa Monica, CA: RAND Corporation, 1991), 152.

79. Cited in Wolf, *Promoting Democracy*, 196.

80. USAID, *20 Years of USAID Economic Growth Assistance*, 59–70.

81. Peter Murrell, "Multinational Corporations in the Eastern European Economic Transition," in *Multinational Corporations in the New Europe and Global Trade in the 1990s*, ed. M. Klein and P. Welfens (New York: Springer, 1991), 154.

82. See the data appendices to USAID, *20 Years of USAID Economic Growth Assistance*.

83. For an overview of the literature, see Godwin Okafor and Allen Webster, "Foreign Direct Investment in Transition Economies of Europe and the Former Soviet Union," in *Palgrave Dictionary of Emerging Markets and Transition Economies*, ed. Jens Hölscher and Horst Tomann (London: Palgrave Macmillan, 2015), 413–436.

84. Martin Bijsterbosch and Marcin Kolasa, "FDI and Productivity Convergence in Central and Eastern Europe: An Industry-Level Investigation" (European Central Bank Working Papers No. 992, January 2009). For a more skeptical view, see Katarina Bačić, Domagoj Račić, and Amina Ahec Šonje, "FDI and Economic Growth in Central and Eastern Europe: Is There a Link?" (Munich Personal RePEc l Archive Working Paper No. 83136, 2004), https://mpra .ub.uni-muenchen.de/83136/1/MPRA_paper_83136.pdf.

85. Jonathan G. S. Koppell, "The Challenge of Administration by Regulation: Preliminary Findings Regarding the U.S. Government's Venture Capital Funds," *Journal of Public Administration Research and Theory* 9, no. 4 (1999): 641–666, at 648.

86. For background, see Congressional Research Service, *Enterprise Funds and U.S. Foreign Aid Policy* (Washington, DC: Library of Congress, 3 January 1996); and Koppell, "The Challenge of Administration."

87. USAID, *20 Years of USAID Economic Growth Assistance*, 6.

88. On the controversies, see Congressional Research Service, *Enterprise Funds;* and Doug Bandow, "Uncle Sam as Investment Banker: The Failure of Washington's Overseas Enterprise Funds" (Cato Institute Policy Analysis No. 260, September 19, 1996), https://www.cato.org/policy-analysis/uncle-sam-investment -banker-failure-washingtons-overseas-enterprise-funds.

89. USAID, *20 Years of USAID Economic Growth Assistance*, 29–30.

90. John Birkelund, "Doing Good while Doing Well: The Unheralded Success of American Enterprise Funds," *Foreign Affairs* 80, no. 5 (September–October 2001): 14–20, at 16.

91. See "The U.S Russia Investment Fund," USAID Semi-Annual Review, Moscow, 9 September 2008, https://pdf.usaid.gov/pdf_docs/PBAAE067.pdf.

92. See Tomas Marcinak, Jurica Novak, and Marcin Purta, "Central and Eastern Europe Needs a New Engine for Growth," McKinsey & Co., 14 November 2018, https://www.mckinsey.com/featured-insights/europe/central-and-eastern -europe-needs-a-new-engine-for-growth.

93. For an official history, see Andrew Kirkpatrick, *After the Berlin Wall: A History of the EBRD,* vol. 1 (Budapest: Central European University Press, 2020).

94. Weber, "Origins of the European Bank," 15.

95. Weber, "Origins of the European Bank," 15.

96. U.S. Congress, House of Representatives, *Proposed U.S. Participation,* 9.

97. U.S. Congress, House of Representatives, *Proposed U.S. Participation,* 5.

98. U.S. Congress, House of Representatives, *Proposed U.S. Participation,* 3.

99. U.S. Congress, House of Representatives, *Proposed U.S. Participation,* 34.

100. This point is emphasized in Weber, "Origins of the European Bank." On the US belief that small-hold farming was a bulwark of democracy, see Ethan B. Kapstein, *Seeds of Stability: Land Reform and U.S. Foreign Policy* (New York: Cambridge University Press, 2017).

101. U.S. Congress, House of Representatives, *Proposed U.S. Participation,* 2.

102. Eric Ipsen, "EBRD: Very Model of a Bank," *International Herald Tribune,* 7 April 1995, https://www.nytimes.com/1995/04/07/business/worldbusiness /IHT-ebrd-very-model-of-a-bank.html.

103. See U.S. Treasury, "Report to Congress on Evaluation Standards and Practices at the Multilateral Development Banks," August 2018, https:// home.treasury.gov/system/files/206/US-Treasury-Report-to-Congress-on -MDB-Evaluation-August-2018.pdf. EBRD evaluations can be found at https://www.ebrd.com/what-we-do/evaluation-overview.html, accessed 31 August 2020.

104. Jason Saving, "Privatization and the Transition to a Market Economy," Federal Reserve Bank of Dallas, *Economic and Financial Policy Review* (Fourth Quarter 1998): 17–25.

105. John McMillan and Christopher Woodruff, "The Central Role of Entrepreneurs in Transition Economies," *Journal of Economic Perspectives* 16, no. 3 (Summer 2002): 153–170, at 154.

106. McMillan and Woodruff, "The Central Role of Entrepreneurs," 158; see also Elena Nikolova, Frantisek Ricka, and Dora Simrov, "Entrepreneurship in the Transition Region" (EBRD Working Paper No. 141, February 2012).

107. Nikolova, Ricka, and Simrov, "Entrepreneurship in the Transition Region."

108. See also Saving, "Privatization and the Transition to a Market Economy."

109. Joel Hellman, "Winners Take All: The Politics of Partial Reform in Post-Communist Transitions," *World Politics* 50, no. 2 (January 1998): 203–234.

110. Ruchir Sharma, "The Rise of Eastern Europe is Forgotten Economic Success Story," *Financial Times,* 14 September 2021.

111. John Nellis, "The World Bank, Privatization and Enterprise Reform in Transition Economies: A Retrospective Analysis" (Center for Global Development Background Paper, n.d.), 9.

112. Anders Aslund, *How Capitalism Was Built: The Transformation of Central and Eastern Europe, Russia, the Caucasus, and Central Asia* (New York: Cambridge University Press, 2013), 164.

113. Aslund, *How Capitalism Was Built,* 164.

114. On the ideational debate, see Bruce Kogut and J. Muir MacPherson, "The Decision to Privatize as an Economic Policy Idea: Epistemic Communities, Palace Wars, and Diffusion" (unpublished manuscript, June 2004).

115. USAID, *20 Years of USAID Economic Growth Assistance,* 36.

116. USAID, *20 Years of USAID Economic Growth Assistance,* 36–45.

117. In addition to Kogut and MacPherson, "Decision to Privatize"; and Nellis, "The World Bank," see Janos Kornai, "Ten Years after 'the Road to a Free Economy': The Author's Self-Evaluation," paper prepared for the World Bank Annual Conference on Development Economics, 18–20 April 2000 (Washington, DC: World Bank, 2000).

118. Nellis, "The World Bank."

119. Andrei Kolesnikov and Denis Volkov, "Pragmatic Paternalism: The Russian Public and the Private Sector" (Carnegie Moscow Center, 18 January 2019), https://carnegie.ru/commentary/78155.

120. See Joel Hellman, Geraint Jones, and Daniel Kaufman, "Seize the State, Seize the Day: State Capture, Corruption, and Influence in Transition" (World Bank Working Papers, September 2000), https://elibrary.worldbank.org/doi/pdf/10.1596/1813-9450-2444.

121. European Bank for Reconstruction and Development (EBRD), *25 Years of the EBRD: The People's View on Transition* (London: EBRD, 2016), 11.

122. On rising inequality, see Branko Milanović, *Capitalism, Alone: The Future of the System That Rules the World* (Cambridge, MA: Belknap Press of Harvard University Press, 2019).

123. Sharma, "The Rise of Eastern Europe," note 112.

6. Exporting Capitalism to Fragile States

1. John Podesta and John Norris, "The Role of the US Government in Private Sector Development" (Brookings Blum Roundtable Policy Brief, 2013), 44.

2. Tom had the note published in *Foreign Policy*. See Thomas Ricks, "Letter from Afghanistan," *Foreign Policy,* 8 July 2010, https://foreignpolicy.com/2010/07/08/letter-from-afghanistan-some-bright-spots-and-how-to-encourage-them/.

3. Graham Greene, *The Quiet American* (New York: Penguin, 1991).

4. Sune Engel Rasmussen, "Afghanistan's Economic Meltdown Leaves Ordinary Citizens Scrambling to Survive," *Wall Street Journal,* 18 September 2021, 1.

5. Adam Smith, "Lectures on Domestic Policy," *Econ Journal Watch* 14, no. 3 (September 2017): 434–473, at 435. Smith gave these lectures in 1763–1764.

6. Cordell Hull, *Memoirs* (New York: Macmillan, 1948).

7. Jacob Javits, "Introduction of Bill to Establish a Peace by Investment Corporation," *Congressional Record—Senate*, 1 May 1968, 11151. This idea, in fact, originated in a proposal from Javits's brother Benjamin (to whom Jacob was very close; indeed, they were law partners), who already in 1950 had published a book titled *Peace by Investment*. Senator Javits proclaimed that encouraging foreign direct investment in developing countries was "in the interest of world peace through mutual economic progress."

8. John Dowdy, "Stabilizing Iraq: A Conversation with Paul Brinkley," *McKinsey on Government*, Spring 2010, 44–49, at 46.

9. In Special Inspector for Afghanistan Reconstruction, *Private Sector Development and Economic Growth: Lessons for the US Experience in Afghanistan* (Washington, DC: Special Inspector General of Afghanistan Reconstruction, April 2018), 6.

10. See Paul Brinkley, *War Front to Store Front: Americans Rebuilding Trust and Hope Under Fire* (New York: Wiley, 2014). Brinkley directed the TFBSO from its inception.

11. Brinkley, *War Front to Store Front*, 76.

12. Charles Maier, "The Politics of Productivity: Foundations of American International Economic Policy after World War II," in *Between Power and Plenty: Foreign Economic Policies of Advanced Industrial States*, ed. Peter Katzenstein (Madison: University of Wisconsin Press, 1978), 23–50, at 31.

13. Eli Berman, Joseph Felter, and Jacob N. Shapiro, *Small Wars, Big Data: The Information Revolution in Modern Conflict* (Princeton, NJ: Princeton University Press, 2018), 260.

14. World Bank, *Strategy for Fragility, Conflict and Violence* (Washington, DC: World Bank, n.d.), 111.

15. USAID, "Economic Growth Policy" (draft for public comment) (Washington, DC: USAID, July 2019), 7.

16. Douglass North, *Institutions, Institutional Change, and Economic Performance* (New York: Cambridge University Press, 1990).

17. See Douglass North, John Wallis, and Barry Weingast, *Violence and Social Orders* (New York: Cambridge University Press, 2009).

18. Jakob Svensson, "Investment, Property Rights, and Political Instability: Theory and Evidence," *European Economic Review* 42 (1998): 1317–1341.

19. Alberto Alesina and Eliana La Ferrara, "Ethnic Diversity and Economic Performance," *Journal of Economic Literature* 43, no. 3 (2005): 762–800.

20. Arnold Lubasch, "Mafia Runs Fulton Fish Market, US Says in Suit to Take Control," *New York Times*, 16 October 1987, https://www.nytimes.com/1987/10/16/nyregion/mafia-runs-fulton-fish-market-us-says-in-suit-to-take-control.html.

21. David Stasavage, "Private Investment and Political Institutions," *Economics and Politics* 14, no. 1 (March 2002): 41–63, at 43.

22. David Fielding, "Modeling Political Instability and Economic Performance: Israeli Investment During the Intifada," *Economica* 70 (2003): 159–186, at 160.

23. Fielding, "Modeling Political Instability," at 177.

24. Quan Le, "Political and Economic Determinants of Private Investment," *Journal of International Development* 16 (2004): 589–604, at 593.

25. See Timothy Besley and Hannes Mueller, "Predation, Protection, and Productivity: A Firm-Level Perspective," *American Economic Journal: Macroeconomics* 10, no. 2 (2018): 184–221.

26. See Chang-Tai Hsieh and Benjamin A. Olken, "The Missing 'Missing Middle,'" *Journal of Economic Perspectives* 28, no. 3 (2014): 89–108.

27. Spencer Ackerman, "What Surge? Afghanistan's Most Violent Places Stay Bad, Despite Extra Troops," *Wired*, 23 August 2012, https://www.wired.com/2012/08/afghanistan-violence-helmand/.

28. Besley and Mueller, "Predation, Protection, and Productivity."

29. John Speakman and Annoula Rysova, *The Small Entrepreneur in Fragile and Conflict-Affected Situations* (Washington, DC: World Bank, 2015).

30. Massimo Guidolin and Eliana La Ferrara, "Diamonds Are Forever, Wars Are Not: Is Conflict Bad for Private Firms?," *American Economic Review* 97, no. 5 (December 2007): 1978–1993.

31. See Joshua Blumenstock et al., "Insecurity and Industrial Organization: Evidence from Afghanistan" (World Bank Policy Research Working Paper No. 8301, January 2018).

32. See Ethan Kapstein, *The Insecure Alliance: Energy Crises and Western Politics since 1944* (New York: Oxford University Press, 1990).

33. Rajiv Chandresakaran, *Imperial Life in the Emerald City: Inside Iraq's Green Zone* (New York: Knopf, 2006), 115.

34. US Senate, Committee on Foreign Relations, *Policy Options for Iraq* (Washington, DC: Government Printing Office, 2006), 155.

35. Special Inspector General for Iraqi Reconstruction (SIGIR), *Learning from Iraq* (Washington, DC: SIGIR, March 2013), 114.

36. World Bank, *State-Owned Enterprises Reform in Iraq* (Washington, DC: World Bank, 26 July 2004), v.

37. World Bank, *Iraq: Systematic Country Diagnostic* (Washington, DC: World Bank, 3 February 2017), 13.

38. On American planning (or the lack thereof) for the postwar occupation of Iraq, see Nadia Schadlow, *War and the Art of Governance: Consolidating Combat Success into Political Victory* (Washington, DC: Georgetown University Press, 2017), chap. 5.

39. Chandresakaran, *Imperial Life in the Emerald City*, 115.

40. Robert Looney, "The Neoliberal Model's Planned Role in Iraq's Economic Transition," Strategic Insight, Naval Postgraduate School, 1 August 2003, https://apps.dtic.mil/dtic/tr/fulltext/u2/a525789.pdf.

41. Chandresakaran, *Imperial Life in the Emerald City*, 117.

42. The argument is made by the former head of the DoD Task Force of Business and Stability Operations. See Brinkley, *War Front to Store Front*.

43. Christopher Foote, William Block, Keith Crane, and Simon Gray, "Economic Policy and Prospects in Iraq," *Journal of Economic Perspectives* 18, no. 3 (Summer 2004): 47–70, at 58.

44. Richard E. Neustadt and Ernest R. May, *Thinking in Time: The Uses of History for Decision-Makers* (New York: Free Press, 1986).

45. Foote et al., "Economic Policy and Prospects in Iraq," 59.
46. James Dobbins, Seth G. Jones, Benjamin Runkle, and Siddharth Mohandas, *Occupying Iraq: A History of the Coalition Provisional Authority* (Santa Monica, CA: RAND Corporation, 2009), 206.
47. See Coalition Provisional Authority (CPA), *State-Owned Enterprise Action Plan* (Baghdad: CPA, 2 May 2004).
48. See Coalition Provisional Authority, *State-Owned Enterprise Action Plan.*
49. Coalition Provisional Authority, *State-Owned Enterprise Action Plan.*
50. Foote et al., "Economic Policy and Prospects in Iraq."
51. Foote et al., "Economic Policy and Prospects in Iraq," 60.
52. See *Congressional Record* 149, no. 144 (15 October 2003) [House], H9431–H9440.
53. See Emanuel's remarks in *Congressional Record* 150, no. 29 (9 March 2004) [House], H907–H913.
54. Chandresakaran, *Imperial Life in the Emerald City*, 124.
55. Coalition Provisional Authority Order Number 39, Foreign Investment, 19 September 2003.
56. Dobbins et al., *Occupying Iraq*, 212–215.
57. Foote et al., "Economic Policy and Prospects in Iraq," 64.
58. Anne Henderson, *The Coalition Provisional Authority's Experience with Economic Reconstruction in Iraq: Lessons Identified* (US Institute of Peace, Special Report 138, April 2005).
59. John Dowdy, "Stabilizing Iraq: A Conversation with Paul Brinkley," *McKinsey on Government*, Spring 2010, 44–49, at 44.
60. Brinkley, *War Front to Store Front*, 46.
61. This point is powerfully made in Stephen Biddle, "Seeing Baghdad, Thinking Saigon," *Foreign Affairs* 85, no. 2 (March–April 2006): 2–14.
62. World Bank, *Iraq: Enterprise Survey 2011* (Washington, DC: World Bank, 2011); World Bank, *Bringing Back Business in Iraq: An Analytical Note* (Washington, DC: World Bank, 2018).
63. Special Inspector General for Iraqi Reconstruction, *Learning from Iraq*, 116.
64. USAID, *Izdihar Final Report: October 2004–March 2008* (Washington, DC: USAID, 2008), 2.
65. USAID, Office of Inspector General, *Audit of USAID/Iraq's Economic Governance II Program*, Audit Report No. E-267-09-004-P (Washington, DC: USAID, 3 June 2009), 3.
66. World Bank, *Bringing Back Business in Iraq*, 1.
67. World Bank, *Bringing Back Business in Iraq*, 13.
68. *Prime Minister's Advisory Commission* (Baghdad, 2014).
69. *Prime Minister's Advisory Commission.*
70. *Prime Minister's Advisory Commission.*
71. Irene Costantini, "A Neoliberal Rentier System: New Challenges and Past Economic Trajectories in Iraq," *The International Spectator* 52 no. 1 (2017): 61–75, DOI: 10.1080/03932729.2017.1262502.
72. Costantini, "A Neoliberal Rentier System," 67.

73. World Bank, *Breaking Out of Fragility: A Country Economic Memorandum for Diversification and Growth in Iraq* (Washington, DC: World Bank, 2020), 28.

74. World Bank, "Afghanistan Systematic Country Diagnostic: An Analysis of a Country's Path toward Development," 9 May 2016, 1, https://www.worldbank.org/en/news/feature/2016/05/10/afghanistan-systematic-country-diagnostic-an-analysis-of-the-countrys-path-toward-development.

75. For the background, see Barnett Rubin, *Afghanistan from the Cold War through the War on Terror* (Oxford: Oxford University Press, 2013).

76. On the distribution of violence within Afghanistan, see Berman, Felter, and Shapiro, *Small Wars, Big Data.*

77. World Bank, *Afghanistan Enterprise Survey 2014* (Washington, DC: World Bank, 2014).

78. Richard Ghiasy, Jiayi Zhou, and Henrik Hallgren, *Afghanistan's Private Sector: Status and Way Forward* (Stockholm: Stockholm International Peace Research Institute, 2015), 6.

79. CIA, *The World Factbook,* https://www.cia.gov/library/publications/the-world-factbook/geos/af.html, accessed 31 July 2020.

80. Ghiasy, Zhou, and Hallgren, *Afghanistan's Private Sector,* 14.

81. US Department of State, "2018 Investment Climate Statement: Afghanistan," https://www.state.gov/reports/2018-investment-climate-statements/afghanistan/, accessed 16 December 2020. This section relies heavily on the pioneering work of Paul Fishstein and his colleagues at SIGAR. See Special Inspector for Afghanistan Reconstruction, *Private Sector Development and Economic Growth: Lessons for the US Experience in Afghanistan* (Washington, DC: SIGAR, April 2018).

82. World Bank, "Afghanistan: Systematic Country Diagnostic, 2016" (Washington, DC: World Bank, 2016), 1.

83. U.S. Army, Center for Lessons Learned, *Commander's Guide to Money as a Weapons System: Tactics, Techniques, and Procedures,* April 2009, https://usacac.army.mil/sites/default/files/publications/09-27.pdf.

84. Grant McLeod, "Responding to Corruption and the Kabul Bank Collapse" (Washington, DC: US Institute of Peace, 2016).

85. This review is drawn from Special Inspector for Afghanistan Reconstruction, *Private Sector Development and Economic Growth,* xii–xiv.

86. For an excellent overview, see Schadlow, *War and the Art of Governance,* chap. 5.

87. RAND Corporation, *Task Force on Business and Stability Operations: Lessons from Afghanistan* (Santa Monica, CA: RAND Corporation, 2016), xiii.

88. RAND Corporation, *Task Force on Business and Stability Operations,* xiii.

89. L. Leonardo and L. Robertson, *Assessment of Corruption in Afghanistan* (Washington, DC: USAID, 2009), http://pdf.usaid.gov/pdf_docs/Pnado248pdf.

90. U.S. Department of State, *Investment Climate Survey: Afghanistan* (Washington, DC: U.S. Department of State, 2017).

91. U.S. Department of State, *Investment Climate Survey.*
92. See Joshua Blumenstock et al., "Insecurity and Industrial Organization: Evidence from Afghanistan" (World Bank Policy Research Working Paper No. 8301, January 2018).
93. See Blumenstock et al., "Insecurity and Industrial Organization."
94. Cited in Kathy Gilsinan, "The Pottery Barn Rule: Syria Edition," *The Atlantic,* 30 September 2015, https://www.theatlantic.com/international/archive/2015 /09/the-pottery-barn-rule-syria-edition/408193/.

7. Dueling Capitalisms?

1. Press briefing on the launch of the US International Development Finance Corporation, 14 August 2019, https://www.state.gov/press-briefing-on-the-launch -of-the-u-s-international-development-finance-corporation/.
2. John Ratcliffe, "China Is National Security Threat No. 1," *Wall Street Journal,* 3 December 2020, https://www.wsj.com/articles/china-is-national-security -threat-no-1-11607019599.
3. Ratcliffe, "China Is National Security Threat No. 1."
4. Amy Kazmin, Benjamin Parkin, and Farhan Bokhari, "China Plots Influence Push as India Battles Covid Crisis," *Financial Times,* 28 April 2021.
5. See International Finance Corporation (IFC), *International Finance Institutions and Development through the Private Sector* (Washington, DC: IFC, 2011).
6. On the influence of neoliberalism, see Quinn Slobodian, *Globalists: The End of Empire and the Birth of Neoliberalism* (Cambridge, MA: Harvard University Press, 2018).
7. George Ingram and Robert Mosbacher, "Development Finance: Filling Today's Funding Gap," prepared for the 2018 Brookings Blum Roundtable.
8. Organisation for Economic Co-operation and Development, "Financing for Stability in the Post-2015 Era" (OECD Development Policy Paper No. 10, February 2018), 5.
9. See International Finance Corporation, *International Finance Institutions and Development through the Private Sector.*
10. Daniel Runde and Aaron Milner, *Development Finance Institutions: Plateaued Growth, Increasing Needs* (Washington, DC: Center for Strategic and International Studies, February 2019).
11. Nargiza Salidjanova, "Going Out: An Overview of China's Outward Foreign Direct Investment," U.S.-China Economic and Security Review Commission, 30 March 2011. For a review of different perspectives on Chinese economic statecraft, see Ethan B. Kapstein, "Economic Statecraft: Continuity and Change," in *Economic Statecraft,* ed. David Baldwin (Princeton, NJ: Princeton University Press, 2020), 405–428.
12. The phrase "political capitalism" is drawn from Branko Milanović, *Capitalism, Alone: The Future of the System That Rules the World* (Cambridge, MA: Belknap Press of Harvard University Press, 2019).
13. See Milanović, *Capitalism, Alone.*

14. Development Finance Corporation, "Congressional Budget Justification: Fiscal Year 2021," 1, https://www.dfc.gov/sites/default/files/media/documents /FY2021_DFC_CBJ-Final-04222020.pdf, accessed 21 September 2021.

15. "Remarks by Vice President Michael Pence on the Administration's Policy towards China," Hudson Institute, Washington, DC, 4 October 2018, https:// www.whitehouse.gov/briefings-statements/remarks-vice-president-pence -administrations-policy-toward-china/.

16. Reuters Staff, "China's August Forex Reserves Rise to $3.165 trillion," Reuters, 7 September 2020, https://www.reuters.com/article/us-china-economy-forex -reserves/chinas-august-forex-reserves-rise-to-3-165-trillion-idUSKBN 25YoU7.

17. Aaron L. Friedberg, "Globalisation and Chinese Grand Strategy," *Survival* 60, no. 1 (2018): 7–40, at 23.

18. Andrew Chatzky and James McBride, "China's Massive Belt and Road Initiative," Council on Foreign Relations Backgrounder, 28 January 2020, https://www.cfr.org/backgrounder/chinas-massive-belt-and-road-initiative.

19. US-China Economic and Security Review Commission, "Hearing on China's Belt and Road: Five Years Later" (Washington, DC: U.S. Congress, 25 January 2018).

20. Ethan Kapstein and Jacob Shapiro, "Catching China by the Belt and Road," *Foreign Policy* 20 (April 2018), https://foreignpolicy.com/2019/04/20/catching -china-by-the-belt-and-road-international-development-finance-corp-beijing -united-states/.

21. For a recent analysis by a Chinese scholar along these lines, see Lü Shirong, "Marx's Thoughts on Economic Globalization," *Social Sciences in China* 37 no. 2 (2016): 5–19.

22. David Dollar and John L. Thornton, "Is China's Development Finance a Challenge to the International Order?," paper presented at the JCER conference, Tokyo, October 2017.

23. U.S. Department of State, *Congressional Budget Justification: Department of State, Foreign Operations, and Related Programs, Fiscal Year 2020* (Washington, DC: U.S. Department of State, 2019), https://www.state.gov/fy-2020 -congressional-budget-justification-department-of-state-foreign-operations -and-related-programs/.

24. Daniel Kliman, Rush Doshi, Kristine Lee, and Zack Cooper, "Grading China's Belt and Road" (Washington, DC: Center for a New American Security, April 2019), 2, https://www.cnas.org/publications/reports/beltandroad.

25. These are among the questions that Audrye Wong seeks to examine in her pioneering work. See Audrye Wong, "Crafting Payoffs: Strategies and Effectiveness of Economic Statecraft" (unpublished manuscript, 2020).

26. For an article that does so, see Ann-Sofie Isaksson and Andreas Kotsadam, "Chinese Aid and Local Corruption," *Journal of Public Economics* 159 (March 2018): 146–159.

27. Francois de Soyres, "The Growth and Welfare Effects of the Belt and Road Initiative on East Asia Pacific Countries," *Macroeconomic, Trade and Investment Practice Notes* no. 4 (Washington, DC: World Bank Group, October 2018), http://documents.worldbank.org/curated/en/896581540306960489

/The-Growth-and-Welfare-Effects-of-the-Belt-and-Road-Initiative-on-East
-Asia-Pacific-Countries.

28. Leah Lynch, Sharon Andersen, and Tianyu Zhu, *China's Foreign Aid: A Primer for Recipient Countries, Donors, and Aid Providers* (Washington, DC: Center for Global Development, July 2020).

29. Lili Kang, Fei Peng, Yu Zhu, and An Pan, "Harmony in Diversity: Can the One Belt One Road Initiative Promote China's Outward Foreign Direct Investment?," *Sustainability* 10 (2018): 1–28.

30. Chengchun Li, Yun Luo, and Glauco De Vita, "Institutional Difference and Outward FDI: Evidence from China," *Empirical Economics* 58 (2020): 1837–1862.

31. U.S.-China Economic and Security Review Commission, *Hearing on China's Belt and Road: Five Years Later* (Washington, DC: U.S. Congress, 25 January 2018), 6, https://www.uscc.gov/hearings/chinas-belt-and-road-initiative -five-years-later.

32. There is not yet a comprehensive study of the topic, although some monographs are starting to appear. See, for example, Xueli Huang and Ying Zhu, *Managing Chinese Outward Foreign Direct Investment: From Entry Strategy to Sustainable Development in Australia* (London: Palgrave Macmillan, 2016).

33. For a recent review, see Bijun Wang, Rui Mao, and Qin Gou, "Overseas Impacts of China's Outward Direct Investment," *Asian Economic Policy Review* 9 (2014): 227–249.

34. There is also, of course, a richer literature on FDI within China. For a fairly recent overview, see Michael Enright, *Developing China: The Remarkable Impact of Foreign Direct Investment* (New York: Routlege, 2017).

35. For a recent discussion, see Xueyan Wu, "China's Political Risk Insurance for Outward FDI within the Context of Belt and Road Initiative," in *A Legal Analysis of the Belt and Road Initiative: Towards a New Silk Road?,* ed. Giuseppe Martinico and Xueyan Wu (London: Palgrave Macmillan, 2020), 185–197.

36. For an introduction to the "going global" policy, see Leonard K. Cheng and Zihui Ma, "China's Outward Foreign Direct Investment," in *China's Growing Role in World Trade,* ed. Robert C. Feenstra and Shang-Jin Wei (Chicago: University of Chicago Press, 2010), 545–578.

37. Cheng and Ma, "China's Outward Foreign Direct Investment."

38. Ana Lucia Abeliansky and Inmaculada Martínez-Zarzo, "The Relationship between the Chinese 'Going Out' Strategy and International Trade" (Kiel Institute for the World Economy, Economics Discussion Papers No. 2018-10, 19 February 2018), http://www.economics-ejournal.org/economics/discussion papers/2018-20.

39. Wang, Mao, and Gou, "Overseas Impacts of China's Outward Direct Investment."

40. Riccardo Crescenzi and Nicola Limodio, "The Impact of Chinese FDI in Africa: Evidence from Ethiopia" (unpublished manuscript, February 2020).

41. Chunyang Pan, William X. Wei, Etayankara Muralidharan, Jia Liao, and Bernadette Andreosso-O'Callagh, "Does China's Outward Direct Investment

Improve the Institutional Quality of the Belt and Road Countries?," *Sustainability* 12 (2020): 1–21.

42. Congressional Research Service, *African Growth and Opportunity Act (AGOA): Background and Reauthorization* (Washington, DC: Library of Congress, 22 April 2015).

43. See Daniel Runde, "U.S. Foreign Assistance in the Age of Strategic Competition" (Washington, DC: Center for Strategic and International Studies, May 2020), 1.

44. For a balanced assessment, see Anthony Cordesman, "President Trump's New National Security Strategy" (Washington, DC: Center for Strategic and International Studies, 18 December 2017).

45. President Donald J. Trump, "National Security Strategy of the United States," December 2017, 25, https://www.whitehouse.gov/wp-content/uploads/2017/12/NSS-Final-12-18-2017-0905.pdf.

46. See "Biden's New China Doctrine," *The Economist*, 17 July 2021, https://www.economist.com/leaders/2021/07/17/bidens-new-china-doctrine.

47. Michael Pence, "Remarks by Vice President Michael Pence on the Administration's Policy towards China," 4 October 2018, https://www.whitehouse.gov/briefings-statements/remarks-vice-president-pence-administrations-policy-toward-china/.

48. For an excellent study that provides somewhat different alternatives for US strategy, see Gal Luft, "Silk Road 2.0: U.S. Strategy towards China's Belt and Road Initiative" (Washington, DC: Atlantic Council, 2017). A real strength of this paper is how Luft breaks down the BRI into its constituent parts and outlines possible US strategies for each one of them.

49. Mike Gallagher, "Yes, America Is in a Cold War with China," *Wall Street Journal*, 7 June 2020, https://www.wsj.com/articles/yes-america-is-in-a-cold-war-with-china.

50. Pence, "Remarks by Vice President Michael Pence."

51. Stephanie Findlay and Farhan Bokhari, "Pakistan Revives Belt and Road Projects under Chinese Pressure," *Financial Times*, 10 December 2019.

52. Daniel Kliman, "To Compete with China, Get the New U.S. Development Finance Corporation Right" (Washington, DC: Center for a New American Security, February 2019), 3.

53. U.S. International Development Finance Corporation, "Developing DFC's New Development Performance Measurement System: What Is Impact Quotient (IQ)?," https://www.dfc.gov/sites/default/files/media/documents/DFC-IQ-PerformanceMeasurement_062020_1.pdf.

54. See the DFC project map, which is updated every forty-five days, at https://www3.opic.gov/ActiveProjectsMap/Default.aspx, accessed 29 December 2020.

55. Development Finance Corporation, *Starting Strong: A Report on DFC's First Year* (Washington, DC: Development Finance Corporation, n.d.), accessed 21 September 2021, https://www.dfc.gov/sites/default/files/media/documents/DFC_2020_Annual_Report.pdf.

56. See Development Finance Corporation, *DFC's Roadmap for Impact: DFC's Inaugural Development Strategy, January 2020–December 2025* (Washington, DC: Development Finance Corporation, n.d.), 6, https://www.dfc.gov/sites/default/files/media/documents/DFC%27s%20Roadmap%20for%20Impact.pdf, accessed 21 September 2021.

57. This section draws from Ethan B. Kapstein and Jacob N. Shapiro, "Catching China by the Belt and Road," *Foreign Policy,* 20 April 2018, https://foreignpolicy.com/2019/04/20/catching-china-by-the-belt-and-road-international-development-finance-corp-beijing-united-states/.

58. See U.S. Department of State, "Blue Dot Network," https://www.state.gov/blue-dot-network/, accessed 18 December 2020.

59. For contemporary policy statements on tied aid from the OECD's Development Assistance Committee, see OECD, "Untied Aid," https://www.oecd.org/dac/financing-sustainable-development/development-finance-standards/untied-aid.htm, accessed 8 June 2020.

60. Tom Wright and Bradley Hope, "China Offered to Bail Out Troubled Asian Fund in Return for Deals," *Wall Street Journal,* 7 January 2019, https://www.wsj.com/articles/how-china-flexes-its-political-muscle-to-expand-power-overseas-11546890449.

61. See Philip Zelikow, "The Rise of Strategic Corruption: How States Weaponize Graft," *Foreign Affairs,* September / October 2020, https://www.foreignaffairs.com/articles/united-states/2020-06-09/rise-strategic-corruption.

62. See the website of the Blue Dot Network: U.S. Department of State, "Blue Dot Network," https://www.state.gov/blue-dot-network/, accessed 18 December 2020.

63. Bruce Stokes, "Americans, Like Many in Other Advanced Economies, Not Convinced of Trade's Benefits: Emerging Market Publics More Likely to Link Trade to More Jobs, Better Wages," Pew Research Center, 26 September 2018, https://www.pewresearch.org/global/2018/09/26/americans-like-many-in-other-advanced-economies-not-convinced-of-trades-benefits/.

64. Indeed, elite educations became no more attainable in 2020 than they had been decades earlier. If anything they were become less available, as rising tuitions conspired with reduced availability of adequate funding, which had once sustained entry to these institutions. Of course, if poor and middle-class students did gain entry to university education, it was often accompanied by crushing levels of debt that would be hard to relieve, particularly in times of economic crisis. See Raj Chetty, Nathaniel Hendren, Patrick Kline, and Emmanuel Saez, "Where Is the Land of Opportunity? The Geography of Intergenerational Mobility in the United States" (NBER Working Paper No. 19843, June 2014).

65. See, for example, President Bill Clinton's speech "The Job of Ending Discrimination in This Country Is Not Over," *Washington Post,* 16 July 1995, https://www.washingtonpost.com/wp-srv/politics/special/affirm/docs/clintonspeech.htm, where he emphasizes "equal opportunity," but not income redistribution.

66. Cited in "Elizabeth Warren on Free Trade," On the Issues, https://www.onthe issues.org/2020/Elizabeth_Warren_Free_Trade.htm, accessed 8 August 2020.

8. The Future of Private Sector Development

1. See cites to Pisar in U.S. Senate, Committee on Foreign Relations, *Hearings on Multinational Corporations and U.S. Foreign Policy, Part 2* (Washington, DC: Government Printing Office, 1973), 517.

2. On Macron's economic views, see Philip Askenazy, "The Contradictions of Macronism," *Dissent* (Winter 2018), https://www.dissentmagazine.org/article /emmanuel-macron-contradictions-neoliberalism.

3. Leila Abbod, "COVID-19 Hastens French Push to Bring Home Medicines Manufacture," *Financial Times,* 29 July 2020.

4. See "Build Back Better: Joe Biden's Jobs and Economic Recovery Plan for Working Families," https://joebiden.com/build-back-better/, accessed 18 December 2020.

5. "The Biden-Harris Administration Immediate Priorities," The White House, https://buildbackbetter.gov/priorities/economic-recovery/, accessed 18 December 2020.

6. The Australian government provides a good overview of the RCEP at the following website: "Regional Comprehensive Economic Partnership," Department of Foreign Affairs and Trade, Australian Government, https://www.dfat .gov.au/trade/agreements/not-yet-in-force/rcep, accessed 18 December 2020.

7. An official EU analysis of the agreement can be found on the following website: "Key Elements of the EU-China Comprehensive Agreement on Investment," https://ec.europa.eu/commission/presscorner/detail/en/IP_20_2542, accessed 2 January 2021.

8. Louis Hartz, *The Liberal Tradition in America* (New York: Harcourt, Brace, 1955).

9. See Ethan B. Kapstein and Rene Kim, "Sourcing Locally for Impact," *Stanford Social Innovation Review* (Fall 2011): 49–53; and Ethan B. Kapstein, "Africa's Capitalist Revolution," *Foreign Affairs* 88, no. 4 (July–August 2011): 119–128.

10. Again, these were first highlighted in David Baldwin, *Economic Development and American Foreign Policy: 1943–1962* (Chicago: University of Chicago Press, 1966).

11. The data may be found at "Worldwide Activities of U.S. Multinational Enterprises: Preliminary 2018 Statistics," https://www.bea.gov/worldwide -activities-us-multinational-enterprises-preliminary-2018-statistics, accessed 23 March 2021.

12. For a recent study that examines the (positive) long-run effects of the pro-market policies promoted by Reagan administration official James Baker on developing countries, see Anusha Chari, Peter Blair Henry, and Hector Reyes, "The Baker Hypothesis" (NBER Working Paper No. 27708, August 2020). But for a prominent study that casts doubt upon the positive effects of FDI on economic growth in Latin America, see Ricardo Hausman and Eduardo Fernandez-Arias, "Foreign Direct Investment: Good Cholesterol?," paper prepared for

the seminar "The New Wave of Capital Inflows: Sea Change or Just Another Tide?," Annual Meeting of the Board of Governors, Inter-American Development Bank and Inter-American Investment Corporation, March 26, 2020, https://publications.iadb.org/publications/english/document/Foreign -Direct-Investment-Good-Cholesterol.pdf.

13. See Kapstein and Kim, "Sourcing Locally for Impact," 49–53.

14. Tomas Havranek and Zuzana Irsova, "Estimating Vertical Spillovers from FDI: Why Results Vary and What the True Effect Is," *Journal of International Economics* 85 (2011): 234–244, at 234.

15. Havranek and Irsova, "Estimating Vertical Spillovers from FDI," 244.

16. The authors, however, may have confounded credit to the private sector at the "macro" level with credit available to individual firms. Thus, while Romania overall has low levels of credit to the private sector, it is entirely possible that firms that service multinational corporations do have access to credit. Thus, local firms with banking relationships gain a competitive advantage over those that do not.

17. For what makes Latin America "different" in terms of the effects of FDI, see Kevin Williams, "Foreign Direct Investment in Latin America and the Caribbean: An Empirical Analysis," *Latin American Journal of Economics* 52, no. 1 (May 2015): 57–77.

18. For an overview of the literature, see Jeffrey Frankel, "The Natural Resource Curse: A Survey" (NBER Working Paper No. 15836, March 2010).

19. Albert Hirschman, "A Generalized Linkage Approach to Development, with Special Reference to Staples," in *The Essential Hirschman,* ed. Jeremy Adelman (Princeton, NJ: Princeton University Press, 2013), 155–194, at 178. As with everything Hirschman, he then goes on to complicate this story, showing how commodity dependence can also, over time and in certain environments, and depending on the introduction of new technologies, foster development.

20. Werner Baer, "Evaluating the Impact of Brazil's Industrialization," *Luso-Brazilian Review* 15, no. 2 (Winter 1978): 178–190.

21. Kapstein and Kim, "Sourcing Locally for Impact."

22. Kapstein and Kim, "Sourcing Locally for Impact."

23. Cited in Donor Committee for Enterprise Development, "The Political Economy of Business Environment Reform: An Introduction for Practitoners" (May 2011), 9, https://www.enterprise-development.org/wp-content/uploads /Political_Economy_An_Introduction_for_Practitioners.pdf.

24. See Eli Berman, Joseph Felter, and Jacob N. Shapiro, *Small Wars, Big Data: The Information Revolution in Modern Conflict* (Princeton, NJ: Princeton University Press, 2018).

25. For a relatively recent critique, see William Easterly, *The White Man's Burden: Why the West's Efforts to Aid the Rest Have Done So Much Ill and So Little Good* (New York: Penguin, 2007).

26. Raghuram Rajan and Arvind Subramanian, "Aid, Dutch Disease, and Manufacturing," *Journal of Development Economics* 94, no. 1 (January 2011): 106–118.

27. See Ethan B. Kapstein, *Seeds of Stability: Land Reform and U.S. Foreign Policy* (New York: Cambridge University Press, 2017), for a discussion of this issue.

28. See the discussion in Berman, Felter, and Shapiro, *Small Wars, Big Data*.

29. For an excellent, relatively recent contribution, see Nathan Jensen, "Political Risk, Democratic Institutions, and Foreign Direct Investment," *Journal of Politics* 70, no. 4 (October 2008): 1040–1052.

30. Sunil Sinha, Johan Holmberg, and Mark Thomas, *What Works for Market Development: A Review of the Evidence* (Stockholm: Swedish International Development Agency, 2013), 20.

31. For an overview of these issues from an aid policy perspective, see Donor Committee for Enterprise Development, "The Political Economy of Business Environment Reform."

32. Cited in Donor Committee for Enterprise Development, "The Political Economy of Business Environment Reform," 6.

33. Cited in Donor Committee for Enterprise Development, "The Political Economy of Business Environment Reform," 9.

34. World Bank, Independent Evaluation Group, *Private Sector Development: Recent Lessons from Independent Evaluation* (Washington, DC: World Bank Group, 2016), 4, https://ieg.worldbankgroup.org/sites/default/files/Data/reports/fpd-summaries_2.pdf.

35. The IFC's programs in China can be found at IFC, "IFC in China," https://www.ifc.org/wps/wcm/connect/region__ext_content/ifc_external_corporate_site/east+asia+and+the+pacific/countries/ifc-in-china, accessed 23 August 2020.

36. Nicholas Bloom et al., "Does Management Matter: Evidence from India" (NBER Working Paper No. 16658, January 2011).

37. Nicholas Bloom, Benn Eiferrt, Aprajit Mahajan, David McKenzie, and John Roberts, "Management Practices across Firms and Countries" (NBER Working Paper No. 17850, February 2012).

38. James Silberman, Charles Weiss, and Mark Dutz, "Marshall Plan Productivity Assistance: A Unique Program of Mass Technology Transfer and a Precedent for the Former Soviet Union," *Technology in Society* 18 no. 4 (1996): 443–460, at 446.

39. Michela Giorcelli, "The Long-Term Effects of Management and Technology Transfers," *American Economic Review* 109, no. 1 (2019): 121–152.

40. Silberman, Weiss, and Dutz, "Marshall Plan Productivity Assistance."

41. See Branko Milanović, *Capitalism, Alone: The Future of the System That Rules the World* (Cambridge, MA: Belknap Press of Harvard University Press, 2019), 3.

42. For a review of the debate, see Julio Garin, Robert Lester, Eric Sims, and Jonathan Wolff, "Without Looking Closer, It May Seem Cheap: Low Interest Rates and Government Borrowing," *Economic Letters* 180 (2019): 28–32.

43. Davide Furceri and Ricardo Sousa, "The Impact of Government Spending on the Private Sector: Crowding-out versus Crowding-in Effects," *Kyklos* 64, no. 4 (November 2011): 516–533.

44. On growing economic concentration, see Thomas Philippon, *The Great Reversal: How America Gave Up on Free Markets* (Cambridge, MA: Harvard University Press, 2019).

45. Braden Kelner, "Leading US Investment in Developing Nations," *Wharton Magazine* 7 (January 2020), https://magazine.wharton.upenn.edu/digital /leading-us-investment-in-developing-nations/.

46. Gillian Tett, "Global Trade Was Slowing Down before the Tariff War Started," *Financial Times,* 18 July 2019.

47. See "Remarks by President Biden at Signing of an Executive Order on Supply Chains," The White House, 24 February 2021, https://www.whitehouse.gov /briefing-room/speeches-remarks/2021/02/24/remarks-by-president-biden-at -signing-of-an-executive-order-on-supply-chains/.

48. See Andrew Phillips and J. C. Sharman, *Outsourcing Empire: How Company-States Made the Modern World* (Princeton, NJ: Princeton University Press, 2020).

49. Agatha Kratz, Allen Feng, and Logan Wright, "New Data on the 'Debt Trap' Question," Rhodium Group, 29 April 2019, https://rhg.com/research/new -data-on-the-debt-trap-question/.

50. See Lingling Wei, "China Eyes Shrinking Jack Ma's Business Empire," *Wall Street Journal,* 29 December 2020.

51. See U.S. Department of Health and Human Services, "Fact Sheet: Explaining Operation Warp Speed," 16 June 2020, https://www.hhs.gov/about/news /2020/06/16/fact-sheet-explaining-operation-warp-speed.html.

52. Congressional Research Service, "Global Research and Development Expenditures: Fact Sheet" (Washington, DC: Library of Congress, 29 April 2020), 1.

53. Nancy Lee and Asad Sami, "Trends in Private Capital Flows to Low-Income Countries: Good and Not-So-Good News" (Center for Global Development Working Paper 151, July 2019), 5.

54. See Bruce Stokes, "Americans, Like Many in Other Advanced Economies, Not Convinced of Trade's Benefits," Pew Research Center, 26 September 2018, https://www.pewresearch.org/global/wp-content/uploads/sites/2/2018/09/PG _2018.09.26_global-trade_FINALupdated.pdf.

55. Soeren Henn and James Robinson, "Africa's Latent Assets" (NBER Working Paper No. 28603, March 2021).

56. Kapstein, "Africa's Capitalist Revolution."

57. It should be emphasized that some scholars have cast doubt upon Packenham's list as an accurate reflection of policy beliefs. For a detailed critique, see David Baldwin, *Economic Statecraft,* new ed. (Princeton, NJ: Princeton University Press, 2020), chap. 10.

58. Robert Packenham, *Liberal America and the Third World: Political Development Ideas in Foreign Aid and Social Science* (Princeton NJ: Princeton University Press, 1973), 19.

59. For a review of the evidence, see Simon Quinn and Chris Woodruff, "Experiments and Entrepreneurship in Developing Countries," unpublished manuscript, University of Oxford, n.d.

60. Martin Ravaillon, "Inequality and Globalization: A Review Essay," *Journal of Economic Literature* 56, no. 2 (2018): 620–642, at 639.

Index

action, covert, 97. *See also* CIA
advice, 216
Afghan Investment Agency, 177
Afghanistan, 2, 8, 216; Al Qaeda, 175, 178; belief in power of private enterprise and, 183; credit in, 181; data on, 182; economy of, 154, 175–176; growth in, 175; lessons from, 155; natural resources in, 180; obstacles to business in, 181; private sector development in, 174–176, 177–180; property rights in, 159; SOEs in, 177, 179, 181; stabilization efforts in, 176; structural conditions in, 184; Taliban, 174, 175, 178, 180, 183, 216; TFBSO in, 156, 178, 179, 180; United States and, 154, 175, 178, 184; violence in, 174–175. *See also* fragile and conflict-affected states (FCS)
Afghanistan Investment Support Agency (AISA), 177
Africa, 5, 30, 38, 207, 208, 221. *See also* developing world; *individual countries*
Africa Growth and Opportunity Act, 197
African Americans, 203
agencies, bilateral, 8
agricultural associations, 59
agriculture, 24. *See also* land reform
aid, foreign: end of, 54, 66, 86; goals of, 197; government-to-government programs, 21,

96–97; image of, 85, 86; implementers of, 7; lack of support for, 26; limitations on, 30; motivations for, 20 (*see also* communism; security); as mutual bargain, 41; need for, 25, 207; private enterprise and, 5, 78 (*see also* crowding out; firms, local; linkages); resources allocated to, 29, 98; supplanting with private sector development, viii; support for, 87; as temporary, 55. *See also* foreign direct investment (FDI); government, US; interventions; policy
aid, public, 28
aid dependence, 212–213
AISA (Afghanistan Investment Support Agency), 177
Alger, Horatio, 12
Allende, Salvador, 88, 91, 93, 103, 105
Alliance for Progress, 69, 84–91
Al Qaeda, 175, 178. *See also* Afghanistan
Anderson, Jack, 103–104
Arbenz, Jacobo, 77, 79
Argentina, 81, 105, 123, 210. *See also* Latin America
Asia, 18, 30, 90; China's influence in, 198; credit in, 14, 214; diversity in, 38; elites in, 214; emphasis on state-led development in, 40; global supply chains and, 214;

Asia (*continued*)
Latin America compared to, 68; Marshall Plan and, 18, 20, 72; Regional Comprehensive Economic Partnership, 206; security environment in, 39. *See also individual countries*
Asian Development Bank, 143
Asian Infrastructure Investment Bank, 196
Aslund, Anders, 148
assets, fixed, 182
assistance, emergency, 127, 128
Association of Southeast Asian Nations, 206
Attai, Jacques, 144
Australia, 102, 202, 206, 210
autarky, 203, 220
authoritarianism, 125, 151, 188, 213. *See also individual countries*
autocracy, 124
Azerbaijan, 215

Baker, James, 112, 135
Baker Hypothesis, 111
balance-of-payments restrictions, 96
Baldwin, David, 3, 11, 19
Baldwin, Robert, 47
banks, 7; in Afghanistan, 177; inter-American, 77, 78; local, 6, 8; regional development, 69. *See also* US International Development Finance Corporation (DFC); *individual banks*
Barnet, Richard, 93, 94
Bearing Point, 170
Belka, Marek, 165
Belt and Road Initiative (BRI), 1, 185, 186, 188, 190–194, 198–202, 220
Benninghoff, Merrell, 56, 58
Berman, Eli, 157
Bermeo, Nancy, 12
Besley, Timothy, 161
Biden, Joe, 8, 196, 205, 219; China and, 197; encouragement of FDI, 221; protectionism of, 186, 203
Birkelund, John, 141
Blaufarb, Douglas, 85
Bloom, Nicholas, 216–217
Blue Dot Network (BDN), 201, 202
Blumenstock, Joshua, 182–183
Bo, K. S., 59
Boehler, Adam, 219
Bogota Conference, 74
Bolivia, 75, 80, 105. *See also* Latin America
bootstrap economy, 12. *See also* self-help
Bowman, Scott, 12

Brands, Hal, 100, 104
Brazil, 123, 210; FDI in, 75, 83; ISI schemes in, 36; ITT in, 88; Kubitschek, 81, 86; military regime in, 90–91; MNCs in, 82–83; nationalism in, 85; nationalizations in, 75; Operation Pan America, 81; petroleum in, 82, 83–84; São Paulo, 92; SOEs in, 67, 71; US investment in, 72; Vargas, 67, 79; Volta Redonda, 71. *See also* Latin America
Bremer, Paul, 162
Bretton Woods negotiations, 20, 21
BRI (Belt and Road Initiative), 1, 185, 186, 188, 190–194, 198–202, 220. *See also* China
bribery, 192–193. *See also* corruption; kleptocracy
Brinkley, Paul, 168
Britain: postcommunist countries and, 141; privatization in, 148, 149
Broe, William, 103
Brookings Institution, 188, 191
Brooks, Stephen, 122–124
BUILD Act, 1–2
Bureau of Economic Analysis, 207
Bush, George H. W., 119, 124, 127, 128, 129, 130–135, 139, 142
Bush, George W., 164, 184
businesses, American. *See* firms, American; multinational corporations (MNCs)
businesses, multinational. *See* multinational corporations (MNCs)
business leaders, American: International Private Investment Advisory Council and, 96; lack of interest in FDI, 28–29, 198–199; Latin America and, 87–88, 89–90; limits on US policy and, 19; preferences of, ix; support for foreign aid, 87; Task Force on International Private Enterprise, 109. *See also* firms, American; multinational corporations (MNCs); *individual firms*

Canada, 28, 102
capital: access to, 193; flows to developing world, 108–109; global flows of, 220–221; scarcity of, in developing world, 20–21. *See also* finance; foreign direct investment (FDI)
capitalism: exportability of, 12; exporting, viii, 223; future of, 218; hostility to, 81. *See also* market economy; private enterprise; private sector development (PSD)
capitalism, crony, 62, 145, 173, 213. See also *chaebol*

capitalism, political, 188
capitalism, state, 220. *See also* China
Caribbean Basin Initiative (CBI), 95, 112, 113–114
Carter, Jimmy, 95, 106–107, 109, 115
Case, Clifford, 93
CBI (Caribbean Basin Initiative), 95, 112, 113–114
cell phone data, 162, 182–183
Center for a New American Security (CNAS), 154, 191, 199
Center for Global Development, 220
Center for Strategic and International Studies, 5, 197
Central America: CBI, 95, 112, 113–114; conflict in, 95, 112–113; FDI encouraged in, 8, 221. *See also* developing world; Latin America; *individual countries*
Central and Eastern Europe (CEE), 118; advanced nations in, 147; cost of reforming economies of, 119; FDI's importance to, 208; investment in, 138; linkages in, 138; opposition to Washington Consensus, 128; outcomes in, 151–152; private enterprise in, 144–145; uprisings in, 198; US firms in, 137. *See also* developing world; market economy; postcommunist countries; postcommunist transition; *individual countries*
chaebol, 61, 62, 64
Chamber of Commerce, US, 1
Chan, Vei-Lin, 55
Chandresakaran, Rajiv, 163, 166
change, systemic: elites and, 184; fallacy of composition and, 223; interventions and, 199, 216; limits of foreign assistance in promoting, 153; as mission in Iraq, 162–164. *See also* Afghanistan; democracy; Iraq; market economy: transition to
change, theory of, 9, 213, 223
Cheng, Tun-jen, 63
Chiang Kai-shek, 39, 40, 41, 43, 45, 56, 66; land reform and, 46; US military advice to, 48; view of economic policies in Taiwan, 49. *See also* Kuomingtang (KMT); Taiwan
Chile: Allende, 90–91, 93, 103, 105; coup attempt in, 104; ITT in, 88, 91, 103–104; MNCs in, 75, 80, 103–104; nationalizations in, 102, 105; Pinochet, 104, 105; political risk insurance and, 103. *See also* developing world; Latin America
China: alternatives to, 202; BRI, 1, 185, 186, 188, 190–194, 198–202, 220;

cooperation with, 202; corruption and, 192, 201–202; developing world and, 38, 99; economic liberalization of, 14; economy of, 186, 190–191; effects of overseas investments, 195–196; expansion of, 206; Going Out/Going Global policy, 188, 195; growth of, viii, 189–190; industrialization of, 12; influence of, 186, 187, 190; investment treaty with European Union, 206; JCCR, 44–45, 46; lack of political freedom in, 14; land reform failure in, 46; Marshall Plan and, 20, 44; OECD and, 201; opening of, to global economy, 116; outward FDI, 194–195, 196; policy coherence of, 188; political capitalism of, 188–189; postwar trajectory of, 203; in RCEP, 206; as revisionist power, 197; state capitalism of, 220; state-led model of economic growth, viii; in Sub-Saharan Africa, 207; tax breaks and, 26; threat posed by, 18, 187; US clash with, 186; US response to, 187, 198–202, 203; violation of international norms by, 200; welfare gains in, 221. *See also* Chiang Kai-shek; communism; Taiwan
China Aid Act of 1948, 44
China Productivity Center (CPC), 52
Chinese Communist Party (CCP), 186, 220
chocolate, 24
Church, Frank, 98
CIA, 27, 214; Chile and, 91, 93, 103–104, 105; on economic nationalism, 102; Latin America and, 77, 85, 103–104; on nationalizations, 102
CIA World Factbook, 176
Clayton, William, 21
climate change, 185, 206, 211
Cloud, John, 134
CNAS (Center for a New American Security), 154, 191, 199
Coalition Provisional Authority (CPA), 162–163, 164, 165, 167, 168–169. *See also* Iraq
Cold War: competition in developing world during, 36; emergence of, 18; end of, 116 (*see also* postcommunist countries; postcommunist transition); FDI during early years of, 7–8; foreign economic policy during, 3; Latin America and, 84; productivity programs during, 217–218; promise of inclusive growth during, 203; theory of change during, 9. *See also* communism; Soviet Union

Colombia, 73. *See also* Latin America

colonialism, foreign private capital as form of, 36. *See also* decolonization; developing world; imperialism

COMAP (Commerce Committee for the Alliance for Progress), 89

Commerce Committee for the Alliance for Progress (COMAP), 89

Commerce Department, US, 89

commodity dependence, 13. *See also* natural resource curse; natural resources; structural conditions

communism: appeal of, 12; collapse of, 118 (*see also* Central and Eastern Europe [CEE]; postcommunist countries; postcommunist transition); countering threat of, 2–3, 39 (*see also* Cold War; security); decolonization and, 18; domino theory, 105; economic grievances and, 20; Eisenhower's views on, 29; Reagan and, 112. *See also individual countries*

conditions, local, 45, 56. *See also* elites; institutions; politics, domestic; social infrastructure; structural conditions

conflict, ix, 13, 16, 211–212, 213; in Central America, 95, 112–113; effects of, on investment, 171; growth's ability to reduce, 156; location of firms and, 160–161. *See also* Afghanistan; fragile and conflict-affected states (FCS); Iraq; politics, domestic; structural conditions; *individual conflicts*

conflict resolution, 206

Congress, US: M&E and, 223; postcommunist transition and, 129, 131–132, 133, 135; protectionism of, 25, 30; skepticism about foreign aid officials, 139; undermining of development programs, 24. *See also* government, US; policy

Congressional Research Service, 98, 131, 220

consultation services. *See* technical assistance

Cooper, Richard N., 2, 107

Corker, Bob, 1

coronavirus, 185, 187, 205, 218, 219, 220

corruption, 145, 196, 200; in Afghanistan, 180; BRI and, 192, 201–202; effects of, 192–193; natural resources and, 209. *See also* kleptocracy

Costantini, Irene, 172–173

cotton, 52. *See also* textiles

Council for United States Aid (CUSA), 53

Counts, Alex, 8

COVID-19 pandemic, 185, 187, 205, 218, 219, 220

CPA (Coalition Provisional Authority), 162–163, 164, 165, 167, 168–169

Crane, Keith, 162

credit, 6; in Afghanistan, 181; in Asia, 14, 214; FDI's association with, 14; in Iraq, 171; in Japan, 62; in Korea, 62; in post-communist countries, 138; property rights and, 158–159

cronyism, 62, 145, 173, 213. See also *chaebol*

crowding out, 78, 90, 212–213, 218. *See also* firms, local

Cuba, 70, 71, 72, 112. *See also* Latin America

Cuban Revolution, 69, 84, 87, 88, 89, 90. *See also* communism

Cullather, Nick, 45, 50, 53

Cumings, Bruce, 42

currencies, local, 26. *See also* exchange rates

Czechoslovakia, 198

Czech Republic, 147

Darnton, Christopher, 87

data, 162, 171–172, 182–183

debt: BRI and, 191; G-20 initiative to reduce, 201, 202; Latin America and, 70, 115–116. *See also* Belt and Road Initiative (BRI)

debt crisis, 95, 106, 108–111, 115–116, 121, 144

debt-equity swaps, 111, 122

decolonization, 17, 18. *See also individual countries*

defense budgets, 44, 119

defense conversion, 117

Defense Department, US. *See* Department of Defense, US (DoD)

deglobalization, 219

Dell, Sidney, 82

democracy: EBRD and, 143; exportability of, 12–13; firm growth's relationship with, 148; investment climate and, 213; in postcommunist countries, 147–148, 151; private enterprise and, 136, 147–148; privatization and, 149; SMEs and, 143. *See also* change, systemic

Democracy in Eastern Europe Act, 132

Department of Defense, US (DoD), 156; Afghanistan and, 177, 178, 179; CPA and, 168–169; in FCS, 155; Iraq and, 164, 166; TFBSO, 155–156, 165, 168, 178, 179, 180

dependency theorists, 68
Dependent Development (Evans), 68
developing world, 4, 20; benefits of foreign investment to, 10; capital flows to, 108–109; capital scarcity in, 20–21; Cold War competition in, 36 (*see also* economic offensive, Soviet); commonalities among, 5; communism's appeal to, 12; diversity in, 4–5, 14, 38; economic leverage over, 121; exploitation of, 21; fate of, 225; generating growth in, 2; infrastructure requirements, 188; international trade regime and, 23–24; investment needs of, 25, 188; liberal international economy and, 96; Marshall Plan and, 20; political-economic structures in, 105 (*see also* institutions; politics, domestic; structural conditions); unwillingness to invest in, 19; views of FDI in, 28, 38, 122–124
development, international: reasons for United States to support, 206; responsibility for, 11, 22–23 (*see also* self-help)
development, private sector. *See* private sector development (PSD)
Development Assistance Committee (DAC), 188, 201
development finance, 1. *See also* foreign direct investment (FDI)
development finance institutions (DFIs), 5–6, 8. *See also* banks; *individual banks*
Development Loan Fund (DLF), 37, 50, 51, 63, 86
development policy. *See* policy
DFC (Development Finance Corporation). *See* US International Development Finance Corporation (DFC)
DFIs (development finance institutions), 5–6, 8. *See also* banks; *individual banks*
Dillon, Douglas, 87
diplomatic corps, 30–31
dirigiste state, 40. *See also* Korea; Taiwan
diversification, economic, 210, 211
DLF (Development Loan Fund), 37, 50, 51, 63, 86
DoD (Department of Defense). *See* Department of Defense, US (DoD)
dollar: shortage of, 24–25, 29, 38, 162; strong, 110
dollar diplomacy, 70
domino theory, 105
Drazen, Allan, 125, 128
Dulles, John Foster, 75, 78, 79, 80–81, 82

East Asian miracle, 40. *See also* Asia; Korea; Taiwan
Easterly, William, 25
EBRD (European Bank for Reconstruction and Development), 119, 121, 134, 135, 141, 142–147, 151
ECA (Economic Cooperation Administration), 44, 60, 72. *See also* Marshall Plan
ECLA (Economic Commission for Latin America), 76, 88
Economic and Social Council (EcoSoc), 34
Economic Commission for Latin America (ECLA), 76, 88
economic conditions. *See* conditions, local; institutions; structural conditions
Economic Cooperation Administration (ECA), 44, 60, 72, 139. *See also* Marshall Plan
economic freedom, 13–14
economic grievances: communism and, 20; eliminating, 47 (*see also* equity); insurgency and, 164, 166, 169; in Korea, 57; political instability and, 20; in postcommunist countries, 136–137; social grievances and, 13; US security and, 60. *See also* unemployment
economic nationalism. *See* nationalism, economic
economic offensive, Soviet, 18, 28, 29, 79, 97
economic power, 40, 43
economics, neoclassical, 125–126
economic structure. *See* elites; institutions; structural conditions
economies, emerging/transition, viii. *See also* Central and Eastern Europe (CEE); postcommunist countries; postcommunist transition
economy, global, 116, 121. *See also* globalization
economy, international, 96
economy, postwar, 24–26, 38; in Europe, 72; planning for, 20–21; in Taiwan, 44–45. *See also* Marshall Plan
EcoSoc (Economic and Social Council), 34
education, 42, 69, 86, 166, 221
efficiency, 126, 127
Egypt, 36, 141
Eisenhower, Dwight D., 2, 25, 29–32, 213; communist threat and, 29; emphasis on free trade, 30; foreign aid and, 5, 26; IFC and, 33, 34, 82; Korea and, 60, 61; Latin America and, 69, 77, 82, 84, 91; loans and, 36–37; on promoting economic growth, 12; on socialized state, 9; taxation and, 31

Eisenhower, Milton, 81
Ekbladh, David, 58
electricity production. *See* power generation
electronics, consumer, 55
elites, ix, 13, 209; change and, 184; economically diversified, 214; in former Soviet states, 150; knowledge of, need for, 56; political capitalism and, 188; property rights and, 158. *See also* leaders, of developing world; structural conditions
El Salvador, 112–113, 114
Emanuel, Rahm, 166
England. *See* Britain
enterprise, private. *See* private enterprise
enterprise funds, 118–119, 133, 134, 139–141, 158, 166
entrepreneurs / entrepreneurship, 144; distrust of, 173; local government's role in promoting, 8–9; obstacles to, 181; in postcommunist countries, 121, 145–147; in Taiwan, 65. *See also* private enterprise; small and medium-sized enterprises (SMEs)
environment, 185, 192, 202, 206, 211, 221
EPZ (export processing zone), 54, 55, 63
equity, 40, 47, 122, 126, 218. *See also* inequality; social justice
Estonia, 147, 151
EU (European Union), 119, 121, 124, 206
Europe: contributions to international development, 86; funding for, 30; investment in CEE, 138; postcommunist transition and, 130; postwar economic problems, 72. *See also* Central and Eastern Europe (CEE); Marshall Plan; *individual countries*
European Bank for Reconstruction and Development (EBRD), 119, 121, 134, 135, 141, 142–147, 151
European Central Bank, 138
European Union (EU), 119, 121, 124, 206
Evans, Peter, 68
exceptionalism, American, 156, 206
exchange, foreign, 10
exchange rates, 213. *See also* currencies, local
EXIM (Export-Import) Bank. *See* Export-Import (EXIM) Bank
exploitation, 21. *See also* natural resource curse
Export-Import (EXIM) Bank, 6, 26, 74; investment guarantee program and, 27; Latin America and, 71, 76, 77, 78, 80,

89; postcommunist transition and, 118, 132, 137
export pessimism, 36, 69
export platforms, 122
export processing zone (EPZ), 54, 55, 63
exports, 10; from Afghanistan, 175; encouraging, 26; Taiwan and, 47, 50, 54
expropriations, 88, 92, 96, 100–106, 115, 123. *See also* multinational corporations (MNCs); political risk insurance

fallacy of composition, 153, 199, 216, 223
farmers, empowerment of, 59. *See also* land reform
Fascell, Dante, 132
FCN (Treaty of Friendship, Commerce, and Navigation), 22, 28
FCS (fragile and conflict-affected states). *See* fragile and conflict-affected states (FCS)
FDI (foreign direct investment). *See* foreign direct investment (FDI)
Federal Reserve Bank, 144
Federal Reserve Board, 33, 34
Felter, Joseph, 157
fertilizer production, 51
Fielding, David, 159–160, 171
finance, access to, 180–181, 212, 215. *See also* capital
Financial Times, 187
firms, American: claims of manipulation by China, 197–198; concerns of, 21; in Eastern Europe, 137; new market opportunities for, 206; in postcommunist transition, 138; in Russia, 141. *See also* business leaders, American; foreign direct investment (FDI); multinational corporations (MNCs)
firms, local: aid dependence and, 212–213; creation of, viii; infrastructure projects and, 191, 202; injecting funds into, 8; learning from, 208–209; natural resources and, 209. *See also* crowding out; linkages; small and medium-sized enterprises (SMEs)
firms, monopolistic, 219
firms, multinational. *See* multinational corporations (MNCs)
FOA (Foreign Operations Administration), 31, 77–78
food aid, 24, 129
foreign aid. *See* aid, foreign; policy
Foreign Assistance Act of 1969, 98

foreign assistance policy. *See* aid, foreign; policy

Foreign Corrupt Practices Act, 95, 110, 202

foreign direct investment (FDI), viii, x, 1, 155; belief in power of, 9–10, 91; change in attitude toward, 122–124; change in nature of, 124; concerns about, 21, 38; countries targeted for, 3–4 (*see also* developing world; governments, local/recipient; *individual countries; individual regions*); emphasis on, 19; as essential to development, 10; flows of, 35, 38, 47–48, 54, 108–109, 110, 111, 138; importance of, to recipients, 208; incentives for, 19, 25–28; lack of interest in, 19, 28–29, 36; need for local support, 152; opposition to, 67–68, 80, 167; political influence and, 67–68; purposes of, 22; risks associated with, 21 (*see also* investment guarantees; political risk insurance); usefulness of, 11. *See also* firms, American; multinational corporations (MNCs)

Foreign Investment Advisory Service, 216

Foreign Investment Policy Committee, 21, 22

Foreign Operations Administration (FOA), 31, 77–78

fossil fuels, 151, 211. *See also* natural resources; oil; petroleum

foundations, 7

fragile and conflict-affected states (FCS), 211–212; building private enterprise in, 157–162; characteristics of, 157; Chinese aid to, 193 (*see also* Belt and Road Initiative [BRI]); distrust in, 183; firms in, 160–161, 182–183; investment in, 159–160; limitations of US policy in, 157; market access in, 159; natural resource curse in, 212; political economy of, 157; promoting reform in, 222; property rights in, 212; SMEs in, 160; studying private sector in, 161–162; violence exacerbated by aid in, 213. *See also* Afghanistan; conflict; Iraq; peace; security; violence

freedom, economic, 13–14

freedom, political, 13–14

FREEDOM Support Act, 136

free enterprise. *See* private enterprise

free market. *See* market economy; private enterprise

Frei, Eduardo, 102

Fried, Daniel, 134

Friedberg, Aaron, 190

Friedman, Milton, 13–14

Frondizi, Arturo, 81

Fulbright, J. William, 95

Gates Foundation, 7

GATT (General Agreement on Tariffs and Trade), 47, 122

Geneen, Harold, 88, 103

General Agreement on Tariffs and Trade (GATT), 47, 122

Germany, 130, 156

Gerrity, E. J., Jr., 103

Gerschenkron, Alexander, 80

Ghana, 210

Ghiasy, Richard, 176

Gilpin, Robert, 4, 93, 94

Giorcelli, Michela, 217

Glickman, Lawrence, 12

globalization, 122, 124, 151, 186, 203, 219, 220, 221

Global Reach (Barnet and Muller), 93

Goldman Sachs, 202

Gonzalez Amendment, 104

Good Neighbor Policy, 70, 71

Goodwin, Richard, 88

Gorbachev, Mikhail, 131, 133, 135

government, US: inability to steer investments of MNCs, 19, 198–199; insistence on promoting private enterprise, 9–15; insurance against political risk, 26 (*see also* political risk insurance); relationship with MNCs, 93–94, 104; totalitarian mind-set of, 12. *See also* aid, foreign; Congress, US; policy; United States; *individual presidents*

governments, local/recipient: aid preferred by, 21, 28; disinterest in ideas of investor government, 48; doubts about private investment, 21; investment treaties and, 27; limits on US policy and, 19; receptivity toward foreign investment, 4, 36; role of, in promoting entrepreneurship and private enterprise, 8–9. *See also* developing world; leaders, of developing world; politics, domestic; *individual countries; individual leaders; individual regions*

Grace, Peter, 89

Grameen Foundation, 8

grants, 35

Gray, Kevin, 47

Great Depression, 71

Green, Mark, 1

Greene, Graham, 154

Grey Report, 9
grievances, economic. *See* economic grievances
Griffith-Jones, Stephany, 86, 87
growth: American beliefs about, 222; barriers to, 24 (*see also* structural conditions); conflict and, 156; dependence on private vs. state capital, 11; focus on, 156; foundations/drivers of, viii, 157, 207 (*see also* foreign direct investment [FDI]; institutions; private enterprise; private sector development; property rights; self-help); generating in developing world, 2 (*see also* foreign direct investment [FDI]); inclusive, 203; investment needed for, 25
guarantees, investment, 25, 26–27, 54, 199. *See also* political risk insurance
Guatemala, 77, 79, 105. *See also* Central America; Latin America
Gu family, 50
gunboat diplomacy, 27

Haggard, Stephan, 52, 53, 54, 57, 59, 62, 63, 64
Hallgren, Henrik, 176
Hamilton, Gary, 50
Hamilton, Lee, 132
Hardesty, Marion, 76
Hardy, Benjamin, 17
Hartz, Louis, 12, 156, 206
Havranek, Tomas, 208
health care, 69, 166, 218. *See also* social infrastructure
Hellmann, Joel, 147
Henn, Soeren, 221
Herter, Christian, 23, 37, 81
Hickenlooper, Bourke, 88
Hickenlooper Amendment, 88, 101, 103, 104
Hirschman, Albert, 10–11, 209, 210
Ho, Samuel, 47
Hodge, John K., 56
Hoffman, Paul, 44
Holland, Henry, 78
Hong Kong, 54
Hull, Cordell, 71, 155
human capital, 138–139, 141, 152, 160, 209
humanitarian impulses, 206
Humphrey, George, 34, 78, 79, 213
Hungary, 131, 147, 153, 198; American firms in, 137; assistance to, 129, 132;

Bush and, 124; enterprise funds for, 133, 134, 139–140. *See also* postcommunist countries; postcommunist transition
Hussein, Saddam, 135, 173. *See also* Iraq
Hutchings, Robert, 126, 127
Hwang, Sang-In, 64

IADB (Inter-American Development Bank), 69, 80, 81, 82, 84, 143
IBRD (International Bank for Reconstruction and Development). *See* World Bank
ideologues, 14
ideology, 14, 55, 98, 165
IEG (Independent Evaluation Group), 216
IFC (International Finance Corporation). *See* International Finance Corporation (IFC)
IMF (International Monetary Fund), 20, 72, 108, 116, 144, 201
Impact Quotient (IQ), 199
imperialism, 18, 104, 208. *See also* decolonization
imports, 10, 110, 178
import-substituting industrialization (ISI), 10, 24, 36, 61, 63, 68, 69, 71
income. *See* equity; inequality
independence, postcolonial. *See* decolonization
Independent Evaluation Group (IEG), 216
India, 206, 221
industrial development/industrialization, 12; in Korea, 59, 61–62; land reform and, 58, 59; in Poland, 127; in Taiwan, 46–48, 50–51, 62
inequality, 152, 210, 218. *See also* equity
inflation, 59, 107, 110, 115, 127, 128
influence, building, 56
infrastructure, 188, 202. *See also* Belt and Road Initiative (BRI)
infrastructure, social. *See* social infrastructure; structural conditions
Ingalls, 51
Inland Steel Company, 30
innovation, 123
inputs, 10
insecurity. *See* fragile and conflict-affected states (FCS)
instability, economic, 127. *See also* economic grievances
instability, political: economic grievances and, 20; as obstacle to business, 181; relationship with investment and growth, 158. *See also* fragile and conflict-affected states (FCS); *individual countries*

institutions: in BRI nations, 196; efforts to export, 13; growth and, 157; importance of, 92; judiciaries, independent, viii; lack of, in postcommunist transition, 120, 125, 126; needed for private enterprise, 120; need to invest in, 152. *See also* property rights: enforceable; social infrastructure; structural conditions

insurance, political risk, 13, 26, 96, 101, 102, 103, 137, 141. *See also* guarantees, investment

insurgency, economic grievances and, 164, 166, 169

Inter-American Defense Conference (Rio Conference), 72–73, 77, 78–79. *See also* Rio Conference

Inter-American Development Bank (IADB), 69, 80, 81, 82, 84, 143

Inter-American Highway, 76

interest rates, 107–108, 110, 115

International Bank for Reconstruction and Development (IBRD). *See* World Bank

International Coffee Agreement, 78

International Finance Corporation (IFC), viii, 32–33, 110, 210; effects of, 35–36; Eisenhower and, 33, 34, 82; enterprise funds and, 141; focus of, 16; founding of, 19; Reagan and, 108

International Labor Organization, 172

International Monetary Fund (IMF), 20, 72, 108, 116, 144, 201

International Petroleum Corporation, 101

International Private Investment Advisory Council, 96

international relations, 22

International Telephone & Telegraph (ITT), 88, 91, 93, 103–104

International Trade Organization, 24

internet, 123

interventions: fallacy of composition and, 153, 199, 216, 223; macro, 153, 215; micro, viii, 152–153, 199, 215, 216; monitoring/evaluating, 144, 170, 214–215, 223. *See also* aid, foreign; foreign direct investment (FDI); technical assistance

investment: effects of conflict on, 171; as irreversible, 159; levels of, 159, 160; long-term, 49, 50, 99, 184; savings and, 10, 157; types of, 159–160

investment, private sector-led. *See* foreign direct investment (FDI); private sector development

investment climate, viii, 11; in Afghanistan, 180, 181–182; democracy and, 213; developing/improving, 8, 37, 207; in FCS, 212; identifying factors of, 215; in Latin America, 75, 89; in postcommunist countries, 137–138; self-help and, 23

investment companies, local, 8

investment destinations, 15, 22, 23, 43, 80. *See also* developing world; governments, local/recipient

investment gap, 25, 26, 29, 35, 38

investment guarantees, 25, 26–27, 54, 199. *See also* political risk insurance

investors: concerns of, 21; diplomatic support for, 31. *See also* business leaders, American; foreign direct investment (FDI); multinational corporations (MNCs)

Iranian Revolution, 107

Iraq, 3, 8, 124, 135; access to finance in, 171; conditions in, 164–165; CPA, 162–163, 164, 165, 167, 168–169; credit in, 171; data on, 171–172; dependence on United States, 184; economy of, 163; entrepreneurship in, 170, 173; FDI and, 166–167; insurgency in, 169; lessons from, 169; obstacles to business in, 169; oil sector in, 166, 169, 172–174, 184; private enterprise in, 163, 169–174, 183; property rights in, 159, 174; rebuilding, 162–169; security and, 164–165, 169, 170–171; SMEs in, 172; SOEs in, 14, 163, 164, 165–166, 174; structural conditions in, 164–165, 184; TFBSO in, 156; unemployment in, 164. *See also* fragile and conflict-affected states (FCS)

Irsova, Zuzana, 208

ISI (import-substituting industrialization), 10, 24, 36, 61, 63, 68, 69, 71

Islamic State, 169, 170

isolationism, 94

Israel, 36, 106, 160, 171

ITT (International Telephone & Telegraph), 88, 91, 93, 103–104

Izdihar, 170

Jacoby, Neil, 48, 49

Japan, 202, 220; colonialism and, 40, 42; credit in, 62; Instruments of Surrender from, 57; Korea and, 58, 63; land reform in, 58; postwar economy of, 156; in RCEP, 206; Taiwan and, 42, 48, 54

Javits, Jacob, 96, 98, 99, 155

JCCR (Joint Commission on Rural Reconstruction), 44–45, 46, 53
J.G. White Engineering Corporation, 52
Johnson, Lyndon, 95–96, 98, 101
Johnson, Ralph, 132
Joint Commission on Rural Reconstruction (JCCR), 44–45, 46, 53
Joint Economic Committee, 88
judiciaries, independent, viii. *See also* institutions
judo strategy, 200–202

Kao, Cheng-Shu, 50
Kaufman, Burton, 29
Kaufman, Henry, 218
Kazakhstan, 202. *See also* postcommunist countries; postcommunist transition
Kennedy, John F., 64, 69–70, 84–91
Kenney, Martin, 55
Kim, June-Dong, 64
Kim, Rene, 210
Kim, Taekyoon, 41
Kissinger, Henry, 98, 105
Kleiman, Daniel, 199
kleptocracy, 121, 124, 125, 189, 193, 214, 215; BRI and, 192; enrichment of, 184; in FCS, 161; market access in, 192; in postcommunist countries, 151, 152, 153; property rights in, 192; in Russia, 150. *See also* corruption
KMT (Kuomingtang), 41, 42–44, 46, 48, 49, 52, 53, 64. *See also* Chiang Kai-shek; Taiwan
Koh, B. C., 60
Koppell, Jonathan, 139
Korea, 56–66, 214; aid's importance to, 59, 60–61, 62; assistance packages for, 40–41; *chaebol* in, 61, 62, 64; communism and, 39, 43, 61; conditions in, 40; conflict in, 63 (*see also* Korean War); credit in, 62; defense requirements, 41; division of, 56, 57; economic grievances in, 57; economy of, 60; end of US aid to, 63; FDI in, 62, 63–64, 65, 68; import substitution in, 61, 63, 68; industrial development in, 59, 61–62; inflation in, 59; instability in, 56–57, 62–63; institutions in, 40; Japan and, 58, 63; labor in, 58; land reform in, 57–59; limits on US influence in, 41; local officials' influence on policy, 42; Marshall Plan aid for, 20; policy vs. reality in, 41–42; politics in, 56; private enterprise in, 64, 65–66; PRK

government, 57, 58; relationship with United States, 65; Rhee, 40, 56, 57, 59, 60, 61, 63, 64, 65, 66; security and, 39, 65; technical assistance in, 42; US relations with, 56, 60
Korean Provincial Government, 56
Korean War, 18, 29, 43, 59, 60
Krasner, Stephen, 100
Kubitschek, Juscelino, 81, 86
Kuomingtang (KMT), 41, 42–44, 46, 48, 49, 52, 53, 64. *See also* Chiang Kai-shek; Taiwan
Kuwait, 124, 135

LaFalce, John, 143
land reform, 40, 86; failure of, in China, 46; industrialization and, 58, 59; in Japan, 58; in Korea, 57–59; in Latin America, 85, 86, 112–113; in North Korea, 58; in Taiwan, 42, 45, 46–47, 49, 50, 58–59. *See also* property rights
Land-to-the-Tiller program, 50
Laos, 202
Larosiere, Jacques de, 144
Latin America: Alliance for Progress, 69, 84–91; Asia compared to, 68; Bogota Conference, 74; Cold War and, 84; communism in, 69, 73–74, 79, 84, 87, 88, 89, 90, 105; conditions in, 92; debt-equity swaps in, 122; debts and, 70, 115–116; diversity in, 4, 38; ECLA, 76, 88; economic integration in, 123–124; economic policy goals, 76; EXIM Bank and, 71, 76, 77, 78, 80, 89; expropriations in, 88, 92, 100–106; FDI in, 28, 35, 68, 70–71, 72, 76, 80, 82–83, 87–89, 110; foreign aid and, 76, 78, 86, 91; governments in, 79 (*see also* leaders, Latin American); Great Depression and, 71; growth in, 71, 89; hostility to American-style capitalism in, 81; IADB and, 69, 82; income distribution in, 77, 210; investment climate in, 75; ISI in, 10, 36, 69, 71; lack of aid to, 74; linkages in, 83, 91–92; loans and, 76, 77, 78, 89; MNCs in, 75, 77, 80, 92 (*see also* International Telephone & Telegraph); nationalism in, 85; Organization of American States, 74; political instability in, 90–91 (*see also* leaders, Latin American); private enterprise in, 74, 75–84; protectionism in, 209; Reciprocal Trade Agreements and, 71; regional development bank in, 69, 77, 80, 81, 82; Rio Conference,

72–73, 77, 78–79; social infrastructure in, 69; SOEs in, 89; structural conditions in, 92; tax breaks and, 26; United States and, 68–69, 72, 80, 100; US investment in, 71–72, 208; US market access in, 113; World War II and, 72. *See also* Central America; leaders, Latin American; *individual countries*

Latvia, 147

LDCs (less-developed countries). *See* developing world; *individual countries; individual regions*

Le, Quan, 160

Leach, Jim, 143

leaders, American. *See* business leaders, American; Congress, US; government, US; *individual presidents*

leaders, Latin American, 213–214; calls for foreign aid, 86–87; lack of stability and, 90–91; plots/coups against, 77, 79, 88, 91, 93, 104, 105; receptivity toward foreign investment, 81. *See also* developing world; elites; governments, local/recipient; politics, domestic; *individual leaders*

leaders, of developing world: foreign aid and, 55; interest in Soviet economic model, 27–28; local politics and, 105; preferences of, ix; view of FDI, 5. *See also* developing world; elites; governments, local/recipient; leaders, Latin American; politics, domestic; *individual leaders*

legal frameworks, 147

less-developed countries (LDCs). *See* developing world; *individual countries; individual regions*

liberty, individual, 12

LIBOR (London Inter-Bank Offer Rate), 107

Lim, Wonhyuk, 61

linkages, 8, 14, 208–209; in CEE, 138; described, 10; in East Asia, 214; in Iraq, 167; in Latin America, 83, 91; MNCs and, 221; natural resources and, 210; promoting, 2; in Taiwan, 55

Lipsey, Robert, 110

Lipton, David, 127

literacy rate, 42

Lithuania, 147

living standards, 42. *See also* economic grievances; structural conditions

loans, 116; expropriations and, 104; interest rates, 107–108; Latin America and, 76, 77, 78, 89; long-term, 86; MDBs and,

108; SOEs and, 89; soft, 35, 36–37. *See also* Belt and Road Initiative (BRI); debt; debt crisis

Lodge, Henry Cabot, 34

London Inter-Bank Offer Rate (LIBOR), 107

Looney, Robert, 164

Lowe, Nichola, 55

Macron, Emmanuel, 205

Mafia, 159

Maier, Charles, 13, 156

Malpass, David, 201

management techniques, 216. *See also* technical assistance

Mandelbaum, Michael, 118

Mann, Thomas, 87

Mao Tse-tung, 18, 203

market access, 159, 192

market economy: building, 126, 129, 152, 163–164; faith in, 13; foreign economic policy and, 1–3; Iraq and, 163–164; need for institutions, 152; property rights and, 158–159; reforming vs. building, 152; transition to, 144–145, 147 (*see also* Central and Eastern Europe [CEE]; change, systemic; postcommunist countries; postcommunist transition)

market reconstruction, 38

Marshall, George, 73

Marshall Plan, viii, 19, 72, 86, 162; administration of, 44, 60, 97, 139; dollar shortage and, 25; recipients of aid from, 18, 20; technical assistance and, 217

Martin, William McChesney, 34

Marx, Karl, 103

Mason, Edward, 61

Matlock, Jack, 133

McCone, John, 103

McGhee, George C., 89–90

McLellan, David, 23

McMillan, John, 145–146, 147

McNamara, Robert, 101

McPherson, Peter, 162, 164, 165, 167

MDBs (multilateral development banks), 108

MENA (Middle East and North Africa) region, 169, 181. *See also* Iraq

Mercosur, 123–124

Mercy Corps, 7

meritocracy, 203

Mexican Revolution, 70

Mexico, 55, 70, 72, 86, 108

microfinance, 8, 170, 171
micro interventions, viii, 153, 199, 216.
  See also interventions
Microsoft, 8
Middle East and North Africa (MENA)
  region, 169, 181. See also Iraq
Mikesell, Raymond, 27
Milanović, Branko, 118, 189, 218
military power, 155. See also Afghanistan;
  Iraq; Korean War; Vietnam War
Milner, Aaron, 5
minerals, 102. See also natural resources
minorities, 203
Mitterrand, François, 142
mobile phone data, 162, 182–183
modernization theory, 2, 85
monitoring and evaluation (M&E), 144,
  170, 214–215, 223
Monlin, Chiang, 45
monocultures, 173
monopolistic firms, 219
Mosbacher, Robert, 135
Moyer, Raymond, 45
MSM/C (Mutual Security Mission to
  China), 50, 51
Mueller, Hannes, 161
Mulford, David, 143
Muller, Ronald, 93, 94
multilateral development banks (MDBs),
  108
multilateralism, 86, 87
multinational corporations (MNCs), 3, 7,
  94; as beneficiaries of FDI, 94; in Brazil,
  82–83; bribery by, 95; during Carter
  administration, 106–107; in Chile,
  103–104; controversy over, 115; as
  development agencies, 221; domestic
  politics and, 94, 106; encouraged to
  invest in Central America, 8; export
  pessimism and, 36; in FCS, 161; foreign
  policy and, 93–94; government's inability
  to steer investments of, 198–199; ICT
  and, 123; interest in developing world,
  4, 207–208; International Private Investment Advisory Council and, 96; investment destinations of, 15; in Latin
  America, 75, 77, 80, 92 (see also expropriations; International Telephone &
  Telegraph); new climate for, 122; in
  postcommunist transition, 121; reluctance to invest in developing world,
  15; technical assistance provided by,
  217; US government and, 93–94, 104.

See also business leaders, American;
  expropriations; firms, American;
  nationalizations
Murrell, Peter, 138
Murthy, Narayan, 124
Mutual Security Agency, 31
Mutual Security Mission to China
  (MSM/C), 50, 51

NAC (National Advisory Council), 33, 34
NAFTA (North American Free Trade
  Agreement), 123
Nasser, Gamal, 36
National Advisory Council (NAC), 33, 34
National Association of Manufacturers, 120
National Foreign Trade Council, 33
nationalism, 85
nationalism, economic, 79, 99, 187; CIA
  on, 102; demands for, 203–204; in Latin
  America, 69; in United States, 205–206,
  220. See also protectionism
nationalizations, 96; in Bolivia, 75, 80; in
  Brazil, 75; in Chile, 102, 105; CIA and,
  102; in Peru, 101; of Suez Canal, 36;
  in Taiwan, 50. See also multinational
  corporations (MNCs); political risk
  insurance
National Security Council (NSC), 18, 77, 79,
  126, 127; on expropriations, 102–103;
  Latin America and, 73, 75, 76, 81
National Security Strategy (2017), 197
natural resource curse, 172–174, 209–211,
  212
natural resources, ix, 13, 15–16, 36, 115,
  222; in Afghanistan, 180; CEE's lack of,
  152; FDI in, 32, 102; fossil fuels, 151,
  211; linkages with local firms and, 210.
  See also oil; petroleum; raw materials;
  structural conditions
Nellis, John, 148
Nelson, Douglas, 47
neoclassical economics, 125–126
neoliberalism, 108, 119–120, 122, 187.
  See also Washington Consensus
Netherlands, 106
New Deal, 58
New International Economic Order, 94, 99,
  106
Newmont Mining Corporation, 210
new world order, 119, 124. See also post-
  communist transition
New Zealand, 206, 210
Nicaragua, 112

nightlights, 162
Nikolova, Elena, 147
Nixon, Richard, 96–106, 115, 135; experience of, 97–98; expropriations and,
100–102, 104; foreign policy of, 94–95;
on government-to-government programs,
96–97; Hickenlooper Amendment and,
88; Latin America and, 81, 82, 91; OPIC
and, 97–99, 139
norms, international, 200, 201
North, Douglass, 157, 158
North American Free Trade Agreement
(NAFTA), 123
NSC (National Security Council). See National Security Council (NSC)

ODA (official development assistance), 19
OECD (Organisation for Economic Cooperation and Development), 117, 188,
193, 201, 210, 218
OFDI (outward foreign direct investment),
194–195, 196
official development assistance (ODA), 19
oil, 210, 211; embargo, 105–106, 107, 115;
Iraq and, 166, 169, 172–174, 184; in
Venezuela, 90. See also fossil fuels; natural resource curse; natural resources
oligarchs, in Russia, 149, 150
openness, in postcommunist transition, 124
Operation Desert Storm, 135. See also Iraq
Operation Pan America, 81
OPIC (Overseas Private Investment Corporation). See Overseas Private Investment
Corporation (OPIC)
opportunity, 126
Organisation for Economic Co-operation
and Development (OECD), 117, 188,
193, 201, 210, 218
Organization of American States, 74, 112
Oriental Chemical Industry (OCI), 63
outcomes, variability of, viii
outputs, 10
outward foreign direct investment (OFDI),
194–195, 196
Overseas Private Investment Corporation
(OPIC), x, 1, 97–99, 189, 199; creation
of, 91, 139; investment guarantee program
and, 27; political risk insurance and, 101,
102, 103, 137, 141; postcommunist
transition and, 118, 132

Packenham, Robert, 222
Pakistan, 187, 198, 200

pandemic, COVID-19, 185, 187, 205, 218,
219, 220
Paraguay, 81, 123
Park, Hun Joo, 40
peace, 155, 156, 212. See also conflict;
fragile and conflict-affected states (FCS);
violence
Pence, Mike, 1, 197, 198
People's Republic of Korea (PRK), 57, 58.
See also Korea
Pepsi-Cola, 103
perestroika, 130
Peru, 101, 105. See also Latin America
Petrobras, 67, 75
petroleum, 107; in Brazil, 82, 83–84; FDI
in, 102; in Latin America, 82; nationalizations and, 101. See also fossil fuels;
natural resources
Pew Research Center, 221
Pinochet, Augusto, 104, 105
Pisar, Samuel, 205
Point Four program, 18, 97, 98, 217;
clarifying, 22–23; Latin America and,
74; resources allocated to, 29; role of
government vs. business in, 23. See also
technical assistance
Poland, 124, 131, 147, 153, 165; assistance
to, 129, 131–132; debt crisis and, 121;
enterprise funds for, 133, 134, 139–140;
entrepreneurship in, 121, 146; industrialization in, 127; inflation in, 127; request
for assistance, 133; Round Table Agreement, 131; USAID funding for, 136
policy, viii, 2; ability to impose, 4; change in,
1; China challenge and, 198–202; during
Cold War, 3; confusion about, 198;
constraints on, 19, 30; contemporary,
196–197; contradiction in, 25; end of
Cold War and, 119; expropriations and,
102, 104; fiscal concerns and, 19; ideology
and, 1–3, 165; international norms and,
201; inward, 204; isolationism, 94; MNCs
and, 94, 104; pragmatic, 14, 136; vs.
reality, 41–42, 45 (see also institutions;
structural conditions); social, 69. See also
aid, foreign; Congress, US; government,
US; Marshall Plan; protectionism
policy coherence, 55, 204, 213, 223;
China's, 188; countering China and, 200;
importance of, 66; Taiwan and, 52
policy incoherence, 68, 103, 178, 222,
223
Polish-American Enterprise Fund, 132, 141

political economy, ix, 10–11, 120. *See also* institutions; structural conditions
political freedom, 13–14
political risk insurance, 13, 26, 96, 101, 102, 103, 137, 141. *See also* guarantees, investment
politics, domestic, 97, 103–104, 106, 214. *See also* CIA; Korean War; leaders, Latin American; Vietnam War
"Politics of Productivity, The" (Maier), 13
Pollard, Robert, 24, 28
populism, 151
postcommunist countries: credit in, 138; democracy in, 147–148, 151; EBRD and, 119, 121, 134, 135, 141, 142–147, 151; enterprise funds in, 139–141; entrepreneurship/start-ups in, 145–147; expectations for, 153; inequality in, 152; kleptocracy in, 151, 152; outcomes in, 146–147, 151–152; privatization in, 121, 122, 124, 148–151; USAID, 129, 136, 137–138, 139, 141
postcommunist transition, 111, 118, 119; aid to Soviet Union during, 135–136; backlash to, 127, 128; Congress and, 131–132; cost of, 119; debates over process for, 120; effects on foreign policy, 119; efficiency in, 127; Europe and, 130; EXIM Bank and, 118, 132, 137; factors shaping US response to, 129–136; Germany and, 130; industrial production in, 127, 128; inflation in, 127, 128; influence on CPA, 165–166, 168; innovation and speed in, 118; instability in, 127; lack of institutions for, 120, 125, 126; liberalization in, 124; long-term nature of, 127–128; magnitude of, 125; market principles in, 125; MNCs in, 121; as opportunity, 130, 131; outcomes of, 120, 124–125; political economy of, 125–128; politics in, 124; private enterprise and, 120, 136–141; privatization in, 121, 122, 124, 148–151; productivity assistance in, 217; response to, 129, 130–131, 134–135; SEED Act, 129, 133–135, 139; social welfare programs and, 117–118; structure needed for, 120; support for, 129–136; theoretical frameworks vs. local reality in, 126; uncertainty in, 125; unemployment in, 127, 128. *See also* Bush, George H. W.; *individual countries*
poverty reduction, viii, 8, 136, 221, 223. *See also* economic grievances

Powell, Colin, 184
power, 40, 43, 222
power generation, 51, 52, 57. *See also* public utilities
Prebisch, Raul, 24, 86
Prebisch-Singer hypothesis, 24
price liberalization, 126–127
price stabilization schemes, 78
private enterprise: American view of, 12; belief in power of, 155, 183; defined, 6; democracy and, 136, 147–148; emphasis on, 18, 19, 37; encouraging in developing world, viii; growth and, 207; institutions needed by, 120; optimism concerning, 74; organic promotion of, 8; relationship with foreign aid, 5; as source of development, 2, 143; threats to, 219; track record of, 3. *See also* business leaders, American; capitalism; entrepreneurs/entrepreneurship; foreign direct investment (FDI); market economy; private sector development
private investment, 88, 113. *See also* foreign direct investment (FDI)
private sector: definitions of, 6; local government's role in promoting, 8–9; providing capital injections to, 8; reputation of, 173; separation from public, 151, 220; skepticism about role of, 35, 36. *See also* private enterprise
private sector development (PSD), viii; barriers to (*see* structural conditions); China's, 188 (*see also* Belt and Road Initiative [BRI]); constraints on, 15; described, 6–8; emphasis on, 187; expansion of, 7; future of, 218–224; geostrategic importance of, 2, 189 (*see also* communism; security); peace and, 212; as policy goal, 187; structural conditions and (*see* institutions; structural conditions); supplanting foreign aid with, viii; supplementing with foreign aid, 16. *See also* aid, foreign; foreign direct investment (FDI); policy; private enterprise
privatization: in Afghanistan, 177; in Britain, 148, 149; in CEE, 144–145; democracy and, 149; EBRD and, 143; foreign investment and, 111; forms of, 149–150; in Iraq, 164, 165–166; outcomes of, 150–151; politics of, 148–151; in postcommunist transition, 121, 122, 124, 148–151; in Taiwan, 49, 50; vouchers, 149, 150
PRK (People's Republic of Korea), 57, 58

productivity, 216–218
productivity spillovers, 208–209
programming. *See* interventions
property rights: elite and, 158; enforceable, viii, 40, 157–159; in FCS, 212; in Iraq, 159, 174; in kleptocracy, 192; market access and, 159; as private good, 158, 215–216; in Taiwan, 42. *See also* institutions; land reform; structural conditions
protectionism, 16, 25, 29, 30, 36; American, 186, 203; discouragement of foreign investors by, 24; in Latin America, 209. *See also* import-substituting industrialization (ISI); nationalism, economic
PSD (private sector development). *See* private sector development (PSD)
public goods, voter preferences for, 218
public sector, separation from private, 151, 220. *See also* state-owned enterprises (SOEs)
public utilities, 82. *See also* power generation
Putin, Vladimir, 125, 151

Quiet American, The (Greene), 154

R&D, global, 220
Rabe, Stephen, 78
Rajan, Raghuram, 213
Randall, Clarence, 30
Randall Commission, 30–31
RAND Corporation, 112, 137, 179
Ratcliffe, John, 186, 187, 198
Ravaillon, Martin, 223
raw materials, 24, 29, 96, 102. *See also* natural resources
Reagan, Ronald, 95, 106, 107–114, 115, 119, 122, 204
Reaganomics, 107
reality, 98, 126. *See also* institutions; politics, domestic; structural conditions
recession, 107, 115
Reciprocal Trade Agreements, 71
reform, 222. *See also* land reform; tax reform
Regional Comprehensive Economic Partnership (RCEP), 206
regionalism, 72
regional trade agreements, 123–124, 206
relationships, need for, 56
rent extraction, vs. long-term investment, 184
Republic of Korea. *See* Korea
reshoring, 219
resource extraction, 209. *See also* natural resource curse

responsibility for development, 22–23. *See also* self-help
Rhee, Syngman, 40, 56, 57, 59, 60, 61, 63, 64, 65, 66. *See also* Korea
Rice, Condoleezza, 134
Ricks, Thomas, 154
Rio Conference, 72–73, 77, 78–79
risk, 54. *See also* guarantees, investment; political risk insurance
Robinson, James, 221
Rockefeller, David, 87, 89
Rockefeller, Nelson, 33
Rogers, William, 96
Roosevelt, Franklin D., 13, 17, 70, 71
Roosevelt, Theodore, 70
Rostow, W. W., 2, 29, 32, 85–86
Rubottom, Richard, 79
Runde, Daniel, 5, 197
Russia, 125; American firms in, 141; entrepreneurship in, 146; expanding influence of, 200; kleptocracy in, 150; market principles in, 125; oligarchs in, 149, 150; privatization in, 149, 150; Putin, 125, 151; USAID funding for, 136; US-Russia Investment Fund, 141. *See also* postcommunist countries; postcommunist transition; Soviet Union
Ruttan, Vernon, 119, 131
Rwanda, 215

Sachs, Jeffrey, 127
Sanders, Bernie, 203
savings, 10, 25, 157. *See also* investment gap
Scheurch, William, 127
Schive, Chi, 55
Schreiber, Jordan, 54
science and technology, 220
sector, private. *See* private sector
security: China and, 187, 191; economics and, 60, 112; expropriations and, 101; growth in developing world and, 2; importance of, 184, 186; SMEs and, 160. *See also* fragile and conflict-affected states (FCS); *individual countries*
SEED (Support for East European Democracy) Act, 129, 133–135, 139
self-help, 22–23; American development policy and, 25; emphasis on, 18, 37, 66; growth and, 207; investment climate and, 23; Latin America / Caribbean and, 74, 113, 114; in postcommunist transition, 132, 134
self-reliance, 11

Sewell, Bevan, 76
Shapiro, Jacob N., 157
Sharma, Ruchir, 147, 152
Shin, Yong-Ha, 59
shock therapy, 120, 168
short-term perspective, 99, 173
SIGAR (Special Inspector General for Afghanistan Reconstruction), 155, 178
SIGIR (Special Inspector General for Iraq Reconstruction), 163
Silberman, James, 217
Singer, Hans, 24
skills, upgrading of, 22. See also technical assistance
Slovak Republic, 147
Slovenia, 147, 151
small and medium-sized enterprises (SMEs): democracy and, 143; enterprise funds for, 118–119; in FCS, 160; injecting funds into, 8; in Iraq, 172; local banks and, 6; in postcommunist countries, 138, 145. See also entrepreneurs/entrepreneurship; firms, local
Small Industry Loan Program, 51
Smith, Adam, 155
Smith, H. Alexander, 37
social grievances, 13
social infrastructure, 42, 69, 84, 85, 86, 87, 166, 221. See also conditions, local; institutions; structural conditions
social justice, 58, 122. See also equity; land reform
social policy, 69
Social Progress Trust Fund, 84
social welfare programs, 117–118, 122
society, local. See conditions, local
socio-political instability (SPI). See instability, political
SOEs (state-owned enterprises). See state-owned enterprises (SOEs)
Solidarity, 131. See also Poland
sourcing, local, 210. See also firms, local
South African Brewing Company, 210
sovereignty, 104, 191
Sovereignty at Bay (Vernon), 93
Soviet Union, 18; aid to, 129, 135–136; apparent economic success of, 27; attempts to preserve, 135; collapse of, 118, 128, 130; defense conversion, 117; developing world and, 38; EBRD and, 142–143; economic offensive, 18, 28, 29, 79, 97; foreign aid from, 28; foreign investment in, 133; industrialization of, 12; Korea and,

57; lack of institutions in, 133; Latin America and, 79; property in, 133; views of Rio Conference, 73. See also Cold War; communism; postcommunist countries; postcommunist transition; Russia
Sparkman, John, 89
Special Inspector General for Afghanistan Reconstruction (SIGAR), 155, 178
Special Inspector General for Iraq Reconstruction (SIGIR), 163
Special UN Fund for Economic Development (SUNFED), 34, 37
Spector, Ronald, 58
SPI (socio-political instability). See instability, political
stabilization, 126, 127, 147
Stages of Economic Growth, The (Rostow), 85
stagflation, 115
Stalin, Joseph, 29
start-ups. See entrepreneurs/entrepreneurship
Stasavage, David, 159
Stassen, Harold, 31–32, 77–78
state capitalism, 220. See also China
State Department, US, 33; on Afghanistan, 180, 181–182; budget of, 191; enterprise fund and, 139; Latin America and, 78
state-led development, viii, 40. See also Korea; Taiwan
state-owned enterprises (SOEs): in Afghanistan, 177, 179, 181; development through, 89; financial support of, 6; in Iraq, 14, 163, 164, 165–166, 174; in Latin America, 67, 71, 89; privatization of (see privatization); support for, 179; in Taiwan, 44, 51; US policy and, 207
Statute for Encouragement of Investment of 1960, 54
Steinberg, David, 59, 62
Stockholm International Peace Research Institute, 176
Stone, Robert, 12
Stroessner, Alfredo, 81
Strong, Robert, 43
structural conditions, ix, 4, 13, 14, 15; aid dependence, 212–213; as barrier to growth, 24; democracy vs. authoritarianism, 213; importance of, 92; interventions' reflection of, 222; private enterprise and, 4, 120. See also conditions, local; conflict; elites; fragile and conflict-affected states (FCS); institutions; natural resource curse; natural resources

structuralist school, 69
Subramanian, Arvind, 213
Suez crisis, 36
sugar, 113
Suk Tai Suh, 57
Sun Yat-sen, 43
supply chains: in FCS, 161; global, 124, 214; local, 221; reshoring, 205; vulnerabilities of, 219
Support for East European Democracy (SEED) Act, 129, 133–135, 139
Sustainable Development Goals, 221
Svensson, Jakob, 158
Swansbrough, Robert, 70
Swedish International Development Agency, 215

Taft, Robert, 30
Taft, William Howard, 70
Taiwan, 42–56, 214; access to US market, 47; aid to, 18, 40–41, 47, 54, 72; colonial legacy in, 42; conditions in, 40, 41–42, 45, 64; containment of communism and, 39; CUSA in, 53; DLF loans to, 51; ECA in, 44; economic policies in, 43–44; entrepreneurship in, 51, 65; equity in, 47; exports and, 47, 50, 54; geopolitical importance of, 39, 41, 43, 46, 48; growth in, 64–65; import needs, 46; industrial development in, 46–48, 50–51, 62; investment in, 47–48, 49, 50, 51, 53–55, 65, 68; ISI in, 68; land reform in, 42, 45, 46–47, 49, 50, 58–59; limits on US influence in, 41; linkages in, 55; local officials in, 42; Marshall Plan aid for, 18, 72; mixed economy in, 53; nationalizations in, 50; policy coherence and, 52; policy in, 48–49; policy vs. reality in, 41–42; postwar recovery of, 44–45; power generation in, 51; private enterprise in, 41, 48, 49, 53, 65–66; privatization in, 49, 50; property rights in, 42; security and, 39, 41, 46; SOEs in, 44, 51; state-led development in, 40, 41; structural conditions in, 42; technical assistance in, 42, 52; threats to, 43. See also Asia; Chiang Kai-shek; Kuomingtang (KMT)
Taiwan Cement Corporation, 50, 51
Taliban, 174, 175, 178, 180, 183, 216. See also Afghanistan
tariffs, 24, 30, 31, 78, 113, 122, 210–211
Tasca, Henry, 60–61

Task Force of Business and Stability Operations (TFBSO), 155–156, 165, 168, 178, 179, 180
Task Force on Foreign Economic Policy, 85
Task Force on International Private Enterprise, 109
tax breaks, 25–26
taxes, 10, 31
taxpayers, US, 39, 99, 101, 140, 141
tax reform, in Latin America, 85, 86
technical assistance, 42, 52, 86, 98, 109, 137–138, 170, 216–218
technocrats, 189
technology, upgrading of, 22. See also technical assistance
technology transfer, 55
textiles, 24, 52, 113
TFBSO (Task Force of Business and Stability Operations), 155–156, 165, 168, 178, 179, 180
Thatcher, Margaret, 120, 122, 148
theory of change, 9, 213, 223
Third World. See decolonization; developing world
Thorp, Rosemary, 71
totalitarian mind-set, 12
trade, free, 30
trade, global, 219. See also globalization
trade, international, 23–24, 203
trade agreements, multilateral, 30
trade agreements, regional, 123–124, 206
trade deficit, 110
trade policy. See policy
training programs, 109. See also technical assistance
transfer pricing, 10, 115
transition economies, viii. See also Central and Eastern Europe (CEE); postcommunist countries; postcommunist transition
transparency, 191, 201, 202, 219, 223
transportation projects, 51, 52
Trask, Roger, 74
Treasury Department, US, 33, 34, 78, 108, 142, 144
treaties, investment, 22, 25, 27–28
Treaty of Friendship, Commerce, and Navigation (FCN), 22, 28
Truman, Harry S., 17–18, 25, 217; on communism, 20, 43; FDI and, 25–28; foreign aid under, 29; IFC concept and, 33; inability to create support for foreign aid, 26; Latin America and, 72–73, 74. See also Point Four program

Trump, Donald J., 78, 139, 186, 196, 203, 205; DFC set up by, 189; economic nationalism of, 220; foreign aid spending and, 197; protectionism of, 203
trust, building, 56
Tsai, Pan-Long, 41
Tucker, Nancy, 48, 49
Tunisia, 141

Uganda, 210
UN (United Nations). *See* United Nations (UN)
uncertainty, 125, 128, 158. *See also* instability
UNCTAD (United Nations Conference on Trade and Development), 210
unemployment: insurgency and, 166; in Iraq, 164; in postcommunist transition, 127. *See also* economic grievances
United Fruit Company, 75, 77
United Kingdom (UK). *See* Britain
United Nations (UN), 5, 72; calls for New International Economic Order at, 94; "Decade of Development," 86; EcoSoc, 34; growth of, 18; SUNFED, 34, 37
United Nations Conference on Trade and Development (UNCTAD), 210
United Nations Investment Board, 21
United States: cost of military forces, 63; economic nationalism in, 203–204; postwar trajectory of, 203. *See also* Congress, US; government, US; *individual presidents*
United States Agency for International Development (USAID), 1; budget of, 191; definition of private sector, 6; on DLF, 37; on economic freedom, 14; enterprise funds and, 140; establishment of, 19; FCS and, 155, 157; on importance of private enterprise, 12; investment guarantee program and, 27, 54; Iraq and, 170; Latin America and, 89; political risk insurance and, 96; in postcommunist countries, 129, 136, 137–138, 139, 141; privatization and, 149–150; on self-reliance, 11; skepticism about, 139
Uruguay, 123
USAID (United States Agency for International Development). *See* United States Agency for International Development (USAID)
US Development Loan Fund (DLF), 37, 50, 51, 63, 86

US Export-Import (EXIM) Bank. *See* Export-Import (EXIM) Bank
US International Development Finance Corporation (DFC), x, 3, 9, 204; Boehler, 219; budget of, 198, 200; countries active in, 199–200; creation of, viii, 1, 139, 189, 196, 207; Impact Quotient, 199; lack of CEO for, 196; lessons from CBI, 114; purpose of, viii, 1–2, 99; response to China and, 187, 198–202; role of, 189; roots of, 19
U.S. Power and the Multinational Corporation (Gilpin), 93
USSR. *See* Russia; Soviet Union

vaccines, 187, 218, 220
Vandevelde, Kenneth, 22
Vargas, Getulio, 67, 79
Venezuela, 90; FDI in, 75; MNCs in, 80; petroleum in, 82; US investment in, 72. *See also* Latin America
venture capital firms, 141
Vernon, Raymond, 93, 94
Vietnam, 95, 97
Vietnam War, 94, 95, 100
Violence, aid and, 213. *See also* fragile and conflict-affected states (FCS)
Volcker, Paul, 107, 115
Volta Redonda, 71

Walesa, Lech, 133
Wall Street Journal, 201
Warren, Elizabeth, 203–204
Warsaw Pact, 127, 128
war-torn economies, opportunities in, 156. *See also* Afghanistan; conflict; fragile and conflict-affected states (FCS); Iraq
Washburne, Ray, 1
Washington Consensus, 108, 122, 126–127, 128. *See also* neoliberalism
Weber, Steven, 130, 142, 144
welfare gains, 193, 221
White, Harry Dexter, 21
Whitman, Marina von Neumann, 26
women, in workforce, 182
Wong, Audrye, 192
Woodhouse, Charles, 23
Woodruff, Christopher, 145–146, 147
World Bank, 72, 101, 143, 196; on Afghanistan, 175, 181, 182; on BRI, 193; China and, 201; on credit to private sector, 6; establishment of, 20; on firms in FCS, 161; Independent Evaluation Group, 216;

Iraq and, 163, 169, 171, 174; Latin America and, 76, 80; micro approach of, 216; objective of, 20; private sector development and, 32; privatization and, 148, 150; Reagan and, 108. *See also* International Finance Corporation (IFC)

World Trade Organization (WTO), 111, 122, 177–178, 196, 201

World War I, 70, 71

World War II: economic devastation caused by, 24–25; Instruments of Surrender from Japan, 57; Latin America and, 71, 72;

postwar economy (*see* economy, postwar; Marshall Plan)

WTO (World Trade Organization), 111, 122, 177–178, 196, 201

Wu, Yongping, 43

Xi Jinping, 190

Yom Kippur War, 105–106

Zeuli, Kimberly, 119, 131

Zheng, Yu, 54

Zhou, Jiayi, 176